The "Spider Web"

House chamber, 1869. Only extant photograph with Speaker's desk in position. Courtesy Library of Congress. Division of Prints and Photographs.

Margaret Susan Thompson

The "Spider Web"
Congress and Lobbying in the Age of Grant

Cornell University Press, Ithaca and London

First published 1985 by Cornell University Press.

International Standard Book Number 0-8014-1815-1
Library of Congress Catalog Card Number 85-47706

Printed in the United States of America

Librarians: Library of Congress cataloging information
appears on the last page of the book.

The paper in this book is acid-free and meets the guidelines for
permanence and durability of the Committee on Production Guidelines
for Book Longevity of the Council on Library Resources.

The Gilded Age was an era in which substantially revised economic and social conditions suggested that many aspects of older values were not always suitable. Newer ideas and new methods seemingly would achieve traditional goals far more effectively . . . but resistance was encountered on all fronts. In very few areas did the new ideas and the new values achieve immediate fruition. . . . But the old order was changing.

A.W.T. (1964)

Contents

8 Contents

Tables, Figures, and Illustrations

9

FIGURES

ILLUSTRATIONS

Acknowledgments

Allan G. Bogue must head any list of those whose advice, expertise, and encouragement contributed to whatever merits this book may possess. He has been both a demanding and supportive mentor, with the intuitive wisdom to know when it was best to wield either the carrot or the stick. For his great insight, humor, and, especially, profound patience I am most grateful.

Others, too, have helped to spin this spider web. Paul Glad, now of the University of Oklahoma; Austin Ranney, now of the American Enterprise Institute; and Barbara Hinckley, of the University of Wisconsin, all helped to shape the work from which the current volume is derived. Allen Weinstein graciously gave me access to most of the data he collected for his *Prelude to Populism,* including extensive notes from the now-closed John Percival Jones Papers. Harry James Brown, professor emeritus at Michigan State University, gave microfilm, his unpublished dissertation on the National Wool Manufacturers' Association, and invaluable advice to a graduate student he had never met, and later provided me with several offprints, *The Garfield Orbit,* and volume 4 of the *Garfield Diary.* He will always represent to me the model of professional collegiality.

Several people have read and commented upon parts or the entirety of this study; these include Ballard Campbell, J. Morgan Kousser, Richard L. McCormick, William G. Shade, and Joel H. Silbey. Past and present colleagues who have done so are Rodney Davis and Stephen

11

Bailey of Knox College; J. Roger Sharp, Linda Fowler, and William Stinchcombe of Syracuse University; and Bernard Barber and Robert K. Merton, both of Columbia University, who were visiting scholars at the Russell Sage Foundation during my year as a postdoctoral fellow.

Every librarian and archivist I encountered in the course of my research was unfailingly courteous and helpful. I cannot list all the institutions where I worked, but special appreciation is due to personnel at the following: the State Historical Society of Wisconsin, the National Archives, the Iowa State Department of History & Archives, the Henry E. Huntington Library, the New Hampshire Historical Society, the Rutherford B. Hayes Presidential Library, the Massachusetts Historical Society, the Van Pelt Library of the University of Pennsylvania, and the Newberry Library. I am indebted to many people at the Library of Congress, particularly the staffs of the Manuscript and Reader Services Divisions, who were of great help both during my early research and during my tenure as J. Franklin Jameson Fellow. Two persons deserve special mention: Dennis Reynolds, Research Librarian at Knox College from 1977 to 1979, whose unusual perspicacity and skill, particularly in locating items through interlibrary loan, were qualities I did not appreciate fully until he was no longer around; and Pauline Rothstein of Russell Sage, who was most helpful during my final year of writing.

Several grants facilitated completion of this project. I am thankful to the State Historical Society of Wisconsin for its Alice Smith Fellowship, to the Newberry Library for a research subsidy, to the National Endowment for the Humanities for a 1980 summer stipend, and to the Library of Congress and the American Historical Association for the Jameson Fellowship. Knox College provided yearly support from its faculty research fund during my tenure there. As an American Political Science Association Congressional Fellow, I was able to spend a year working in and observing the modern House, from which my research derived both direct and indirect benefit; I am particularly grateful to Thomas Mann of the American Political Science Association, to Maureen Drummy, and to the late Representative William A. Steiger (R-Wis.), in whose office I worked and whose love for and insight into the House immeasurably enriched my understanding. Finally, my thanks to the Russell Sage Foundation for the postdoctoral fellowship that enabled me to complete revision of this manuscript under most stimulating and generous auspices.

I also thank Vivian Kaufman of Russell Sage, who typed much of this manuscript, and Lawrence Malley and Peter Agree of Cornell University Press.

At this point, many scholars (usually male) express undying gratitude to spouses for their myriad and often decisive contributions. So perhaps it should be said that I did my own cooking, cleaning, laundry, research, writing, indexing, rewriting—and most of my own typing. I do, however, owe profound debts to many friends, for reasons each of them will appreciate. Some have been mentioned already; others include my grandparents Mary and Jacob Siegel, Kathryn Clarke, Manning Dauer, Gerard DiSenso, Daniel Field, Ruth McQuown, Charles O'Connell, Phyllis A. Price, Margaret Ellen Traxler, and the members of the Friday Night Group and of the Greater Syracuse National Organization for Women.

The dedication acknowledges my greatest human debt.

MARGARET SUSAN THOMPSON

Syracuse, New York

Prologue

> After a time there is a slightly perceptible unanimity in the getting up and sitting down and walking about of the uneasy crowd [of members on the floor] which indicated that a vote is being taken. Amid the confusion, the Speaker again brings his mallet down on the top of his desk and says:—"The ayes seem to have it, the ayes have it"; and the clerks appear to be attending to the further details.
>
> "What did they do?" you ask.
>
> Well, just then the House voted to spend $224,000,000 in round numbers. If you had a copy of the bill you would see that it contained about 150 pages of closely-printed matter. . . . It is to balance accounts for the fiscal year. . . . The Appropriations Committee is presumed to have examined this bill; it has been read and printed, and read again and printed, and read again, and now it is passed. We chanced to see the last process of the operation.
>
> MRS. JOHN A. LOGAN, *Thirty Years in Washington*

In this account by a knowledgeable and perceptive contemporary observer of the nineteenth-century Congress, the legislative roll call is viewed from a proper and balanced perspective. A vote was necessary to release the $224 million. But the move to appropriate funds in the first place, and decisions as to the specific number of dollars to request and the purposes for which they were to be spent, were made elsewhere and by different participants. The roll call was only the culmination of a long series of events that took place off, and long before, those on the floor.[1]

Most historians in recent decades have tended to slight such preliminary machinations. The still-definitive work on nineteenth-century committees, for example, was written by Lauros McConachie in 1898, and Mary P. Follett's *The Speaker of the House of Representatives* (1896)

---

1. Mrs. John A. Logan, *Thirty Years in Washington, or Life and Scenes in Our National Capital* (Hartford, 1901), p. 110.

continues to be authoritative on that subject. The last full-length overview of House activities came out just six years after the overthrow of
Joseph Cannon, and its author was a politician, not a scholar.[2] Collat-
eral topics such as lobbying, meanwhile, generally have been relegated
to the domains of fiction, muckraking, and "popular" history.

What Mrs. Logan referred to as "the last process of the operation," in
contrast, has received more than its share of attention. A precursor to
this historiographic trend was Orin G. Libby's seminal address before
the American Historical Association in 1896, "A Plea for the Study of
Votes in Congress." Libby's plea remained largely unanswered until
nearly three-quarters of a century later, with the emergence of com-
puter technology capable of facilitating calculations derived from such
data. Pioneering works by both Thomas Alexander and Joel Silbey
appeared in 1967; since then, few legislative studies have been without
at least a token scalogram, a little factoring, or a smattering of Rice and
Riker indexes.[3]

Roll-call analysts, in short, have virtually taken over. In doing so, they
have immeasurably enriched our understanding of coalition-building,
individual and aggregate voting decisions, legislative partisanship, and
similar aspects of on-the-floor behavior. But their methodology permits
merely a partial and unidimensional view of activity in the congressional system. As one scholar has commented: "[These] studies exist in
a curious vacuum, as though the only business of Congress was to
supply future historians with roll call data with which to reconstruct
our political past."[4]

My purpose here is not to deliver a full-scale critique of vote-based
scholarship, for numerous examples of that are available elsewhere. It

2. Lauros G. McConachie, *Congressional Committees: A Study of the Origins and Development of Our National and Local Legislative Methods* (1898; New York, 1973); Mary P. Follett,
The Speaker of the House of Representatives (New York, 1896); DeAlva S. Alexander, *History
and Procedure of the House of Representatives* (New York, 1916). Alexander was a Republican
Representative from New York, serving from 1897 to 1911.

3. Orin G. Libby, "A Plea for the Study of Votes in Congress," *Annual Report of the
American Historical Association* (Washington, 1896), pp. 323–34; Thomas B. Alexander,
*Sectional Stress and Party Strength: A Study of Roll Call Voting Patterns in the United States House
of Representatives, 1836–1860* (Nashville, 1967); Joel H. Silbey, *The Shrine of Party: Congres-
sional Voting Behavior, 1841–1852* (Pittsburgh, 1967); Allan G. Bogue, *Clio & the Bitch
Goddess* (Beverly Hills, Calif., 1983); Margaret Susan Thompson and Joel H. Silbey,
"Research on 19th Century Legislatures: Present Contours and Future Directions," *Legis-
lative Studies Q.,* 9 (1984), 319–50; J. H. Silbey, "Congressional and State Legislative Roll-
Call Studies by U.S. Historians," *Legislative Studies Q.,* 6 (1981), 597–607; and "'Delegates
Fresh from the People': American Congressional and Legislative Behavior," *J. of Interdis-
ciplinary History,* 13 (1983), 606–27.

4. Robert Zemsky, "American Legislative Behavior," in *Emerging Theoretical Models in
Social and Political History,* ed. Allan G. Bogue (Beverly Hills, Calif., 1973), p. 58.

is appropriate, however, to note three particular limitations of that literature. First, it contains a built-in bias toward divisive issues, since interesting scales and factor analyses can rarely be derived from consensus. When this is combined with historians' natural preference for studying situations in which "something happened," the result is a portrait of the past in which "great" and controversial issues play a greater part than they in fact did. Second, roll calls focus on a certain kind of policy option: the successful survivors of long and arduous filtration that can take months or even years to run its course. Attention solely to these necessarily obscures both discarded alternatives and the process by which they were eliminated. Finally, many types of activity—including organizational decisions, patronage distribution, and committee deliberations—hardly ever come to the floor or are subjects of balloting, despite their prominent place in the legislative arena. Clearly, we need to know of such matters if we propose to understand the entirety of representative governance. But if historians remain preoccupied with roll calls, that understanding is unlikely to come about.

These concerns played a major part in my decision to focus on lobbying in my analysis of Congress. Lobbying illuminates many things that roll calls do not. It affects not just the public culmination of the legislative process, but all stages of it, every kind of decision that is made, including those that never come up for floor vote. At the same time, lobbying is a form of advocacy that can transcend partisanship, sectionalism, and similar bases of ongoing coalitions and alignments: the very phenomena most accessible to (and most exhaustively discussed by) students of roll calls. Lobbying is also an attractive subject because, to an even greater extent than parties, it is basically an informal phenomenon—although not, like parties, extraconstitutional. In politics in general and Congress in particular, informal norms and practices are at least as important as entrenched structures, procedures, rules, and rituals.

To political scientists, especially those whose research, while grounded in theory, is based primarily on empirical observation, I owe my appreciation of the role of informal mechanisms in government. To them, too, I owe my conviction that sound analysis derives as much from "feel" as from facts, that conclusions must not only be sustained by data but must also be intuitively acceptable. Thanks to them, I began to learn what questions to ask about both lobbying and legislatures.[5] But if political science opens doors and suggests questions for the historian,

5. Four of these political scientists are Austin Ranney, Ralph K. Huitt, Barbara Hinckley, and Richard Fenno.

the disparities between its purposes and those of history are great. The image of nineteenth-century evidence reflected by the twentieth-century mirror of political science is badly distorted. Political scientists predicate their study of present behavior on a set of assumptions that simply do not apply to the nineteenth century. For while the basic functions of legislatures have not changed tremendously, the conditions under which those functions are carried out have. In Table 1, which summarizes what I see as the most crucial differences, the left-hand list can be taken to represent the assumptions that are implicit in modern analysis.[6]

Models dependent on the existence of a seniority system, for instance, or a stable "careerist" membership or clearly established sources of internal expertise and leadership, cannot serve to explain the Congress that sat in Washington a hundred years ago. What is needed is theory suited to the circumstances of that time, informed by an intrinsically historical perspective. One subset of the political science canon that deliberately incorporates the past into its coverage—longitudinal works on institutional development—brings this home with some force. The main objective of these works is not strictly historical, but rather to discern and locate the origins and evolution of current structures and norms. In doing that, however, they inevitably highlight the distinctions between conditions today and those that came before, even if the latter are treated incidentally. Moreover, by choosing matters like careerism, professionalization, and committee composition as their foci, the authors lend witness to the present importance of these phenomena—and, implicitly, to the importance of their absence in other times.

6. Nelson W. Polsby, "The Institutionalization of the U.S. House of Representatives," *APSR*, 62 (1968), 144–68, and Polsby, Miriam Gallaher, and Barry S. Rundquist, "The Growth of the Seniority System in the U.S. House of Representatives," *APSR*, 63 (1969), 787–807; H. Douglas Price, "The Congressional Career—Then and Now," in *Congressional Behavior*, ed. Nelson W. Polsby (New York, 1971), pp. 14–27, "Congress and the Evolution of Legislative 'Professionalism,'" in *Congress in Change: Evolution and Reform*, ed. Norman J. Ornstein (New York, 1975), pp. 2–23, and "Careers and Committees in the American Congress: The Problem of Structural Change," in *The History of Parliamentary Behavior*, ed. William O. Aydelotte (Princeton, 1977), pp. 28–62; Garrison Nelson, "Change and Continuity in the Recruitment of U.S. House Leaders, 1789–1975," in Ornstein, *Congress in Change*, pp. 155–83, and "Partisan Patterns of House Leadership Change, 1789–1977," *APSR*, 71 (1977), 918–39; Joseph Cooper, *The Origins of the Standing Committees and the Development of the Modern House* (Houston, 1970); Michael Abram and J. Cooper, "The Rise of Seniority in the House of Representatives," *Polity*, 1 (1968), 53–85; Morris P. Fiorina et al., "Historical Change in House Turnover," in Ornstein, *Congress in Change*, pp. 24–57; Peter Swenson, "The Influence of Recruitment on the Structure of Power in the U.S. House, 1870–1940," *Legislative Studies Q.*, 7 (1982), 7–36.

Table 1. Significant differences between nineteenth- and twentieth-century legislatures

Twentieth century	Nineteenth century
Stable membership; high average tenure.	High turnover; largely inexperienced membership.
Careerist orientation of most members; professional commitment to the legislative institution.	Legislative service seldom a lifetime career; few die in office or spend the major share of their professional lives in the legislature.
Formal and differentiated leadership structure; floor leaders chosen by party caucuses not speaker.	No formal leadership structure apart from the speakership; floor leaders are products of committee assignments, made by the speaker alone.
A formal seniority system that determines members' ranks in the committees on which they serve; initial assignments determined by groups in the respective parties and not solely by the speaker; relatively little movement by senior members.	No formal seniority system; speaker retains exclusive authority over both majority and minority assignments; high levels of movement by senior members and no guarantees of jurisdictional continuity.
Extensive sources of substantive expertise, including large professional staffs for members and committees, support agencies.	No provisions that guarantee internal sources of substantive expertise; little or no professional staff for either members or committees.
Orchestration of the floor agenda by a Committee on Rules, explicitly separate from speakership.	No Rules Committee or else one chaired by the speaker; in either case, speaker retains control over the agenda.
Breakdown of partisan voting behavior; replaced by individual, constituency, and substantive interest orientation.	Partisan voting behavior.
Decline of ideology.	Ideological dimension in voting behavior.

Source: Margaret Susan Thompson and Joel H. Silbey, "Research on 19th Century Legislatures: Present Contours and Future Directions," *Legislative Studies Quarterly,* 9:2 (1984), 335.

Both recent historiography and the forays of political science into history leave unasked or incompletely answered such questions as: How were committee assignments given out, if not on the basis of seniority? What were the consequences of a largely unstable, inexperienced membership? Where did power reside, and with whom? What was the shape of the legislative agenda, and how was business affected by lack of both procedural and substantive know-how? What, in short, was Congress really like, as a political body charged with policy making and representation responsibilities? And how, if at all, did its nineteenth-century character either enhance or impede the influence of lobbying?

Because there is no ready-made model of the historical House, one has to be made; and since the House is not a static institution, the one chosen for analysis has to be that of a specific period, not some amorphous "premodern" entity. Having determined this much prior to my research and writing, I had no hesitation about the time to choose. It would be the 1870s, the early Gilded Age, the years of Ulysses Grant's tenure in the White House.

The logic that guided this decision as well as most of the others that shaped this project was born of the creative tension in my background, which was on the borderline between two disciplines. The longitudinal studies in political science, for instance, suggested, if sometimes only implicitly, that the 1870s were a crucial time of transformation in the evolution of the federal legislature; historians, for their part, had long regarded the era as one in which the lobbyist "reigned supreme." Other sources, too, primary and secondary, affirmed the decade's political significance. Washington's agenda underwent unprecedented expansion as the persisting legacies of Civil War and Reconstruction collided with the imperatives of industrialization, technological innovation, and transcontinental settlement. Any period appears transitional in retrospect, of course, but citizens and officeholders alike in the days of Grant seemed unusually self-conscious about the "newness" of things— and both stimulated by and suspicious of ensuing challenges.

Students of national development, here and elsewhere, have argued that such circumstances are precisely the sort that encourage, indeed necessitate, political innovation, including the integration of new interests and groups into the polity.[7] Formerly effective modes of problem solving no longer work, even as new ones to replace them remain elusive. And stopgap measures that suffice in the interim, some of which eventually evolve into permanent solutions, tend to be greeted initially with doubt or even condemnation. These considerations led me to hypothesize—correctly, I now believe—that the 1870s would be an especially good period to study for an understanding of the informal and highly flexible phenomenon of lobbying and the workings of representative government. The door was also opened to my conviction that lobbying's bad reputation is at least partly unearned: that it

---

7. Samuel P. Huntington, *Political Order in Changing Societies* (New Haven, 1968), pp. 59–63; J. S. Nye, "Corruption and Political Development: A Cost-Benefit Analysis," *APSR*, 61 (1967), 417–27; J. C. Scott, *Comparative Political Corruption* (Englewood Cliffs, N.J., 1972); Morton Keller, "Corruption in America: Continuity and Change," and Ari Hoogenboom, "Did Gilded Age Scandals Bring Reform?" in *Before Watergate: Problems of Corruption in American Society*, ed. A. S. Eisenstadt et al. (Brooklyn, 1978).

derived as much from the novelty of lobbying's prevalence and power, and from change-related confusion, as from any actual corruption or illegitimacy.

As the chapters that follow will reveal, both these ideas and the analysis they generated are substantially at odds with the hitherto almost universally accepted depiction of Congress and lobbying in the Grant years. Although that vision was fleshed out and popularized by Matthew Josephson and Richard Hofstadter, its provenance may be impossible to pinpoint exactly. I believe, however, that it can be traced substantially to two still-cited accounts that date from the Gilded Age itself: the most provocative and thorough contemporary efforts to illuminate activities in the capital. The first of them began as an 1879 essay in the *International Review;* its author was an aspiring young lawyer and student of politics who signed himself Thomas W. Wilson. Entitled "Cabinet Government in the United States," the piece contained themes that within six years would receive more extensive treatment in *Congressional Government;* by then its author had dropped his first name and was calling himself Woodrow Wilson. He had also become acquainted with a like-minded English peer who, following an extended American tour, hoped to produce a book of his own, aimed at "portraying the whole political system of the country, in its practice as well as its theory." That ambition was more than realized in 1888, when James, Lord Bryce published his two-volume epic, *The American Commonwealth.*[8]

The rest, as they say, is history—or historiography. A century later, Wilson and Bryce still cast a long shadow over what is written on the Gilded Age polity. Yet shadows, although derived from light, manifest themselves in darkness. Today, therefore, Wilson's and Bryce's legacy does more to obscure than to illuminate the 1870s. Although *Commonwealth* and *Government* cannot be ignored, the motives behind their writing and the implications of their influence need reassessment.

8. Matthew Josephson, *The Politicos* (New York, 1938); Richard Hofstadter, "The Spoilsmen: An Age of Cynicism," in *The American Political Tradition and the Men Who Made It* (New York, 1957), pp. 164–85; Woodrow Wilson, "Cabinet Government in the United States (1879)," in *The Papers of Woodrow Wilson,* ed. Arthur S. Link (Princeton, 1966), 1:493–510 (originally published under the name of Thomas W. Wilson in the *International Review,* 6 [1879], 146–63), and *Congressional Government: A Study in American Politics* (1885; Cleveland, 1956); James Bryce, *The American Commonwealth,* 2 vols. (London, 1888), 1:2. On relationship between Wilson and Bryce, see Henry Wilkinson Bragdon, *Woodrow Wilson: The Academic Years* (Cambridge, 1967), pp. 121, 138, 179–80; Ray Stannard Baker, *Woodrow Wilson, Life and Letters: Youth, 1856–1890* (Garden City, N.Y., 1927); H. A. L. Fisher, *James Bryce,* 2 vols. (New York, 1927).

Wilson, for instance, professed nothing but disdain for so-called experts who "are still reading the *Federalist* as an authoritative manual." As a remedy, he proposed to expose "the modifications which have been wrought in the federal system and which have resulted in making Congress the omnipotent power in the government, to the overthrow of the checks and balances to be found in the 'literary theory.'" Thus, he wrote to his fiancée, when he began to write *Congressional Government:* "I want to contribute to our literature what no American has ever contributed, studies in . . . the practical and suggestive philosophy which is at the core of our governmental methods; their use, their meaning, 'the spirit that makes them workable.' I want to divest them of the theory that obscures them and present their weakness and their strength without disguise." The future president regarded most of the extant literature as "irrelevant or already antiquated." "An observer who looks at the living reality," he declared, "will wonder at the contrast to the paper description."⁹ What he intended, then, was an account at once descriptive and analytic; what he wrote, however, fell short in both respects.

Even as an undergraduate, Wilson had been guided in his political theorizing by explicitly utilitarian principles and (even more) by a fondness for prescription. Thus, as early as 1879, probably as he prepared his essay for the *International Review,* he entered into a "solemn covenant" with a classmate, pledging "that we would school our powers and passions for the work of establishing the principles we held in common; that we would acquire knowledge that we might have power; and that we would drill ourselves in all the arts of persuasion . . . that we might have the facility in leading others into our purposes." Both "Cabinet Government" and *Congressional Government* were, then, intended not merely to portray politics as it was but to proselytize in behalf of how Wilson believed it should be. More specifically, Wilson was urging transformation of the American system into one modeled after the British parliamentary one: "Simply to give to the heads of the Executive department . . . seats in Congress, with the privilege of the initiative in legislation and some part of the unbounded privileges now commanded by the Standing Committees."¹⁰

Wilson's admiration for English institutions and his belief in their superiority over those of the United States dated from his first political consciousness. At the age of fifteen, he hung a portrait of Gladstone

---

9. Wilson to Ellen Axson, 1 Jan. 1884 and 30 Oct. 1883, in Baker, *Wilson,* pp. 213–14.
10. Bragdon, *Wilson,* p. 51; Wilson, "Cabinet Government," p. 498.

over his desk and, in what might be regarded as the ideological equivalent of a mixed metaphor, "dreamed of becoming the American Burke, whose writings would exercise a 'statesmanship of opinion.'" This predilection intensified rather than diminished over the years; at Princeton, the young Anglophile wrote a senior thesis entitled "Our Kinship with England." Yet perhaps the most important episode in his intellectual development occurred one year earlier, in 1878, when he read Walter Bagehot's *The English Constitution*. Later, Wilson would refer to that author as "my master," and would call him "the most vivacious, the most racily real, of writers on life." Not surprisingly, then, when the American commenced his own scholarly career, his methodological and ideological indebtedness to the Britisher was obvious in his work; as Gamaliel Bradford would remark in a review of *Congressional Government*, "His book is evidently modeled on Mr. Bagehot's 'English Constitution,' and it will, though the praise is so high as to be almost extravagant, bear comparison with that inestimable work."[11]

Conventional wisdom has it that Wilson—who, at the time he wrote *Congressional Government*, was halfway through his two years as a graduate fellow at Johns Hopkins—never traveled the forty miles from Baltimore to Washington to observe Congress in action. He certainly had not observed Parliament. His monograph was sparsely documented, but those references he did cite were principally British texts such as Bagehot's, law books, and articles by like-minded and similarly Anglophilic liberal reformers of his day, including George Frisbie Hoar, Henry Adams, and Bradford. Wilson also relied heavily upon the official Rules of the House and Senate, and the most persuasive passages of *Congressional Government* are those describing the intricacies and potential uses and abuses of legislative procedure. These, Wilson argued, imposed insurmountable constraints upon Congress, and especially the House, because they inhibited the kind of impressive oratory that Wilson saw as the main path by which "natural leaders" emerged. For this reason, too, he despised the authority of the congressional committees and, despite his obsession with leadership, the Speaker who appointed them, because they did not meet publicly— and, hence, inspired no oratory—and because they diffused responsibility and influence widely among members, most of whom the scholar regarded as intellectually weak and politically unsophisticated.

---

11. Bragdon, *Wilson*, pp. 13, 59–61, 202, 422; Baker, *Wilson*, pp. 202, 211; Editorial Note preceding "Cabinet Government" in Link, *Papers of Wilson*, 1:492; Gamaliel Bradford, "Wilson's Congressional Government," *Nation*, 40 (12 Feb. 1885), 142.

In short, what emerges most clearly from the work is Wilson's un-
disguised and unapologetic elitism; his book amounts to a polemic
against a system that appeared to operate in ways inhibitory to the rise
of "great men," "fit" to hold the reins of power.[12]

The portrait in *Congressional Government* of how this system worked is
both arid and superficial. Throughout, Wilson seems to forget that
legislative machinery exists for reasons more compelling than the institutional need to organize and control the deliberations of House and
Senate. These bodies did not meet simply to sustain themselves or to be
symbols of "greatness"; they were supposed to formulate and implement legislation and to perform other practical tasks. But in only one
chapter, "Revenue and Supply," did Wilson discuss the policy function,
and even there he was less concerned with the outcomes of decision
making than with reiterating his arguments against the power of committees and the relative powerlessness of cabinet and executive.

Indeed, Wilson's treatment of the relationships among legislative and
other political actors, when he dealt with them at all, was rather cursory.
True, his book did contain one chapter, oddly unrelated to the main
body of the monograph, entitled "The Executive." Only minimal attention was paid to the interplay of the executive with the legislature, and
here, ironically, the future president appeared incapable of getting
beyond the most formal dimensions of the relationship. Yet that superficial treatment was more than any other element of the political system
received. Not even the judiciary was discussed, although it is a constitutionally ordained component of federalism and, thus, well within the
bounds of institutionalism. Nor was the citizenry, in an electoral or any
other capacity. And lobbyists, of course, apart from one slur, are
practically ignored—although greater inclusion of them, at least in
their popular guise, might have amplified and reinforced Wilson's
negative thrust. As it was, his account suggested that Congress func-
tioned almost in a vacuum, eschewing much interaction with anyone or
anything else.

Thus, controlled by his proscriptive purpose and dependent for
firsthand observations upon the commentary of others no more disin-

12. For Bradford, see "Congressional Reform," *NAR*, 111 (1870), 330–41, and "Shall the
Cabinet Have Seats in Congress?" *Nation*, 16 (3 Apr. 1873), 233–34. In the notes to
Congressional Government, Wilson refers to Adams's pieces on Congress for the *North
American Review* as "incisive" and "brilliant"; similarly, he refers often to Hoar's "Conduct
of Business in Congress" (*NAR*, 128 [Feb. 1879], 113–34), at one point acknowledging it as
a piece "to which I am indebted for many details . . . in the text." Wilson, *Congressional
Government*, pp. 218–19; see also pp. 59–62, 63ff., 174ff., 193–215.

terested than himself, the man who wanted to analyze American government in its "rough practice" and not its "literary theory" produced an incontrovertibly unempirical study. Despite his desire to explain things "as they really are," Wilson instead allowed his sources and his sentiments to define the dimensions of his subject. Personally unfamiliar with the vitality and human energies of Capitol politics, he took too seriously its organization chart. He lacked both the substantive and instinctual bases for drawing distinctions between reality and form, and the two became congruent in his mind and in his work. For Wilson, ultimately, form *was* reality, and the only reality he perceived in Congressional Government.

If Wilson's book suffers from an excess of proscription and a scarcity of empirical insights, at least the latter cannot be said of *American Commonwealth*. In two volumes with 116 chapters, Bryce probably mentioned every aspect of American life that bore any discernible relationship to politics. His discussion encompassed the state and local, as well as federal, levels and contained descriptions of the roles of ex officio participants, too: journalists, schools and universities, churches, railroads—and lobbyists. Bryce employed a wide variety of source materials, including the sorts of written works used by Wilson and *Congressional Government* itself.[13] To these, however, he added interviews, newspapers, and—most important—extensive firsthand observation. Furthermore, he made a conscious effort to understand how the various pieces interacted with one another: to describe a system, not piecemeal institutions. And within this scheme, Congress received more attention than any other systemic component. For Bryce, like Wilson and most political writers of his time, recognized the hegemony that House and Senate exercised within the mid-nineteenth-century federal universe. *American Commonwealth*, therefore, contains a plethora of information, observations, and asides about the Capitol arena—its personnel, responsibilities, politics, and organizational structure—all extremely useful to anyone trying to get a feel for Gilded Age Washington.

Yet Bryce did not, strictly speaking, provide a *model* for explaining

13. Bryce called *Congressional Government* "a lucid and interesting book from which I have derived much help in this and the two following chapters" (chaps. 15–17); *American Commonwealth*, 1:157. That his debt to Wilson was more extensive than that is demonstrated throughout, especially in the contents and title of chap. 8: "Why Great Men Are Not Chosen Presidents." Wilson, in turn, would write an extremely positive review of *Commonwealth* for the *Political Science Quarterly*, 4 (March 1889), 153–69, and Bryce would ask Wilson for help when he revised *Commonwealth* in 1891; Bragdon, *Wilson*, pp. 179–80.

behavior and policy making. Generally, the images he presented were static ones: "[His] book was a photograph . . . not a history, a picture . . . of the American democracy as it presented itself to the eye of a brilliant and scrupulous observer in 1888." Bryce said he saw himself more as reporter than as scholar; he had no intention of devising a framework or set of theories that could be applied to other times or circumstances. That, he believed, was impossible: "America changes so fast that every few years a new crop of books is needed to describe the new face which things have put on, the new problems that have appeared . . . the new and unexpected developments."[14] Beyond this, the ongoing friendship between this author and Wilson was indicative of their common genteel elitism, which—all prefatory protestations to the contrary—inevitably limited *Commonwealth*'s explanatory power. Amidst the plethora of detail, the Englishman's attitudes are unmistakable, and inhibiting.

We are left, therefore, with two accounts that are superficially dissimilar and yet alike in many of their authors' conclusions about the then-current state of congressional politics. And the combined force of these impressions, particularly in the absence of substantial alternatives, has effectively determined most of the subsequent one hundred years' popular and scholarly wisdom. This is not to say, of course, that there have been no reinterpretive efforts; David Rothman's and Allan G. Bogue's work on the Senate, and some sections of Morton Keller's *Affairs of State*, certainly qualify.[15] But after a century, there is practically nothing, beyond DeAlva S. Alexander's impressionistic 1916 volume, that purports to give the Gilded Age House anything like the comprehensive treatment attempted by Bryce and Wilson. It is time, it seems to me, to start to correct that situation.

The intention here, therefore, is to go off the floor and behind the scenes of the House in the 1870s. The emphasis will be on those norms and activities least likely to be illuminated clearly by examining roll calls, since those are already studied so extensively. More specifically, I shall be looking at the House as a representational, policy making, and political body, and analyzing the strengths and weaknesses of its performance in these areas, as well as the factors responsible for shaping

14. Fisher, *James Bryce*, 1:234, 238; Bryce, *Commonwealth*, 1:4.
15. David J. Rothman, *Politics and Power: The United States Senate, 1869–1901* (Cambridge, 1966); Allan G. Bogue, *The Earnest Men: Republicans of the Civil War Senate* (Ithaca, 1981); Morton Keller, *Affairs of State: Public Life in Late Nineteenth Century America* (Cambridge, 1977).

that performance. A secondary objective will be to assess the contributions of lobbying to life in the congressional arena, and to the fulfillment of members' various responsibilities. But while lobbyists will play prominent roles in what is to follow, this is preeminently a book about Congress.

I believe this book is necessary and important. The same could be said, however, about any number of other books I might have written, even in the field of congressional studies. In the end, therefore—and despite every rationalization, however valid, I can think of—the principal reason I wrote this one is that I found that studying Congress and lobbying in the Age of Grant was fascinating, challenging, and fun.

In lobbying, after all, we have a constitutionally guaranteed right of all citizens, a right that has always been exercised energetically, yet that nonetheless has no respectability unless it masquerades under euphemistic aliases. It is a more broadly accessible right than voting, for instance; minors, minorities, aliens, women, even idiots have always been able to employ it. And those who condemn it most vociferously will both use and defend their "right to petition" in behalf of their conception of the "public interest." Such a focus not only allowed but *required* me to read muckraking novels (some dreadful, some surprisingly good), the work of crusading journalists, and self-righteous reform literature that urged Americans to unite to bring pressure to stop the pernicious power of The Lobby. I also encountered lobbyists who moonlighted as haberdashers (or vice versa), men on $10,000 retainers from Jay Gould who donated their spare time to serving widows and former slaves, women who earned many times the highest salaries they could get as federal clerks by engineering the appointments of others, and congressmen who sought office explicitly (and proudly) to represent the cause of private interests.

Thus, while I cannot say conclusively that lobbying is always stimulating or enjoyable, reading about it certainly can be. It is unfortunate that not all of the most amusing things I found could be incorporated here. Still, most of the sense of what I found remains and, I hope, adds to the texture and feel of what follows.

I worked in graduate school with a man who once sought—successfully, I believe—to write about agricultural economics by conveying a feel for the "individual farmer—the man with dirt on his hands and dung on his boots." He obviously had fun, and managed to transmit it. He insisted that his students not just settle for "do-able" topics, and told them to "wait until lightning strikes." I did, and that really is why this book has come about.[16]

Note on Terminology

I have tried to avoid excessive reliance on jargon, both that which commonly creeps into social science literature and that which stems from personal idiosyncrasy. Readers will have to decide for themselves how well I have succeeded, but I should note that two atypical usages are intentional. The first is my capitalization of "Representative(s)" whenever it refers to members of Congress, not just when it functions as a title. A key point in my argument is that lobbyists are also representatives; capitalization therefore reflects a substantive distinction. The second is my use of "Congressional Government" (also capitalized), a phrase taken from the title of Woodrow Wilson's 1885 work. I intend this phrase to mean the entire scope of life that devolved upon Capitol Hill during the Gilded Age: policy making, patronage distribution, internal politicking, the representational relationship, constituent service, electoral connections, and so on. It is also meant to indicate the primacy of the legislature in the late nineteenth-century federal arena. This shorthand is, I believe, useful both as a preventative to repetitious litanies and as a continual reminder of the rich and complex background against which every particular action occurred.

M.S.T.

16. Allan G. Bogue, *From Prairie to Cornbelt: Farming on the Illinois and Iowa Prairies in the Nineteenth Century* (Chicago, 1963), p. 1.

Abbreviations

AHR	*American Historical Review*
APSR	*American Political Science Review*
BDAC	*Biographical Directory of the American Congress* (1961 ed.)
Cong. Dir.	*Congressional Directory*
Cong. Rec.	*Congressional Record*
DAB	*Dictionary of American Biography* (New York, 1928)
D	Democrat
Hse. J.	*House Journal*
Hse. Rpt.	*House Report*
JAH	*Journal of American History*
JSH	*Journal of Southern History*
L.C.	Library of Congress
MVHR	*Mississippi Valley Historical Review*
Nat. Cyc.	*National Cyclopedia of American Biography* (New York, 1898)
NHHS	New Hampshire Historical Society, Concord, New Hampshire
NAR	*North American Review*
R	Republican
Sen. J.	*Senate Journal*
Sen. Rpt.	*Senate Report*

The "Spider Web"

CHAPTER 1

Corruption—or Confusion?
Toward an Understanding
of the Gilded Age Polity

> It was [Ulysses Grant's] misfortune that he came upon the national scene at a moment when our entire national life was going through a process of transition. . . . A new and startlingly different society was evolving. When Grant left the White House in 1877 America was as different from the America of 1861 as the cottage in Galena was different from the Executive Mansion.
>
> WILLIAM B. HESSELTINE, *Ulysses S. Grant, Politician*

On January 6, 1869, Republican Representative Elihu Washburne rose to address his House colleagues on the significance of the national elections two months before. His party had triumphed, the Illinoisan declared, because "it was pledged to honesty and economy, to the upholding of public faith and public credit, and to the faithful execution of the laws." Thus, he predicted, Ulysses S. Grant's accession to the presidency in March would inaugurate "a new departure"; he had won because Americans knew him to be "emphatically an honest man and an enlightened statesman, who would [govern] without fear, favor, or affection." But the president could not be asked to act alone in responding to the demand for confidence in government or in ending the "demoralization incident to all great wars." The legislative branch was preeminent in the capital, and so it, the congressman warned, even more than the executive, must be careful not to betray the public trust: "It is time that the Representatives of the people were admonished that they are the servants of the people and are paid by the people; . . . that their position and their power are to be used for the benefit of the people whom they represent, and not for their own benefit and the benefit of the lobbyists, the gamblers, and the speculators who have come to Washington to make a raid upon the Treasury. . . . Never has the country in time of peace looked to Congress with more intense interest than at the present time." Nonetheless, Washburne was confident that the country had little cause to worry: "Much is expected of the new Administration, and the public expectation will not be disappointed."[1]

But of course the "public expectation" *was* destined for disappointment. One legislative leader of the time asserted that corruption "never got so dangerous a hold upon the forces of the Government, or upon a great political party, as in the Administration of General Grant." Contemporaries coined the term "Grantism" to connote malfeasance in office, while historians have immortalized the General's tenure with such epithets as the "Great Barbecue" and the "Age of the Spoilsmen" or "Age of Excess." Despite recent publication of two prize-winning reinterpretations of Grant and his governance, historiographic consensus still embodies the perspective of Matthew Josephson, who devoted his 1938 best seller, *The Politicos,* to scathing denunciation of the "saturnalia of plunder" that presumably commenced in the 1870s. It was a time, he alleged, when Americans "witnessed the full flowering of the spoils system in our Government in stronger and purer form than ever before. For seven years, until they faced detection and punishment, the spoilsmen who invaded every branch of the National Government moved in the pursuit of 'beauty and booty' solely. . . . [in] the uninterrupted use and enjoyment of their offices." For over a century, in short, the Grant years have been regarded generally as synonymous with corruption and, specifically, as years when lobbyists, who personified that corruption, presumably controlled the corridors of power.[2]

1. *Congressional Globe*, 40th Cong., 3d sess., part I (6 Jan. 1869), 216.
2. George F. Hoar, *Autobiography of Seventy Years*, 2 vols. (New York, 1903), 1:305. A representative contemporary critique is Edward Winslow Martin [James Dabney McCabe], *Behind the Scenes in Washington* (Philadelphia, 1873). "Great Barbecue" is from Vernon L. Parrington, *The Beginnings of Critical Realism in America* (New York, 1930). Richard Hofstadter, "The Spoilsmen: An Age of Cynicism," in *The American Political Tradition and the Men Who Made It* (New York, 1948), pp. 164–85; Ray Ginger, *Age of Excess: The United States from 1877 to 1914* (New York, 1965). Recent reinterpretations are William Gillette, *Retreat from Reconstruction, 1869–1879* (Baton Rouge, 1979), and William S. McFeely, *Grant: A Biography* (New York, 1981). Matthew Josephson, *The Politicos, 1865–1896* (New York, 1938), p. 100. Current consensus is reflected in college history textbooks, e.g., John M. Blum et al., *The National Experience*, 4th ed. (New York, 1977), pp. 274, 341–45; Winthrop D. Jordan et al., *The United States*, 5th ed. (Englewood Cliffs, N.J., 1982), pp. 389–91; and Mary Beth Norton et al., *A People and a Nation* (Boston, 1981), pp. 550–54.

No one would deny that a series of scandals plagued the national scene during Grant's two terms. The most well known was that of the Credit Mobilier, a Pennsylvania-chartered "dummy" corporation that was controlled by officials of the federally subsidized Union Pacific Railroad. And while shareholding companies were neither unusual at the time nor illegal, this one clearly overstepped the bounds of propriety. Oakes Ames, a director of both concerns and a Republican congressman from Massachusetts, was the principal culprit. He boasted to his business partners that he would ensure their fortunes by distributing Credit Mobilier stock "where it will produce the most good to us"—namely, among strategically placed colleagues of his in the Capitol. When the scheme was exposed in 1872, the list of alleged recipients included eighteen current or former legislators from both parties. Among them were House Speaker James G. Blaine; Schuyler Colfax and Henry Wilson, Grant's two vice-presidents; Treasury Secretary George S. Boutwell; Ways & Means Committee chairman Henry L. Dawes; Democratic leader James Brooks; and James A. Garfield, chairman of Appropriations and future president.

Naturally, this affair incited widespread public outrage. Although only two persons, Ames and Brooks, were formally censured, lingering clouds of suspicion attached themselves to many others. But Credit Mobilier was not solely responsible for the tainted legacy that has attached itself to the Age of Grant. Within a week of condemning Ames and Brooks, for instance, Congress voted itself a pay raise, increasing legislators' remuneration from $5000 to $7000 per year. The sum probably was justifiable—Washington, then as now, was not an inexpensive city—but the measure became infamous because it was to apply retroactively. That is, members were to receive "back pay" for the entire Forty-second Congress, even though the bill authorizing it was passed on the last day of that Congress and over half the men who would benefit were lame ducks. The "Salary Grab" joined Credit Mobilier in the litany of scandal; popular condemnation of it was so intense that it was repealed as soon as Congress reconvened.[3]

By 1877 several more discreditable items could be added to the list. Secretary of War William Belknap would be impeached for selling Indian trading posts to the highest bidders. Investigations into the so-called "Whiskey Ring," which involved tax evasion, and into an extra-

3. Standard accounts of these episodes are in William A. Dunning, *Reconstruction Political and Economic, 1865–1877* (New York, 1907), pp. 231–35; Ellis Paxson Oberholtzer, *A History of the United States since the Civil War,* 5 vols. (New York, 1926), 3:70–81; and James Ford Rhodes, *History of the United States from the Compromise of 1850 to the Final Restoration of Home Rule at the South in 1877,* 7 vols. (New York, 1906), 7:1–21. See also Martin, *Behind the Scenes,* pp. 248–301.

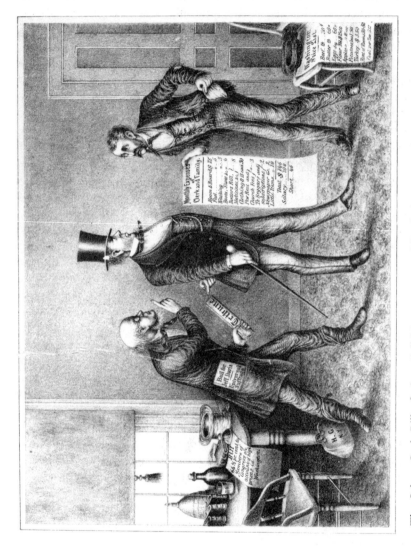

The Salary Grab Bill of 1873: Politicians prosper while clerks starve. Figure on left is Horace Greeley's ghost. Courtesy Library of Congress, Division of Prints and Photographs.

legal venture to annex the Caribbean island of San Domingo revealed unsavory facts about the president's personal secretary, Orville Babcock. Railroad magnates including Collis P. Huntington of the Central Pacific and Texas & Pacific's Thomas Scott reportedly spent hundreds of thousands of dollars in efforts to obtain subsidies for their competing routes to California. Then there were the Sanborn Contracts, problems in various custom houses, the Pacific Mail Steamship Company frauds, and numerous contested elections in which candidates or their supporters were charged with attempting to bribe voters or with using intimidation to keep them from the polls. And three well-publicized sex scandals added further fuel to public outrage: one involving the influential clergyman Henry Ward Beecher; another involving two senators—presidential hopeful Roscoe Conkling (R-N.Y.) and the alcoholic William Sprague of Rhode Island—and the latter's wife, Chief Justice Salmon Chase's glamorous daughter Kate; and the third linking Grant himself with the wife of his attorney general (ironically, a proposed nominee to succeed Chase).[4] All in all, the period hardly stands out as one of probity, political or otherwise.

Nonetheless, to recognize that the times were corrupt is to see them

4. Hofstadter, "The Spoilsmen"; William B. Hesseltine, *Ulysses S. Grant, Politician* (New York, 1938), chaps. 12, 14, 22, 24; Allan Nevins, *Hamilton Fish: The Inner History of the Grant Administration* (New York, 1936), chaps. 14, 27, 32, 33; Lewis B. Lesley, "A Southern Transcontinental Railroad into California: Texas and Pacific versus Southern Pacific, 1865–1885," *Pacific Historical Review*, 5 (1936), 52–60; Wallace D. Farnham, "The Weakened Spring of Government," *AHR*, 68 (1963), 662–80. On sexual scandals, see *Tilton vs. Beecher, Action for Criminal Conversations, Verbatim Report by the Official Stenographer*, 3 vols. (New York, 1875); Charles F. Marshall, *The True History of the Brooklyn Scandal* (Philadelphia, 1874); Milton Rugoff, *The Beechers: An American Family in the Nineteenth Century* (New York, 1981); Ishbel Ross, *Proud Kate: Portrait of an Ambitious Woman* (New York, 1953). On Grant and Kate George (Mrs. George F.) Williams, most accounts are very oblique: Oberholtzer, *History of the United States*, 3:128; James H. Whyte, *The Uncivil War: Washington during the Reconstruction, 1865–1878* (New York, 1958), p. 192. But the following is most revealing: "Williams' appointment [to succeed Chase] . . . is more horrible perhaps than even you know it to be. He Williams, has said within two days that *his wife* knew of Grant's purpose to nominate him on Saturday night—that he did not learn it till Monday morning—Who is his wife? She was a handsome adventuress in San Francisco known as Kate George—publicly kept as a mistress by one George a prosperous stage proprietor. She has a son in the Maryland Penitentiary, a convict for the crime of robbery, his second offence—The old Senators and Representatives who 'know' things in Washington believe that Kate 'screwed' her husband into the Attorney Generalship—One of the shrewdest of the old Senators said yesterday in conversation about this appointment—Mrs. W. has the most profitable c——t that has been brought to Washington in my day—." Letter from "S" [Jerome B. Stillson, reporter, New York *Sun*] to Charles Dana, 3 Dec. 1873, enclosed in Dana to Manton Marble (editor, New York *World*), 4 Dec. 1873; Marble Papers, L.C.

simply on a single, superficial level. Scandal was only part of what was going on in the Grant years; there also was profound reorientation in the purposes and practices of government. That, over the long run, would prove to be of far greater consequence, and once this is understood, it becomes possible to put the intrigues of the era, as well as the public's obsession with them, into proper perspective. For corruption, real and alleged, was not an independent phenomenon. It was rather a by-product of larger systemic change, which would transform the American polity forever.

Congressman James A. Garfield was one man of the seventies who considered himself a reformer. Nonetheless, in the year following Grant's second inauguration, he often found himself discomfited by contemporaries' preoccupation with the seamier side of politics. His discomfiture was, of course, less than disinterested. This former college president and war hero, this lay preacher who relaxed by reading classical philosophy in the original Greek and Latin and by corresponding with many of the leading theologians and secular thinkers of the day, had been implicated in Credit Mobilier and, if only because he chaired the Appropriations Committee that authorized it, in the Salary Grab as well. Many of his constituents were appalled; in the months after the Forty-second Congress adjourned, the beleaguered member was forced to spend most of his time in his district, disseminating oral and written defenses of his character and actions. For the first time, the Ohioan complained, he experienced "the injustice with which an excited people will treat a Representative . . . being blamed for what is not blameworthy and for what I have not done." On more than one occasion during the spring and summer of 1873, Garfield considered resigning and ridding himself from what he had come to feel were the "odious burdens of public life." He finally decided to remain, but only, he said, because he was "not willing to appear to be driven from it by mere clamor."[5]

Meanwhile, as fall began, Garfield found the nation's affairs to be at least as unsettling as his own. On September 18, the collapse of the powerful banking firm of Jay Cooke & Company had precipitated a major financial panic that eventually would result in over 5000 business failures. Within six weeks the U.S.S. *Virginius* was captured by a Spanish gunboat off the coast of Cuba, and eight of the Americans on board

5. *The Diary of James A. Garfield,* ed. Harry James Brown and F. D. Williams, 4 vols. (East Lansing, Mich., 1967–81), 2:162, 164 [hereafter, *Garfield Diary*]; Allan Peskin, *Garfield* (Canton, Ohio, 1978), pp. 354–86.

were executed. By late October, the efforts of Garfield and others could not prevent Democratic victory in the Buckeye State elections, and, while some critics initially blamed the congressman personally for his party's woes, it soon became clear that the Ohio contest was no isolated phenomenon. Not since before the Civil War had Republican hegemony been so threatened in so many formerly unshakable strongholds. The resulting defeats, combined with "redemption" of all except four ex-Confederate states, raised the frightening possibility that, after fifteen years of ascendancy, the G.O.P. might even lose control of the federal House in 1874.[6]

It was not surpising, therefore, that Garfield was deeply disturbed when he returned to Washington on November 12 to prepare for the convening of Congress three weeks later. As he wrote in his diary that night: "I look upon the coming session as the most troublesome and uncertain of any that I [have] ever seen at this distance from it. . . . There will be a babble of opinion and remedies laid before the public, with great uncertainty as to the outcome. Everything is tended to saturate the public mind with suspicion and unfaith and no man is wise enough to see the path through the entanglements. It is a bad time to be in public life."[7]

Clearly, circumstances seemed greatly changed from those of ten years earlier, when the Ohioan began his service in the Capitol. Then the nation, or what remained of it, was suffering the trauma of Civil War and Garfield had been elected in absentia, while on duty with the Union Army. He had been reluctant to leave the front, but his partisans, abetted by President Lincoln, persuaded him that the House— and the country—could use the insights of one with combat experience. Appropriately, the general so recently in the field was placed on the Committee on Military Affairs. There, he became involved immediately in the most pressing decisions of the day.[8]

After Appomattox, however, and as Reconstruction progressed, the locus of federal attention shifted. Garfield was one of the first to anticipate the change, and within months of Lee's surrender he requested and received a middle-level place on Ways & Means. From then

6. *Garfield Diary*, 2:225–35; and Horace Samuel Merrill, *Bourbon Democracy of the Middle West, 1865–1896* (Seattle, 1953), chap. 5.

7. *Garfield Diary*, 2:243.

8. Peskin, *Garfield*, pp. 146–48, 224–46; Theodore Clarke Smith, *The Life and Letters of James Abram Garfield*, 2 vols. (New Haven, 1925), 1:220–36, 381–86. On Washington life, see Harry James Brown, "Garfield's Congress," *Hayes Historical Journal*, 3 (1981):57–77; see also Henry Adams, *The Education of Henry Adams* (1918; New York, 1931), chap. 16.

on, except in the Fortieth Congress (when he chaired Military Affairs), his principal assignments would always be on panels with economic jurisdiction; as the Forty-third Congress convened in 1873, he was about to begin his second term at the helm of Appropriations. As head of a preeminent committee, and as one of the most experienced members of the House, Garfield was viewed as a likely successor to Speaker James G. Blaine if, as was expected, the Maine Republican ran for the presidency in 1876. Yet despite his power and influence, the Ohioan was far from happy. He wrote frequently in his diary of feeling "jaded," and of "not much being accomplished." His days were full ("I am worked beyond all measure"), but mainly with the routine responsibilities of constituent service. His committee, meanwhile, met frequently in mundane and often unproductive sessions and was "not as hard working a body of men as the Committee of last Congress."[9] Thus, in retrospect his November prediction had not been far from the mark. There was no shortage of things to do, but the course was indeed "troublesome and uncertain"; it was "a bad time to be in public life."

Garfield was not alone in his frustration. Many of his colleagues later wrote fulsome autobiographies, and the mid-1870s rarely figured largely in their tales. Speaker Blaine, for instance, devoted a total of only thirty pages in his two-volume memoir to the Forty-third and Forty-fourth Congresses, while New York Democrat S. S. Cox and Massachusetts Republicans George Frisbie Hoar, George S. Boutwell, and Benjamin Butler were similarly succinct. Even Ohio's John Sherman, one of the most accomplished and respected members of the Senate, could think of little to say; he suggested in his *Recollections* that, although he was chairman of the important Finance Committee, his greatest achievement during this period was probably sponsorship of a resolution to complete the Washington Monument. To men like these, Capitol service during Ulysses Grant's second term apparently was forgettable not because it was corrupt but because it seemed so unproductive. As Francis Curtis, an early Republican Party historian, would conclude: "the[se] session[s] were unimportant. . . . a large amount of legislation failed to pass both Houses."[10]

9. Committee assignments from *Cong. Dir.*, 38th–43d Congs. (Washington, 1864–74). *Garfield Diary*, 2:298, 274, 280, 282, 285, and passim; Smith, *Life of Garfield*, 1:387–97.

10. James G. Blaine, *Twenty Years of Congress: From Lincoln to Garfield*, 2 vols. (Norwich, Conn., 1886), 2:537–66; Samuel S. Cox, *Union-Disunion-Reunion: Three Decades of Federal Legislation* (Providence, 1885); Hoar, *Autobiography;* George S. Boutwell, *Reminiscences of Sixty Years in Public Affairs*, 2 vols. (New York, 1902); Benjamin F. Butler, *Butler's Book: A Review of His Legal, Political, and Military Career* (Boston, 1892); John Sherman, *Recollec-*

Some contemporary observers, however, analyzed the situation very differently. According to Gamaliel Bradford, a Boston reformer and active student of public affairs, politicians and citizens who expected governance to be as grandly compelling in 1870 as during the Rebellion were destined to disappointment; postwar problems were more complex and demanding than those of the preceding decade, but they challenged the intellect, not emotions. Writing in the *North American Review,* he argued: "The questions of slavery and the war were perfectly simple. The people comprehended them. In contrast, the questions which are now pressing upon us are technical, and call for the exercise of statesmanship . . . the people do not understand the subjects, and require to be led." Similarly, New York *Tribune* editor Whitelaw Reid referred to "the more difficult issues of this more critical time" in an 1873 speech that he delivered on several college campuses. By expressing such insights, these men showed cognizance of something few would understand so well without benefit of hindsight: in policy terms, the 1870s constituted a turning point.[11] On one level, this meant that, while war-related activity would persist for at least awhile, it would have to share center stage and eventually relinquish it to other subjects of national concern. Fundamentally, though, the coming transformation was more profound than even Reid and Bradford knew. The magnitude and success of the Union war effort had created new appreciation for the activated potential of federal governance, and, once hostilities ended, the public would insist that that potential be used in new and unprecedented ways. At the same time, commercial and territorial expansion resulted in heavy demand for traditional public services: courts and law enforcement, post offices, customs agents, internal improvements, and so on. Thus, both the amount and scope of Wash-

---

tions of Forty Years in the House, Senate, and Cabinet: An Autobiography, 2 vols. (Chicago, 1895), 1:547–48; Francis Curtis, *The Republican Party: A History of Its Fifty Years' Existence and a Record of Its Measures and Leaders, 1854–1904,* 2 vols. (New York, 1904), 2:37–40. Along these lines, Henry Adams said of Rep. Abram S. Hewitt (D-N.Y.), whom he admired greatly, that he "was the more struck by Hewitt's saying, at the end of his laborious career as legislator, that he left behind no permanent result except the Act consolidating the Surveys. Adams knew no other man who had done so much except Mr. Sherman." Adams, *Education,* pp. 294–95.

11. Gamaliel Bradford, "Congressional Reform," *NAR,* 111 (1870), 334; Reid quoted in Royal Cortissoz, *The Life of Whitelaw Reid,* 2 vols. (New York, 1921), 1:256–57. See also George F. Hoar, "The Conduct of Business in Congress," *NAR,* 128 (1879), 120. Only an individual as smug as Henry Adams would be able to assert, as early as 1870: "to say that the government of the United States is passing through a period of transition is one of the baldest complacencies of politics"; "The Session," *NAR,* 111 (1870), 29.

ington policy making would change dramatically during the course of Grant's tenure. The capital and the country were moving, albeit tentatively and not entirely consciously, toward development of a modern national state.

The road to modernity was not smooth, however, especially at its inception. It grew wide and then narrow, twisted, turned, and sometimes even regressed; only occasionally did it proceed easily or uncompromisingly. To begin with, although pressures to address new economic and social questions were intense, it was impossible for Congress to neglect persistent problems from the past, including many that resulted from the Civil War. Currency was one such matter. In order to finance the Union effort, the Treasury had suspended specie payments and authorized issuance of legal tender notes, or "greenbacks." By mid-1866, over $450 million of this paper was circulating, the national debt equaled a staggering $2.8 billion (or nearly one-half the gross national product), and inflation was rampant. These consequences of sectional crisis would affect the course of monetary policy during the Grant years and, indeed, for the remainder of the century.[12]

Finance was not the only sector of the agenda that felt the reverberations of battle. Conditions in at least three Southern states remained so jeopardous that, through the mid-seventies, the president would have to consider activating troops to restore order; Louisiana, probably the most unstable of all, would be unable until December 1877 to decide peaceably on a governor or on an incumbent for one of its two Senate seats. Investigations of continued unrest would preoccupy at least a dozen standing and select committees of the House alone throughout Grant's second term.[13] Indeed, remnants of rebellion had their impact on the entire legislative calendar. Of the 833 laws enacted during the Forty-third Congress, for example, 441 (or 52.9 percent) were private bills, almost all for relief of parties injured by the war. Many provided pensions, while others allotted reparations to businesses, churches and schools, homesteads, and other properties sustaining military damage. Five House committees and four committees in the Senate confined their deliberations primarily to this kind of work, and while only 18.8

---

12. Walter T. K. Nugent, *The Money Question during Reconstruction* (New York, 1967), esp. chap. 2; Robert P. Sharkey, *Money, Class, and Party: An Economic Study of Civil War and Reconstruction* (Baltimore, 1959), esp. chap. 1; and Irwin Unger, *The Greenback Era: A Social and Political History of American Finance, 1856–1879* (Princeton, 1964).

13. Gillette, *Retreat from Reconstruction*, chaps. 5–7; Joe Gray Taylor, *Louisiana Reconstructed: 1863–1877* (Baton Rouge, 1974), esp. chaps. 7 and 11; and Agnes S. Grosz, "The Political Career of Pinckney Benton Steward Pinchback," *La. Hist. Q.*, 27 (1944), 527–612.

percent of the House membership served on such panels, they were responsible collectively for over 60 percent of all introduced bills.[14] But even that extensive activity did not comprise the sum of congressional involvement in relief. For although the Bureaus of Claims and Pensions handled routine cases—by far the majority—they were agencies staffed principally by beneficiaries of legislative patronage who, by law as well as popular sentiment, were predominantly old soldiers. Members therefore bore the burden of getting jobs for as many qualified constituents as they could, and then of working with these appointees to oversee disposition of applications for aid from other residents of their districts.[15]

Thus, persistent concerns stemming directly from the war contributed to an enlarged Washington workload in the 1870s. But such tasks alone do not explain the great expansion in congressional activity (Table 2). Rather, the aftermath of rebellion coincided and combined with other phenomena—immigration, westward settlement, technological innovations, and acknowledgment of the potential utility of public assertiveness and federal hegemony over the states—that were at least equally significant. The result was growth within three distinct, albeit interrelated, policy dimensions whose content and size owed little if anything to sectional conflict. First was the "traditional" domain, encompassing things like patronage, tariffs, internal improvements, and law enforcement: business that long had been considered intrinsic to federal jurisdiction and resolution. Next, there was what might be

14. Figures on legislation compiled from information in the Index to the *Cong. Rec.,* 43d Cong. are: 543 laws enacted, of which 292 (53.8 percent) were private. The smaller number of laws in the 44th Cong. was due mainly to divided party control. Figures on committee membership compiled from information in the *Cong. Dir.,* 43d Cong., 1st sess.; five relevant House committees were Claims, War Claims (called "Revolutionary Claims" prior to 1873), Invalid Pensions, Revolutionary Pensions (whose business increased as older veterans sought to climb aboard the gravy train established for Civil War soldiers; it also handled business related to the War of 1812 and Mexican War, many of whose survivors were, by the 1870s, elderly and needy), and Private Land Claims. See also "Work of the Forty-third Congress," *The Republic* 2 (1874), 203; and James, Lord Bryce, *The American Commonwealth,* 2 vols. (London, 1888), 1:671–72.

15. On veterans' preference, see *U.S. Statutes at Large,* 13 (1865–67), 571; Mary R. Dearing, *Veterans in Politics: The Story of the G.A.R.* (Baton Rouge, 1952), pp. 53–56; and Leonard D. White, *The Republican Era, 1869–1901: A Study in Administrative History* (New York, 1958), pp. 389–90. See *Politics and Patronage in the Gilded Age: The Correspondence of James A. Garfield and Charles E. Henry,* ed. James D. Norris and Arthur H. Shaffer (Madison, Wis., 1970), for a member's typical experience with patronage and bureaucracy; see also *Garfield Diary;* White, *Republican Era,* chap. 4; and correspondence of congressmen, especially those who were themselves veterans, e.g.: the Papers of James A. Garfield, Benjamin F. Butler, Nathaniel P. Banks, and (Sen.) John A. Logan, all L.C.

Table 2. Amount of federal legislation, by decade, 1789–1958

Years	Congresses	Average no. of bills per Congress	Total	As % of all bills	Public acts	Private acts	Private as % of acts
					Legislative enactments		
1789–1799	1–5	147	107	72.8	92	15	14.0
1799–1809	6–10	204	103	50.5	87	16	15.5
1809–1819	11–15	425	220	51.8	144	76	34.5
1819–1829	16–20	535	250	46.7	130	120	48.0
1829–1839	21–25	1,077	431	40.0	141	289	67.1
1839–1849	26–30	1,093	317	29.0	120	197	62.1
1849–1859	31–35	1,320	325	24.6	118	208	64.0
1859–1869	36–40	1,847	485	26.3	265	222	45.8
1869–1879	41–45	6,171	739	12.0	345	394	53.3
1879–1889	46–50	12,384	1,060	8.6	342	717	67.6
1889–1899	51–55	15,482	1,134	7.3	411	722	63.7
1899–1909	56–60	28,885	3,222	11.2	470	2,752	85.4
1909–1919	61–65	32,421	601	1.9	415	206	34.3
1919–1929	66–70	20,745	1,047	5.0	685	362	34.6
1929–1938	71–75	18,173	1,255	6.9	687	567	45.2
1939–1948	76–80	10,734	1,435	13.4	790	645	44.9
1949–1958	81–85	15,090	1,813	12.0	852	961	53.0

Source: *Historical Statistics of the United States: Colonial Times to 1957* (Washington, 1961), pp. 959–60.

termed the "adoptive" agenda, which embraced responsibilities that formerly had been handled by state, or even local, authorities. Finally, there was an amorphous and almost infinitely expandable sphere of "discretionary" initiatives, bringing matters into the arena of governance that, until then, had not been deemed properly public at all.

Despite the toll of battle, for instance, nearly 15,000,000 more people inhabited the country in 1876 than when Lincoln took office fifteen years earlier; among them were 4.2 million immigrants. While the majority of aliens went to established cities, some joined the wave of migration to the far West, where population almost trebled between 1860 and 1880. And close behind the pioneers were the locomotives. Operational rail milage more than doubled between Grant's acceptance of Lee's surrender and his departure from the White House scarcely over a decade later, while total railroad property investment and capital quadrupled. Only eighteen years after the first federal land grant railroad was chartered in 1851, the Golden Spike at Utah's Promontory Point signaled completion of the first transcontinental route, whereupon this and other lines spurred settlement of newly accessible territory that promised agricultural and mineral riches. So in the years from 1850 to 1870 nine new territories were organized and seven states admitted to the Union.[16] This led to skyrocketing demands for routine services: post offices; law enforcement and judicial personnel; revenue, land, pension, and customs agents; internal improvements; and so on. Table 3 reveals the dimensions of this rise in federal activity, as well as that the increase was more massive in the 1870s than in the preceding decade of war. The Age of Grant, in short, experienced an unprecedented boom in both the size and range of the national public sector, insofar as traditional business was concerned.

This same popular and territorial expansion, in combination with advances in industrial and other technology, also impelled a nationalization of business previously within state or local jurisdiction. For not only had American endeavor generally become greatly enlarged, its geographic, social, and economic sectors exhibited increasingly complex interrelationships that only the centralized authority of Washington could contend with adequately. The impact of railroads typified this. As their place in the national economy grew more prominent, railroads were at once welcomed for the progress they signified and feared for the commercial power they represented. Thus, by the late

16. Figures from *Historical Statistics of the United States, Colonial Times to 1957* (Washington, 1961), pp. 7, 12–13, 45, 427–28.

Table 3. Increase of civilian federal employees, 1861–1881

Year	Total federal	Outside Washington	Post Office Department only
		Types of employees	
1861	36,672	34,473	30,269
1871	51,020	44,798	36,696
% increase, 1861–71	39.1	30.1	21.2
1881	100,020	86,896	56,421
% increase, 1871–81	96.0	94.0	53.8
% increase, 1861–81	172.7	152.1	86.4

Source: *Historical Statistics of the United States, Colonial Times to 1957* (Washington, 1961), p. 710.

1860s efforts were initiated to regulate mass transportation. Such efforts began in the states, as had previously been the case with ante-bellum land grants and subsidies; but as the rapid failures of the Granger Laws showed, local regulation could not control an activity that had no respect for boundaries. Washington had no choice. It had to assume responsibility for oversight of interstate commerce, and the first proposal to do so passed the House in 1874.[17] To be sure, creation of the Interstate Commerce Commission did not occur until 1887. Still, railroad regulation—as well as responsibility for routes, rail gauges, patents, and so on—typified the Grant years' emerging awareness of the necessity for federal policy coordination; it was an early, but not isolated, precedent for the capital's soon-to-burgeon "adoptive" agenda.

Discretionary initiatives, meanwhile, were already increasing during the 1870s, although just a few of them would achieve fruition right away. The Petition Files now in the National Archives, as well as contemporary journalism, offer potent testimony to the range of concerns that citizens had begun to bring to Washington; one reporter for the *Republic*, in 1876, was able to crowd two columns of his magazine with selective listings.[18] To a great extent, the Civil War could be credited with inspiring the plethora of new demands, as it stood and was recognized as a demonstration of the potential power lodged along the

17. Gabriel Kolko, *Railroads and Regulation, 1877–1916* (Princeton, 1965), chap. 1; William J. Cunningham, *American Railroad: Government Control and Reconstruction Policies* (Chicago, 1922), p. 10; Balthasar Henry Meyer, *Railway Legislation in the United States* (New York, 1903), pp. 191–94; *Hse. Rpts.*, 43d Cong., 1st sess., no. 26; *Hse. Jnl.*, 43d Cong., 1st sess., 665.
18. "Work of the Forty-fourth Congress," *Republic*, 6 (1876), 69.

Potomac's banks.[19] And Reconstruction had served to expand the boundaries of acceptable public action even further. The variety of freedmen's programs, for instance, comprised an unprecedented foray into the realm of social policy making that almost immediately led other groups to turn to Washington for redress of their grievances. Just as antebellum feminists had been inspired by abolition, their postwar sisters attempted to correlate their own demands for suffrage and civil rights with those of the former slaves; while they were explicitly excluded from the Fourteenth and Fifteenth amendments, the 1872 Republican platform expressed cautious sympathy for their goal and the first amendment to allow females to vote was introduced in 1878.[20] Indeed, the very emphasis on political objectives that characterized the late nineteenth-century Woman Movement reflected a more general popular enthusiasm for public solutions to what formerly had been considered private problems suited to moral suasion. Advocates of temperance, labor and civil service reform, scientific agriculture, abolition of capital punishment, and Indian rights were only a few of those who began to petition Washington.[21] Educators found an especially warm welcome there. Convinced that the rebellion had demonstrated the need for an informed citizenry, James Garfield persuaded his colleagues in 1867 to establish both a House Committee on Education & Labor and a federal Department of Education. Five years later, under his sponsorship, the House passed its first bill authorizing national aid to education.[22]

The Freedmen's Bureau was disbanded by the mid-1870s, of course,

19. Morton Keller, *Affairs of State: Public Life in Late Nineteenth Century America* (Cambridge, 1977), chap. 4.

20. *National Party Platforms, 1840–1972*, comp. Donald Bruce Johnson and K. E. Porter (Urbana, Ill., 1975), p. 47; Elizabeth Cady Stanton et al., *History of Woman Suffrage*, 6 vols. (New York, 1881–1922), 2:324, 360, and passim; Ellen Carol DuBois, *Feminism and Suffrage: The Emergence of an Independent Women's Movement in America, 1848–1869* (Ithaca, 1978).

21. An excellent, if incomplete, indicator of the scope of the discretionary agenda is the Legislative Petitions File, Legislative and Judicial Division, National Archives, Washington. Petitions are filed by congress, chamber, committee of reference, and, when appropriate, subject. There are forty-one linear feet of petition files for the House alone during the second Grant administration.

22. Peskin, *Garfield*, pp. 291–97; Rep. Thomas E. Petri (R-Wis.), "James A. Garfield and Education," speech [written by M. S. Thompson], *Cong. Rec.*, 96th Cong., 2d sess. (1 Oct. 1980), H10423; James A. Garfield, "National Aid to Education," speech of 6 Feb. 1872, in *The Works of James Abram Garfield*, ed. Burke A. Hinsdale, 2 vols. (Boston, 1883), 2:19–25. The Senate failed to concur in this action. During the 1870s, the House defeated on several occasions a more rigorous bill sponsored by George F. Hoar; Hoar, *Autobiography*, 1:265; Richard E. Welch, Jr., *George Frisbie Hoar and the Half-Breed Republicans* (Cambridge, 1971), pp. 22–25.

and the Education Department would be demoted to a bureau; temperance, woman suffrage, and effective labor reform would not reach fruition until the twentieth century. Still, the Reconstruction social programs were more than aberrrant, war-related experiments. A number of specific initiatives survived and prospered: Howard University (1867) and Hampton Institute (1868) for blacks, Gallaudet College for the Deaf (1864), soldiers' homes and pensions for veterans, land grant colleges, and so on. More important, the mere assertion of such varied new demands, as well as the consideration—however limited—accorded to them, suggested a new willingness to extend the potential boundaries of what might be called the discretionary policy agenda. Over time, many concerns raised first in the 1860s and 1870s would be reintroduced, and, along with others not yet conceived, would succeed. Then the foundations laid earlier would serve effectively as precedent, as usable legislative history and justification.[23]

Nonetheless, few discretionary initiatives achieved fruition during the Grant years, partly because of as yet ineradicable doubts as to the wisdom of a broader public sector.[24] Such doubts may be inevitable accompaniments to major shifts in the polity; at any rate they almost certainly contributed to the ambiguous message conveyed by the data in Table 2. On the one hand, more bills were being dropped into the hopper during the seventies than ever before, as the Capitol dockets expanded almost five times faster than in any previous decade. Moreover, as those years were followed by another period of growth, the typical session of the 1880s saw over nine times the number of proposals introduced than had been the case in the 1850s. Thus, Ohio's Garfield was not far off the mark when, in 1873, he estimated that "the business of a member of Congress must have more than quadrupled during the last twenty years." No wonder he felt "jaded" and "worked beyond all measure"![25]

One fact was indisputable. The bulk of big government's newly assumed burden would fall upon the shoulders of Congress. This was,

---

23. Keller, *Affairs of State*, chap. 5; Walter I. Trattner, *From Poor Law to Welfare State: A History of Social Welfare in America* (New York, 1974), p. 78.

24. Keller, *Affairs of State*, chap. 8; John G. Sproat, *"The Best Men": Liberal Reformers in the Gilded Age* (New York, 1968), chaps. 3, 6; Edward C. Kirkland, *Dream and Thought in the Business Community, 1860–1900* (Ithaca, N.Y., 1956), chap. 5; Stephen Skowronek, *Building a New American State: The Expansion of National Administrative Capacities, 1877–1920* (Cambridge, 1982), chaps. 1, 2; and Samuel P. Huntington, *American Politics: The Promise of Disharmony* (Cambridge, 1981), chaps. 1, 2, 5.

25. *Garfield Diary*, 2:225–26, 298, 280, 274.

after all, the decade that Woodrow Wilson immortalized in the succeeding decade as that of "Congressional Government," and, as late as 1895, a senator who first rose to prominence during Reconstruction would declare that "the executive department in a republic like ours should be subordinate to the legislative department."[26] Indeed, the Grant years may have marked the pinnacle of assertiveness from the Capitol, for in the wake of what was widely perceived as Andrew Johnson's abuse of his office, legislative leaders were determined to preserve their own institution's hegemony. In this respect, the ascendance of Ulysses Grant was welcome and appropriate; upon accepting the 1868 Republican nomination, he had called the presidency a "purely administrative" post—and gave every indication of believing it. Just a year after the general was inaugurated, Henry Adams could inform his readers in the *North American Review:* "[Grant's] own idea of his duties as President was always openly and consistently expressed, and may perhaps be best described as that of the commander of an army in time of peace . . . as it was the duty of every military commander to obey the civil authority without question, so it was the duty of the President to follow without hesitation the wishes of the people as expressed by Congress."[27]

But if, as Woodrow Wilson—and Grant—believed, "the legislature is the aggressive spirit" and "the motive power of the government," what did that imply in the 1870s? One must distinguish at the outset between relative institutional *power* (within the overall federal system) and the actual *effectiveness* or *strength* of a body itself (its internal capacity and resources). In the Reconstruction Congress there was surely an abundance of the former, but the latter was far from evident; in the words of Henry Adams: "Congress is inefficient, and shows itself more and more incompetent, as at present constituted, to wield the enormous powers that are forced upon it." The legislature's potency, then, was more apparent than real; it seemed strong only in contrast to a weak and passive executive. Examined independently and purely on its own merits, Congress was—in structural, procedural, and compositional terms—a highly imperfect, ineffectual body. "There is nowhere," declared Senator (and former Representative) George F. Hoar in 1879,

---

26. Woodrow Wilson, *Congressional Government: A Study in American Politics* (1885; Cleveland, 1956); Sherman, *Recollections,* 1:447.

27. Grant's letter in *History of American Presidential Elections, 1789–1968,* ed. Arthur M. Schlesinger, Jr., et al., 3 vols. (New York, 1971), 2:1274. Adams, "The Session," 33–34. See also W. R. Brock, *An American Crisis: Congress and Reconstruction, 1865–1867* (New York, 1963); and Wilfred E. Binckley, *President and Congress* (New York, 1947), chaps. 7–9.

"responsibility for securing due attention to important measures, and no authority to decide between their different claims."[28] To a great degree, therefore, the legislature's vast intragovernmental power persisted *in spite of* severe and concurrent intra-institutional weaknesses. And it was the juxtaposition of these two contradictory conditions that constituted the great and most peculiar irony of post-Civil War "Congressional Government."

By the Age of Grant the Capitol had, in other words, clearly overextended itself. As welfare agency, employment bureau, ombudsman with the bureaucracy for constituents, policy initiator, program implementer, political barometer and partisan testing-ground, oversight watchdog, and self-styled (if only sometime) guardian of the public virtue, the House and Senate had assumed or been asked to handle a range of responsibilities that collectively and, in most cases, individually exceeded dramatically their normal pre–Civil War, peacetime workload. *The Republic* editorialized continuously on the "immense amount of routine business," and suggested that it was impossible for officials to pay attention to even one-tenth of the subjects presented for their consideration and that, in its "essential business," the legislature was always "far behind."[29]

Indeed, the perspective of hindsight suggests that demands upon Congress in the Age of Grant more closely resembled those of the twentieth century than those of the antebellum era. But if the number and diversity of government's tasks were "modern," the institution that attempted to perform them surely was not. There was, at that time, no formal or consistent adherence to a seniority system. Floor leaders were not, as now, elected by their party caucuses; instead, they were products of a committee roster determined by an extremely powerful, sometimes autocratic, speaker. Levels of both parliamentary and substantive expertise were, by present standards, appallingly low, even among the most experienced and influential committee chairmen. And staff—which is widely appreciated now as having enormous importance and authority—was virtually nonexistent.[30]

---

28. Wilson, *Congressional Government*, pp. 35–36, 43; Adams, "The Session," 60; Hoar, "Business in Congress," 134. See also White, *Republican Era*, p. 48; Brock, *American Crisis*, p. 59.

29. *Garfield Diary*, 2:225–26, see also p. 198; *Republic*, 2 (1874), 75, and 6 (1876), 195.

30. See chap. 2, below; on staff, see Michael J. Malbin, *Unelected Representatives: Congressional Staff and the Future of Representative Government* (New York, 1980); Harrison W. Fox, Jr., and S. W. Hammond, *Congressional Staffs: The Invisible Force in American Lawmaking* (New York, 1977); Rochelle Jones and P. Woll, *The Private World of Congress* (New York,

These circumstances, of course, were neither novel nor peculiar to the years just after the Civil War. Rather, they were familiar holdovers from the days when federal responsibilities were not nearly so extensive. But given the sizable enlargement of the legislature's role, its antebellum procedures and modes of behavior had become acutely anachronistic. In other words, Congress could be said to have suffered from an especially pronounced incidence of *time-lag.*

Time-lag is a condition characterized by a developmental gap between (1) the growth, in number and diversity, of the kinds of policy demands with which government is expected to deal, and (2) the public sector's evolution of institutional norms and machinery adequate to meet those demands. Of course, Congress is supposed to be a reactive body, so some amount of time-lag, of disjuncture between pressure and response, is inevitable. But because of unusually vast and rapid development within the federal sector, constraints imposed by time-lag in the 1870s were particularly severe. Henry Adams declared at the beginning of the decade: "This system is outgrown. . . . New powers, new duties, new responsibilities, new burdens of every sort, are incessantly crowding upon the government at the very moment when it finds itself unequal to managing the limited powers it is accustomed to wield."[31] And as Adams, that outspoken and perceptive analyst of his times, was well aware, such an outgrown system was extremely vulnerable to corruption, actual and alleged.

Twentieth-century research into political modernization sustains Adams's perception. While hardly condoning suspicious practices or disputing their disturbing effects, some scholars suggest that high levels of real or purported corruption normally accompany transformations in governance—and may, therefore, be unavoidable. Samuel P. Huntington offers three reasons why this is so. First, change creates new sources of wealth and power. Corruption, then, "may be the means of assimilating new groups into the political system by irregular means because the system has been unable to adapt sufficiently fast to provide legitimate and acceptable means for this purpose." In the America of the 1860s and 1870s, dozens of new social, commercial, racial, industrial, and professional entities were demanding integration into the polity; only a few would find the extant machinery and procedures

————
1979), chap. 4; and J. McIver Weatherford, *Tribes on the Hill* (New York, 1981), esp. pp. 47–55, 61–70, 214–20.

31. Adams, "The Session," 59–60; see also David J. Rothman, *Politics and Power: The United States Senate, 1869–1901* (Cambridge, 1966), p. 4.

adequate to their needs. Second, Huntington notes that governmental development usually involves expansion of the public sector's activities and jurisdiction—again, something clearly characteristic of the post–Civil War federal sphere. In such circumstances, "the multiplication of laws multiplies the possibilities of corruption," especially if enforcement mechanisms are insufficient to handle an enlarged workload or if the profit (material or otherwise) to be made by breaking the law is an attractive enough incentive to do so.

Finally, Huntington contends that systemic change eventually results in new public values and objectives, as old evaluative criteria and practices become inadequate or inappropriate to altered circumstances. For a time, however, *no* agreed-upon standards may be operative because, while traditional methods may no longer be effective, new modes have not yet emerged or achieved consensual acceptance. In that interim—when time-lag is at its most severe—the legitimacy of all norms may be undermined, and the result is likely to be a higher incidence of activity that does not seem to "fit": that might, therefore, be deemed corrupt under either the old rules or the new—perhaps even under both. Within such an environment, charges of corruption may proliferate but mean little. Thus, Huntington concludes, a "modernizing" society's initial response to change usually will take extreme forms: "The ideals of honesty, probity, universalism, and merit often become so overriding that individuals and groups come to condemn as corrupt . . . practices which are accepted as normal and even legitimate in more modern societies."[32]

To understand both Gilded Age corruption and attitudes toward it as accouterments of political evolution is not necessarily to underestimate

32. Samuel P. Huntington, *Political Order in Changing Societies* (New Haven, 1968), pp. 59–63. See also Keller, *Affairs of State*, p. 245; J. S. Nye, "Corruption and Political Development: A Cost-Benefit Analysis," *APSR*, 6 (1967), 417–27; James C. Scott, "Corruption, Machine Politics and Political Change," *APSR*, 63 (1969), 1142–59, and *Comparative Political Corruption* (Englewood Cliffs, N.J., 1972), chaps. 1–2; Morton Keller, "Corruption in America: Continuity and Change," and passim, in *Before Watergate: Problems of Corruption in American Society*, ed. Abraham S. Eisenstadt et al. (Brooklyn, N.Y., 1978); Richard L. McCormick, "Scandal and Reform: A Framework for the Study of Political Corruption in the Nineteenth-Century United States and a Case Study of the 1820s," unpublished paper delivered at the Shelby Cullom Davis Center for Historical Studies, Princeton University, 26 Feb. 1982, and "The Discovery that 'Business Corrupts Politics': A Reappraisal of the Origins of Progressivism," *AHR*, 86 (1981), 247–74. An alternative view is in George C. S. Benson et al., *Political Corruption in America* (Lexington, Mass., 1978), esp. pp. 80–83, 212–15.

their seriousness; some episodes of the 1870s would be considered scandalous by any standard, and contemporaries, who lacked the advantage of Huntington's hindsight, were understandably upset. But for the most part, they also were rather unsophisticated in their notions of what constituted fraud and of why it occurred, as well as in their responses and proposed solutions to it. Subsequent scholarship, meanwhile—especially that of the Josephson school—has served mainly to reinforce and preserve late nineteenth-century naiveté. And nothing reflects this more vividly than persistent prejudices against lobbying.

Today, as a century ago, lobbyists commonly are regarded as premier symbols of corruption, as attractive scapegoats to whom blame can be ascribed for any problems in the body politic.[33] Even modern congressmen, who almost all praise the vast majority of current lobbyists, nonetheless recognize the pejorative connotations that seem indelibly connected to the designation. As Rep. Edward W. Pattison (D-N.Y.) declared in 1975, during testimony before a House committee: "What image arises in the citizen's mind when the idea of lobbying is posed? He thinks of shady deals made in secret rooms, clandestine meetings in restrooms and hotel lobbies, the shoebox full of money passed from one pair of gloved hands to another. The public view of lobbying is that it is an illicit, unfair influence on the government process. The perception is that lobbying is an abuse by special interests, who can buy whatever they want from elected representatives while those who elected them are unable to exert any influence except every 2 or 4 or 6 years."[34]

Popular opinion has changed very little, apparently, over the last one hundred years, since Pattison's statement reflects much the same consensus that existed in the time of Ulysses Grant. Four months after the general's first inaugural, for instance, a reporter for the respected *Nation* defined the professional lobbyist as "a man whom everybody

33. Andrew M. Scott and Margaret A. Hunt, *Congress and Lobbies: Image and Reality* (Chapel Hill, 1966), pp. 3–4; Lester Milbrath, *The Washington Lobbyists* (Chicago, 1963), pp. 15, 65; Lewis Anthony Dexter, *How Organizations Are Represented in Washington* (Indianapolis, 1969), p. 11. See also two book-length "exposés" of lobbying: Kenneth G. Crawford, *The Pressure Boys* (New York, 1939); Karl Schriftgeisser, *The Lobbyists: The Art and Business of Influencing Lawmakers* (Boston, 1951). As Speaker Blaine said during the 1870s: "That is always the cry when anything [unsavory] comes up, 'There is a lobby!'" Gail Hamilton [Mary Abigail Dodge], *Biography of James G. Blaine* (Norwich, Conn., 1895), p. 439.

34. *Lobbying—Efforts to Influence Governmental Actions: Hearings before the Committee on Standards of Official Conduct, House of Representatives (94th Cong., 1st sess.) on H.R. 15 and Related Bills*, Committee Print (Washington, 1976), p. 163.

suspects; who is generally during one half of the year without honesst means of livelihood; and whose employment by those who have bills before a legislature is only resorted to as a disagreeable necessity." Edward Winslow Martin, author of a sensational 1873 exposé, *Behind the Scenes in Washington,* reacted similarly, if more bluntly: "Their plan is to rob the public treasury." Such derogatory comments were not, to be sure, without their antebellum antecedents. In 1856, poet Walt Whitman had castigated "lobbyers" as "crawling serpentine men, the lousy combings and born freedom sellers of the earth," and fifteen years before that, James Silk Buckingham told of "agents, selected for their skill in the arts of deluding, persuading, and bribing members" of legislative bodies.[35] But the 1870s were different. Just as they witnessed an unprecedented expansion in the public sector, so too did they experience an unprecedented wave of obsession with, and antipathy toward, lobbying.

The concurrent appearance of these two phenomena, growth of government and concern about lobbying, was hardly coincidental. For although federal officials had made clear a willingness to widen the scope of their activities, they lacked capacity to cope successfully with the amount of business that ensued. As a result, many who tried to deal with Washington became frustrated by the lack of responsiveness they found there. Traditional channels of communication, especially those between legislators and their constituents, were clogged; such executive agencies as the Pension Office and Bureau of Claims were overloaded. In their impatience, people began to look for ways of breaking through the logjam. Some of them turned to lobbyists, and discovered a marked improvement in their chances for substantive satisfaction.

Lobbyists, of course, had always been around, but because government was trying to do more than it had in the past and because those who petitioned it were increasingly numerous, there was a correspondingly greater demand for lobbying services. At the same time, larger segments of the general population started to realize that a newly expanded policy agenda had the potential to affect their lives directly; what went on by the Potomac mattered concretely to them in ways it

35. "Existence of Lobby," *Nation,* 9 (1869), 64; Martin, *Behind the Scenes,* p. 217. See also "Is There Anything in It?" *Continental Monthly,* 3 (1863), 688; Walt Whitman, "The Eighteenth Presidency!" (1856) in *Walt Whitman: Complete Poetry and Selected Prose and Letters,* ed. Emory Halloway (London, 1938), p. 592; and James Silk Buckingham, *America: Historical, Statistic, and Descriptive,* 2 vols. (New York, 1841), 2:421.

never had before. Consequently, their attention was more intently focused on the capital.[36] Not only, then, were lobbyists more active than in antebellum days, but there was more extensive popular awareness of their presence. And as an interested but troubled citizenry observed a public arena that seemed riddled with confusion, inefficiency, and corruption, the participation of lobbyists—a relatively unfamiliar and, therefore, suspect element—emerged as a credible, even compelling, explanation for the problems that infested the polity.

The lobby was a plausible scapegoat for many reasons. First, its members were undeniably involved in many, though not all, of the era's most notorious scandals, and particularly in some (Credit Mobilier, for example) that were intended to result in large-scale private profit.[37] Second, while the right of petition enjoyed clear constitutional protection, there was both intuitive and legal doubt as to the legitimacy of employing outside advocates to plead in behalf of individuals or "special interests." Similarly, while there were established procedures for holding both elected officials and bureaucrats accountable—a fact that the generation of Johnson's impeachment would not forget—no such constraining instrument seemed to exist for lobbyists. The public, consequently, felt powerless to control what in its view was at best an extralegal phenomenon.[38] Finally, and in some ways most important, by blaming lobbyists for what ailed the body politic, others could deny their own culpability. Voters, for instance, could say that they were not responsible for the alleged corruption of their Representatives; rather, these men were being tampered with by something beyond the purview of the ballot box. Officials, meanwhile, could and sometimes did defend themselves against charges of "jobbery" by pleading innocence or ignorance of behind-the-scenes goings-on—and by simultaneously calling for investigations of outsiders who were attempting to debase the system.[39] And by identifying lobbying as some kind of corrosive alien

36. On lobbying in the early United States, see Schriftgeisser, *Lobbyists*, pp. 3–5; Martin, *Behind the Scenes*, pp. 24–28; and Kenneth R. Bowling, "The Bank Bill, the Capital City and President Washington," *Capitol Studies*, 1 (1972), 59–71. On Gilded Age public awareness, see Martin, *Behind the Scenes*, p. 5; Frank Luther Mott, *American Journalism, a History: 1690–1960*, 3d ed. (New York, 1962), chaps. 20–22, 25, 29, 30, and *A History of American Magazines, 1865–1885* (Cambridge, Mass., 1938), chap. 10; and Douglass Cater, *The Fourth Branch of Government* (Boston, 1959), pp. 82–83.

37. The Salary Grab was one scandal involving no outside lobbying.

38. See discussion of *Trist v. Child*, below.

39. The most famous cases like this both involved James G. Blaine, first after his implication in Credit Mobilier, and, second, after allegations of similar fraud (revealed in

factor, distinct from traditional political practices, ardent partisans were able to continue supporting besmirched candidates or leaders, who were "more sinn'd against than sinning," as they decried the malevolent forces that had seduced and despoiled them. In this context it was, therefore, neither hypocritical nor illogical for journals like the *Republic* and commentators like Thomas Nast to be both enthusiastic proponents of President Grant and vociferous critics of so-called "Grantism." For, within their frame of reference, the chief executive was as much a victim as was the public.[40]

Attitudes like these received reflection and reinforcement from a number of sources besides the press. One repository of opprobrium was the plethora of political dictionaries and compendia of "Americanisms" that appeared throughout the late nineteenth century; nearly all contained entries on lobbying or its practitioners, of which the following, from Brown and Strauss's 1888 *Dictionary of American Politics,* is typical: "*Lobby, The,* is a term applied collectively to men that make a business of corruptly influencing legislators. The individuals are called lobbyists. Their object is usually accomplished by means of money paid to the members, but any other means that is considered feasible is employed."[41] Woodrow Wilson, meanwhile, lent academic respectability to such charges. The single time "lobbying" appears in *Congressional Government,* it is modified by "corrupt"; in a second reference, the phrase "illegitimate influences" is used as a synonym.[42]

The most effective and influential genre in shaping public opinion, if not historiography, though, was probably political fiction.[43] Authors as

---

the so-called "Mulligan Letters") in 1876. See Hamilton, *Blaine,* pp. 268–93, 335–63; David Saville Muzzey, *James G. Blaine: A Political Idol of Other Days* (New York, 1934), pp. 64–69, 83–100; and James Ford Rhodes, *History of the United States,* 7:1–10, 194–206.

40. Compare, for instance, general articles on President Grant with "The Lobby," *Republic,* 1 (1873), 71–74. See discussion and examples of Nast's work in Albert Bigelow Paine, *Th. Nast: His Period and His Pictures* (New York, 1904); and Morton Keller, *The Art and Politics of Thomas Nast* (New York, 1968). See also Hesseltine, *Grant,* p. 308; Hoar, *Autobiography,* 1:305.

41. Everit Brown and Albert Strauss, *A Dictionary of American Politics* (New York, 1888), p. 253. See also John S. Farmer, ed., *Americanisms Old and New: A Dictionary of Words Peculiar to the United States* (London, 1889), p. 348; Charles Ledyard Norton, *Political Americanisms: A Glossary of Terms and Phrases Current at Different Periods in American Politics* (New York, 1890), p. 66; and John Russell Bartlett, *Dictionary of Americanisms: A Glossary of Words and Phrases Usually Regarded as Peculiar to the United States,* 4th ed. (Boston, 1877), pp. 262–63.

42. Wilson, *Congressional Government,* pp. 132–33.

43. On the illuminative value of political fiction generally, see Gordon Milne, *The American Political Novel* (Norman, Okla., 1966); for this period particularly, Robert Falk, *The Victorian Mode in American Fiction, 1865–1885* (East Lansing, Mich., 1965).

disparate as Henry Adams and Mark Twain used lobbyists as easily recognized symbols of wickedness and corruption; witness Mrs. Samuel Baker of *Democracy* and Colonel Mulberry Sellers and Laura Hopkins of *The Gilded Age*.[44] The book co-authored by Twain and Charles Dudley Warner was quickly adapted into a stage play that enjoyed great popularity, and had so great an impact that, even now, the tawdriness connoted by its title remains synonymous with the era it described. But during the mid-seventies themselves, the undisputed master of pejorative imagery, in the view of no less potent a contemporary than William Dean Howells, was John William De Forest.[45] In three novels and several short stories he used broad strokes to paint unidimensional portraits of lobbyists which left no doubt in anybody's mind that such creatures were agents of the devil: "Men of unwholesome skins, greasy garments, brutish manners, filthy minds, and sickening conversation; men who so reeked and drizzled with henbane tobacco and cockatrice whiskey that a moderate drinker or smoker would recoil from them as from a cesspool; men whose stupid, shameless boastings of their briberies were enough to warn away from them all but the elect of Satan . . . [and] decayed statesmen, who were now, indeed, nothing but unfragrant corpses, breeding all manner of vermin and miasma."

Darius Dorman, a lobbyist in De Forest's *Honest John Vane*, is described as speaking "with spasmodic twinges of cheerless gayety which resembled the 'cracked and thin laughter heard far down in Hell.' . . . Shaking all over with his dolorous mirth, his very raiment, indeed, quivering and undulating with it, so that it seemed as if there might be a twitching tail inside his trousers."[46] *Vane*, to be sure, was intended as a Jeremiad—its author suggested that it might be read as a "perversely reversed and altogether bedeviled rendering of *Pilgrim's Progress*"—but even his more subtle works reflected this demonic vision. Josie Murray, for example, the initially vivacious and almost sympathetically drawn protagonist of *Playing the Mischief*, because of her efforts to secure passage of a fraudulent piece of legislation is forced to undergo a rabid

---

44. Henry Adams, *Democracy, An American Novel* (New York, 1880); Mark Twain and Charles Dudley Warner, *The Gilded Age: A Tale of Today* (Hartford, Conn., 1874).

45. For opinion of Howells and other contemporaries, see James W. Gargano, ed., *Critical Essays on John William De Forest* (Boston, 1981). Howells's assessment is summarized best in "Review of *Honest John Vane*," *Atlantic Monthly*, 34 (1874), 229. See also Milne, *American Political Novel*, chap. 4; Falk, *Victorian Mode*, pp. 32–42; and James F. Light, *John William De Forest* (New York, 1965).

46. John William De Forest, *Honest John Vane* (1875; State College, Pa., 1960), pp. 133–35.

and Dorian Gray-like transformation that leaves her bereft of friends, poverty stricken, and driven virtually to prostitution.[47]

Is it any wonder, then, that almost no one actively sought to be identified as a "parliamentary practitioner," or that a real-life figure such as New Hampshire's William E. Chandler was expected to wince when the epithet of "lobbyist," albeit accurate, was applied to him? Upon introducing the star of the stage version of *Gilded Age* to his father the Speaker, Walker Blaine felt it necessary to assure him that he would find actor John T. Raymond "a more enjoyable acquaintance than you have found Col. Sellers a wrath-provoking one." And one highly respectable capital society lady became furious when she heard a rumor that she was the inspiration for Mrs. Samuel Baker in *Democracy*.[48] In reality, of course, few if any individuals actually lived down to the satanic fictional or journalistic reputations that had been ascribed generically to them. Yet antilobbying propaganda during the Grant years was so ubiquitous and vehement that, with just enough truth behind it to render it plausible, lobbying became a potent political symbol that provided many Americans with a convenient, if simplistic, explanation of why their government was not working properly.

Briefly, the rationale can be summarized as follows: (1) Government is ineffective, and incapable of responding satisfactorily to public demands. (2) Government is infested with corruption. (3) Corruption perverts the purposes of government and prevents it from functioning as it should. (4) Lobbyists are responsible for corruption. Therefore, (5) lobbyists are responsible for ineffective governance. If one accepted this logic, then the solution to the polity's problems was obvious. Rid the system of lobbyists. Castigate them, expose them, and make it impossible for them to operate. As the *Republic* editorialized in 1873: "the only effective cure [is] the complete abolition of the 'third house' by the overwhelming power of organized public opinion."[49] But in offering this proposal, the *Republic*'s writer unintentionally articulated the principal obstacle to its execution. For the methods by which "the

---

47. De Forest, *Honest John Vane*, p. 224, and *Playing the Mischief* (1875; State College, Pa., 1961). Other works by De Forest that deal with Washington or lobbying include *Justine's Lovers* (New York, 1878); "The Colored Member," *Galaxy*, Mar. 1872; and "An Inspired Lobbyist," *Atlantic*, Dec. 1872.

48. E. M. Smith to William E. Chandler, 25 May 1875, Chandler-NHHS Papers; Walker Blaine to James G. Blaine, 16 Jan. 1875, Blaine Papers, L. C.; Marian Hooper (Mrs. Henry) Adams to Robert W. Hooper, 17 Apr. 1881, in *The Letters of Mrs. Henry Adams, 1865–1883*, ed. Ward Thoron (Boston, 1938), pp. 283–85, and note, p. 168.

49. "The Lobby," *Republic*, 1 (1873), 74.

overwhelming power of *organized public opinion*" might make itself felt
came uncomfortably close to those of the "third house" it aimed to
eradicate.[50] It was through a massive lobbying campaign, in other
words, that lobbying was to be destroyed. And here the phrase "in
other words" is more than incidental, because neither the journalist
who produced this piece nor citizens who might follow his suggestion
would describe what they intended as lobbying. "Lobby," after all, was
an epithet, so how could their moralistic crusade possibly fall within its
rubric? To them, the distinction literally was as clear as that between
good and evil. A century later, two Washington insiders would delineate it this way: "1. If you agree with the aims of the group, it is a
'crusader in the public interest,' a 'voice of the people,' or a 'force for
good.' 2. If you're indifferent to its cause, it is a 'special interest group.'
3. If you disagree with its position, it's a 'lobby.' "[51]

What both the *Republic's* editorial, albeit unintentionally, and the
modern epigram suggest is this: it is acceptable to engage in lobbying so
long as one does it in the interests of a "good cause" (usually self-
defined)—and so long as one calls it something else. Such logic was so
persuasive to Gilded Age Americans that persons involved in what
anybody today would recognize as lobbying were able to deny in all
sincerity that they were doing anything of the kind. Thus, the New
York Central Railroad's general counsel could write alternately to the
line's president like this: "If we surrender to [the lobby], we are gone
forever. . . . We are determined not to be fastened upon by the lobby—
anything rather than that. . . . I would not consent to employ the class
of men who hang about the Legislature and form the lobby"; and like
this: "We are very much in want of *some really good man* to attend solely
to legislative matters. . . . I [am] perfectly willing to employ competent
respectable persons who would avow their positions to look after our
interests and to pay them fairly for it."[52] Similarly, President William K.
Ackerman of the Illinois Central hired "with compensation" a Mr.

50. A. R. Spofford, "Lobby," in *Cyclopaedia of Political Science, Political Economy, and of the Political History of the United States,* ed. John J. Lalor, 3 vols. (Chicago, 1886), 2:779–80.

51. Austin H. Kiplinger and Knight A. Kiplinger, *Washington Now* (New York, 1975), p. 203. As one turn-of-the-century journalist put it: "The Lobby's . . . presence in all legislative halls has become so familiar . . . that no one now needs to be told that it exists, or what are its functions"; J. M. Bulkley, "The Third House," *Overland Monthly,* 39 (1902), 903; see also Scott and Hunt, *Congress and Lobbies,* p. 4.

52. John Pruyn to Erastus Corning, 7 Jan., 15 and 19 Feb., and 12 Mar. 1858, in Appendix to Thomas C. Cochran, *Railroad Leaders, 1845–1890: The Business Mind in Action* (Cambridge, Mass., 1953), pp. 451–52. Positive and negative comments appear alternately, and sometimes in the same letter: e.g., that of 12 March.

Hamill to "look after the Washington interests" of the Land Grant Roads. He noted that Hamill "appears to be a gentleman of integrity" although, the corporate official admitted, "My experience with that class of men in Washington has been such as to impress me with the necessity of being cautious." So before dispatching his agent to the capital, he warned Hamill that, "so far as our company was concerned, we were not willing to pay a single dollar to any lobbyist." Northern Pacific President George Washington Cass, on the other hand, eschewed intermediaries. As he wrote to one of his company's directors in 1875: "It is necessary that we have the presence of each member of our Board in Washington to convince the members of Congress that it is a responsible body and not a lobby."[53]

Even the United States Supreme Court could not distinguish clearly between functions and symbolic connotations. It is indicative of the transformation of governance that was going on during the Grant years that the Court issued its first decision to deal explicitly with the legitimacy of lobbying in October 1874. The Court's ruling on *Trist v. Child*, as expressed in the opinion written by Justice Noah H. Swayne, was: "A contract to take charge of a claim before Congress, and prosecute it as an agent and attorney for the claimant (the same amounting to a contract to procure by 'lobby services'—that is to say, by personal solicitation by the agent, and others supposed to have personal influence in any way with members of Congress—the passage of a bill providing for the payment of the claim), is void."[54] The dispute had involved efforts by two attorneys, Linus and L. M. Child, to collect fees they had allegedly earned as agents of N. P. Trist. Trist had successfully petitioned for private legislation to reimburse him for his role in negotiating the 1848 Treaty of Guadelupe-Hidalgo, and his initial agreement with the two attorneys stipulated that they would work on a contingency basis, their fee to equal 25 percent of any award granted to him. When Trist got his money, however, he refused to pay the fee— whereupon L. M. Child (Linus having died) persuaded the Treasury Department to suspend payment of the $14,559 award to the claimant. Subsequently, the District of Columbia Supreme Court upheld Child's right to $3639, plus interest, and decreed that Trist should receive nothing until that debt was cancelled.

53. Ackerman to W. Butler Duncan, 24 Sept. 1877, and Cass to William Moorhead, 15 Jan. 1875, in Appendix to Cochran, *Railroad Leaders*, pp. 237, 287; documentation of Cass's employment of lobbyists is in two other letters on p. 287.

54. *Trist v. Child*, 21 Wallace (1875), 441–53: all quotations relating to this decision are to be found here.

In reversing the lower tribunal's decision, the U.S. Supreme Court weighted heavily a letter written by L. M. Child to Trist on February 20, 1871, exactly two months before Congress passed the necessary special bill.[55] As even Trist's attorney admitted, "[no] bribe had been offered or ever contemplated," and Child's counsel, one of whom was Congressman Benjamin F. Butler (R-Mass.), argued: "We are not asking the court . . . to give aid to that which is known as 'lobbying,' and is properly denounced as dishonorable." Nevertheless, the Court ruled that the contract between Trist and the Childs was not binding, since it involved procurement of legislation through what the Justices considered to be "lobby services." Swayne recognized that the Childs had performed some "legitimate" functions: drafting the petition, setting forth the claim, collecting facts, preparing arguments and submitting them to the proper authority (in this case, a congressional committee), and so on. But he believed that the February 20 letter, which documented personal contact between Child and some legislators, stood as "clear" proof of "lobby tactics" and therefore rendered the entire agreement null and void. As the justice put it, citing Roman law, "a promise made to effect a base purpose . . . is not binding." The "base purpose," he specified, consisted of the use of "personal influence" by Child and others not directly interested in the legislation.

Therefore, it was not the use of influence itself that the Court saw as improper. Nor did it rule absolutely against the right of claimants to employ counsel. What it did find illegitimate was employment of an agent who acted as an intermediary within the context of the representational relationship. In other words, a lobbyist—who, of course, denied through his attorney here that he *was* a lobbyist—was perceived not as a facilitator of communication between citizens and the government they petitioned but, instead, as an inhibitor of a direct relationship between representatives and the represented.[56]

55. The letter read as follows: "Everything looks very favorable. I found that my father has spoken to C___ and B___, and other members of the House. Mr. B___ says he will try hard to get it before the House. . . . A___ will go in for it. D___ promises to go for it. I have sent your letter and report to Mr. W___ of Pennsylvania. It may not be reached til next week. Please write to your friends to write immediately to any member of Congress. Every vote tells; and a simple request to a member may secure his vote, he not caring anything about it. Set every man you know at work, even if he knows a page, for a page often gets a vote. The most I fear is indifference." *Trist v. Child*, p. 443.

56. Counsel Benjamin Butler noted that Trist was ill at the time his bill reached the House in 1871; he was also "old and infirm." Therefore, he was incapable of arguing his own case: "What principle of either morals or policy, public or private, was there to prevent him (being thus old, infirm, sick, and away from Washington) from employing an honorable member of the Massachusetts bar to do the same thing for him? What

Where, though, did one draw the line? When did "submission [of facts and arguments] either orally or in writing to a committee or other proper authority, with other services of like character intended to reach only the understanding of the persons sought to be influenced"—all of which was permissible—become lobbying, the "personal solicitation by the agent, and others supposed to have personal influence in any way with members of Congress"—which was prohibited? The distinction was hardly precise, and this 1874 judgment could offer no clear guidelines to any agent or petitioner who wanted to act safely within the limits of established precedent. Nevertheless, despite the Court's rejection of the legitimacy of "lobby services," so-called, Swayne's opinion suggested that at least some lobbying *functions* were acceptable. In other words, so long as activities were carried out by someone with a respectable title, such as "counsel," and so long as that agent used expertise and formal conduct to present a case, lobbying—albeit not by name—was all right. This all may seem very confusing because, of course, it was. But the kind of ambiguous rationalization evident in the *Trist v. Child* decision is not unusual in times of transition, especially when phenomena are involved that are as evocative of suspicion as was the lobby.

Regardless of popular fiction, crusading journalists, and the Supreme Court, lobbying was hardly going to be displaced from the 1870's polity; it offered services that were valuable to both clients and officials of an overburdened and underequipped federal sector. Citizens had turned to lobbyists in the first place because their expert advocacy helped to focus policymakers' attention on demands that might otherwise have gone unnoticed permanently amid so many others. Legislators, meanwhile, found themselves listening to such agents because they were desperately in need of assistance as they tried to work through the spider web of clogged agendas, cumbersome committees, obsolete procedures, and amateurism that was early Gilded Age Congressional Government. Representatives as well as their constituents were products of the same political culture that had engendered De Forest, Edward Winslow Martin, and the *Republic's* editorialist, and no matter how well their substantive interests might be served by lobbying they remained inhibited from recognizing its legitimacy by name; they could not have escaped some awareness of the

---

principle to prevent him from doing by attorney that which he had himself the right, but from the visitation of God, had not himself, and at that time, the physical ability to do?" *Trist v. Child,* p. 445.

potential utility of lobbying, however euphemistically described—or at least of the fact that outside advocates were becoming an inevitable part of Capitol life. Thus it was neither hypocritical nor inappropriate in this time of transition that the Grant years produced the first three congressional initiatives to regulate and, therefore, indirectly to legitimate the functional dimensions of lobbying.

The first such measure appeared just three months after Justice Swayne handed down his decision. On January 22, 1875, Massachusetts Senator George S. Boutwell introduced a bill "to provide for the organization of a bar of the two Houses of Congress." It was based on precedent in Great Britain, where so-called parliamentary practitioners already were part of the official governmental structure. Boutwell wanted to accredit similar persons in the United States, hoping thereby to eradicate the allegedly powerful and corrupt "claims lobby." Membership in Boutwell's bar would be restricted to "respected and qualified" attorneys, who would be bonded and registered with the House and Senate clerks, and who would be permitted to represent petitioners' interests before Congress and its committees.[57] Attorneys, in other words, would be able to serve as legislative advocates for their clients—assuming much of the role, if not the title, of lobbyists. Despite his expressed abhorrence for the claims lobby, then, the senator had no real intention of ending its activities. Rather, he hoped merely to confine such business to pursuit by honorable gentlemen.

Boutwell's bill was referred to the Senate Judiciary Committee, where it languished for the remaining six weeks of the session. No action was taken and neither Boutwell nor anyone else reintroduced the bill when Congress reconvened. In the meantime, however, Representative Ellis H. Roberts (R-N.Y.) had reported a more sweeping measure from the House Ways & Means Committee that was destined to become the first lobby registration initiative ever to win endorsement from either chamber. During the first several weeks of 1875, Ways & Means had been engaged in an investigation of alleged bribery connected with a campaign by the Pacific Mail Steamship Company to obtain a federal subsidy. Roberts's bill, H.R. 4849, was a product of that effort; it was intended "to regulate the appearance of agents and attorneys prosecuting claims or demands before Congress and the Executive Departments of the Government." Essentially, it would have required all lobbyists to register with the House and Senate clerks, as

57. *Cong. Rec.,* 43d Cong., 2d sess. (1875), 648. See also Bryce, *American Commonwealth,* 1:671, 674, 676; and "Lobbying and Its Remedy," *Century Magazine,* 31 (1886), 961–63, esp. p. 963 ("Senator Boutwell's Plan").

well as with the clerks of any committees or agencies they wanted to deal with, and to provide an account of their expenditures. Unlike the Boutwell plan, its coverage was not limited to the claims' sphere, or even to the Capitol, but rather was meant to encompass all forms of interest advocacy. As might be expected, the word "lobbying" appeared nowhere in it. Even so, the general terms of this proposal were remarkably like those of the Lobby Registration Act, still operative today, that would be adopted seventy-one years later.[58]

Roberts made his initial report on February 27, 1875, at which time H.R. 4849 was recommitted to Ways & Means. But on March 3, by a teller vote of 113 to 31, the House passed the bill. Since this was the last day of the Forty-third Congress, the Senate had no time to act; consequently, H.R. 4849 failed to be enacted into law. Still, the margin of the teller vote reflected an impressive amount of support for the benefits of registering—and, therefore, recognizing—outside advocates. Among other things, Roberts's procedure would have addressed what many contemporaries believed was the most obnoxious aspect of outside advocacy: the secrecy with which it supposedly was conducted.[59] So it is not surprising that, scarcely more than a year after this symbolic victory, a form of registration—albeit temporary and less inclusive than that which H.R. 4849 would have authorized—was effected within the federal House.

On May 20, 1876, Rep. George Frisbie Hoar introduced a resolution for the Judiciary Committee, which passed that day by voice vote: "*Ordered,* that all persons or corporations employing counsel or agents to represent their interests in regard to any measure pending at any time before this House, or any committee thereof, shall cause the name and authority of such counsel or agent to be filed with the Clerk of the House; and no person whose name and authority are not so filed shall

---

58. On the Pacific Mail Steamship Company affair, see Oberholtzer, *History of the United States*, 3:131–32; Lately Thomas, *Sam Ward: "King of the Lobby"* (Boston, 1965), pp. 367–73; *Hse. Rpts.*, 43d Cong., 2d sess. no. 268; and weekly articles in the *Nation*, 17 Dec. 1874–4 Feb. 1875. Text of H.R. 4849 is in *Cong. Rec.*, 43d Cong., 2d sess. (1875), 2235; the *Record* stated that it was introduced "in connection with the Pacific Mail investigation." Text of the current lobbying law is in "Federal Regulation of Lobbying Act: Title III of the Legislative Reorganization Act of 1946 (Public Law 601, 79th Cong., 2nd sess., 2 U.S.C. 261–270)," Printed for the Use of the Secretary of the Senate (Washington, 1969).

59. *Cong. Rec.*, 43d Cong., 2d sess. (1875), 1884, 2235; *Hse. Jnl.*, 43d Cong., 2d sess., 582, 639. On secrecy, see Bradford, "Congressional Reform"; and Thomas M. Cooley, *A Treatise on the Constitutional Limitations Which Rest upon the Legislative Power of the American Union* (Boston, 1878), pp. 166–68.

appear as counsel or agent before any committee of this House." Hoar explained that the Judiciary Committee submitted such a resolution because it had been bombarded with "counsels," all of whom asserted that they had been retained in regard to a bill the panel was considering. The members simply did not know whom to believe (suggesting, of course, that "authorized" agents would be listened to), or what the interests of the various parties were. Therefore, the congressman declared, "it seems to us that it would be a great protection to members of the committee and of the House to require that any person or corporation who employ [sic] an agent to represent his or its interest here to file the name of that agent with the House, so that the House may know who is the responsible agent in such cases."[60]

The substantive impact of the Hoar Resolution was slight. It applied only to the House. It expired at the end of the Forty-fourth Congress, and was not renewed; it neither contained nor was supplemented by enforcement mechanisms for the prosecution of those who failed to abide by its terms. Still, for the first time, a branch of Congress was granting quasi-official status to certain activities that could be described only as lobbying—and it did so by consensus. The terminology was guarded, of course. "Counsel" and "agent" were less offensive labels than "lobbyist" to legislators and their constituents. Euphemisms aside, though, the implications were clear. The Hoar Resolution, along with the Boutwell and Roberts bills that preceded it, marked a turning point in the functional acceptance of lobbying. In polite circles the word "lobbying" might remain taboo, but the three initiatives of the mid-1870s were indicative of political transformation. They signified efforts to assimilate newly important actors into the policy arena, and to regularize their participation.

It should be clear by now that the interrelationships among corruption, lobbying, and Congressional Government were far more complex than either contemporary rhetoric or traditional historiography has allowed. The Age of Grant was a period of fundamental changes in political institutions and behavior, and the rising role of the Lobby was a consequence of those developments. Corruption existed as a perhaps unavoidable concomitant to evolution; when governmental machinery is inadequate and jurisdiction is expanding, as Huntington has suggested, some unscrupulous persons inevitably attempt to take advantage of the resultant confusion and others, frustrated by the slowness with which decisions are being made, resort to expedient shortcuts that

60. *Cong. Rec.*, 44th Cong., 1st sess. (1876), 3230–31.

may not be entirely honest.[61] But growing pains in the polity, and not the phenomenon of lobbying, were primarily responsible for a relatively high incidence of corruption during the 1870s. Over the years, as time-lag became less acute and the federal sector advanced on its course toward modernity, the kinds of fraud that so plagued the early Gilded Age inevitably grew less pronounced. Lobbying, meanwhile, came to occupy an ever larger and, gradually, more acceptable place within the policy arena.

To a great extent, then, the obsession with lobbying—and, indeed, with corruption itself—during the Grant years represented an effort to reduce to simple terms the almost incomprehensible changes that were taking place within the purview of governance. Antipathy toward "jobbery" or the "Third House" was a way of expressing fear of the unknown and untraditional. Like De Forest with his demons and Henry Adams with his futile nostalgia for a genteelly beneficent past that really never was, a bewildered public used symbols and codewords to rationalize what was going on and to absolve itself from any direct responsibility for systemic problems. Had people looked more closely at the functional and behavioral dimensions of contemporary circumstances, however, they might have obtained an even greater sense of reassurance than such totems were able to provide. They might have discovered that a lot of what they abjured was neither inherently evil nor outside their control. It simply was new.

Britain's Lord Bryce was one individual who did delve beneath the surface as he conducted the observations for his *American Commonwealth* (1888). Perhaps his status as an outsider and practical politician was what accounted for his perceptiveness; in any event, Bryce's two-volume epic is still probably the most thorough and insightful chronicle of late nineteenth-century public life, and his chapter on corruption is one of its best features.[62] He began by noting that Europeans, drawing upon impressions "that the loose language of many Americans sanctions," generally believed that fraud was the New World norm. But after spending a lot of time in both Washington and several state capitals, the Englishman concluded that, on the whole, the "level of

61. In an insightful essay, Ari Hoogenboom noted that one reason so much is known about corruption in the Gilded Age is that it was investigated so thoroughly: "The steps that Gilded Age Americans took to prevent corruption have been less publicized [than the scandals]. In many instances exposure of corruption produced more lasting results than satisfying a desire to 'turn the rascals out.' The age of reform began in the corrupt Gilded Age." "Did Gilded Age Scandals Bring Reform?" in Eisenstadt, ed., *Before Watergate*, p. 125; see also Scott, *Comparative Political Corruption*, p. 23.

62. Bryce, *American Commonwealth*, 2:121–33.

integrity" in the civil service—that notorious bastion of patronage—especially in the federal sector, was "as high as that of England or Germany," and higher than that in France. As for bribery, it "exists in Congress, but is confined to a few members, say five per cent of the whole number."

Bryce believed that Americans' obsession with allegedly extensive corruption derived not so much from fact as from the practical impossibility of living up to "the excellence . . . of the frame of the Constitution." Thus, he observed, "in the case of America men are inclined to apply an ideal in politics, and setting . . . a higher ideal than most European monarchies. Yet it must be remembered that in a new and large country . . . conditions are not the most favourable to virtue. If recognizing the fact that the path of the politician is in all countries thickly set with snares, we leave ideals out of sight and try America by an actual standard, we shall find that . . . her Federal and State administration, in spite of the evils flowing from an uncertain tenure, is not, in point of integrity, at this moment markedly inferior to the administrations of most European countries."[63]

These conclusions about corruption follow an exhaustive account of political and governmental affairs, of their enormity and their unsettled state in a time of national expansion and assertiveness. Bryce was optimistic about the American polity and its future. But he warned that immature institutions still engendered serious problems and that the federal sector had a long way to go before it would be able to exercise effective control over the plethora of responsibilities within its purview. Here Congress, because of its dominance over the other branches, disturbed the Englishman most deeply; despite its preeminent power, he thought it remained parochial, amateurish, and, on the floor and in nearly all its committees, grossly unsystematic in its deliberations.[64] He focused much of his criticism on high turnover, both among the membership at large and in the composition of legislative panels: "There are few walks of life," the lord declared, "in which experience counts for more than it does in parliamentary politics." Until Congress, and the polity generally, overcame such weaknesses and developed the resources necessary to cope with constituent demands, Bryce feared that the frustration generated by the gap between expectations and performance would persist, and maybe even increase.[65]

---

63. Ibid., 2:128, 132–33.
64. Ibid., 1: chaps. 13–16, 19.
65. Ibid., 1:193.

Commonwealth does not contain suggested remedies for all the difficulties it details.[66] One exception, however, is located in a lengthy note on "the Lobby." Bryce was not entirely immune to perjorative imagery, so his essay contains the inevitable references to corrupt practitioners and their tactics. Nonetheless, although the author writes that the designation "is commonly used in what Bentham calls a dyslogistic sense," he goes on to argue that lobbying "does not necessarily impute any improper motive or conduct." Furthermore, he suggests that "advocacy of this kind is needed in order to bring the facts fairly before the legislature" and that it might, therefore, serve to alleviate some of the institutional weaknesses resulting from its lack of intrinsic expertise.[67]

In offering this interpretation, Bryce depended heavily on Librarian of Congress Ainsworth R. Spofford's "The Lobby," an article in *Lalor's Cyclopoedia of Political Science* (1886). One of Spofford's main points was that "corruption is frequently wholly absent in cases where the lobby is most industrious, numerous, persistent, and successful." For, he continued, "what the legislator most needs is light upon every subject that can come before him; and whatever contribution to his knowledge of the numerous and complicated subjects with which he has to deal, and of which he must often be profoundly ignorant, is of value." In other words, Spofford concluded, "bad legislation . . . is the fruit of ignorance, not of corruption"—ignorance both among congressmen and among a mass public too vulnerable to simplistic totems.[68]

Spofford and Bryce published their works a decade after Ulysses Grant left the White House, but neither the attitudes nor the substantive problems that characterized governance during the General's tenure had dissipated completely in that time. Lobbying continued to be denounced by most people, as Congress continued to be overworked and underequipped. And as late as 1892, Hamlin Garland could write a pedantic novel entitled *Member of the Third House* that sounded remarkably like the more extreme of De Forest's earlier efforts.[69] Near the end of this rather dreadful parable, Garland's villain, a Mr. Brennan who lobbied for the Air Line Railroad, testifies in court in a manner that clearly is intended to incite moral outrage among readers.

66. Ibid., 1:4.
67. Ibid., 1:673–78.
68. Spofford, "Lobby," pp. 779–80.
69. Hamlin Garland, *A Member of the Third House: A Dramatic Story* (1892; Upper Saddle River, N.J., 1968). Compare the following description of the effects of lobbying, spoken by the novel's hero, with De Forest's imagery: "I swear, sometimes I feel as if nothing but some cataclysm of nature would be powerful enough to cleanse our political dens, reeking with moral slime" (p. 98).

The prosecutor asks him, " 'Do you consider the work you've done here for the Air Line . . . legitimate?' 'Yes, sir, and more, it was necessary,' replied Brennan, with engaging frankness."[70] Garland may have been appalled by such a self-defense, but, in light of what Spofford and Bryce had to say, it rings with a note of truth. Lobbying was necessary, it was legitimate, and, despite occasional abuses, the legislative process benefited from its presence.

70. Ibid., pp. 152–53.

INTERIOR OF THE HOUSE OF REPRESENTATIVES AT WASHINGTON—THE HOUSE IN SESSION—SKETCHED BY THEODORE R. DAVIS.—[SEE PAGE 182.]

The House at work. Wood engraving by Theodore R. Davis, from *Harper's Weekly*, 20 March 1868. Courtesy Library of Congress, Division of Prints and Photographs.

CHAPTER 2

The Inner Workings
of Congress

What is "the House"? An aggregation of vigorous elements having different objects, antagonistic notions, and selfish interests,
centered about indefinite party policies and moved by personal,
political, and sometimes patriotic purposes.

REPRESENTATIVE DEALVA S. ALEXANDER,
History and Procedure of the House of Representatives

On December 1, 1873, newly reelected Speaker James G. Blaine convened the House into the first session of the Forty-third Congress.
Perhaps, as he assumed the podium, he reflected on the absence of
many notable and notorious men who had been present during the
preceding term. Many, of course, had retired voluntarily, while others
were victims of their districts' policies of rotating representation. A few
were dead, among them Oakes Ames (R-Mass.) and James Brooks (D-
N.Y.), who, disgraced by exposure of their involvement in the Credit
Mobilier scandal, had allegedly lost their wills to live. Several had
sought reelection unsuccessfully. Two of these, at least, would return in
the Forty-fourth Congress: antebellum Know-Nothing Speaker
Nathaniel P. Banks as an Independent Liberal Republican, for the
seventh of an eventual nine terms, and Michael C. Kerr of Indiana as
the first Democratic Speaker since 1859. And one former member,
California's Aaron Sargent, had been elevated by his legislature to the
Senate.[1]

---

1. Facts on congressional membership in this and the succeeding paragraph are from
the *BDAC*.

Perhaps, on the other hand, Blaine wondered about the freshmen who comprised a majority of those before him. Who were the potential leaders, and would any of them stay in the House long enough to make significant contributions to its activities? What was he to do with the growing number of ex-Confederates, including Lucius Q. C. Lamar, the venerable Alexander Stephens, and thirty who had borne arms against the Union? Or perhaps the Speaker preferred to focus on the familiar. He could see Eugene Hale and William P. Frye, two fellow Republicans from Maine. Other allies, too, were scattered about: Ohio's Garfield, Tennessee's Horace Maynard, Wisconsin's Jerry Rusk and Philetus Sawyer, William A. Wheeler of New York, and the ardent workingmen's protectionist from Philadelphia known to one and all as "Pig Iron" Kelley. As usual, and despite Banks's defeat, Massachusetts had returned an impressive delegation; Blaine could spot Ways & Means chairman Henry L. Dawes, the wealthy Sam Hooper, genteel George Frisbie Hoar with his older brother, the former attorney general E. Rockwood Hoar, and—deliberately seated next to Josiah Walls, the black Representative from Gainesville, Florida—that not-always-welcome intimate of Grant, Benjamin F. "Black Ben" Butler. Finally, the man from Maine could not ignore his adversaries—even if, like Pennsylvania's Sam Randall, they chose inconspicuous desks in the back row. The impetuous New Yorker, Samuel S. ("Sunset") Cox, had no desire to be unobtrusive; he sat self-importantly in the very front. And midway between was Fernando Wood: also from the Empire State, Democracy's nominee for speaker, and Blaine's next-door neighbor on Fifteenth Street. Perhaps they had ridden to the Capitol together on that Monday morning, reminiscing about old times and catching up on news of each others' families.[2]

Blaine unfortunately left no record of his thoughts on that occasion.[3]

2. Blaine's attitudes toward his colleagues are in his *Twenty Years of Congress: From Lincoln to Garfield*, 2 vols. (Norwich, Conn., 1886), 2: esp. chap. 23; and *The Letters of Mrs. James G. Blaine*, ed. H. S. Blaine, 2 vols. (New York, 1908), vol. 1. Information on Blaine and Wood is in Gail Hamilton [Mary Abigail Dodge], *Biography of James G. Blaine* (Norwich, Conn., 1895), p. 223; their addresses on 15th Street, N.W. (Blaine at 821, Wood at 825) are from the *Cong. Dir.*, 43d Cong., 1st sess., 135, 139. Seat locations in the chamber are from DeB. Randolph Keim, *Washington and Its Environs: An Illustrated, Descriptive and Historical Hand-Book to the Capital of the United States of America*, revised annually (Washington, 1874), chart, pp. 110–11.

3. He wrote only one sentence about the day in his memoirs: "The Forty-third Congress organized on the first Monday in December, 1873." Blaine, *Twenty Years of Congress*, 2:539.

But as he surveyed the scene before him, it is unlikely that he was either surprised or very pleased by what he saw. From his perspective, the sea of faces must have seemed much like those he had confronted for the last four years, ever since his speakership began. It was, for the most part, an inexperienced group. Only four men present had been in the House continuously for more than a decade, and just one of those— Henry Dawes of Massachusetts—had entered before the Civil War. This was to be expected, of course; high rates of turnover were a fact of mid-nineteenth-century congressional life. How could Blaine, or anyone, anticipate that three of those in the chamber that day would still be there twenty-seven years later to greet the twentieth century? Their persistent presence would be evidence of a process that political scientist H. Douglas Price one day would call "professionalization": a process with roots that can be discerned retrospectively in the period of Blaine's ascendance. Neither that process nor the larger development described as "institutionalization" by Nelson Polsby was evident to observers in the Grant years; to them, the Forty-third House and its successors would not appear noticeably dissimilar to the preceding ones. Evolution, after all, is something that becomes visible only with hindsight.[4]

The body over which Blaine presided is best understood as one suffering acutely from time-lag. Changes occurred within it, to be sure, but they were essentially reactive rather than prospective—initiated mainly in response to immediate problems, and not with an eye to the future. The House, in other words, was a fundamentally antebellum institution endeavoring, with limited success, to cope with the enlarged federal purview of postwar America. Outmoded norms and machinery severely constrained its ability to adjust to new conditions and respond to intensified demands. Its rules were complex, and too few members were sufficiently versed in their intricacies. Both power and expertise were at once too concentrated and too diffuse to be very useful, and

---

4. Data on careers from the *BDAC*. H. Douglas Price, "The Congressional Career— Then and Now," in *Congressional Behavior,* ed. Nelson W. Polsby (New York, 1971), pp. 14–27, and "Congress and the Evolution of Legislative 'Professionalism,'" in *Congress in Change: Evolution and Reform,* ed. Norman J. Ornstein (New York, 1975), pp. 2–23; Nelson W. Polsby, "The Institutionalization of the House of Representatives," *APSR,* 62 (1968), 144–68; Polsby et al., "The Growth of the Seniority System in the U.S. House of Representatives," *APSR,* 63 (1969), 787–807. See also Allan G. Bogue, et al., "Members of the House of Representatives and the Process of Modernization," *JAH,* 63 (1976), 275–302; Michael Abram and Joseph Cooper, "The Rise of Seniority in the House of Representatives," *Polity,* 1 (1968), 53–85; Morris P. Fiorina et al., "Historical Change in House Turnover," in Ornstein, *Congress in Change,* pp. 24–57; and Peter Swenson, "The Influence of Recruitment on the Structure of Power in the U.S. House, 1870–1940," *Legislative Studies Q.,* 7 (1982), 7–36.

neither served effectively to focus or direct legislative deliberations. And if congressional parties were emotively strong, they also were substantively weak; neither Democrats nor Republicans were able to convert their adherents' organizational and rhetorical loyalties into coherent and comprehensive programmatic agendas.

This was the environment in which Blaine and his fellows had to operate and, as members of the federal sector's preeminent branch, to bear the heaviest burden of Washington's expanding jurisdiction and workload. But environmental conditions alone would not determine the quality of legislative policy making. To a great extent that was dependent upon the sorts of men whom the electorate chose to represent it—and whom, in December 1873, the Speaker confronted from the podium. These individual legislators were, in effect, the raw material from which the Capitol machinery would be built: they would write its bills, populate its committees, provide constituent service, and, occasionally, vote upon measures that made it to the floor. So before examining the House as an institution, it might be well to look at its members. Responsibility for many of the weaknesses of Congressional Government was in fact primarily, and firmly, within their ranks.

A total of 477 men—249 Republicans, 216 Democrats, five Conservatives, three Independents, and four assorted others—served in the House for all or part of the second Grant administration.[5] Even the most cursory assessment of their backgrounds suggests at least some of the reasons for the lower chamber's inefficiency during the 1870s. As Tables 4 and 5 reveal, fewer than half the Representatives in either Congress had prior congressional experience. The majority—which bore responsibility for filling the speakership, chairing the committees, and so on—in both cases contained a higher percentage of greenhorns than the minority; during the Forty-fourth, more than two-thirds of the dominant Democrats were freshmen. The injurious effect of so many

5. Party affiliations from the *BDAC*. All except one Independent in the 44th Congress (Julius H. Seelye of Mass.) caucused with the Democrats; in the tables throughout this chapter, all members are classified according to the party with which they caucused (R = 250, D = 227). Totals here and in tables, unless otherwise indicated, reflect House membership at the beginning of the second session of each Congress—by which time most, if not all, electoral contests had been settled. Because of subsequent contest decisions, deaths, resignations, and so on, a few further changes occurred after that point, of course. In all, a total of 513 individuals sat for at least part of a term during the second Grant administration, including delegates from 9 territories (8, after Colorado was admitted to statehood in 1876) and, in the 43d, the District of Columbia; delegates are not included in the statistical analysis.

Table 4. Incidence of prior and later service in Congress among members of the 43d House

	All members			South*			Non-South		
	Total	D	R	Total	D	R	Total	D	R
Total number of members	292	92	200	105	55	50	187	37	150
Prior House experience:									
Number with experience	145	46	99	47	25	22	98	21	77
% of total with experience	49.7	50.0	49.5	44.8	45.5	44.0	52.4	56.6	51.3
Total years experience	597	194	403	162	89	73	435	105	330
Av. yrs. exper. (all members)	2.04	2.11	2.02	1.54	1.62	1.46	2.27	2.84	2.20
Av. yrs. exper. (among those with exper.)	4.12	4.22	4.07	3.45	3.56	3.32	4.44	5.00	4.29
Later House experience:									
Number with experience	133	53	80	45	33	12	88	20	68
% of total with experience	45.5	57.6	40.0	42.9	60.0	24.0	47.1	54.1	45.3
Total years experience	672	294	378	223	198	25	449	96	353
Av. yrs. exper. (all members)	2.30	3.20	1.89	2.12	3.60	0.50	2.40	2.59	2.35
Av. yrs. exper. (among those with exper.)	5.05	5.55	4.73	4.96	6.00	2.08	5.10	4.80	5.19
Later Senate experience:									
Number with experience	21	8	13	7	7	—	14	1	13
% of total with experience	7.2	8.6	6.5	6.7	12.7	—	7.5	2.7	8.7
Total years experience	237	47	190	43	43	—	194	4	190
Av. yrs. exper. (all members)	0.81	0.51	0.95	0.41	0.82	—	1.04	0.11	1.27
Av. yrs. exper. (among those with exper.)	11.29	5.88	14.62	6.14	6.14	—	13.86	4.00	14.62

Source: Biographical Directory of the American Congress, 1774–1961 (Washington, 1961).
*Includes all former slave states except Delaware, i.e.: Alabama, Arkansas, Florida, Georgia, Kentucky, Louisiana, Maryland, Mississippi, Missouri, North Carolina, South Carolina, Tennessee, Texas, Virginia, West Virginia.

Table 5. Incidence of prior and later service in Congress among members of the 44th House

	All members			South*			Non-South		
	Total	D	R	Total	D	R	Total	D	R
Total number of members	293	182	111	105	87	18	188	95	93
Prior House experience:									
Number with experience	126	59	67	48	37	11	78	22	56
% of total with experience	43.0	32.4	60.4	45.7	42.5	61.1	41.5	23.2	60.2
Total years experience	512	244	268	161	120	41	351	124	227
Av. yrs. exper. (all members)	1.75	1.34	2.41	1.53	1.38	2.28	1.87	1.31	2.44
Av. yrs. exper. (among those with exper.)	4.06	4.14	4.00	3.35	3.24	2.73	4.50	5.64	4.05
Later House experience:									
Number with experience	169	144	55	74	68	6	95	46	49
% of total with experience	57.7	62.6	49.5	70.5	78.2	33.3	50.5	48.4	52.7
Total years experience	875	585	290	401	383	18	474	202	272
Av. yrs. exper. (all members)	2.99	3.21	2.61	3.82	4.40	1.00	2.52	2.13	2.92
Av. yrs. exper. (among those with exper.)	6.18	5.13	5.27	5.42	5.63	3.00	4.99	4.39	5.55
Later Senate experience:									
Number with experience	21	12	9	9	9	—	12	3	9
% of total with experience	7.2	6.6	8.1	8.6	10.3	—	6.4	29.5	9.7
Total years experience	207	84	123	56	56	—	151	28	123
Av. yrs. exper. (all members)	0.71	0.46	1.11	0.53	0.64	—	0.80	0.29	1.32
Av. yrs. exper. (among those with exper.)	9.86	7.00	13.67	6.22	6.22	—	12.58	9.33	13.67

Source: Biographical Directory of the American Congress, 1774–1961 (Washington, 1961).
*Includes all former slave states except Delaware, i.e.: Alabama, Arkansas, Florida, Georgia, Kentucky, Louisiana, Maryland, Mississippi, Missouri, North Carolina, South Carolina, Tennessee, Texas, Virginia, West Virginia.

Table 6. Members of the House with prior legislative experience, 43d and 44th Congresses (federal and/or state)

	43d			44th		
	Total	*D*	*R*	*Total*	*D*	*R*
Number of members	292	92	200	293	182	111
Number with experience	217	70	147	209	119	90
% with experience	74.3	73.5	76.1	71.3	65.4	81.1

Source: Biographical Directory of the American Congress, 1774–1961 (Washington, 1961).

novices was mitigated to some extent by the fact that a lot of them had sat in their state Assemblies or Senates and thus had some previous tenure in a legislature (Table 6). But as most observers realize, every representative body has its own distinctive norms, modes of behavior, and procedures. So Congressman James Brooks was not too far from the mark when he declared that the postwar federal House was a veritable "sea of inexperience."[6]

Further analysis of the data in Tables 4 and 5, moreover, displays yet another trait typical of this era: if one looks at the figures on subsequent service, it is evident that only a handful of incumbents were going to accrue extensive future Capitol tenure, either. There was, then, little in the way of professional commitment to Congress, an attribute that is one of the most characteristic and significant norms governing federal legislators today. In the 1870s, few people explicitly set out to make a career in Washington. Of six freshmen in the Forty-third House whom Blaine regarded as "conspicuous additions," for example, two stayed for merely one term and another, Hugh Jewett of Ohio, resigned after scarcely a year to become president of the Erie Railroad. Thus, only three of them would "acquire additional distinction by subsequent service," and just one—Democrat William R. Mor-

6. Brooks quoted in W. R. Brock, *An American Crisis: Congress and Reconstruction, 1865–1867* (New York, 1963), p. 55. On norms, impact of inexperience, and socialization, see James, Lord Bryce, *The American Commonwealth*, 2 vols. (London, 1888), 1:145, 190–92; Heinz Eulau et al., "The Political Socialization of American State Legislators," *Midwest J. of Political Science*, 3 (1959), 188–206; Kenneth Prewitt et al., "Political Socialization and Political Roles," *Public Opinion Q.*, 30 (1966–67), 569–82; Charles G. Bell and Charles M. Price, *The First Term: A Study of Legislative Socialization* (Beverly Hills, 1975), and "Pre-Legislative Sources of Representational Roles," *Midwest J. of Political Science*, 13 (1969), 254–70; Herbert B. Asher, "The Learning of Legislative Norms," *APSR*, 67 (1973), 499–513, and *Freshman Representatives and the Learning of Voting Cues* (Beverly Hills, 1973).

rison, a future chairman of Ways & Means—would remain longer than two additional terms.[7]

Even those whose many years of representation might suggest professional commitment did not always display the attitudes or enjoy the advantages normally associated with careerists. Democrat S. S.Cox, after ten years as a member from two states and prior to serving for eighteen years more, decided in 1870 that he was "frustrated" with politics and suggested to editor Manton Marble of the New York *World* that he might like to become a foreign correspondent. Even just getting renominated was by no means automatic; Cox himself had come to New York in the mid-sixties only after being gerrymandered out of his original district in Ohio. Iowa's William B. Allison, who spent four terms in the House before embarking in 1872 on a Senate career that would span three-and-a-half decades, had had to defy his state's two-term rotation tradition when he ran for his third nomination to the lower chamber in 1866. Charles Willard of Vermont was less fortunate in 1874 when, after a six-year tenure, his party denied him its endorsement. Still, as he wrote to a colleague, "my defeat was not unexpected. . . . You know my work was, much of it, hardly pleasant enough to be desirable, and I cannot say that I am sorry at the prospect of soon being out of it." Even James A. Garfield, whose nine terms in the House constituted a record nearly unmatched by any of his contemporaries, agonized every two years as to whether or not he should stand again as a candidate, and reacted to a difficult victory in 1874 by taking it as a sign that he could retire honorably to the practice of law.[8]

In fact, only 139 of the 477 men who were in the House during the second Grant Administration would accumulate three or more terms of consecutive service. The average amount of prior experience for non-freshmen members alone was barely over four years; this figure is more than cut in half if all members of the body are counted. To some extent, the lack of accrued tenure in the Forty-fourth House is explained by the transition from Republican to Democratic control; with such a shift, one would expect to find a relatively high proportion of

7. Margaret Susan Thompson and Joel H. Silbey, "Research into Nineteenth Century Legislatures: Present Contours and Future Directions," *Legislative Studies Q.*, 9 (1984), 319–50; Blaine, *Twenty Years of Congress*, 2:541. See also sources cited in n. 4, above; Barbara Hinckley, *Stability and Change in Congress* (New York, 1971), p. 67; and David Mayhew, *The Electoral Connection* (New Haven, 1974).

8. David Lindsey, *"Sunset" Cox: Irrepressible Democrat* (Detroit, 1959), p. 125; Leland L. Sage, *William Boyd Allison: A Study in Practical Politics* (Iowa City, 1956), p. 81; Charles Willard to Henry L. Dawes, 17 Aug. 1874, Henry L. Dawes Papers, L.C.; Thomas Clarke Smith, *The Life and Letters of James Abram Garfield*, 2 vols. (New Haven, 1925), 1:582.

first-termers. But the turnover rate for the Forty-third House was not substantially lower than that for its predecessor, which had the same partisan cast. As shown in Table 7, twenty-two of thirty-seven states in it—including ten of the thirteen largest—were represented mainly by inexperienced members; even in the Forty-fifth House, the only one that contained a non-freshman majority, fewer than half the states sent delegations to Washington containing a preponderance of men with prior service.

Furthermore, few Representatives left to assume higher political positions (Tables 8 and 9). Nor did many die in office or decline further service as a result of advanced age (Table 10). Most men, rather, retired voluntarily after a term or two and simply returned, at least temporarily, to private life—or sought other, not necessarily more prestigious political offices back home. Only twenty-one members in each of these two Congresses went on to serve in the Senate, and several of them served only partial terms, filling temporary vacancies. The majority who held any offices after their tenures in the House occupied lesser posts, at the state or local level.

Nonetheless, there are indications of transition in this era; things were beginning to change. The Forty-third Congress was the last in which first-generation Republicans, whose roots were in the antislavery movement and who had helped to found or had joined their party in its infancy, were to be preeminent. Democracy triumphed in the 1874 election, and the debates on amnesty and civil rights during the lame-duck session that followed might be regarded as the Old Guard's swan song. The mid-seventies would witness the passing-on of the handful of early leaders who had endured; some, like Charles Sumner in the Senate and Sam Hooper in the House, would die, and a few, like Dawes, George F. Hoar, and Blaine, would be elevated to the Senate. Others associated with radicalism, such as Ben Butler, would be defeated or would pursue new concerns like currency or trade, while those such as Garfield who remained in the House would never again hold formal leadership positions. Republicans from the Old Confederacy were a disappearing breed, as well; only three continued to sit in the House after the Forty-fifth Congress adjourned in 1879. And while there would be only two years prior to 1901 in which no black legislators came to Washington, none served in the Forty-fifth House.[9]

9. William Gillette, *Retreat from Reconstruction, 1869–1879* (Baton Rouge, 1979), esp. chaps. 9–11; James M. McPherson, "Abolitionists and the Civil Rights Act of 1875," *Western Political Q.*, 18 (1965), 763–75; Samuel Denny Smith, *The Negro in Congress, 1870–1901* (Chapel Hill, 1940), pp. 5–6. There were seven black Representatives in the

Table 7. Distribution of returning and new House members, by party, region, and state, 43d–45th Congresses

	Deleg. size	43d Total D	43d Total R	43d Old D	43d Old R	43d New D	43d New R	44th Total D	44th Total R	44th Old D	44th Old R	44th New D	44th New R	45th Total D	45th Total R	45th Old D	45th Old R	45th New D	45th New R
South																			
Ala.	8	3	5	1	1	2	4	6	2	1	1	5	1	8	0	3	0	5	0
Ark.*	4	0	4	0	1	0	3	4	0	2	0	2	0	4	0	3	0	1	0
Fla.	2	0	2	0	1	0	1	1	1	0	1	1	0	1	1	0	0	1	1
Ga.	9	6	3	1	1	5	2	9	0	4	0	5	0	9	0	9	0	0	0
Ky.	10	10	0	5	0	5	0	9	1	3	0	6	1	10	0	5	0	5	0
La.	6	1	5	0	3	1	2	4	2	0	1	4	1	4	2	2	1	2	1
Md.	6	4	2	2	0	2	2	6	0	2	0	4	0	6	0	4	0	2	0
Miss.	6	1	5	0	2	1	3	4	2	1	1	3	1	6	0	3	0	3	0
Mo.	13	9	4	2	2	7	2	13	0	7	0	6	0	9	4	9	0	0	4
N.C.	8	5	3	2	2	3	1	7	1	4	0	3	1	7	1	6	0	1	1
S.C.	5	0	5	0	2	0	3	0	5	0	2	0	3	2	3	0	3	2	0
Tenn.	10	3	7	1	3	2	4	9	1	3	1	6	0	8	2	8	1	0	1
Tex.	6	6	0	3	0	3	0	6	0	2	0	4	0	6	0	6	0	0	0
Va.	9	4	5	1	2	3	3	8	1	2	1	6	0	8	1	7	0	1	1
W.Va.	3	2	1	2	0	0	1	3	0	2	0	1	0	3	0	1	0	2	0

Non-South

	Calif.	Col.**	Conn.	Del.	Ill.	Ind.	Iowa	Kans.	Maine	Mass.	Mich.	Minn.	Nebr.	Nev.	N.H.	N.J.
	4	1	4	1	19	13	9	3	5	11	9	3	1	1	3	7
	1		1	0	5	3	0	0	0	0	0	0	0	1	1	1
	3		3	1	14	10	9	3	5	11	9	3	1	0	2	6
	0		1	0	2	2	0	0	0	0	0	0	0	1	1	0
	1		3	0	3	6	4	1	3	6	2	2	0	0	0	1
	1		0	0	3	1	0	0	0	0	0	0	0	0	0	1
	2		0	1	12	4	5	2	2	5	7	1	1	0	2	5
	3	0	3	1	12	8	1	1	0	5	2	0	0	0	2	5
	1	1	1	0	7	5	8	2	4	6	7	3	1	1	1	2
	1	0	1	0	2	1	0	0	0	0	0	0	0	0	0	1
	1	0	1	0	5	2	5	1	4	3	6	2	1	0	0	1
	2	0	2	1	10	7	1	1	0	5	2	0	0	0	2	4
	0	1	0	0	2	3	3	1	1	3	1	1	0	1	1	1
	1	1	3	1	8	4	0	0	0	1	1	0	0	0	1	4
	3	0	1	0	11	9	9	3	5	10	8	3	1	1	2	3
	1	0	3	1	6	2	0	0	0	0	1	0	0	0	1	3
	1	0	1	0	4	4	2	1	2	4	2	2	0	0	1	1
	0	1	0	0	2	2	0	0	0	1	0	0	0	0	0	1
	2	0	0	0	7	5	7	2	3	6	6	1	1	1	1	2

Table 7—*continued*

	Deleg. size	43d Total		43d Old		43d New		44th Total		44th Old		44th New		45th Total		45th Old		45th New	
		D	R	D	R	D	R	D	R	D	R	D	R	D	R	D	R	D	R
Non-South																			
N.Y.	33	10	23	5	10	5	13	16	17	4	7	12	10	17	16	8	5	12	11
Ohio	20	7	13	1	4	6	9	13	7	4	6	9	1	8	12	5	5	3	7
Ore.	1	1	0	0	0	1	0	1	0	0	0	1	0	0	1	0	0	0	1
Pa.	27	5	22	3	10	2	12	17	10	2	6	15	4	10	17	8	7	2	10
R.I.	2	0	2	0	2	0	0	0	2	0	1	0	1	0	2	0	2	0	0
Vt.	3	0	3	0	2	0	1	0	3	0	1	0	2	0	3	0	3	0	0
Wis.	8	2	6	2	4	0	2	3	5	0	2	3	3	3	5	1	2	2	3

Source: Biographical Directory of the American Congress, 1774–1961 (Washington, 1961). Figures reflect members serving at the beginning of the 2d session of each Congress. "Old" refers only to those members serving at the end of the preceding Congress—not to all men with some previous tenure.

*Apparent discrepancy between Arkansas figures for the 43d and 44th Congresses due to changes in occupants of two seats late in the 2d session of the 43d Congress.

**Colorado not admitted to statehood until the middle of the 44th Congress (1876).

Table 8. Noncongressional political experience among members of the 43d House

Office or position**	Prior*			Later*			Both*		
	Total	D	R	Total	D	R	Total	D	R
President or vice president	0	0	0	2	0	2	0	0	0
State governor	4	1	3	8	3	5	0	0	0
Territorial governor	0	0	0	1	0	1	0	0	0
Mayor	16	5	11	1	1	0	1	0	1
U.S. cabinet	1	0	1	7	1	6	0	0	0
Diplomatic appointment	5	0	5	12	4	8	1	0	1
Judge: federal	1	0	1	6	1	5	0	0	0
Judge: state	18	4	14	12	4	8	6	4	2
Judge: local	24	4	20	4	2	2	2	1	1
State legislature	142	41	101	6	2	4	11	2	9
Other federal appointive post	34	9	25	44	17	27	10	0	10
Other state elective post	24	5	19	5	4	1	0	0	0
Other state appointive post	40	11	29	21	9	12	5	1	4
Other local elective post	91	27	64	4	1	3	2	1	1
Other local appointive post	26	14	12	4	1	3	0	0	0

Source: Biographical Directory of the American Congress, 1774–1961 (Washington, 1961).
*Categories are exclusive. If a member had prior and later experience, he is counted under "Both," *only.* So the sum of "Prior" and "Both" equals the number who came to Congress with any particular type of experience.
**Categories are exclusive; a local judge, for instance, is not counted under other local categories. If a member held more than one position in a single category, he is counted only once.

Table 9. Noncongressional political experience among members of the 44th House

Office or position**	Prior*			Later*			Both*		
	Total	D	R	Total	D	R	Total	D	R
President or vice president	0	0	0	4	2	2	0	0	0
State governor	7	5	2	9	5	4	0	0	0
Territorial governor	1	1	0	3	3	0	0	0	0
Mayor	19	13	6	7	6	1	1	0	1
U.S. cabinet	1	0	1	8	3	5	1	1	0
Diplomatic appointment	4	2	2	6	2	4	1	0	1
Judge: federal	0	0	0	6	3	3	0	0	0
Judge: state	19	9	10	14	10	4	1	1	0
Judge: local	23	13	10	7	5	2	0	0	0
State legislature	153	87	66	6	3	3	8	5	3
Other federal appointive post	29	14	15	41	24	17	6	1	5
Other state elective post	16	9	7	5	3	2	1	1	0
Other state appointive post	45	21	24	20	15	5	4	1	3
Other local elective post	84	48	36	6	4	2	2	2	0
Other local appointive post	19	13	6	5	3	2	1	1	0

Source: Biographical Directory of the American Congress, 1774–1961 (Washington, 1961).

*Categories are exclusive. If a member had prior and later experience, he is counted under "Both," *only*. So the sum of "Prior" and "Both" equals the number who came to Congress with any particular type of experience.

**Categories are exclusive; a local judge, for instance, is not counted under other local categories. If a member held more than one position in a single category, he is counted only once.

Table 10. Remaining years of life of 477 Representatives after leaving the House

Number of years*	Number of members	% of total
0–4	63	13.2
5–9	56	11.7
10–14	77	16.2
15–19	67	14.0
20–24	60	12.6
25–29	63	13.2
30–	91	19.1

Source: Biographical Directory of the American Congress, 1774–1961 (Washington, 1961).
*Calculated from end of continuous House service (or service containing only one term out of office prior to return), not from the end of the 43d or 44th Congress.

Some might argue, however, that Radical Reconstruction, given the types of officials it elevated to prominence, was by definition an aberration in American politics. If that is the case, the decline of radicalism and its adherents does not say much about the long-range evolution of legislative careers, although it was a serious concern among contemporaries.[10] Longitudinal data regarding House turnover, on the other hand, do provide evidence of the transitional significance of the mid-seventies. Morris Fiorina has calculated that twenty-eight Congresses prior to 1873, including eighteen of the preceding twenty, contained freshman majorities. The Forty-third and Forty-fourth Houses both resembled their predecessors in that regard. But the Forty-fifth could boast of an experienced majority, like all but two of its successors.[11] And while the literature on modernization offers only hypotheses as to why this change might have occurred, it supports the inference that such phenomena usually result at least partly from developments within the larger polity. Nelson Polsby expressed it this way: "As the responsibilities of the national government grew, as a larger proportion

43d House and eight in the 44th. Blanche K. Bruce (R-Miss.) served in the 46th Senate, when no blacks were in the House.

10. Lawrence N. Powell, "Rejected Republican Incumbents in the 1866 Congressional Nominating Conventions: A Study in Reconstruction Politics," *Civil War History*, 19 (1973), 219–37; see also Michael Les Benedict, "The Route of Radicalism: Republicans and the Elections of 1867," *Civil War History*, 18 (1972), 334–44.

11. Fiorina, "Historical Change in House Turnover," pp. 29–30. Fiorina defines a "first-termer" as anyone who did not sit in the immediately preceding Congress (but who might have served at an earlier time). Nelson Polsby and others have defined "first-termer" to include only those with no past experience at all; see Polsby, "Institutionalization." Use of the latter criterion yields a lower apparent turnover. For justification of the first technique, see Fiorina, pp. 27–29.

of the national economy was affected by decisions taken at the center, the agencies of the national government institutionalized." Polsby located the time of these events some years after the 1870s.[12] Yet intentionally or not, he was describing conditions that obtained during the Age of Grant, which then were manifested in Capitol demography.

Disaggregating the data reveals additional details and subtler trends. Although the number of longer-tenured members was rising overall, for example, the increase was most pronounced among southern Democrats (Tables 4 and 5). Northerners who desired lengthy political careers at the national level, especially if they were Republicans, tended to pursue them outside the House. A greater proportion of northerners subsequently served in offices of higher status: the Senate, cabinet, foreign ministeries, and so on. By contrast, southern Democrats were more likely to remain Representatives: over one-third of those serving in 1877 eventually would accrue tenures of at least a decade. It was through this sort of persistence that the so-called Southern bloc came into existence—and came to exert an institutional power and influence that would be a dominant force within the House until the mid-twentieth century. In other words, by repeatedly seeking reelection, by accumulating experience and expertise, and by acquiring substantial seniority as well as places within the leadership out of all proportion to their numbers, men from the former slave states came to exercise the authority of a "concurrent majority." Or, to use a term more widely employed today, they became the first sizable, cohesive, and identifiable group to exhibit the traits of modern congressional professionalism.[13]

Dixie's influence was just starting to surface by the mid-1870s, of course; the proportion of novices generally was too high—even among southerners—and the number of men with extensive tenures too small for this period to stand as a giant step forward on the road to professionalization. Still, however small the reduction in turnover was during the later Grant years, it nonetheless signaled the beginning of a trend that eventually would transform the House. An experienced membership is perhaps the single most essential prerequisite to evolution of

12. Polsby, "Institutionalization," p. 164; an alternative view, but one that also locates the period of significant change later than the 1870s, is in Peter Swenson, "The Influence of Recruitment on the Structure of Power in the U.S. House," *Legislative Studies Q.*, 7 (1982), 7–36.

13. David M. Potter, *The South and the Concurrent Majority*, ed. D. E. Fehrenbacher and C. N. Degler (Baton Rouge, 1972), esp. chap. 2; Fiorina, "Historical Change in House Turnover," pp. 34–39. See also Price, "Professionalism."

practices and norms that have the potential, at least, to provide for effective governance in a complex polity. Such a membership inevitably contains greater substantive and procedural expertise, and offers greater likelihood of efficiency and continuity in policy making, than a fluid body like the post–Civil War federal House.[14] It can form the foundation for an institution that is intrinsically both knowledgeable and confident enough to handle a large and diversified workload. It is a resource that probably could have contended with, if not avoided, many of the problems and frustrations that typified early Gilded Age Congressional Government—and that so bothered both contemporary observers and officials.

During the 1870s, though, and for quite some time to come, instability would continue to characterize the House; it was not until 1900 that the incidence of freshmen first fell below 30 percent. In the meantime, the erosion-like impact of short tenures and amateurism remained cumulative and severe. One Reconstruction-era member complained that "under our . . . miserable system of representation, every two or four years, after a man has been educated to a place in this body, after he has come to know its rules, and understand his duties, after he has been trained and educated as a statesman, then at that hour the political wheel rolls him out, and a green man comes here."[15] Thus, the House had to cope continuously with an acute shortage of both procedural and substantive expertise. Committee chairmanships reflected this; the foremost nineteenth-century authority on the subject discovered that some 1300 chairmanships prior to 1895 lasted for fewer than six years, and only 70 exceeded that length. James Garfield spent only four years at the helm of Appropriations, but still recognized the value of on-the-job experience, however brief. On December 8, 1874, in the middle of his second term in that position, he was able to write to a friend that he had "succeeded in getting five of my appropriations bills introduced, which is, I believe, more than has ever been done on the first day of the session in the history of the government." The Ohioan believed strongly that his effectiveness had increased over time; indeed, after the Democrats took over in 1875, he confided to another correspondent that Speaker Michael C. Kerr left him off Appropriations "avowedly on the ground that my thorough knowledge

14. Bryce, *American Commonwealth*, 1:192–93; Price, "The Congressional Career—Then and Now"; Polsby, "Institutionalization" and "Seniority System."

15. Fiorina, "Historical Change in House Turnover," p. 30; Rep. James Brooks, quoted in Brock, *American Crisis*, p. 55.

of the matter would be an embarrassment to the [new] chairman."[16]
Similarly, Rep. Washington Townsend (R-Pa.) reflected the jaundiced
view of many experienced members when he wrote to a fellow Republican survivor of the 1874 Democratic landslide that they would "be
relieved of some responsibility in the next Congress and from the back
seats that will be assigned to us we can overlook the antics of the
democracy, with philosophic eye, as they endeavour to inaugurate their
wild schemes of finance, revenue, and Southern regeneracy. Fortunately the Senate can act as a breakwater against them for some time
to come." Shortly afterward, another congressman would write: "At
every party change ignorance displaces efficiency and experts give way
to blunderers." Then he added, in disgust, "The error of such a system
is daily disclosed."[17]

To be sure, minority status could not deprive experienced and skillful men of all influence. Gilded Age Democrats, for example, after
years of opposition, were well versed in the tactics of criticism and
obstruction, of which they often had made good use. Toward the end of
the Forty-third Congress, Garfield was one of many adversaries who
accused Sam Randall, "Sunset" Cox, and others of imposing "tyranny"
in their filibuster against the 1875 Civil Rights bill, and urged "a change
in the rules as shall not make such obstruction possible."[18] In a similar
vein, a man like Blaine in no way lost all his power simply by being
denied the Speaker's gavel. Upon his initial venture as minority leader
in the Forty-fourth, his skill at demoralizing the new majority provoked
widespread comment; one newspaper went so far as to say that, by
virtue of his shrewdness, "Mr. ex-Speaker Blaine, by himself alone,
constitutes the majority of the House."[19] And a year later, the cover of

---

16. Lauros G. McConachie, *Congressional Committees: A Study of the Origins and Development of Our National and Local Legislative Methods* (1898; New York, 1973), p. 142; James A.
Garfield to Burke A. Hinsdale, 8 Dec. 1874, in *Garfield-Hinsdale Letters, Correspondence
between James Abram Garfield and Burke Aaron Hinsdale*, ed. Mary L. Hinsdale (Ann Arbor,
1949), p. 299 (see also p. 301). On Garfield's reaction in 1875, see Smith, *Garfield*, 1:524,
590; since his replacement was Samuel J. Randall, this doubtless reflects Garfield's
personal pique—although it is true that Randall had no experience on Appropriations.
17. Washington Townsend to George F. Hoar, 6 Nov. 1874, George F. Hoar Papers,
Mass. Historical Society, Boston; Alexander, *History of the House*, pp. 97–98.
18. Garfield to Hinsdale, 1 Feb. 1875, *Garfield-Hinsdale Letters*, p. 316.
19. Quoted in Hamilton, *Blaine*, pp. 321–22, 379. A similar comment was made about
Randall a decade later; on 1 Dec. 1885, after he was no longer Speaker, the Washington
Post declared that "Congress has too long consisted of the Senate and Sam Randall";
quoted in Albert V. House, "The Contributions of Samuel J. Randall to the Rules of the
National House of Representatives," *APSR*, 29 (1935), 840.

the New York *Daily Graphic* commemorated him and his procedural triumphs in verse:

> Here Blaine, the spider sly, doth weave his web
> Of threads all spun with old historic lines,
> Of meshes parliamentary and traps,
> Round Democratic flies his coils he twines.
>
> Hill buzzed his wings but once, and now, alas!
> A hill of empty skin inane he lies;
> Still, with their gaudy wings Lamar and Cox,
> Randall and Wood, do sport like wanton flies.
>
> Sport on, ye insects fine; your fate is sure!
> Blaine is your "daddy" with his web and claw;
> And e'en old flies like Wood, or fighting Cox,
> Must stuff at last yon spider's hungry maw.[20]

Blaine's sort of ascendancy was rare, of course, and open only to that small cohort of old hands who were intimately acquainted with the intricacies of parliamentary methods. George F. Hoar spoke for the more typical member when he said that the House was "governed by a complicated and artificial system of rules, so difficult to be understood that many able men of great national fame go through . . . terms of service without professing to understand it."[21]

Indeed, it would not be overstating matters to argue that the most critical factor distinguishing insiders from the rank-and-file was the former's familiarity with and mastery of congressional procedure. But such men were always scarce, and the combination of a generally inexperienced and transient membership and a rigid set of legislative rules produced a decision-making universe in which real power was concentrated in an extremely small number of hands. Reformers like Henry Adams commented angrily, "The rules have become so complicated as to throw independent members entirely into the background." Those with longer than average tenure were at a natural advantage, although they did not achieve proficiency automatically, or simply by putting in time. Expertise required intelligence as well as endurance, so inside status effectively was restricted to a tiny percentage of the chamber's personnel, who collectively wielded a disproportionate amount of

---

20. New York *Daily Graphic*, 10 Feb. 1876, p. 1.
21. George F. Hoar, "The Conduct of Business in Congress," *NAR*, 128 (1879), 113.

Speaker James G. Blaine, Republican, Maine. Courtesy Library of Congress,
Division of Prints and Photographs.

weight. In the words of George Frisbie Hoar: "The strength of the personal influence of able and popular men is and must be very great in a body composed as is our House of Representatives."[22]

At the center of this select circle, one usually found the Speaker. The latter third of the nineteenth century witnessed a gradual politicization of and aggregation of power in the speakership, culminating in the turn-of-the-century "czardom" of Joseph G. Cannon. But foundations for such a tradition were laid by progenitors like James G. Blaine and Samuel J. Randall. Between them, Blaine and Randall chaired the House for most of the 1870s. Both were strong and capable leaders who were wise enough to enhance their authority further by choosing skilled and respected colleagues as their lieutenants. Blaine relied heavily on men like Garfield and Dawes, while Randall appreciated the assistance of Fernando Wood, Richard Bland (D-Mo.), and William S. Holman (D-Ind.), among others.[23]

It took more than able deputies, however, to make a good Speaker. The rigidity and complexity of House rules notwithstanding, there were interpretive loopholes and plenty of other options for a sufficiently shrewd and knowledgeable chieftain to exploit. As one observer has noted: "The power exerted by the chair always depends on who is the [incumbent]; the office can be made whatever the holder has the capacity to make of it."[24] In particular, two of the Speaker's responsibilities gave him extensive opportunities to influence the course of legislative affairs. These were his right to orchestrate activities on the floor and, more significant, his power to designate the committees.

Both Blaine and Randall made ample use of all available procedures—and developed a few of their own—to enhance their considerable native talents for administration and political persuasiveness.

22. Henry Brooks Adams, "The Session," *NAR*, 111 (1870), 60; McConachie, *Committees*, p. 156; Hoar, "Conduct of Business," p. 133. Although it is rather obvious, the point should be made that citizens vote for congressional candidates on grounds other than intelligence. Thus, those who endure for long tenures may or may not be talented enough to acquire the skills of "insiders."

23. Mary P. Follett, *The Speaker of the House of Representatives* (New York, 1896); Neil MacNeil, *Forge of Democracy* (New York, 1963), pp. 28–29; Albert V. House, "The Political Career of Samuel Jackson Randall" (Ph.D. diss., University of Wisconsin–Madison, 1934), p. 135, and "Contributions of Randall to the Rules," p. 837; David Saville Muzzey, *James G. Blaine: A Political Idol of Other Days* (New York, 1934), p. 62. It should be noted that both Cannon (who entered Congress in 1873) and Thomas B. Reed (R-Maine) acquired their early congressional skills under Blaine and/or Randall's leadership; Reed was also a Maine protégé of Blaine's.

24. Floyd M. Riddick, *The United States Congress: Organization and Procedure* (Manassas, Va., 1949), p. 64.

The Republican, for example, was notorious for what the *Nation* termed his "bargaining with members for recognition"; he had no qualms about denying Representatives the floor if he disagreed with their policy positions. Randall operated in a similar fashion and, in 1881, made the definitive ruling on this matter: "There is no power in the House itself to appeal from the recognition of the chair. The right of recognition is just as absolute in the chair as the judgment of the Supreme Court of the United States is absolute as to the interpretation of the law."[25] Of course, long before the Pennsylvanian's proclamation, adversaries of both men were aware of their "iron-fisted" use of prerogatives. Genial Democrat "Sunset" Cox, for instance, in notifying Blaine that he was about to take a week off in the midst of the session, declared that it made no difference whether or not he was there because, if he asked for a chance to present his views, "you would 'put me down.' "[26]

Blaine was famous in his day for using the discretionary power of the chair to advance the interests of his party and his policies. And Randall, who augmented the official House rules with his own lengthy and privately composed "Speaker's manual," had effective methods, too. One was to urge reference of bills he disliked to the committees least disposed to their passage; since this was something any congressman could request, he began to do it while still in the minority. After winning the podium, he continued to use this device and supplemented it with others. Among his favorites was to convene the Committee of the Whole whenever sizable appropriations were on the agenda. This maneuver enabled Randall, who was a strong advocate of retrenchment, to leave the chair to speak, thereby permitting him to actively rally support for his position.[27]

An adroit presiding officer tried, however, to avoid having to resort to such parliamentary wiles by preventing the progress of objectionable matters onto the House calendar in the first place. Various alternatives were open to him, like the referral method mentioned above; a negative report from a hostile committee usually was enough to prevent House consideration of a measure. But in order to ensure the kind of report he desired, the leader could do more than simply to decide

25. Alexander, *History of the House,* pp. 58–59; A. V. House, "Contributions of Randall to the Rules," pp. 838–39.

26. S. S. Cox to Blaine, 6 May 1874, James G. Blaine Papers, L.C.

27. Randall's private manual is in Box 220 of the Samuel J. Randall Papers, Van Pelt Library, University of Pennsylvania, Philadelphia; see also A. V. House, "Political Career of Randall," pp. 38, 204–5.

under whose jurisdiction each proposal should fall. For the rules stipulated that as Speaker he, and he alone, had the power to appoint members to committees and, therefore, to construct panels that reflected his views. Thus, it was at that preliminary stage, even sometimes before the House had convened or begun its deliberations, that a smart leader began to operate.

The political uses of committee assignments will be considered in detail later on. For now, it is important only to recognize that such means lay exclusively in the presiding officer's hands, and that he could and did exploit them to augment the extent of his authority. Turn-of-the-century Representative DeAlva S. Alexander (R-N.Y.) remarked that "this power soon made the Speakership a citadel about which factional strife and party warfare continually raged. Instead of being impartial boards as originally intended, committees became actively partisan, being framed to safeguard party policies." As Mrs. James G. Blaine, whose husband usually is credited—or blamed—for "politicizing" this process, wrote confidentially to her son two months before the Forty-second House convened: "Your father and [his secretary] are desperately busy over the committees. It is the secret of the power of the Speaker."[28]

The committees were also centers of power and activity within the legislative body as a whole. Woodrow Wilson saw this in 1885, and his commentary has become virtually a cliché: "The House sits . . . to sanction the conclusions of the committees. . . . It legislates in its committee-rooms; not by the determinations of majorities, but by the resolutions of minorities; so that it is not far from the truth to say that Congress in session is Congress on public exhibition, whilst Congress in its committees is Congress at work."[29] Thus, the Speaker's initial leverage over the committee system was responsible for much of his ascendancy. Yet there was a consequent and concomitant irony: because the committees themselves enjoyed such hegemony within the legislative process, the appointment of competent and effective panels, and especially clever and experienced chairmen, created potent competition for the presiding officer. As Lauros McConachie said, "The power of the great committee chairmen tempers the Speaker's power." Wilson

28. Alexander, *History of the House*, p. 66; Mrs. Blaine to Walker Blaine, 9 Oct. 1871, in *Letters of Mrs. Blaine*, 1:41.

29. Woodrow Wilson, *Congressional Government: A Study in American Politics* (1885; Cleveland, 1956), p. 69. In one of the few notes to *Congressional Government*, Wilson acknowledged his debt to George Frisbie Hoar's 1879 essay "The Conduct of Business in Congress" for its insight into congressional committees.

put it even more forcefully when he wrote that "[The Speaker] appoints the leaders of the House, but he is not himself its leader. The leaders of the House are the chairmen of the principal Standing Committees."[30]

So the very institutional characteristics that began by focusing or narrowing the base of congressional clout—a largely transient and unskilled membership, complicated rules, and so on—led also to an inevitable diffusion of authority. Power filtered away from a tightly controlled inner circle concentrated around and dependent upon the Speaker toward "committees which constitute small, independent, exclusive councils." Each of these, according to George Frisbie Hoar, "almost comes to regard itself as a little legislature, and contends with great jealousy against encroachments on its own authority."[31]

Even in the earliest days of the Republic, it was impossible for each Representative personally to consider and evaluate every piece of proposed legislation. Committees were introduced to effect the more efficient disposition of House business and, as such, have been an integral part of the American Congress since its first session.[32] By 1800 the House contained six committees, and as the programmatic and jurisdictional interests of government grew, the committee system was enlarged to reflect and deal with new issues. At the start of the Forty-third Congress, it numbered forty-six panels; the all-time high of sixty-one would not be reached until 1901.[33]

Over time, committees came to assume extensive functions. According to House rules, each was responsible only for studying all bills that fell within its jurisdiction and, in order to facilitate its deliberations, was empowered to call witnesses to appear before it and to solicit written testimony. Upon completion of these tasks, the committee was to make its report to the House, recommending passage or rejection of each measure it had considered. At that point its formal obligations were over. In fact, however, committees did a great deal more. They served

30. McConachie, *Committees*, p. 165; Wilson, *Congressional Government*, p. 58.

31. Adams, "The Session," p. 59; Hoar, "Conduct of Business," p. 131.

32. McConachie, *Committees*, chaps. 1 and 2; George B. Galloway, *History of the House of Representatives* (New York, 1961), pp. 64–67; Noble E. Cunningham, Jr., *The Process of Government under Jefferson* (Princeton, 1978), chap. 10; see also Jack N. Rakove, *The Beginnings of National Politics: An Interpretive History of the Continental Congress* (New York, 1979), pp. 194–96, 204–5.

33. For instance, the Committee on Public Lands was formed in 1805, in response to the Louisiana Purchase; McConachie, *Committees*, p. 40; George B. Galloway, *The Legislative Process in Congress* (New York, 1953), pp. 273–75.

as bodies of reference for the thousands of petitions, memorials, and other such communications sent by the public to their Representatives. As they weighed[34] and reviewed this material, committee members also had to deal with concentrated "informational" campaigns, conducted by outsiders interested in matters before them. Further, because of supposed familiarity with its policy purview, a committee's members generally were expected to act as (and were perceived by their colleagues as) in-House experts—or "cue-givers"—when relevant measures came to the floor.[35] Once an initiative became law, panels assumed oversight responsibility for implementation of programs they had authorized. And they wrote legislation, as well. Of the 4112 House bills introduced during the first session of the Forty-fourth Congress, for example, 414 (10.1 percent) were written in committee, including all of the major appropriation bills.[36]

Of course, inevitably a much larger number of bills were introduced in each session than could possibly be considered, even at the committee level. So panels also had control over ordering and directing the agendas in their respective fields of jurisdiction. Members had to decide which proposals should be allowed to die on the docket and which

34. The word "weigh" is meant literally. In going through the forty-one linear feet of extant petitions for the 43d and 44th Houses in the National Archives, I found many with their seals unbroken (they are no longer in that condition). If these particular documents got any consideration at all, it must have been due to their bulk and not their contents; Petition Files, 43d and 44th Congs., House, Legislative and Judicial Division, National Archives.

35. Cue giving is the process by which one member decides to vote on a measure by determining how another, whose judgment on the matter she or he trusts, is going to vote. "Negative cues" are also employed, with a member voting against someone she or he usually disagrees with. Givers and takers of cues commonly vary from issue to issue. Cues can also be used for purely informational reasons—to gather facts nonjudgmentally as the basis for independent decisions. Cue giving is one of the primary motivating forces behind many informational or "social" congressional organizations. It provided much of the impetus for formation of the House Democratic Study Group, in which the process has become formalized (with, for example, the distribution of position papers). It also functions in such Republican clubs as Chowder & Marching, SOS, and the Wednesday Group (all of which attempt to get as many committees as possible represented among their members, so as to enhance their collective expertise), as well as in "common interest" groups like the Black and Women's Caucuses, Energy Caucus, and New England Caucus. I am grateful to the late Rep. William A. Steiger (R-Wis.) and to Reps. Thomas E. Petri (R-Wis.), David Obey (D-Wis.), and Joel Pritchard (R-Wash.) for their comments on cue giving today. See also Burdett A. Loomis, "Congressional Caucuses and the Politics of Representation," in *Congress Reconsidered,* ed. Lawrence C. Dodd and Bruce I. Oppenheimer, 2d ed. (Washington, 1981), pp. 204–20; Asher, *Freshman Representatives and Cues.* On cue giving in the Gilded Age, see below.

36. Figures calculated from information in the Index to *Cong. Rec.,* 44th Cong., 1st sess.

would be pushed to the floor. They served, in other words, as filters in the legislative machinery, screening out frivolous, ungermane, or (from their perspectives) "undesirable" policy options to prevent them from cluttering up the House calendar. Through its decentralized authority, then, the committee system should have played an important role in the maximization of congressional efficiency.

But did it? Only a qualified "yes" can be given to that question. To answer "yes" without equivocation we would need to presume, for instance, that committees contained enough expertise to competently execute their various functions: determining priorities, evaluating alternatives, assessing submitted information, setting agendas, and so on; or that the Speaker's principal motive in appointing members to their places was to obtain substantively responsible and efficient "little legislatures"; or perhaps that the larger institutional environment, within which the committees operated collectively and individually, permitted them to perform effectually. Yet even a brief examination of the system, employing only these of many possible criteria, should reveal its inherent weaknesses.[37]

To begin with, substantive expertise or competence was only one of many factors, albeit an important one, that the Speaker considered in constructing his committees; he also had to consider members' preferences, geographic balance, national party interests, and personal political or programmatic outlooks. Furthermore, the leeway that a Speaker had in making his decisions was related directly to his own job security. Blaine, who was the unanimous choice of his fellows, clearly had greater freedom of action than did Kerr and Randall, survivors of serious contests who needed to reward their supporters with choice positions. And a House leader was restricted by the resources embodied among his colleagues; legislative and substantive know-how invariably were scarce commodities, which had to be disbursed with care.

These constraints, together with the chieftains' policy, political, and procedural requirements, determined the standards by which assignments would be distributed. First, the Speaker had to try to achieve some degree of regional balance within each committee, among committees, and among types of committees. Second, insofar as it was possible, he needed to put members, particularly in his own party, who agreed with him on panels where they could help him to achieve his

37. Much of the discussion that follows, on committee status and committee types, is condensed from Margaret Susan Thompson, "Before the Floor: Preliminary Steps in Legislative Decision-Making," unpublished paper delivered before the Social Science History Association, Philadelphia, 1976.

goals, and to prevent those in opposition from doing too much damage. Third, he sought to make the most effective use that he could of his institutionally experienced personnel—his long-tenured insiders. And finally, he wanted to make the most effective use that he could of his substantively expert personnel: those with specialized knowledge in particular policy areas.

Objectives like these were not easy to meet. For while individually they might appear fairly straightforward, collectively they were far from that. The demands they imposed often were contradictory. It could easily happen, for example, that the bulk of institutionally experienced members were from one or two regions, or that they were in ideological disagreement with the Speaker. Furthermore, and more important, putting the most procedurally talented Representatives in positions of maximum institutional utility might keep them from acquiring substantive expertise; given their small number, it might prove more efficient to shift them around from term to term, instead of allowing them to sit on particular committees long enough to become jurisdictional specialists. For the leader could not forget that the majority of men almost surely would be inexperienced or nearly so and, whatever guidelines he followed, such persons inevitably would end up with around half of all committee slots.

Thus the ideals a presiding officer envisioned for his committees were unlikely to bear more than a remote resemblance to reality. As Mary Follett put it, "A Speaker can do no better than his material allows"—which, during the 1870s, was not particularly encouraging.[38] Since it clearly was impossible, given the limitations of House membership, to have Representatives with institutional and/or substantive expertise in large numbers on all committees, Speakers had to take care to put them where they could do the most good. This meant that not all assignments could be distributed according to the same criteria. And if one assumes that leaders' decisions were neither random nor irrational, then they must have conformed to certain logical and comprehensible patterns—in other words, to behavioral norms, however informal they might have been, that were intended to effect the leaders' purposes.

By applying three separate measures to committee lists from the 1870s (42d–46th Houses, inclusive), I was able to discover some of these norms, and to learn that they remained consistent regardless of who was Speaker or which party was in control.[39] The first measure, de-

---

38. Follett, *Speaker*, p. 104.
39. I confined the analysis to 1871–81 in order to avoid interference from disruptive

veloped by Warren Miller and Donald Stokes to "status rank" twentieth-century committees, is the ratio of House-experienced members moving onto a committee to the number moving off (but remaining in Congress); the greater this ratio, the higher a committee's "prestige" is assumed to be.[40] For a variety of reasons, this is not a fully satisfactory index to apply, at least in isolation, to Gilded Age behavior.[41] Nevertheless, it does permit one to trace the careers of long-tenured Representatives. The other two indexes are both simpler to compute and of greater explanatory power for nineteenth-century data. The Index of Seniority is the percentage of nonfreshmen on any given committee; the Index of Stability is the percentage of a committee's members in a given Congress who served on the same panel in the preceding Congress.

These calculations reveal, to begin with, that there was relatively little correlation between seniority and stability; the seniority *system* with which we are familiar today did not operate a century ago. Although 50.7 percent of all committee slots were filled by men with House experience, only 16.6 percent were occupied by men who had served before on the same panel (Table 11). Similarly, as shown in Table 12, of 189 chairmanships that could have been given to members with previous committee tenure, just 81 (or 53.9 percent) were so assigned, and during the Forty-third, Forty-fifth, and Forty-sixth Congresses (when

---

events on either side of the period. The 42d was the first post–Civil War Congress in which the South was fully represented. Beginning with the 47th Congress, the shape of the committee system was altered by the 1880 revision of the House rules. All committee lists are taken from the *Cong. Dir.* for each House session; data on members' careers and tenures are from the *BDAC*. All committees, standing and select, that existed in all five congresses (as well as Expenditures in the Department of Justice, created in the 43d) have been included.

40. The formula for computing this Index is $[(B/(A + B)] \times 100$, where A = number of returning members moving *off* a committee and B = number of returning members moving *onto* a committee. (N.B.: This Index ignores three categories of members [in Congress and on each committee]: 1. those who stay on a committee from one Congress to the next; 2. those who are freshmen, defined as anyone not serving in the immediately preceding Congress; 3. those retiring from Congress entirely.) I am grateful to Professor Barbara Hinckley of the University of Wisconsin–Madison for making available the dimensions of this measure.

41. It is inappropriate in isolation because it assumes: 1. that members have some degree of control over their movements, and can choose to stay where they were before—or that such stability is the norm; 2. that there is a sizable pool of experienced, directly-motivated potential "movers"; 3. that professionalism and a seniority system exist, combining to produce many long-tenured members (and few freshmen) and to make for very few openings on "prestigious" committees. Obviously, these assumptions are not valid for the Gilded Age.

Table 11. Committee membership experience, 43d–46th Houses

	43d		44th		45th		46th		Total	
	N	%	N	%	N	%	N	%	N	%
Total number of committees	48		48		47		47		190	
Total number of slots	446		443		447		488		1,824	
Slots held by members with *House* experience	220	49.3	179	40.4	267	59.7	257	52.7	923	50.7
Slots held by members with *committee* experience	83	18.6	46	10.4	86	19.3	87	17.8	302	16.6

Sources: Congressional Directory for the 42d–46th Congresses (Washington, 1872–80).

Table 12. Congressional and committee tenure of chairmen, 43d–46th Houses

Committee	House tenure (in yrs.)[a]				Committee tenure[b]			
	43d	44th	45th	46th	43d	44th	45th	46th
Ways & Means	16	4	16	18	*	—	x	*
Appropriations[c]	10	12/4	6	8	*	—/—	*	*
Rules[d]	10	8/12	14	16	*	—/x	*	*
Naval Affairs	10	4	6	8	*	x	*	*
Judiciary	6	4	6	8	x	—	*	*
Accounts	12	0	2	2	*	—	x	—
Indian Affairs	2	2	4	6	x	—	*	*
Commerce	6	4	6	8	—	—	x	*
Exp. in War Dept.	6	2	2	4	*	—	x	*
Military Affairs	6	2	4	4	*	—	*	—
Banking & Currency	13	14	4	6	—	—	—	*
Printing	2	0	8	10	—	—	x	*
Library	2	2	16	0	—	x	—	—
Militia	6	0	2	4	—	—	—	*
Post Office & Post Roads	4	2	6	4	—	—	x	x
Enrolled Bills	4	2	2	2	—	x	x	x
Foreign Affairs	8	6	8	18	—	—	*	x
Public Buildings	3	8	4	6	x	—	x	*
Invalid Pensions	2	0	2	3	—	—	x	—
Pacific Railroad	8	5	2	4	—	—	x	—
Coinage, Wts. & Measures	12	18	20	22	*	—	*	*
Public Lands	4	2	6	0	x	—	—	—
Claims	4	4	6	8	—	—	*	*
District of Columbia	2	2	2	6	x	—	—	x
Mileage	2	0	0	2	—	—	—	*
Patents	14	2	4	6	—	—	*	*
Exp. in Treasury Dept.	4	2	4	8	x	—	—	—
Elections	2	6	8	4	—	—	*	x
War Claims	0	4	6	2	—	—	*	—
Exp. in Navy Dept.	0	0	2	2	—	—	—	—
Mississippi Levees	4	0	0	2	*	—	—	*
Territories	4	2	2	2	x	—	x	x
Exp. in Interior Dept.	2	0	2	2	—	—	—	—
Exp. in P.O. Dept.	3	2	2	0	*	—	—	—
Exp. in Justice Dept.	0	0	0	6	NA[e]	—	—	—
Public Expenditures	2	2	4	2	—	—	x	x
Private Land Claims	4	1	3	5	—	—	*	*
Education & Labor	2	0	2	4	x	—	*	*
Civil Service Reform	4	2	2	0	—	x	—	—

Table 12—*continued*

Committee	House tenure (in yrs.)[a]				Committee tenure[b]			
	43d	*44th*	*45th*	*46th*	*43d*	*44th*	*45th*	*46th*
Agriculture	4	2	2	2	x	—	—	x
Exp. on Pub. Bldgs.	6	0	3	0	—	—	—	—
Railways & Canals	4	4	2	4	—	—	x	x
Revolutionary Pensions	2	2	2	0	—	—	—	—
Exp. in State Dept.	4	0	2	6	—	—	*	—
Mines & Mining	2	2	2	2	—	—	—	—
Manufactures	2	2	4	0	—	—	—	—
Revision of Laws	6	2	2	10	x	—	—	—

[a] In some cases, accumulated tenure is nonconsecutive.

[b] Meanings of symbols:— no prior service on committee; x prior service on committee; * prior service as chairman of committee.

[c] J. D. C. Atkins took over the Appropriations Committee from S. J. Randall when Randall became Speaker of the House.

[d] Randall took over the Rules Committee from M. C. Kerr when he became Speaker upon Kerr's death.

[e] The Committee on Expenditures in the Department of Justice was established during the 44th Congress.

party control did not change), a mere 44 panels (or 31.4 percent) were led by the same persons as in the preceding House.[42]

Nonfreshman Representatives were not, however, distributed randomly throughout the roster. Those with institutional and/or substantive expertise were concentrated in a fairly small proportion of the committees, the identity of which remained constant regardless of partisan majority or Speaker. Thus if it is assumed that efforts were made to utilize expertise responsibly—an assumption supported strongly by contemporary accounts and subsequent scholarship—it is possible to combine the measures of membership to produce a "status continuum," appropriate to the Gilded Age, by which the committees can be ranked (Table 13).[43] Assignments throughout the careers of 139

42. Figures computed from information in *Cong. Dir.* and *BDAC.*

43. Bryce, *American Commonwealth,* 1: chap. 15; Wilson, *Congressional Government,* chap. 3; Price, "Professionalism"; Polsby, "Institutionalization" and "Seniority System"; Abrams and Cooper, "Rise of Seniority." These data also demonstrate that Gilded Age legislators attached little or no significance to the distinction between consecutive and nonconsecutive service. Members who had earned tenure in the past, and who returned after a break, were still regarded as "experienced," as their assignments reveal. Thus, N. P. Banks, who did not sit in the 43d, was immediately placed on Rules when he returned in the 44th (this event, plus the return of Speaker Kerr—who also did not sit in the 43d—explains the relatively low ranking of Rules according to the Miller-Stokes Index). Even Alexander Stephens (D-Ga.) was accorded all the respect due to a sixteen-year House veteran when he returned in 1873—despite the fact that he had interrupted his tenure to serve as vice president of the Confederacy!

Table 13. Index values and cumulative rank orderings of committees, 42d–46th Houses

Committee	Sum Rank	Miller-Stokes Value	Miller-Stokes Rank	Stability Value	Stability Rank	Seniority Value	Seniority Rank
Ways & Means	1	80.77	1.5	41.3	3	87.0	3
Appropriations	2	74.29	3	35.4	4	89.6	2
Rules	3.5	62.50	11	65.0	1	90.0	1
Naval Affairs	3.5	73.33	4	43.2	2	68.2	7
Judiciary	5	80.77	1.5	25.0	7.5	68.8	6
Accounts	6	63.64	9	30.0	5	65.0	8
Indian Affairs	7.5	72.73	5	23.4	11	57.4	13
Commerce	7.5	64.29	8	22.9	12	63.1	9
Exp. in War Dept.	9	66.67	6.5	13.6	27	77.3	4
Military Affairs	10.5	60.78	12	24.4	10	55.6	16.5
Banking & Currency	10.5	60.00	14	20.5	14.5	61.4	10
Printing	12	57.14	19.5	25.0	7.5	58.4	12
Library	13	50.00	29.5	25.0	7.5	75.0	5
Militia	14	60.00	14	20.5	14.5	54.5	19
Post Office & Post Roads	15.5	57.58	18	15.9	21	59.1	11
Enrolled Bills	15.5	60.00	14	16.7	19.5	55.6	16.5
Foreign Affairs	17	50.00	29.5	25.0	7.5	56.8	14
Public Bldgs. & Grounds	18	54.17	21.5	22.7	13	52.3	23
Invalid Pensions	19	63.18	10	18.2	17.5	40.9	34.5
Pacific Railroad	20	52.50	26	15.4	22	55.8	15
Coinage, Wts. & Measures	21	58.62	17	13.6	27	52.3	23
Public Lands	23	53.12	24	15.2	23	52.2	25
Claims	23	59.38	16	9.1	33	52.3	23
District of Columbia	23	46.67	35	20.0	16	53.3	21
Mileage	25	66.67	6.5	5.0	39	45.0	29
Patents	26	48.00	32.5	18.2	17.5	45.5	28
Exp. in Treasury Dept.	27	54.17	21.5	7.1	37	53.6	20
Elections	28	52.78	25	10.4	30	47.9	27
War Claims	29	50.00	29.5	9.1	33	50.0	26
Exp. in Navy Dept.	30.5	52.17	21.5	0.0	47	54.6	18
Mississippi Levees	30.5	48.00	32.5	14.3	25	40.9	34.5
Territories	32	40.62	42	16.7	19.5	43.8	31
Exp. in Interior Dept.	33	57.14	19.5	4.5	41.5	40.9	34.5
Exp. in P.O. Dept.	34	53.33	23	4.5	41.5	40.9	34.5
Exp. in Justice Dept.	35	47.62	34	7.4	36	44.4	30
Public Expenditures	36	45.00	36	6.8	38	21.3	46
Priv. Land Claims	37	44.12	37	9.1	33	43.2	32
Education & Labor	38	40.74	41	13.6	27	38.6	37.5
Civil Service Reform	39	41.94	39	9.1	33	38.6	37.5
Agriculture	40	33.33	45.5	14.6	24	33.3	40.5
Exp. on Pub. Bldgs.	41	50.00	29.5	3.8	45	38.5	39
Railways & Canals	42	40.00	43	9.1	33	31.8	39
Revolutionary Pensions	43	29.63	47	11.6	29	30.2	44
Exp. in State Dept.	44	42.86	38	4.5	41.5	31.8	42.5
Mines & Mining	45	41.18	40	4.2	44	33.3	40.5
Manufactures	46	33.33	45.5	4.5	41.5	20.5	47
Revision of Laws	47	34.27	44	2.3	46	29.5	45

long-time members—those with three or more terms of consecutive House service—reflect consistent movement up the status ladder. During their first terms, the average value of these Representatives' highest-ranking committees is 20.16; during their second it is 13.54; and in their third it is 11.71. Beyond that, five-eighths of the ninety-six who sat continuously in the House for more than six years eventually served on one of the top five panels, while nearly all of the rest either chaired or held ranking minority slots on committees of only slightly lower status.[44]

Merely to state that some committees were more "important" or "prestigious" than others, however, does not explain why such differences occurred. Why, for instance, was it considered necessary to assign more experienced members to some, rather than other, committees? Why was committee tenure, but not House tenure, deemed expendable in certain cases? When, if ever, did geographic distribution enter into the picture? And how did the Speaker cope with all those hordes of inexperienced, and generally indistinguishable, freshmen? Answers to these questions can be derived by drawing *functional* distinctions among the panels. They fell into four basic categories, and, except for the third, they tended to form identifiable cohorts along the status continuum that has been presented.

The first category consisted of what might be called the innovative, or major policy, committees.[45] They had jurisdiction over design of the most significant federal programs: revenue collection and disbursement; military and naval establishments, including veterans' homes and the patronage-rich navy yards; internal improvements (authorized, during this period, by the Commerce Committee); and so on. Over three-fifths of all public bills were referred to panels in this group.

44. Figures calculated from committee histories that were constructed for each of the 139 "core" members. Raw data from *Cong. Dir.* and *BDAC.*

45. *Allocative* decisions (see below) determine how finite resources are distributed (who will get funds from a fixed appropriation, for example, or to whom patronage positions shall be awarded); *innovative* decisions involve initiation of new programs or policy thrusts. To illustrate: the decision to bake a pie is innovative; decisions as to what size(s) its pieces should be, or as to whom they should be given, are allocative. For further discussion of this distinction, see Theodore J. Lowi, "American Business, Public Policy, Case Studies and Political Theory," *World Politics,* 16 (1964), 677–715; Charles O. Jones, *An Introduction to the Study of Public Policy* (Belmont, Calif., 1970), pp. 140–44; and Robert J. Salisbury, "The Analysis of Public Policy: A Search for Theories and Roles," in *Political Science and Public Policy,* ed. Austin Ranney (Chicago, 1968), pp. 151–75; some of these authors use slightly different terms. Of course, committee time, floor time, and the like are also finite resources that also must be allocated; thus, allocative decisions can be either substantive or procedural.

Accordingly, these committees controlled and determined most of the House's substantive agenda. And their functions were facilitated by Rules, which served as the chamber's de facto steering committee and which also belonged in this classification.[46] Because the work of these committees comprised the core of congressional responsibility, it was essential that their members have legislative experience. Yet that alone was not sufficient; the intricacies of the policy areas with which they dealt demanded specialized knowledge, as well. Acquisition of this took time and required a certain measure of political, as well as programmatic, insight. Consequently few Representatives won seats on these panels until they had been around for awhile learning the ropes and developing a degree of professional commitment, if only that made evident by a willingness to return to the chamber.[47]

To a great extent, committees in the first cohort parallel those that, since 1946, have been designated as "exclusive" assignments: that is, persons who sit on them do not ordinarily serve anywhere else. And those in the second Gilded Age category might be regarded as equivalent to the "semi-exclusive" places of today—in other words, the secondary policy committees.[48] Nearly all remaining public measures belonged within their jurisdictions, and these sometimes included proposals of great salience. So, for example, Railways & Canals, normally a rather inactive body, produced the first initiative to regulate interstate transportation, and homesteads, an intermittently pressing issue, were under the purview of Public Lands. But unlike panels of the first order, these only occasionally occupied center stage. Furthermore, they did not enjoy—as did Ways & Means, Appropriations, and certain other principal committees—standing rules that permitted them to circumvent the calendar and report to the House at any time.[49] Thus, while these panels investigated many items that fell within the discretionary legislative agenda, they rarely had the opportunity, or clout, to achieve

46. Administrative significance also explains the relatively high ranking of such committees as Accounts and Enrolled Bills.

47. James K. Pollock, Jr., "The Seniority Rule in Congress," *NAR*, 222 (1925), 235–45; Alexander, *History of the House*, chap. 5.

48. On the distinction between exclusive and semiexclusive committees, see Nicholas A. Masters, "Committee Assignments," in Polsby, *Congressional Behavior*, pp. 161–63 [reprinted from *APSR*, vol. 55]; George Goodwin, Jr., *The Little Legislatures: Committees of Congress* (Amherst, Mass., 1970), pp. 66–68. Together, these two categories parallel most of the panels included in Alexander's list of "Important Standing Committees"; Alexander, *History of the House*, Appendix E, pp. 399–410.

49. Privileged status is discussed in McConachie, *Committees*, pp. 172–84; Alexander, *History of the House*, pp. 276–77; Lewis A. Froman, Jr., *The Congressional Process: Strategies, Rules, and Procedures* (Boston, 1967), pp. 49–52.

implementation. Rather, most of their business consisted of routine oversight of ongoing programs. In an era of vast federal expansion, of course, this was not a negligible task, and partly for that reason, secondary policy committees usually had at least a few members with both tenure and substantive expertise. A congressional insider sometimes chose to stay on such a committee, either because he had a personal interest in its programmatic areas or because its jurisdiction was of special relevance to his constituency (which could easily be the case with committees such as Pacific Railroads, Agriculture, and Mississippi Levees).[50] Committees of this kind were also effective proving grounds for men in their first or second terms—who, if they demonstrated ability and stayed in the House, could then move from them to major panels.

The third category includes committees like Claims and Invalid Pensions, which handled most of Congress's distributive business. These were the House workhorses, for over half the bills introduced every session (and more than half of those that passed) were on the private calendar. These matters occasionally went before major committees, especially Military Affairs, but usually they were referred to one of the six House panels devoted almost exclusively to such problems.[51] Despite their burden, members of these boards exhibited less institutional or substantive expertise than could be found among those who sat on major committees. This was because their jobs were fairly routine and demanded little in the way of specialized knowledge, such as that, for instance, which was needed among those writing tariff legislation on Ways & Means. So long as the chairman had sufficient House experience to present his panel's decisions on the floor, the rest of its members might just as well be freshmen. And both the heavy workload and its repetitive quality discouraged returning men from seeking reassignment in this area. Even their chairmanships, therefore, frequently went to members who had never served on them previously—but who, usually by their second or third terms, had demonstrated diligence and promise.

Collectively, the first three categories contained a bit more than half

50. Frequent references to such members and their committee preferences can be found in relevant biographies, and in the invaluable compendium: William Horatio Barnes, *The American Government: Biographies of Members of the Forty-Third Congress*, 3 vols. (New York, 1874), vols. 2 and 3.

51. The six committees were: Claims, Invalid Pensions, Patents, Private Land Claims, Revolutionary Pensions, and War Claims. Private measures comprised 52.9 percent (43d) and 53.8 percent (44th) of all bills enacted into law. Galloway, *History of the House*, p. 304; see also Table 3 in chap. 1, above.

of all House committees and handled nearly all of the body's business. The remaining panels did little or nothing; many considered *no* bills during session after session, while others made minor contributions to the routines of government. Consequently, this final group, by far the largest, can be called the repository or "do-nothing" class.[52] It was here that one found the heaviest concentrations of first-termers. Often the only experienced members would be the chairmen, although freshman chairmen were not unheard of. Repositories, however, did have their political and institutional uses. Their chairs, for example, were cheap prizes that could be awarded to incompetent but loyal old-timers, to second-termers of modest ability, or to insiders who served on but did not head major policy committees. Recipients of these positions, meanwhile, had reason to be grateful; in an era before personal staffs and office buildings, access to the committee clerks and rooms within the Capitol that accompanied such slots was a highly sought-after perk.[53] And it was through these chairmanships that Speakers often attempted to achieve some approximation of geographic equity. Nineteenth-century authority Lauros McConachie noted that because of regional imbalances within each party, and within many partisan factions, most important and responsible assignments went to men from just one or two parts of the country. But he found that shrewd presiding officers were able to maintain appearances of overall fairness through judicious distribution of minor chairs.[54]

Thus, Gilded Age Speakers tried, insofar as they were able, to employ rational and consistent norms as they organized the House. But how well, after assignments were made, did the committee system actually work? In many ways, and at its best, it unquestionably improved the quality and effectiveness of congressional deliberations. When, for example, a newcomer arrived with specialized professional expertise, the committee system could and often did work to enhance

---

52. Concerning the eight Committees on Expenditures in the Departments, for example, McConachie said: "their names have usually been by-words with the Representatives; and the speaker . . . blesses them as convenient shelving places for the members with whose unfitness as legislators he has been impressed"; McConachie, *Committees*, p. 234. Information on lack of bills is from the Index to the *Cong. Rec.*

53. As Alexander put it: "Several of these committees seemed to exist for no other purpose than to furnish rooms for their chairmen—a highly prized perquisite in the absence of an office building." He noted that many of these "repositories" were abolished after the first House office building was erected in 1909; Alexander, *History of the House,* p. 233.

54. McConachie, *Committees*, pp. 44–53; see also Alexander, *History of the House,* chap. 5.

the speed and directness with which his skill or knowledge was put to use. In this manner, freshman John H. Burleigh (R-Maine), a former sea captain, lent an insider's perspective to the Committee on Naval Affairs. Hosea W. Parker (D-N.H.), who had studied law with a former U.S. commissioner of patents, was endorsed by leaders of both parties and was placed immediately on the Patents Committee. And William W. Phelps (R-N.J.), a freshman in 1873 who had been counsel to many banks and who was a published authority on monetary matters, right away brought to his work on Banking & Currency a background that "so well equipped him for the consideration of all financial questions that he was able to give assistance to the oldest and most experienced members of his committee."[55]

Similarly, the differentiation among panels allowed Speakers to make good use quickly of novices who had established their political savvy elsewhere, or who were fortunate enough to have secured impressive endorsements from powerful colleagues or other respected public figures. So Democrat Henry Watterson, famous and influential editor of the *Louisville Courier-Journal,* came in halfway through the Forty-fourth House to replace someone who had died, and went directly onto Ways & Means. Republican Charles Foster of Ohio started there, too, in 1871, and Blaine told him later that he was put there expressly because Horace Greeley had urged that "a gentleman who could carry a democratic district . . . must naturally possess elements that justified his being given a higher place on committees than is usually granted to new members."[56] Sam Randall kept Blaine informed of machinations within both parties' delegations from Pennsylvania, and on at least one occasion the G.O.P. leader took his advice as to which Keystone State Republican belonged on Appropriations. Four years later, when the situation was reversed, Speaker Randall accepted Blaine's request that his Maine protégé, the freshman Thomas Reed, be given a choice assignment.[57]

---

55. Barnes, *Biographies of Members,* 2:13–14, 23–24. On Republican support for Parker, see C. H. Roberts to William E. Chandler, 21 Nov. 1873, William E. Chandler Papers, New Hampshire Historical Society, Concord; Hugh M. Herrick, *William Walter Phelps: His Life and Public Services* (New York, 1904), pp. 42–43.

56. On Watterson, see *BDAC,* p. 207, and *Cong. Dir.* for the 1st and 2d sessions of the 44th Cong.; the man he replaced, Edward Y. Parsons, had served on Private Land Claims and Coinage, Weights & Measures; see also Joseph F. Wall, *Henry Watterson: Reconstructed Rebel* (New York, 1956), and Henry Watterson, *"Marse Henry": An Autobiography,* 2 vols. (New York, 1919). On Foster, see *Nat. Cyc.,* 1:139.

57. S. J. Randall to J. G. Blaine, 29 Sept. 1873, Blaine Papers; Blaine to Randall, 8 Oct. 1877, Randall Papers.

nents of greenhorns were reliable, however. Illinois's
m, for instance, wrote Blaine a long letter before the
se convened to tell him about the new men from his
several were praised as "clever" and "shrewd," one was
nctorily as "a sort of lawyer—don't think very heavy
owerhouse and Speaker Joseph G. Cannon![58] Thus,
freshmen rarely got preferential treatment at the expense of those men
who managed to stay in Congress—even, occasionally, on the same
committee—long enough to acquire procedural and substantive expertise. William Holman (D-Ind.), an ardent advocate of retrenchment
known as the "Watchdog of the Treasury," developed great influence
through several terms on Appropriations, and the name of Pennsylvania's "Pig Iron" Kelley became synonymous with protectionism during his unprecedented twenty-year continuous tenure on Ways &
Means.[59] Men such as these, far more than knowledgeable greenhorns,
could both direct the work of their committees and act as reliable cue-
givers on the floor. By remaining a workhorse, for example, Claims
chairman William Washburn (R-Mass.) engineered his measures ably
through the House; as colleague George Frisbie Hoar recalled, "He was
universally respected. Every man felt safe in following his recommendation in any matter which he had carefully investigated. . . . He very
soon acquired the confidence of the House so completely that his
judgment became its law in matters within the jurisdiction of his committee." And there was the credible, if probably apocryphal, story of
Illinois's William R. Morrison, a Democrat who chaired Ways & Means
under Speakers Kerr and John G. Carlisle. A biographer alleged that
"there was probably no man in Congress in Morrison's day . . . who was
as much sought after for his advice," and reported the following incident: "One day an honest old German representative from Pennsylvania, a Republican, was unknowingly blundering through the tellers
in the House when he was asked how he voted. 'Vell, vell,' he said, 'I
knows nodink aboud de question. How did Bill Morrison vote?' On
being informed that Bill Morrison voted 'aye' he nodded his head in
satisfaction and called out, 'aye.' "[60]

58. Shelby M. Cullom to Blaine, 6 Sept. 1873, Blaine Papers.

59. On Holman, see Barnes, *Biographies of Members*, 3:111–12; *Nat. Cyc.* 5:457; *DAB*,
9:158–59. On Kelley, Barnes, *Biographies of Members*, 2:175–83; *Nat. Cyc.*, 6:53; *DAB*, 10:
299–300.

60. George F. Hoar, *Autobiography of Seventy Years*, 2 vols. (New York, 1903), 1:226;
Franklin D. Scott, "The Political Career of William R. Morrison," *Illinois State Historical
Society Transactions*, 33 (1926), 144–45.

Such authorities, because of their influence over their colleagues, did help to make the "inner workings" of Congress run more smoothly; in that sense, they clearly enhanced legislative efficiency. For no individual conceivably could inform himself on all policy areas and measures on which he eventually would have to vote; without even the twentieth-century advantage of a personal staff, congressmen in the Age of Grant had to depend heavily—and probably more than members today—on the advice and expertise of others. Yet how reliable was that advice; how sure could a member be that, in following it, he was serving the best interests of his constituency or country? Democrat Fernando Wood once persuaded the House to reject a clause "about to pass without debate" in an army appropriation bill ostensibly because he had heard that the secretary of war had made a secret contract with "an unscrupulous and ignorant man" who would have benefited from the decision. As a reporter from the *Overland Monthly* put it, "[Wood] was one of the most dignified and impressive members of the House. . . . For such a personage to . . . discourse thus upon a subject of which no man on the floor knew anything, could not fail to produce an effect." But he added darkly that the New Yorker's motives turned out to be less than honorable, for "it developed later that Wood was leading a lobby for another scheme with which [this proposal] had interfered."[61]

The incident may have been atypical; in any event, I do not mention it to draw a generalization about all influential members.[62] Still, the possibility for abuse existed, and given the general lack of knowledge among Representatives in the 1870s, when it occurred it was often impossible to detect. Furthermore, the diffused power delegated by the House to its committees, their chairmen, and other selected cue-givers may actually have increased the likelihood that abuses would take place. From the perspective of late nineteenth-century reformer Gamaliel Bradford, this system "greatly simplified the labors [of] private interests, which would be almost powerless if they had to deal with the whole body of members." The committees, in contrast, enabled such interests to focus their efforts on only a handful of legislators and, having won

61. J. M. Bulkley, "The Third House," *Overland Monthly,* 39 (1902), 906–7.
62. This theme—the process by which "honorable" men were deceived or entrapped into acting as front men for "dishonorable" interests—was, of course, a common one in the political fiction of the era, as discussed in chap. 1. See, for example, John W. De Forest, *Honest John Vane* (1875; State College, Pa., 1960); Henry Adams, *Democracy, An American Novel* (New York, 1880); and Hamlin Garland, *A Member of the Third House: A Dramatic Story* (1892; Upper Saddle River, N.J., 1968).

them over, to "govern not only the manner of treatment, but the subjects themselves to be treated."[63]

Despite Bradford's concern, committees, in their overall impact upon legislative behavior, doubtless did more good than harm. But if they were "the heart of congressional activity," what did their weaknesses, as well as their strengths, imply for the House as a whole? The fundamental problem may be summarized quite simply. Congress was overloaded, and so were its committees. Congress suffered from time-lag, and so did that part of its machinery peculiar to the committee system. Thus, due to overloading, the filtration function—in other words, the ordering of priorities—became essential within each panel's jurisdiction; and due to time-lag, the wherewithal—in terms of time, talent, and expertise—often did not exist to perform that function properly. Even the best-run, most responsible committee faced competition from nearly four dozen others: for space on the calendar, for floor time, for *access* to the attention of the legislature. "The result," testified George Frisbie Hoar, "is that there is a [constant] struggle between the different leading committees for the opportunity to bring their questions before the House."[64] It was up to the Speaker, as the official source of authority in the body, to determine the outcome of this struggle. But in constructing panels strong enough to engage in this sort of jousting, he effectively abdicated to them a measure of his own potential power. In the words of Woodrow Wilson, "The Speaker . . . stands as near to leadership as any one; but his will does not run as a formative and imperative power in legislation. . . . the hedging cir-

---

63. Gamaliel Bradford, "Congressional Reform," *NAR*, 111 (1870), 331, 333. See also McConachie, *Committees*, pp. 136–37.

64. Hoar, "Conduct of Business," p. 131. Hoar's account of the pressures of overload is striking enough to be quoted at length: "Several thousand bills are introduced in every Congress. . . . The processes by which these bills are strangled will be understood by comprehending the operation of the committees. . . . Each committee is entitled, when it is called, to occupy this morning hour of each of two successive days with the measures which it has prepared, and, if its second morning hour expires while the House is actually considering one of its measures, to have that single measure hold over in the morning hour till it is disposed of. Supposing the two sessions which make up the life of the House to last ten months, and allowing for the holidays, the time taken for organization and appointing committees, and the time when the four privileged subjects . . . take up the attention of the House, so that the morning hour can not be devoted to this call, I suppose one hundred days in two sessions is an unusually large average of days when such a call is had. This gives an average of not more than two hours apiece to the committees of the House to report upon, debate, and dispose of all the subjects of general legislation committed to their charge. From this time is taken the time consumed in reading of the bill, and in calling the yeas and nays, which may be ordered by one fifth of the members present and which requires forty minutes for a single roll-call" (pp. 120–21).

cumstances of his official position as presiding officer prevent his performing the part of active leadership." Hence, even if it were possible to order priorities successfully within a committee, it still was almost impossible to determine them *among* committees—each headed by its own little "lord-proprietor."[65] So despite, and sometimes because of, the committees, the process of legislation continued to be haphazard. To a great degree, it lacked any unified design or direction, and often was inadequate to meet the demands that a growing nation placed upon it.

"Such is Washington, such is Congressional life—a perpetual bubbling of hot water, with almost nothing else in the pot. Of the five hundred bills which were introduced at the beginning of this session, probably not fifty, and perhaps not ten, will pass. . . . Congress used to be a law-making body. Now it is mainly an axe-grinding body." So said "Representative Hollowbread" in John William De Forest's 1875 satire about Congress, *Playing the Mischief.*[66] An overloaded House had to come up with some basis for determining priorities, or it would find itself completely immobilized, and caricature would turn into truth. But where was direction to be found? Ideally it should have come from within the institution itself. But that rarely happened during the Gilded Age. Speaker Blaine, for instance, commented on the "very pronounced . . . division of opinion" among his colleagues. So did James A. Garfield, who, in an 1873 interview with the *New York Tribune,* predicted a session in which the combined efforts of "150 new members" and returnees with "minds like a fleece of wool that have [sic] been left out in the rain" would only produce measures that would be "impracticable, crude, and even absurd." Both of these professionals doubtless would have felt compelled to agree with the astute Gamaliel Bradford, as he summarized the legislative process: "Each [measure] passes through on its own merits, if the word is not a misnomer. . . . Anything like a permanent and comprehensive policy is not possible to Congress and its committees of constantly changing members, mostly little familiar with precedents. . . . [Among them] there is no authority which can distinguish between the wildest fustian and the soundest reasoning based upon experience."[67]

Thus if Congress could not rationalize decision making for itself even through its committees, it would have to look elsewhere for

65. Wilson, *Congressional Government,* p. 58; Galloway, *History of the House,* p. 73.
66. John W. De Forest, *Playing the Mischief* (1875; State College, Pa., 1961), pp. 268–69.
67. Blaine, *Twenty Years of Congress,* 2:561; *The Diary of James A. Garfield,* ed. Harry James Brown and Frederick D. Williams, 4 vols. (East Lansing, Mich., 1967–81), 2:246, n. 171.

guidance if it were not to become paralyzed completely. And there were four sources of potential assistance toward which the legislature could turn. First was the executive branch, particularly the presidency. That, however, was hardly of much help so long as a passive, "purely administrative" officer like Ulysses Grant occupied the White House. Lesser officials, to be sure, at the cabinet level and below, were not only willing but eager to be of service, especially in regard to the funds that should be authorized for their departments. But these men tended to direct their pleas toward Appropriations or toward the particular committees that oversaw their operations, rather than toward the House as a whole. Furthermore, since federal money was not unlimited, demands from such officials actually were in *competition* with one another, and so probably contributed more to confusion and fragmentation than to simplification and rationalization of the legislative policy process.[68]

Political parties, too, might have provided direction to congressional deliberations. But both major parties were in a state of programmatic flux during the Grant years. Although each could operate as an effective electoral instrument and could elicit intense loyalty from its members, neither had yet evolved an internal consensus on issues not connected to the Civil War.[69] Northern Republicans continued to get

68. Wilfred E. Binkley, *President and Congress* (New York, 1948), pp. 146–61; Wilson, *Congressional Government*, chap. 5. Any number of communications between executive officials and Congress exists in the James A. Garfield Papers, L.C., and Randall Papers; both these men were chairmen of Appropriations during the second Grant administration.

69. Recent historiography on late nineteenth-century partisanship, which is both extensive and impressive, tends to argue that parties in this period were rationally organized and embodied distinctive constituencies and outlooks. Most of these studies, however, either concentrate exclusively on state-level activities, deal solely with elections (and not with the governmental consequences, if any, of rational partisanship at the ballot box), or focus on a time later than that of this study. Those scholars, like Ballard Campbell, who find clear partisan voting patterns in state legislatures generally find them in respect to issues (school policy and temperance, for instance) that were not significant at the national level—and do *not* find them on the sorts of economic issues that were prominent in the 1870s Congress. Patterns on national issues such as tariffs and currency tended not to emerge until the 1880s; hence, the findings of Brady, Rothman, and others are not applicable to the Grant years. Thus, Democrats could elect a free trade Speaker (Kerr) in 1875, and follow him with a protectionist (Randall) in 1876; not until 1883 was Randall defeated in caucus for the speakership because his views on the tariff were incompatible with what had become the dominant party policy. But note that, as late as 1896, Democrats could divide over presidential nominees as different on currency as Grover Cleveland and William Jennings Bryan. For recent historiography on partisanship in the late nineteenth century, see Paul Kleppner, *The Third Electoral System, 1853–1892* (Chapel Hill, 1979); Richard Jensen, *The Winning of the Midwest: Social and Political Conflict, 1888–96* (Chicago, 1971); Melvyn Hammarberg, *The Indiana Voter: The*

great mileage out of waving the bloody shirt, and as redemption proceeded, its antithesis worked wonders in the South. Thus, Charles Merriam would conclude that, until at least 1880, "the war issue was still too strong" to permit sufficient attention to other matters, while historian Edgar E. Robinson found that "the activities of Congress seemed again and again to reveal that the legislative membership of both parties was divided upon all of the important questions before the public."[70] In the meantime, Democracy and the G.O.P. alike had free traders and protectionists, greenbackers and resumptionists, spoilsmen and civil service reformers, and antimonopolists and railroad entrepreneurs all within their ranks; little bound these sundry forces together except antipathy toward those in the opposing camp. By 1872, James A. Garfield was not alone in fearing that, as rebellion receded into the past, "we are rapidly reaching that period when the two great political parties must dissolve their present organizations. . . . [Both] still have a great organization, but out of which the informing life has nearly departed." Four years later, the Ohioan still looked forward to the day when "in the south as in the north men may seek their party associates on the great commercial and industrial questions," rather than on views of region and race.[71] In short, early Gilded Age parties hardly were capable of broad-based, substantive agenda setting at the national level, and tended instead to resort to emotional appeals and passionate attacks on the opposition. This grew increasingly common as the election of 1876 drew near. Democrats had a majority in the House,

---

Historical Dynamics of Party Allegiance during the 1870s (Chicago, 1977); Ballard C. Campbell, *Representative Democracy: Public Policy and Midwestern Legislatures in the Late Nineteenth Century* (Cambridge, Mass. 1980); David W. Brady, *Congressional Voting in a Partisan Era: A Study of McKinley Houses and a Comparison to the Modern House of Representatives* (Lawrence, Kans., 1973); and David J. Rothman, *Politics and Power: The United States Senate, 1869–1901* (Cambridge, Mass., 1966). Older scholarship, on the other hand, tends to focus more explicitly on the fluidity of parties in the 1870s, and on the congressional parties of that era: see Bryce, *American Commonwealth*, 1:653–61; William G. Carleton, "The Money Question in Indiana Politics, 1865–1890" and "Why Was the Democratic Party in Indiana a Radical Party, 1865–1890?" *Indiana Magazine of History*, 42 (1946): 107–60, 207–28; see also references in note 70, below, and chap. 5, below.

70. Charles Edward Merriam, *The American Party System: An Introduction to the Study of Political Parties in the United States* (New York, 1923), pp. 204–5; Edgar E. Robinson, *The Evolution of American Political Parties: A Sketch of Party Development* (New York, 1924), pp. 193–94.

71. James A. Garfield to Lyman Hall, 6 Apr. 1872, letter printed in Margaret Leech and Harry J. Brown, *The Garfield Orbit* (New York, 1978), p. 271; quote of 1876 in Stanley P. Hirshson, *Farewell to the Bloody Shirt: Northern Republicans and the Southern Negro, 1877–1893* (Bloomington, Ind., 1962), p. 25; see also J. H. Van Allen to Sen. John Sherman (R-Ohio), 4 Jan. 1876, John Sherman Papers, L.C.

and Republicans controlled the Senate and executive; each attempted to blame the other for government's failure to resolve the nation's problems. But while this provided useful raw material for any number of impassioned speeches and provocative campaign leaflets, and formed the foundation for apparent partisan unity, it scarcely constituted a positive contribution to the course of congressional business.

A third potential source of direction was public opinion. This assumes, of course, that the public could share one opinion on any issue, or that mechanisms existed that could transmit majority sentiments effectively to Representatives—something that rarely if ever occurred. Speaker Blaine complained in regard to economics: "The various propositions in this [Forty-third] Congress fairly illustrate the conflicting views on financial matters held among people. . . . The country looked to Congress for relief, and yet did not agree upon any measure of relief." Thus, any number of members introduced legislation that they believed reflected the desires or best interests of the public—as those members perceived them. In the words of Gamaliel Bradford, "The public stands completely bewildered among the multiplicity of doctors. . . . When we come to Congress the popular confusion is merely concentrated . . . neither Congress nor the country has any clear idea of the method of its actions."[72]

Institutional mechanisms, the executive, the parties, and the public—all proved incapable of providing effective direction to legislative deliberation. Indeed, in the face of all these sources of uncertainty and conflicting pressures—an overloaded agenda, time-lag, diffused authority, and so on—what ultimately may seem most remarkable about early Gilded Age Congressional Government is that it managed to function at all. That it did was owing partly, no doubt, to inertia, and partly to luck. And there were, of course, some very talented and capable men within its ranks. But also instrumental was the one potential external source of assistance that I have not yet examined in this regard, an agency that at least occasionally was able to provide some order out of the chaos—to help Congress, insofar as anything could help, to decide upon a few attainable objectives and priorities from among the demands being made upon it. This helping hand came from the very forces that Gamaliel Bradford and so many others deplored: the "private interests" that, it was alleged, were corrupting the "public interest" that Congress was intended to protect.

Bradford's view was by no means unique and, in fact, was not entirely

72. Blaine, *Twenty Years of Congress,* 2:563; Bradford, "Congressional Reform," p. 342.

without merit. Yet it was not wholly accurate, either. For the two supposed types of interests, public and private, were not inherently or inevitably antithetical. By the Age of Grant, both were coming increasingly under the jurisdiction of federal governance. And both, accordingly, needed and deserved effectual representation.

Representative James A. Garfield, Republican, Ohio. Courtesy Library of Congress, Division of Prints and Photographs.

CHAPTER 3

Constituencies and Clienteles: Toward a Redefinition of Representation

Congress has always been and must always be the theatre of contending opinions; the forum where the opposing forces of political philosophy meet to measure their strength; where the public must meet the assaults of local and sectional interests; in a word, the appointed place where the nation seeks to utter its thought and register its will.

JAMES A. GARFIELD (1877)

Ninety years before Garfield wrote these words,[1] James Madison and about fifty of his contemporaries were gathered in Philadelphia, composing the document that established the Congress in which the Ohioan would later serve. The delegates to the convention, which began in May 1787, very quickly realized that countless disputes stood in the way of consensus. One sore point, however, seemed more fundamental than all the rest, and Madison spoke for many when he declared, on June 19: "The great difficulty lies in the affair of Representation; if this could be adjusted, all others would be surmountable."[2]

1. James A. Garfield, "A Century of Congress," *Atlantic*, 40 (1877), 60.
2. Madison quoted in J. R. Pole, *Political Representation in England and the Origins of the American Republic* (New York, 1966), p. 362. On the Philadelphia Convention, see, for example, David G. Smith, *The Convention and the Constitution: The Political Ideas of the Founding Fathers* (New York, 1965); Gordon S. Wood, *The Creation of the American Republic, 1776–1787* (Chapel Hill, 1969); and Max Farrand, ed., *The Records of the Federal Convention of 1787*, 3 vols. (New Haven, 1923).

Three months later, the conferees had approved a constitution and submitted it to the states for ratification. The "affair of Representation," along with many others, presumably had been adjusted, and the United States was on its way toward becoming a national republic. Yet it is hard to extract from the Constitution itself any details as to the sorts of representation it was intended to foster. Article I outlined the methods by which legislators were to be selected, although it left many particulars of the process to the states, and it gave some delineation to the substantive areas within these officials' jurisdiction. But it offered no guidelines as to how members of Congress were to behave—*how* they were to represent—once they assumed office.

Thus, as later generations were to find out, many matters did not get resolved fully in Philadelphia. Americans in the Grant years were especially aware of lingering uncertainties, for some—most notably the place of slavery and the balance between federal and state authority— had figured significantly in bringing on the Civil War. Controversy over representation generally did not manifest itself so violently.[3] Nonetheless, concern about the quality and obligations of representation was acute during the Gilded Age.

Representation is the means through which citizens in a republic are able to participate in governance. It connects people with public institutions and permits communication among diverse elements in the polity; it is a relationship that can take many forms, both substantive and symbolic.[4] Complex though the subject is, however, all students of representation agree that it is an essential component of public life in virtually every nation-state, and most especially in those that, like the

3. Arthur Bestor, "The American Civil War as a Constitutional Crisis," *AHR,* 69 (1964), 327–52; Harold M. Hyman, *A More Perfect Union: The Impact of the Civil War and Reconstruction on the Constitution* (Boston, 1975), chaps. 1–3. Representation was, of course, an issue of the Civil War and Reconstruction, and often led to violence, particularly where black suffrage was concerned. Similarly, violence has appeared repeatedly in the ongoing campaigns for women's and blacks' civil rights—in which various aspects of representation are central issues.

4. A good starting point for those interested in the history of American representation is Alfred de Grazia, *Public and Republic: Political Representation in America* (New York, 1951). For the early years, see sources in n. 2; Bernard Bailyn, *The Origins of American Politics* (New York, 1967); and Charles Edward Merriam, *A History of American Political Theories* (1903; New York, 1969). For discussion of representational theory, see Hanna Fenichel Pitkin, *The Concept of Representation* (Berkeley, 1967), and H. F. Pitkin, ed., *Representation* (New York, 1969); J. Roland Pennock and John W. Chapman, eds., *Representation* (New York, 1968); and various works by Robert A. Dahl, including *A Preface to Democratic Theory* (Chicago, 1956), *Who Governs?* (New Haven, 1961), and *Dilemmas of Pluralistic Democracy: Autonomy vs. Control* (New Haven, 1982).

United States, can be characterized as "pluralist democracies."[5] Without question, the issue of representation has always been central to American political theory, rhetoric, and practice.

While the concept of representation has ancient roots, it did not assume prominence as a theme in political philosophy until approximately the eighteenth century, and it was the writing of that period that most profoundly influenced the framers of the American Constitution.[6] Some of them, in turn—particularly Madison and Alexander Hamilton, in *The Federalist*—helped to extend representation theory; a principal contribution was the notion that legislative representation is workable within a large and heterogeneous republic, and not simply within a "city-state."[7] Still, *The Federalist* was very much a product of its era and, as such, was more concerned with justifying representation than with its quality. Modern theory, on the other hand, focuses more intently on how representation works and on how it might operate more effectively.

The change in emphasis obviously owed a good deal to experience; the Founding Fathers had no real precedents for their federal experiment and, hence, no basis for empirically grounded predictions as to how it actually would function. Thus, there necessarily were limits to the framers' prescience, and it in no way diminishes their accomplishments to suggest that the system they devised in the 1780s did not prove, over time, to be wholly adequate. For if representation is a component of governance, then it follows that, as government changes—in the size and substance of its purview, in its impact upon citizens' lives and aspirations, and in the roles that its officeholders are supposed to fill—representation must also change. If it is not adjusted, or if contemporaries do not acknowledge or appreciate adjustments that do occur, the polity is apt to grow dissatisfied and disaffected.[8]

5. De Grazia, *Public and Republic*, chaps. 1, 8–9; Dahl, *Dilemmas of Pluralist Democracy*, pp. 1–11.

6. See works cited in n. 2, and those by de Grazia, Bailyn, and Merriam in n. 4. See also Henry Jones Ford, *The Rise and Growth of American Politics: A Sketch of Constitutional Development* (1898; New York, 1967), part 1; and Bernard Bailyn, *The Ideological Origins of the American Revolution* (Cambridge, Mass., 1967). Some scholars would relate the emergent prominence of this political theme to the parallel emergence of capitalism: Albert O. Hirschman, *The Passions and the Interests: Political Arguments for Capitalism before Its Triumph* (Princeton, 1977), part 1.

7. Alexander Hamilton, James Madison, and John Jay, *The Federalist Papers*, ed. Clinton Rossiter (New York, 1961); all citations to this work will be by paper rather than by page, since so many editions are extant.

8. See works cited in n. 4., above, particularly those by Dahl; Terrence E. Cook and

Events during the Age of Grant exemplified this pattern. It was, of course, a time of great change in the federal sector. As the scope of policy grew, more and more interests were affected by it and therefore felt a need to be represented actively in public affairs. This put tremendous pressure on established representational mechanisms: especially the Congress and, more specifically, the popularly elected House, whose resources were inadequate to the expanding number of tasks before it. Not surprisingly, the legislature's incapacity engendered discontent among the citizenry, which often manifested itself in vociferous outcries against "Grantism, jobbery, and corruption." There was no small irony in this situation, however. For the very phenomenon that incited the loudest criticism—lobbying—was also a catalyst that could help to remedy the polity's problems, if only it were understood properly. Its practitioners were able to exercise a wide range of representational responsibilities in behalf of many of those who needed to deal with Washington; they served their clients in much the same way that congressmen served their constituencies. There were differences, to be sure. Legislators enjoyed constitutional sanction, and lobbyists did not. More important—for lack of sanction did not prevent lobbyists from practicing—American legislators are chosen at the polls to represent fixed geographic constituencies, while lobbyists are agents for entities of fluid and self-selected composition, whose substantive interests might or might not have spatial boundaries.

Relatively few items on the crowded agenda of the 1870s were defined exclusively by locale; as a result, the public's concerns and will in regard to them would not necessarily follow the lines of congressional districts. They lent themselves more fittingly, therefore, to promotion by persons outside the formal legislative structure. New representational instruments evolved to take care of them, instruments that could operate concurrently with those the Founding Fathers had devised, and that enabled the electorally determined representation of constituencies to be supplemented by lobbyists' representation of *clienteles.* Concurrency would not mature fully until the twentieth century, when lobbyists' contributions would be recognized as beneficial and, eventually, as essential to the operation of a pluralistic democracy.[9] None-

Patrick M. Morgan, eds., *Participatory Democracy* (San Francisco, 1971); and Peter Bachrach, *The Theory of Democratic Elitism: A Critique* (Boston, 1967).

9. De Grazia, *Public and Republic,* chaps. 8–9; Dahl, *Dilemmas of Pluralist Democracy,* chap. 2; E. Pendleton Herring, *Group Representation before Congress* (Baltimore, 1929); David B. Truman, *The Governmental Process: Political Interests and Public Opinion,* 2d ed. (New York, 1971); Earl Latham, *The Group Basis of Politics: A Study in Basing-Point Legisla-*

theless, concurrency's roots, and its systemic rationale, were founded in the Age of Grant.

Beginning with *The Federalist,* countless treatises have been written that purport to describe congressmen's roles and responsibilities. From them, two points of consensus seem to emerge. The first is that federal Representatives, acting collectively, are to reflect and determine the national will (sometimes referred to as the "general good"). The second is that, individually, each legislator should represent the particular opinions and needs of his or her own constituency.[10] Originally it was assumed that efforts on behalf of the general good would dominate congressional behavior; this is evident not only from the jurisdictional details included in Article I of the Constitution, but also from the arguments of both Madison and Hamilton in *The Federalist,* written in explanation and defense of those details.[11]

The Founders did not completely reject the notion that narrower perspectives might have their place in the national arena. Madison, for instance, referred more than once to the "energizing" force that such interests could inject into the legislature and cited them as part of his justification for geographically based House districts, although he was equally concerned with controlling the influence of those "petty and transitory passions." George Mason, another participant in the Philadelphia debates, was less restrained than his fellow Virginian in affirming the value of representation that reflected constituency orientation; as he saw it, House members actually were delegates who "should sympathize with their constituents, should think as they think and feel as they feel, and for these purposes should even be residents among them."[12] Yet not even Madison or Mason expected that localism or

tion (New York, 1965), chap. 1; Betty H. Zisk, ed., *American Political Interest Groups: Readings in Theory and Research* (Belmont, Calif., 1969); Terry M. Moe, *The Organization of Interests: Incentives and the Internal Dynamics of Political Interest Groups* (Chicago, 1980).

    10. *The Federalist,* Nos. 10, 55–56, 63; Pitkin, *Concept of Representation,* chap. 7; Roger H. Davidson, *The Role of the Congressman* (Indianapolis, 1969), chap. 4.

    11. *The Federalist,* Nos. 23, 27, 35 (all Hamilton), 55–58 (Madison).

    12. *The Federalist,* Nos. 10, 55–56; Mason quoted in George B. Galloway, *History of the House of Representatives* (New York, 1961), p. 2. Hamilton, no advocate of this sort of "actual" representation, argued that the president, because he was the only officer chosen (however indirectly) by the entire citizenry, was in fact the most "representative" federal figure of all; *The Federalist,* Nos. 68–69, 77; see also Gamaliel Bradford, "Congressional Reform," *NAR,* 111 (1870), 334; Ford, *Rise and Growth of American Politics,* chap. 15. In this vein, the following statement from Jimmy Carter's 1976 presidential nomination acceptance speech bears remarkable resemblance to that of George Mason: "We can have an American President . . . who's not isolated from the people, but who feels your pain and shares your dreams, and takes his strength and his wisdom and his courage from you"; *C.Q. Weekly Rpt.,* 34 (17 July 1976), 1933–34.

other forms of particularity would play too great a part in Congress's affairs. For since the body's purview was restricted by design to issues of overriding national interest—security, trade, finance, and so on—there would be scant opportunity or need for parochialism to intrude. Federal governance, in short, was to be concerned with the general good; it was not intended as an arena for the satisfaction of specialized demands, or as a source of great consequences in the mundane affairs of the nation's citizens.

From its inception, of course, the American system operated in ways that bore little resemblance to the framers' ideal. Even before the Constitution was ratified, officials had had to confront the sorts of "petty and transitory passions" that Madison was concerned with, and their presence hardly diminished with time. As government began to deal with matters like tariffs, manufactures, expansion, internal improvements, and slavery, people quickly became aware that central authority was no abstract or symbolic entity but, rather, a force with the power to make a noticeable impact upon their day-to-day existence. This awareness was reflected in Americans' representational expectations; as early as the era of Jefferson's presidency, they wanted their congressmen to act as delegates rather than as trustees without commitment to the interests of localities.[13] That is, when issues came up that were of concern to those back home, members were being explicitly asked to serve as spokesmen for their constituencies' interests, not as guardians of the so-called "general will." By the Gilded Age, this pattern was well established. Indeed, delegate tendencies became stronger after the Civil War than they had been before.

It is clear that the expansion and diversification of Washington's agenda directly affected representation by the time of Grant's tenure in the White House. Citizens in the 1860s and 1870s were more cognizant than their forebears of how the federal sector could affect their lives. The Civil War and its persistent legacies were of course potent demonstrations of its power to do that; but so were currency, tariff, regulatory, and railroad policy—all tremendously important to a people whose economic endeavors were becoming increasingly interdependent and whose "island communities" had started their merger into a "global

13. On the pre-constitutional period, see Jack N. Rakove, *The Beginnings of National Politics: An Interpretive History of the Continental Congress* (New York, 1979), chaps. 6, 9–11, 15. For the early national period, see Noble E. Cunningham, Jr., *The Process of Government under Jefferson* (Princeton, 1978), chaps. 12–13; N. E. Cunningham, Jr., ed., *Circular Letters of Congressmen to Their Constituents, 1787–1829*, 3 vols. (Chapel Hill, 1978).

village."[14] Of course, Washington's influence could be felt in more immediate ways, as well: through internal improvements, local public works, and so on. Its land grants, pensions, claims, patronage, and other personal benefits even touched individuals. On all these levels, the relationship between the public and the public sector was growing more and more intricate and direct. As reporter Edward Winslow Martin put it in 1873, "[Washington] is not only the seat of government, but it is the centre from which radiate the varied influences which affect every citizen of the Republic, from the millionaire to the man dependent on his daily earnings." His countrymen know, the writer continued, that their affairs "must prosper or suffer according to the fidelity and ability with which those who are placed here by the people to watch over and direct them, execute their trust."[15]

Most legislators tried earnestly to hold up their end of the representational relationship by pledging to work explicitly in behalf of what they perceived to be their constituencies' policy interests. Speeches, eulogies, memoirs, journalistic accounts, and, for those who kept them, diaries and correspondence all attest to the pervasiveness of such behavior. Many candidates rode into office on the basis of promises to "serve the district"—and sometimes they meant to do so in very tangible ways. Texas Democrat James W. Throckmorton, for instance, won votes in 1874 by stating that, if elected, he would press for a subsidy for the Texas & Pacific Railroad. When opponents charged that he was a stockholder in the company and on its board of directors, Throckmorton acknowledged as much but denied any impropriety. Rather, *because* he had a personal stake in a project that would benefit his neighbors, he would labor more diligently in their behalf than a disinterested legislator could. He saw his role on the board essentially as that of a "representative of the state's interests," as he put it during his first campaign; "I have worked for Texas since the hour of my connection with this road." His intention in running for Congress, he declared, was merely to extend and improve his representational capacity. As this was the principal issue in the canvass, Throckmorton's victory suggests that an electoral majority endorsed the politician's attitude and objective.

14. Robert E. Wiebe, *The Search for Order, 1877–1920* (New York, 1967), chaps. 1–2; Marshall McLuhan and Quentin Fiore, *War and Peace in the Global Village* (New York, 1968).

15. Edward Winslow Martin [James Dabney McCabe], *Behind the Scenes in Washington* (Philadelphia, 1873), p. 5.

And although Texas & Pacific never got its subsidy, it was not for lack of effort on the Texan's part; during his tenure in the House, he pushed the corporation's claim from the seat he had sought and won on the Pacific Railroad Committee.[16]

Throckmorton may have been more outspoken than most, but he was far from the only member to operate in such a fashion. Ways & Means chairman Henry Dawes defended his connections with textile manufacturers by noting that theirs was an important industry in his district and, by supporting legislation that benefited the companies, he was promoting prosperity for those back home. Philadelphian Charles O'Neill said, early in his thirty-year House career: "I for one, representing in part a city which is largely engaged in manufactures, say I want to stand by our own manufacturers wherever and whenever I can." Even Speaker Blaine, at the height of his power, kept a careful eye on measures affecting the fisheries and Canadian trade of his native Maine.[17]

William Horatio Barnes recorded the typicality of such behavior in an invaluable 1874 compendium, *The American Government: Biographies of Members of the Forty-third Congress.* In its three volumes totaling over a thousand pages, Barnes provided a sketch of every man in the House and Senate at the time of Grant's second inaugural, and virtually all his essays testify to the dedication with which members attempted to serve their districts. Amos Clark (R-N.J.), for example, "performed his duty with great faithfulness . . . to his constituency, irrespective of party" and, while in office, obtained a $50,000 appropriation for harbor improvements. Democrat George Adams of Kentucky worked against the taxation of distilleries; Jay Hubbell (R-Mich.) "was sent to Washington by the people of the copper-mining district to aid in securing a higher tariff on copper, and was successful in securing that result." Eli Perry (D-N.Y.) made a name for himself by helping soldiers' widows to secure pensions and by persuading his fellow members of the Public Buildings & Grounds Committee to authorize $500,000 for a structure

---

16. Claude Elliott, *Leathercoat: The Life History of a Texas Patriot* (San Antonio, 1938), pp. 222–28; see also Grenville M. Dodge to Thomas A. Scott (president, Texas & Pacific Railroad), Nov. 1872, and Dodge to Throckmorton, 5 Jan. 1876, Grenville M. Dodge Papers, Iowa State Department of History & Archives, Des Moines.

17. On Dawes, see DeAlva S. Alexander, *History and Procedure of the House of Representatives* (Boston, 1916), pp. 146–47; and George F. Hoar, *Autobiography of Seventy Years*, 2 vols. (New York, 1903), 1:202–3, 228. O'Neill quoted in William Horatio Barnes, *The American Government: Biographies of Members of the Forty-Third Congress*, 3 vols. (New York, 1874), 2:184. On Blaine, see Gail Hamilton [Mary Abigail Dodge,], *Biography of James G. Blaine* (Norwich, Conn., 1894), p. 310.

in Albany. Democrats Milton Sayler and Henry Banning of Cincinnati "promote[d] the success of the Louisville and Portland Canal Bill, in which [their] constituents were deeply interested," while Charles Williams (R-Wis.) did the same for legislation on behalf of the Wisconsin Central Railroad. Barnes was an avid Republican, but his admiration for aggressive constituency orientation was expressed without regard to party. He was as approving of William Hearndon's (D-Tex.) "many measures of utility and reform, most of which tended to the development and prosperity of his own section" as he was of Leonard Myers (R-Pa.), who "has been among the most efficient in procuring legislation to promote the interests of his city and state." Not everyone shared Barnes's opinion of such behavior, of course. Reformers like Gamaliel Bradford issued scathing denunciations of it, and the Russian observer Moisei Ostrogorski regarded it a short time later as evidence that "the House . . . is simply a diet of representatives of private or local interests," where "every interest is represented . . . except the public interest."[18] Normative judgments aside, however, there is a clear consensus that House members demonstrated awareness of and concern for their constituencies' needs and tried, whenever possible, to act responsively.

Not all legislators did so in the same ways, however, or even for the same reasons. Some, like James Throckmorton—or Charles Clayton (R-Calif.), who went first to Sacramento and then to Washington largely to propound the commercial views of a bipartisan coalition of San Francisco merchants—entered Congress primarily as advocates of specific interests that they alleged were beneficial to their districts. Others, such as Albany's Perry, concentrated on the pork barrel either because opportunity presented itself through fortuitous committee assignments or because they saw it as an easy way of winning popular approbation. And a few were perhaps most strongly compelled by the motive of personal gain—although even they were careful to justify their performances with references to "community good." Into this category fell the remarkable Alvah Crocker of Fitchburg, Massachusetts, who wanted his town to have a direct rail line to Boston: "Chiefly for the purpose of securing the railroad charter, he became a member of the Massachusetts Legislature in 1836"; then he resigned and served as president of the newly created Boston & Fitchburg Railroad. Some

18. Barnes, *Biographies*, 2:116, 160, 187, 3:20, 21, 70, 212, 220, 255. Gamaliel Bradford, "Congressional Reform," *NAR*, 111 (1870), 342; M. Ostrogorski, *Democracy and the Organization of Political Parties*, 2 vols. (New York, 1902), 2:544.

time later, when he wanted a tunnel for the line, he got himself sent to the State Senate, where he secured that charter—and resigned again, as the governor had appointed him to the Hoosic Tunnel Commission, on which he supervised construction of the improvement for which he had won authorization. It is hardly surprising, then, that his neighbors elected him to Congress. Who knows what he might have accomplished there, had he not died in the middle of his first full term![19]

For the majority of members, however, "constituent service" was neither premeditated nor very spectacular. Rather, it was a by-product of the prodigious expansion of federal governance into activities that directly affected citizens' lives, requiring them to deal with officialdom and to call upon their Representatives for help. A new dimension, that of the ombudsman, had entered into the Capitol experience. It reflected phenomena that were entirely outside the Founding Fathers' predictive vision and, as a result, that were not accounted for in their representational design. Ombudsmanship had in fact become a large and essential component of the congressman's role.[20] Roswell Horr (R-Mich.), first elected in 1878, testified four years later that the average member received fifty letters a week or more, and that "growing out of these letters will be found each week a large number of errands, a vast amount of what is called department work." Over two-thirds of the entries in James Garfield's diary for days that the House was in session contain references to efforts of this kind, and extant collections of legislators' mail suggest that his burden was typical. In December 1875, for example, Nathaniel P. Banks (R-Mass.) got 106 letters, of which 53

19. Barnes, *Biographies*, 2:59–60, 269–70; *BDAC*, p. 755. Regarding Clayton (who was English-born), Barnes noted that he was a Republican, but that Democratic merchants had been "instrumental" in his electoral victories; on Crocker, see also Edward Chase Kirkland, *Men, Cities and Transportation: A Study in New England History, 1820–1900*, 2 vols. (New York, 1948), 1:387–432.

20. For general discussion of the ombudsman role, see Davidson, *Role of the Congressman*, pp. 99–104; Walter Gellhorn, *When Americans Complain: Governmental Grievance Procedures* (Cambridge, Mass., 1966), pp. 58–94; Thomas E. Cavanagh, "The Two Arenas of Congress," and John R. Johannes, "Casework in the House," both in *The House at Work*, ed. Joseph Cooper and G. Calvin Mackenzie (Austin, Tex., 1981), pp. 56–96; and Senator William S. Cohen and Kenneth Lasson, *Getting the Most Out of Washington: Using Congress to Move the Federal Bureaucracy* (New York, 1982). For the late nineteenth century, see Leonard D. White, *The Republican Era, 1869–1901: A Study in Administrative History* (New York, 1958), esp. chap. 4; James D. Norris and Arthur H. Shaffer, eds., *Politics and Patronage in the Gilded Age: The Correspondence of James A. Garfield and Charles E. Henry* (Madison, Wis., 1970), esp. Introduction; Stephen Skowronek, *Building a New American State: The Expansion of National Administrative Capacities, 1877–1920* (Cambridge, Mass., 1982), esp. chaps. 2, 5; and chap. 6, below.

related to patronage and 13 to pensions and claims; 6 were lecture invitations, another 6 asked for documents, and 5 were notes of introduction that suggested their subjects had "cases" before the government.[21]

Many congressmen, including a number who performed such tasks regularly and well, resented the extent to which their time was taken up in the minutiae of constituent service; in at least one case, it seemed to have driven an overwhelmed member into immobility and probably to drink.[22] Barnes himself admitted that citizens' requests could "greatly tax" the Representative's energies and "seriously interfere with that attention to the work of legislation which is his first duty." Maryland's John Thomas found it "onerous and self-degrading," while William D. Kelley of Pennsylvania, when running for the sixth of an eventual fifteen terms, threatened in 1870 to reject renomination unless the citizens of Philadelphia stopped regarding him as an "errand boy" or "employment agent."[23] One must suspect, however, that despite his rhetoric, Kelley continued to serve those functions when he returned to Washington. For he, like Blaine, Garfield, and the handful of other Gilded Age congressional careerists, necessarily appreciated what subsequent generations of professionals have discovered, too: a member

21. Horr quoted in White, *Republican Era*, p. 72; Garfield estimate based on examination of relevant entries in *The Diary of James A. Garfield*, ed. Harry James Brown and Frederick D. Williams, 4 vols. (East Lansing, Mich., 1967–81), vols. 2–3; the relevant letters to Banks are in the Nathaniel P. Banks Papers, L.C. Other manuscript collections that confirm the burden of casework include the papers of James A. Garfield, Benjamin F. Butler, Henry L. Dawes, and John Sherman, all L.C.; the George F. Hoar Papers, Massachusetts Historical Society, Boston; the Samuel J. Randall Papers, Van Pelt Library, University of Pennsylvania, Philadelphia; and the William B. Allison Papers, Iowa State Department of History & Archives, Des Moines.

22. Thus, one disgruntled New York state resident wrote to James Garfield: "I have written to our M. C. MacDougall four letters. The last time I sent him a sheet of paper in an envelope, stamped & addressed to me [the franking privilege had recently been abolished], for him to answer my previous letters on. Now I write you to ask you to tell me *frankly*, whether Mac is on a *drunk* or not—Mac is my friend, and if so, you need not hesitate to write it for whatever you say to me will be confidential. The *general* impression here, for he answers *no* letters written him, is, that he is 'bursting it'—If he dont change his tactics and show a *little* attention to his *subjects*, he will fare bad *next* time. If he is *straight*, show him this letter and ask him how you shall answer it?" J. T. Pingree to Garfield, 6 Mar. 1876, Garfield Papers. Garfield's reply has not been preserved, but MacDougall failed in his 1876 bid for renomination; *BDAC*, p. 1248.

23. "Onerous" and "self-degrading" were from comments by Rep. John L. Thomas of Maryland, quoted in White, *Republican Era*, p. 71; Barnes's comments were from an entry criticizing the performance of Rep. Alexander McDill (R-Wis.), and Kelley's threat was from a speech excerpted by Barnes; Barnes, *Biographies*, 2:182–83; 3:267.

who ignores his constituency's particular demands may forfeit his opportunity to concentrate on the "real" business of government—because he will not be returned to the Capitol.[24]

Whether or not he liked it, and whatever he did, the Gilded Age congressman was deluged with constituent demands, demands that he was supposed to consider in both his policy making and ombudsman roles. For even when Representatives found time to deal with matters of substance, they were not immune to constituency pressures. Individuals wrote letters, signed petitions, issued memorials, and talked personally with legislators, attempting to persuade them that particular initiatives or positions were in the best interests of their districts or, at least, of certain of those who lived there.[25] These pressures were more numerous and probably more intense than those that confronted earlier generations of House members, since people felt the effects of government more acutely than in the past and consequently cared about and watched its operation more closely.

In short, the preponderance of evidence suggests that nearly all congressmen tried diligently, if sometimes reluctantly, to be responsive to local desires. Yet despite these efforts, many Americans remained unimpressed by the quality of representation they were getting. Too often, apparently, effort and effectiveness did not seem to go hand-in-hand. The public's political dissatisfaction had more than one cause, of course. But much can be traced to the framework of constituencies into which the people were organized—to the fixed geographic and electoral basis of representation within the congressional system.

James Madison had articulated a detailed defense of constituency-based representation in several papers of *The Federalist,* most notably in

24. On the relationship between successful ombudsmanship and reelection, see Norris and Shaffer, *Garfield-Henry Letters,* p. ix; David R. Mayhew, *Congress: The Electoral Connection* (New Haven, 1974), pp. 108–10; Johannes, "Casework in the House"; Richard E. Fenno, Jr., *Home Style* (Boston, 1978); and House Commission on Administrative Review [Obey Commission] *Final Report,* 2 vols., 95th Cong., 1st sess. (1977), Hse. Doc. 95-272, passim (survey results). While many of these sources question whether there is a measurable relationship between ombudsmanship and electoral success, they do show that most members of Congress believe there is such a relationship—and act accordingly. For other views, see Richard E. Fenno, Jr., "If, as Ralph Nader Says, Congress Is 'the Broken Branch,' How Come We Love Our Congressman So Much?" in *Congress in Change: Evolution and Reform,* ed. Norman J. Ornstein (New York, 1975), pp. 277–87; Margaret S. Thompson, "Ben Butler versus the Brahmins: Patronage and Politics in Early Gilded Age Massachusetts," *New England Q.;* 55 (1982), 163–86.

25. Petitions are to be found in every extant collection of congressional correspondence from the era. The largest collection solely of petitions and memorials is the Petition Files, Legislative & Judicial Division, National Archives.

Numbers 55 and 56. His particular concern was to assuage fears expressed by many of his contemporaries that, under the proposed constitutional system, districts would be too large, and the entire House too small, to "possess a due knowledge" of the people's interests. The Virginian addressed the latter point first, and noted that the House was meant to grow as the nation did; based upon the assumption that constituency size would remain constant (and that blacks always would be counted as three-fifths of their actual number), he suggested that, within fifty years, the chamber would contain 400 seats instead of its initial 65. [In fact, the Twenty-fifth House would number 242 members, from a total of 26 states.] So he dismissed that objection rather quickly and proceeded to focus more seriously on the other. "It is a sound and important principle," he began, "that the representative ought to be acquainted with the interests and circumstances of his constituents." But, he continued, "this principle can extend no further than to those circumstances and interests to which the authority and care of the representative relate. An ignorance of a variety of minute and particular objects which do not lie within the compass of legislation is consistent with every attribute necessary to a due performance of the legislative trust. In determining the extent of information required in the exercise of a particular authority, recourse then must be had to the objects within the purview of that authority." Thus, Madison concluded that districts were and would remain sufficiently contained to reflect those local interests necessary to "energize" the House. No further specificity was required, he believed, since "minute and particular objects" would be outside the scope of legitimate federal jurisdiction.[26]

Just as national governance quickly outstripped the narrow limits that Madison and his fellows prescribed, however, so the concept of constituencies that evolved from their understanding was inadequate to the representational needs of their descendants. Congressional districts have never been completely homogeneous, of course; even in the 1790s, it would have been difficult to find any that were unitary in social, political, or economic composition. To the Founding Fathers this was relatively unimportant, but by the Gilded Age the substance of public policy demanded that legislators attempt to comprehend and to implement the interests of their districts and of those who lived there. Yet the average Representative of 1875 had a constituency three-and-a-half times as large as that of his counterpart eighty years before, and sat in a House with over three times as many members from nearly triple

26. *The Federalist,* Nos. 55, 56; the quotation is from the beginning of No. 56.

the original number of states.[27] Heterogeneity, in short, had increased dramatically both within and among districts—at the same time that the polity required more particularized and reflective representation.

Such circumstances made life difficult for both officials and the general public, and their problems obviously were interrelated. Each congressman could reasonably expect that large numbers of his constituents would have cause to deal with government and would make demands upon him to which they expected tangible responses. But different issues would inspire different sectors of his public, and among those interested in any single matter there might be divergent opinions as to what he should do. It was unlikely, in other words, that everyone in his district would have the same set of policy priorities; in some cases, an individual's desires might be in direct conflict with those of his or her neighbors. Thus, a civil service reformer in Ohio's Fifth District might have more in common with some residents of the Nineteenth—or of Massachusetts—than with the majority of those who lived around him. Others might think that restoration of silver as specie, or woman suffrage, was important, while the foe of patronage might not care about these questions at all or might, in fact, support a gold standard and oppose feminism. Manufacturers and workers in the same town were apt to have sharply antagonistic views on the merits of the eight-hour day, while a village's brewer and its Methodist parson might not be very concerned with that question, but probably felt strongly about temperance. Meanwhile, a dozen war veterans and widows might want federal pensions and might vie for their Representative's help in obtaining them. All in all, hundreds of messages would inundate each man in the Capitol. Some would contradict others, and all would be competing for shares of the finite resources of time, energy, and clout at the individual legislator's command. Clearly, representing "the district's interests" was easier to promise than to practice. For a Representative could not be uniformly responsive to every constituent's demands.

Legislators, therefore, were forced to make choices—to develop representational priorities. They did not necessarily do so consciously; indeed, many members probably were unaware that they drew distinctions. They could continue in good conscience, then, to describe what they did as work in behalf of their constituents. But their behavior

27. *BDAC*, p. 45; *Historical Statistics of the United States: Colonial Times to 1957* (Washington, 1961), pp. 12–13.

might be defined more accurately as effort to represent their various *meaningful* constituencies.[28]

"Constituency," like many other political terms, can mean a variety of things. Legally, it means all residents of a legislator's district. But it can be construed as specifying only full-fledged citizens, that is, those qualified to participate in politics through mechanisms such as the suffrage. Some theories limit the meaning even further, to a member's "realistic" constituency: that subset of the people who actually voted for him.[29] This interpretation resembles, but is not identical to, what Grant McConnell has called the "effective constituency . . . the part of the whole unit which is able to enforce its demands"—a definition that does not necessarily require residence in the officeholder's district.[30] Or one may refer to an "assumed" or "adopted" constituency: a cohort with which the legislator feels particular empathy and whose cause he espouses consciously; it may consist wholly or in part of individuals whom he has no geographic or legal responsibility to represent.[31]

A few examples will show how each specie of "constituency" manifested itself in the 1870s, except for the all-inclusive type, which existed only in the realm of ideals. Most congressmen rarely considered the interests of district residents who were not part of the electorate; this is unsurprising, since Representatives' authority (and, if they had careerist ambitions, their survival) ensued from the ballot box. For this reason, among others, the needs of women, except for some individual soldiers' widows, generally were regarded as expendable. Thus, during the 1873 conference that eventually produced the notorious "Salary Grab," one usually overlooked casualty was a bipartisan House proposal to increase the maximum allowable compensation for female departmental employees to the minimum level authorized for men doing the same jobs. Various House conferees publicly regretted the Senate's refusal to concur in what several called a "manly" gesture;

28. Davidson, *Role of the Congressman*, chap. 4; and Fenno, *Home Style*.
29. Aage Clausen, *How Congressmen Decide: A Policy Focus* (New York, 1973), pp. 126–27.
30. Grant McConnell, *Private Power and American Democracy* (New York, 1966), p. 108.
31. Organized caucuses in the late twentieth-century House attest to the persistence of this behavior; Burdett A. Loomis, "Congressional Caucuses and the Politics of Representation," in *Congress Reconsidered*, ed. Lawrence C. Dodd and Bruce I. Oppenheimer, 2d ed. (Washington, 1981), pp. 204–20. Although many caucuses are composed primarily of members who either belong to the group that is represented or represent districts in which the group is disproportionately strong, this is not universal; the Congresswomen's Caucus, for example, recently was reorganized as the Congressional Caucus on Women's Concerns to permit participation by Congress*men*.

when asked why the other body had rejected the raise, Benjamin F. Butler explained: "It was this, that we put up these salaries of female clerks so high that they came up to [male] clerkships and their places would be sought for by members of Congress for somebody who was a male and had a vote to cast for them, which I think is the best argument in favor of female suffrage I ever heard."[32]

Of course, within a district not all voters were equally important. For obvious reasons, Representatives tended to listen more attentively to supporters than to opponents, especially when it came to distributive decisions—and certainly when it came to patronage. And support often meant more than mere partisanship. In areas where parties were particularly factionalized, such as Boston, unimpeachable personal loyalty to an individual boss or legislator was the litmus test for "realistic" representation.[33] Accordingly, the normally Republican John Coon of Cleveland, Ohio, felt the need to go to James Garfield for assistance in obtaining a medical leave for his ailing brother, who worked in the Second Auditor's Office. He did so even though his own congressman, Richard C. Parsons, was also in the G.O.P.: "while I claim to be an admirer of the 'Rare and Radical Richard,'" he wrote, "it is true that he failed to receive my vote . . . since that failure he has imposed upon himself the deprivation which springs from a total ignorance of existence. So you see, I am in eclipse, as it were."[34]

---

32. *Congressional Globe*, 42d Cong., 3d sess. (3 March 1873), 2099–2105; Butler's remarks are on p. 2102. For discrimination against women in the Gilded Age federal workforce, including some discussion of the relationship between that and disfranchisement, see Mary Clemmer Ames, *Ten Years in Washington: Life and Scenes in the National Capital, as a Woman Sees Them* (Hartford, Conn., 1875), chaps. 30, 31, 34, 35; W. H. Price to J. A. Garfield, 2 Feb. 1876, Garfield Papers; and Cindy S. Aron, "'To Barter Their Souls for Gold': Female Clerks in Federal Government Offices, 1862–1890," *JAH*, 67 (1981), 835-53. The best contemporary fictional account is in John W. De Forest, *Justine's Lovers* (New York, 1878).

33. Thompson, "Butler vs. the Brahmins." In the case of Nathaniel P. Banks, for instance—a man who manifested at least four distinct partisan affiliations during an intermittent congressional career that spanned four decades—petitioners for his assistance would try to emphasize their personal loyalty to him, rather than to a party. Some labeled themselves "Independent Republicans" (Banks's formal designation in the 44th House); another claimant wrote: "You do not know me—much—but, General, I've long known you. I voted for Greeley on y'r recommendation, chiefly. And with a clerkship in view, in the language of a native (black) South Carolinian, 'Fo' de Lawd God, General, I almost thinks I loves ye.'" H. M. Rideout to Banks, 31 Jan. 1876, and Henry C. Fisk to Banks, 7 Feb. 1877, Banks Papers.

34. John Coon to J. A. Garfield, 26 Dec. 1873, Garfield Papers. It is important to remember that the secret ballot was not used generally in the 1870s; thus, persons could not easily conceal how they voted.

Effective constituencies—those, sometimes outside the electorate, that could enforce their demands—generally were more significant in the Senate than in the House, for senators were not chosen directly by the voters. Thus, southern carpetbaggers during Reconstruction might feel more obligation to the northern Radical organization than to many of the natives in the states from which they served. A long series of Nevada senators was handpicked by a group of California banking moguls known as the "Ralston Ring" and answered primarily to them, rather than to the Gemstone State's population.[35] Effective constituencies, however, remained powerful only so long as officials continued to feel beholden to them; it was not uncommon for such legislators to act "insufficiently grateful" once they obtained their seats and arrived in Washington. In such cases their benefactors could say only, as one Chicago-based railroad official did about a recalcitrant Nebraskan: "I regret to say we put him there."[36] Adopted constituencies, on the other hand, tended to receive ardent and persistent advocacy, since members chose these for themselves and often cared quite deeply about them. Many congressmen who had fought for the Union, for instance, acquired well-earned reputations as "friends of the veterans."[37] Garfield, a former college president, and George Frisbie Hoar, with strong family ties to Harvard, were active boosters of education.[38] And most

35. The experience of one such southern Republican is recounted in Blanche B. Ames, ed., *Chronicles from the Nineteenth Century: Family Letters of Blanche Butler and Adelbert Ames*, 2 vols. (Clinton, Mass., 1957); see also relevant correspondence in the papers of Benjamin F. Butler, John Sherman, and William E. Chandler (Exec. Sec., Republican National Committee), all L.C. On Nevada, see George D. Lyman, *Ralston's Ring* (New York, 1937); Gilman M. Ostrander, *Nevada, the Great Rotten Borough* (New York, 1966); and Allen Weinstein, *Prelude to Populism: Origins of the Silver Issue, 1867–1878* (New Haven, 1970), esp. chap. 3.

36. The comment was in regard to Republican Sen. Algernon S. Paddock; Charles E. Perkins (vice-president, CBQ R.R.) to John Murray Forbes (president, CBQ R.R.), 31 July 1880, quoted in Thomas C. Cochran, *Railroad Leaders, 1845–1890: The Business Mind in Action* (Cambridge, Mass., 1953), p. 193; see also David J. Rothman, *Politics and Power: The United States Senate, 1896–1901* (Cambridge, Mass., 1966), chap.7.

37. Benjamin Butler, for example, was president of the Board of the National Soldiers' Homes, James Garfield was president of the "Veterans' National Committee," and John Logan held various offices in the Grand Army of the Republic. See the papers of each (all L.C.); and Mary R. Dearing, *Veterans in Politics: The Story of the G.A.R.* (Baton Rouge, 1952). Sen. John Sherman (R-Ohio), while sympathetic to veterans in his own right, became identified as a particular "friend" by some correspondents (especially those outside Ohio) who confused him with his brother, General William Tecumseh Sherman: e.g., A. Williamson (Ky.) to Sherman, 1 Jan. 1877, Sherman Papers.

38. For Hoar see, for example, communications from the National Education Association, attached to Rep. Washington Townsend (R-Pa.) to M. Warner (instructing him to see Hoar), 23 Dec. 1875; and various long letters from Andrew D. White (president, Cornell

of the handful of black members saw themselves as representatives of black Americans everywhere, not simply of those in their districts; Joseph Rainey (R-S.C.) even extended this sympathy to the Chinese and Indians, and described himself as a "defender of minorities."[39]

In practice, then, "constituency" had always been considered and used in various ways, of which the examples above are suggestive, if not exhaustive. What is more, a legislator could embrace constituencies of more than one kind. An adoptive sympathy for freedmen might determine his position on civil rights, while the presence of shoe factories in his district could shape his views on leather tariffs. Clearly, the home economy had little to do with the first decision, and race was largely irrelevant to the second; each "constituency" was called into being only when it was appropriate. Similarly, a Gilded Age member's avowed friendship for veterans generally provided little guidance if two former boys in blue were candidates for the same postmastership within his gift; additional factors would have to come into play.[40] In other words, when policy "matters" to those back home, the shape and membership of a congressman's meaningful constituency can change from issue to issue, and often from particular decision to decision within a given issue area. A district majority in the 1870s that favored specie resumption, for example, could consist of persons largely distinct from those who opposed subsidies for railroads, so that some residents would find themselves part of the dominant group in one case and not the other. When these two questions came up in the House, the Representative could vote on both in accordance with his perception of the district's "majority will"—but he in fact would be responding to two separate majorities, to two differently defined constituencies.

University) to Hoar—e.g., 20 Dec. 1873 and 12 June 1874 (Hoar Papers). Hoar also worked to procure war damages for William & Mary College of Virginia, which suffered during the Civil War, as a way of promoting both education and national reconciliation; for this he was awarded an honorary degree in 1873 (although the college did not receive its reparations until 1890). Hoar, *Autobiography*, 1:265–66; *Nat. Cyc.*, 1:453; letter to the author from Ms. Lisa Heuvel, Office of University Communications and Information, College of William & Mary, Williamsburg, Va., 22 May 1979; Henry A. Wise (governor of Va.) to Hoar, 13 Feb. 1872, and Benjamin S. Ewell to Hoar, 24 Sept. 1873, Hoar Papers. For Garfield, most of whose active connections with this issue had ended by 1872, see Allan Peskin, *Garfield* (Kent, Ohio, 1978), pp. 291–97; James A. Garfield, speech of 6 Feb. 1872 on "National Aid to Education," in *The Works of James Abram Garfield*, ed. Burke A. Hinsdale, 2 vols. (Boston, 1883), 2:19–25.

39. On Rainey, see Barnes, *Biographies*, 2:272–74; see also Emma Lou Thornbrough, *Black Reconstructionists* (Englewood Cliffs, N.J., 1982).

40. See correspondence in Norris and Shaffer, *Garfield-Henry Letters;* and chap. 6, below.

At the same time, much congressional business is too specilized to activate a pervasive opinion in some—sometimes any—legislative districts. Was anyone outside the Hawkeye State really aroused in the seventies over a possible new federal judgeship for Des Moines?[41] How many Americans cared whether or not there was a tariff on boracic acid (how many knew what boracic acid was)? While a few people crusaded aggressively for abolition of the death penalty, most probably never gave it a moment's thought. On matters like these, the active constituencies might be exceedingly small, but nonetheless outspoken and passionate in seeking satisfaction of their demands.[42] Moreover, the interested parties would not necessarily comprise a consensus; even obscure proposals usually generated opposition as well as support. Legislators in the 1870s, as now, dealt with countless questions like these, questions on which, as one political scientist put it, "there are several mutually inconsistent opinions of different groups of people, and a mass of largely uninterested persons." Yet whatever position members adopted in such cases—and however "representative" of their districts they attempted to be—it seems inappropriate to describe their behavior as reflective of a *constituency* interest since, in the words of an astute observer, "on most questions the [mass] constituency will not be looking. . . . very few of its members will have any opinion" or, consequently, be concerned or involved in the immediately operative representational relationship.[43]

So despite its widespread usage, "constituency" is ambiguous and misleading. Furthermore, because congressmen assert a comprehensive responsibility to it that cannot actually be realized, the term may

41. David B. Henderson to Sen. William B. Allison (R-Iowa), 11 June 1874 (and over a dozen others from Henderson in 1874); Theodore Hawley to Allison, 20 June 1876; O. P. Shiras to Allison, 25 Jan. and 7 Feb. 1876; editor of the Fort Dodge *Messenger* to Allison, 21 and 29 Jan. 1876; E. L. Shugart to Allison, 25 June 1876; M. D. O'Connell to Allison, 20 Jan. 1876; and D. C. Chase to Allison, 14 Feb. 1876 (all in Allison Papers). All were Iowa residents whose interests would be affected directly by the location of a new courthouse. That such local affairs might occasionally arouse attention from citizens elsewhere, especially those who believed their own region was being slighted, is discussed in Terry L. Seip, *The South Returns to Congress: Men, Economic Measures, and Intersectional Relationships, 1868–1879* (Baton Rouge, 1983), pp. 219–27.

42. On boracic acid, see a seven-page letter from L. C. S. Dyer to Nathaniel P. Banks, 17 Jan. 1877, Banks Papers. On abolition of the death penalty, see Marion H. Bovee to W. B. Allison, 19 May and 9 Nov. 1875, Allison Papers; Bovee to N. P. Banks, 7 Jan. 1876, Banks Papers; and 100 or so items in the Marion H. Bovee Papers, Henry E. Huntington Library, San Marino, California.

43. Marek Sobolewsky, "Electors and Representatives: A Contribution to the Theory of Representation," and J. Roland Pennock, "Political Representation: An Overview," in Pennock and Chapman, *Representation*, pp. 106, 22.

invite dissatisfaction and disaffection from citizens who find or feel that they are effectively excluded. A legislator going about his daily routine of doing "the people's" business did not normally have in mind the large, heterogeneous, geographically determined and fixed population that he was sworn to serve. Rather, he sought to represent an indefinite number of ever-changing, overlapping subgroups within his perceived public, each defined and called into being by a different sort of policy question. The composition of these subgroups, unlike that of districts, was fluid: that is, individuals belonged to as many subgroups as were necessary to encompass the range of their particular policy interests. Each cohort constituted the *clientele* for a specific sector of the public agenda. And in practice these clienteles, not unwieldy constituencies, comprised the substantive representational base of the policy-making system.

"Clientele" is a word that may have its own potential for ambiguity, although many political scientists now recognize its utility in their analyses of representation and legislative politics.[44] It facilitates discussion of a policy process in which increasing numbers of decisions are highly specialized, in which diverse forces within the polity demand consideration, and in which congressmen are expected to serve a variety of both legislative and ombudsman functions. Indeed, "clientele" seems especially appropriate to circumstances of the Gilded Age. It offers a convenient and comprehensible alternative to the phrase "interest group," which implies a degree of formal organization among clientele members that normally did not exist in the 1870s.[45] The term

44. Recent examples of the use of "clientele" as it is used here include several references in Richard E. Fenno, *Congressmen in Committees* (Boston, 1973); Aage Clausen, *How Congressmen Decide*, p. 119; and David E. Price, "Policy Making on Congressional Committees: The Impact of 'Environmental' Factors," *APSR*, 72 (1978), 550–51. Some scholars use the term for a narrower phenomenon, however; thus, in a recent anthology, "clienteles" are defined as parties with *persistent, regular,* and *established* relationships with government—i.e., those who are beneficiaries of entitlement programs: Christopher Clapham, ed., *Private Patronage and Public Power: Political Clientelism in the Modern State* (New York, 1982), esp. pp. 4–7. While such persons would not be excluded from the definition that is being used here, they comprise only a small share of those to whom "clientele" will be applied in the present study.

45. The existence of organized groups is the single most important factor that E. Pendleton Herring cited to differentiate the "old" lobby from the "new": *Group Representation before Congress,* chaps. 1–2. Similarly Lester Milbrath, in perhaps the most frequently cited study of modern lobbying, has declared that "lobbyists are group representatives almost by definition," although he broadened his definition in a subsequent essay; Lester W. Milbrath, *The Washington Lobbyists* (Chicago, 1963), p. 28, and "Lobbying," in *International Encyclopedia of the Social Sciences,* ed. David L. Sills (New York, 1968), 9:442. See also chap. 7, below.

can apply to either individuals or groups, and to either geographically localized or dispersed populations and interests. And because it does not have exclusively legislative connotations, it can fit into any of the various contexts in which citizens and officials need to operate and relate to one another. All these factors allow "clientele" to be employed consistently, regardless of the task or issue at hand. Equally critical, as will shortly become evident, it can be used regardless of who is doing the representing.

Seeing representation not as an unvarying and constant relationship between legislators and constituents but rather as a multidimensional interaction among numerous discrete and overlapping clienteles and their agents—who may or may not be members of Congress—illuminates both the context and the complexity of the process. As one political scientist has said, "The task of government . . . is not to express an imaginary popular will, but to effect adjustments among the various special wills and purposes which at any given time are pressing for realization."[46] Yet the type of government to which such a functional definition can be applied is obviously one quite different from that which was envisaged in the 1780s. The "minute and particular objects" that James Madison dismissed so easily in Number 56 of *The Federalist* no longer are entities that can be ignored or expelled from the federal machinery. Instead, collectively they have become legitimate, even necessary, components of the representational fabric.[47] The new definition suggests a government in which both the number and range of policy decisions have been expanded—a government whose citizens perceive it to have concrete and potentially critical effects on their lives. Such a definition also implies that representation should be able to take these many tasks and needs into account. In short, it describes at least theoretically what the American system has now become. But it is not wholly descriptive of conditions during the presidency of Ulysses Grant, when the representational structure that such a system requires was only beginning to evolve.

A polity comprised of clienteles requires appropriate mechanisms of representation, mechanisms that can address public concerns directly

---

46. John Dickinson, "Democratic Realities and Democratic Dogma," *APSR*, 24 (1930), 291.

47. *The Federalist*, No. 56. Cf. Dahl, *Dilemmas of Pluralist Democracy;* Truman, *The Governmental Process;* Harmon Zeigler, *Interest Groups in American Society* (Englewood Cliffs, N.J., 1964), esp. chap. 1; and Graham K. Wilson, *Interest Groups in the United States* (Oxford, England, 1981), chaps. 1, 7.

and effectively. Legislators can do part of the job; they can attempt to identify clienteles that are important within their districts and can try to respond to them. The standing committees, with their substantive jurisdictions, can facilitate matters, too, by providing foci for demands that transcend locale or the resources of single members. These two procedures, combined with advocacy for so-called assumed constituencies, will bring many elements into the policy arena. But even the needs of those elements may not be reflected accurately or sufficiently, and other interests inevitably will be left out. Such limitations are intrinsic to systems of fixed constituencies, whether they are based on geography, as in the United States, or on something else. Alternative formulae that continue to rely upon constituencies, however consituted, may ameliorate but cannot entirely eliminate the essential representational dilemma that is inherent in static and inflexible jurisdictions. The weaknesses of occupational representation, for example—a concept that enjoyed some popularity in late nineteenth- and early twentieth-century America—should be obvious to everyone but the most extreme economic determinists.[48] Even proportionalism, a reform that was subject to both debate and experimentation during the Gilded Age, would fail to resolve the basic problem, since it can enable only certain kinds of relatively large, usually partisan, minorities to enter the decision-making arena.[49]

Clienteles, almost by definition, are no respecters of constituency boundaries. Many have interests that are too specialized to achieve

48. De Grazia, *Public and Republic*, chap. 8, discusses several alternative constituency formulae, including occupationalism, and the interest that late nineteenth- and early twentieth-century Americans had in them. Obviously, the biggest flaws in the occupational system are that (1) individuals' interests are not all defined exclusively (or even primarily) by the work they do and (2) it is extremely difficult to determine lines *between* constituencies (should they be vertical, horizontal, etc.?). A defense of occupationalism can be found in Mary P. Follett, *The New State* (Chicago, 1918), and Robert A. Brady, *Business as System of Power* (New York, 1943), as well as in much of the general literature on pluralism; for an early critique, see Paul Douglas, "Occupational versus Proportional Representation," *American Journal of Sociology*, 29 (1923), 129–57.

49. The literature on proportionalism is vast; an overview in De Grazia, *Public and Republic*, chap. 7, contains extensive references to much of the basic literature. See also Douglas, "Occupational versus Proportional Representation"; John Stuart Mill, *Considerations on Representative Government* (1882; New York, 1958), chap. 7; Thomas Gilpin, *The Representation of Minorities of Electors to Act with the Majority in Elected Assemblies* (1844; *Annals* of the American Academy of Political and Social Science, 168 [1896], 233ff.); Thomas Hare, *The Machinery of Representation* (London, 1857), and *The Election of Representatives, Parliamentary and Municipal* (Philadelphia, 1867); John R. Commons, *Proportional Representation* (New York, 1896); and Select Committee of the U.S. Senate on Representative Reform *Report*, 40th Cong., 3d sess. (1869), Sen. Doc. 271.

sufficient recognition from Representatives with general responsibilities to their districts; exceedingly particular clienteles, such as
pension seekers and candidates for patronage positions, may be so
competitive within individual constituencies that mass satisfaction is
practically impossible. Others may be numerically large but locationally
diffuse, so that their size cannot guarantee attention from even a single
elected official; alternatively, geographic concentration may artificially
inflate the impact of a very small group.[50] Finally, some clienteles, many
of which are especially vulnerable to government action (or inaction),
cannot hope to obtain adequate representation through a system that is
controlled exclusively through elections. This was an extremely serious
matter in the 1870s, when well over half of the adult population—
including all women, most male aliens, Indians and transients, and (as
"redemption" of the South proceeded) many black men—was denied
the vote.

Thus, to be both accessible and appropriate to the purposes of all
clienteles, a representational device must be able to circumvent the
constraints of electoral constituencies. It must provide both fluidity and
precision, so as to reflect the diverse and discrete interests of countless
and overlapping cohorts within the populace. It may be highly organized, but it should by design be informal, since formal integration into
the machinery of governance may lead to inflexibility. It should, however, be compatible with the official decision-making system, since it is
from there, after all, that clienteles must seek and obtain satisfaction of
their demands.[51] It must, therefore, operate in ways that foster cooperation from those within the process: by providing services that are
beneficial to them, for instance, or by facilitating the execution of their
representational responsibilities to heterogeneous constituencies. If it
does all this, at least one systemic consequence should ensue: the
officially sanctioned representational bond, that between constituents
and members of the legislature, should grow stronger.

Lobbying is the device that most closely meets these criteria; it is the
process by which the interests of discrete clienteles are represented

---

50. Dahl, *Dilemmas of Pluralist Democracy*, chap. 3. Obviously a national minority can
comprise majorities in over 50 percent of all legislative districts (thereby controlling the
legislature). A national majority, however, if disproportionally concentrated in a few
locales, may be able to win only a handful of legislative seats. None of this is relevant, of
course, if the majority is disfranchised.

51. Norman Luttbeg and Harmon Zeigler, "Attitude Consensus and Conflict in an
Interest Group: An Assessment of Cohesion," *APSR*, 60 (1966), 655; V. O. Key, Jr.,
Politics, Parties, & Pressure Groups, 5th ed. (New York, 1964), pp. 130–45; Truman, *The
Governmental Process*, esp. chap. 8.

within the policy-making system. Lobbyists, then, can be defined as representatives who act concurrently with, and supplement the capabilities of, those who are selected at the polls. Lobbyists fill roles that in many ways are comparable to those of legislators: helping to transmit and obtain satisfaction for demands upon the government, thereby advancing the substantive interests of those whom they have taken it upon themselves to serve.[52] Both lobbyists and legislators may involve themselves in a variety of programmatic areas, or they may become specialists in single facets of the agenda. Like congressmen, lobbyists may also initiate campaigns on their own, without explicit requests or direction from potential beneficiaries; they may be careerists or amateurs, for whom advocacy may be either an occasional or full-time pursuit. Thus, there is a fair amount of validity to the observation that George B. Galloway, among others, has made: "Congress represents people on a territorial basis, whereas lobbying represents them on a functional basis."[53]

Galloway's comment tells just part of the story, however; it captures the parallels between legislators and lobbyists, but not the most important ways in which they are distinct. Lobbying is potentially more inclusive than congressional representation, for it is accessible to some clienteles, such as the diffused and disfranchised, who otherwise might go unheard within the public sector. Unlike their elected counterparts, whose offices carry with them a broad range of institutional and representational responsibilities, lobbyists find it easier to specialize: to develop substantive and procedural expertise in particular policy areas, if they so choose, and to focus their talents more exclusively upon matters of direct interest to their clients.[54] Such advocates can avoid the constraints of parties, enabling them to work with members of both caucuses and with both Democratic and Republican administrations.[55] And since their tenures cannot be terminated at the ballot box or by

52. While the comparison usually is phrased in terms of the lobbyist's functional similarity to the legislator, some have recognized that the resemblance goes both ways: "Although many Congressmen privately deplore their 'bellboy' activities, others frankly regard themselves merely as 'the people's hired men' and seem reconciled to serving primarily as glorified lobbyists or Washington representatives for their home communities"; George B. Galloway, *The Legislative Process in Congress* (New York, 1953), p. 203.

53. Galloway, *The Legislative Process*, p. 496; see also Key, *Politics, Parties, & Pressure Groups*, p. 143. The points raised in this paragraph are developed in chap. 4, below.

54. Milbrath, *The Washington Lobbyists*, p. 115. Claims agents comprised one Gilded Age group of specialists; see chap. 7, below. For a biography of a railroad specialist, see James C. Olson, *J. Sterling Morton* (1942; Lincoln, Nebr., 1972).

55. Sam Ward, the self-proclaimed "King of the Lobby," was a classic example of this. Although he was a Democrat and a member of the genteel, Swallowtail Manhattan Club,

intrapartisan squabbles or rotation traditions, lobbyists can be a source of persistence and continuity—even as the Capitol's population and internal organization change from term to term.[56]

The features that differentiate lobbyists from legislators are obviously beneficial to clienteles. But they also allow lobbyists to provide certain services that are useful to those within government. Advocates can bring new issues and problems to officials' attention, thereby helping them to formulate and order a public agenda that is responsive to articulated concerns.[57] They can put their substantive expertise at the disposal of decision makers whose own informational and staff resources may be inadequate.[58] Their procedural know-how may expedite the mechanics of policy design and implementation, especially at times when amateurs and novices predominate within government's ranks.[59] And the persistence and continuity of lobbying can help to

---

he maintained close ties not only to various factions in his own party, but to leaders of the several wings of the G.O.P. as well. See letters from Ward in the papers of Democratic editor Manton Marble (New York *World*) and Sen. Thomas Bayard (Del.), both L.C.; Democratic Speaker Samuel J. Randall and party leader Samuel L. M. Barlow, Huntington Library; and in the papers of Republicans like Garfield and James G. Blaine (L.C.). See also Lately Thomas, *Sam Ward: "King of the Lobby"* (Boston, 1965), and discussion of claims agents in chap. 7, below.

56. Lobbyists like Ward and Republican William E. Chandler generally had far more experience in Washington than all except a handful of congressmen. Chandler's experience is documented in the Chandler Papers, both at the L.C. and at the New Hampshire Historical Society, Concord, and in Leon Burr Richardson, *William E. Chandler, Republican* (New York, 1940); see also Key, *Politics, Parties, & Pressure Groups*, pp. 130, 132, 136.

57. Herring, *Group Representation before Congress*, pp. 46–50; Truman, *The Governmental Process*, pp. 104–6 and chaps. 8, 10; Milbrath, *Washington Lobbyists*, chap. 9. Thus, in 1864 the editor of *Moore's Rural New Yorker* urged wool growers among his readers to band together so as to bring their concerns before the government; by doing so, he believed they could prove that "*constituencies* can, on occasion, and in a just cause, make their opinion heard as loudly in Congress as a *few hundred* other persons [i.e., manufacturers]"; quoted in Harry Brown, "The Fleece and the Loom: Wool Growers and Wool Manufacturers during the Civil War Decade," *Business History Review*, 29 (1955), 6–7.

58. Thus, Charles Francis Adams II volunteered to share his expertise on railroad questions with James A. Garfield (soon after, the latter was appointed to the Pacific Railroad Committee): "At all times I am especially anxious to give to Members of Congress any information in my power on the subject of railroads;—should you, in the approaching session, desire on any point to avail yourself of any suggestions in my power to offer you, I hope you will not hesitate to call upon me;—you will always find me most ready to response [sic] to the extent of my ability"; Adams to Garfield, 1 Oct. 1873, Garfield Papers. Members frequently sought this kind of assistance. Sen. Stephen Dorsey (R-Ark.), for example, asked William E. Chandler for help on a technical matter before the District of Columbia Committee; Dorsey to Chandler, 30 May 1876, Chandler Papers, L.C. See also the discussions of David Wells in chaps. 4 and 5, below.

59. See discussion of claims agents in chap. 7, below; and Key, *Politics, Parties, & Pressure Groups*, pp. 132, 138.

stabilize the public sector by offsetting to some extent the disruptive effects of high legislative and bureaucratic turnover.

Thus, lobbyists engage in a variety of activities that collectively should facilitate the articulation and satisfaction of demands. And since this sort of communication is at the heart of political representation, their presence may alleviate tensions and prevent disaffection within the general polity. Lobbyists, then, do not obstruct the relationship between citizens and officials. Their role is complementary and, at least in theory, ought to strengthen the bond between elected Representatives and their publics. Things may not always go smoothly in practice, of course; lobbying is as vulnerable to abuse as any instrument of political power. Nevertheless, policy systems that affect particularized interests must have ways of assimilating their clienteles into the operations of governance. And lobbying is an appropriate instrument for doing so.

Clienteles are inevitable in a pluralistic democracy and, therefore, so is lobbying. But while interest-based advocacy has always been and will remain an important factor within the polity, its extent and significance can fluctuate considerably. There is no question that its contribution was profound during the Grant years; indeed, that era may have marked the pinnacle of lobbying's power to affect the content and direction of policy.

The intensity of lobbying's impact resulted from the transitional nature of the era, and from the time-lag that so seriously strained the decision-making capacity of early Gilded Age Congressional Government. In antebellum America, the smaller scope of national governance activated comparatively few specialized clienteles; in later years, the federal sector would develop its own mechanisms for coping with such interests. Thus, the pre–Civil War Washington agenda contained relatively little that warranted lobbyists' involvement. And although the public sphere of course continued to grow and diversify after 1880, its own institutional and procedural development would begin to counteract at least some of lobbying's potential influence. Both the evolution of a seniority system and the introduction of personal and professional staffs, for instance, gave the legislature indigenous sources of substantive knowledge and expertise.[60] The executive achieved similar results

60. Barbara Hinckley, *The Seniority System in Congress* (Bloomington, Ind., 1971), chaps. 1–2; *Committee Organization in the House: Panel Discussions before the Select Committees*, 93d Cong., 1st sess. (1973), Hse. Doc. 94–187, esp. pp. 525–52; Nelson W. Polsby, "The Institutionalization of the U.S. House of Representatives," *APSR*, 62 (1968), 144–68; Polsby et al., "The Growth of the Seniority System in the U.S. House of Representatives,"

by the increased use of competitive examinations and other techniques for incorporating professionalism into the bureaucracy, by classifying more and more jobs within the rolls of the civil service, and so on.[61] At the same time, many of the distributive tasks that so overloaded the Gilded Age Congress—and that provided such fertile fields for lobbyists to determine outcomes—gradually were transferred from the Capitol to administrative control, where decisions tended to become more routinized and less susceptible to outside pressures.[62] Changes like these could offset and, eventually, would diminish the extent of lobbying's significance; although its practitioners would multiply and would go on serving functions similar to those of their nineteenth-century forebears, they would be operating in a universe greatly altered from that of the Gilded Age. By the mid-twentieth century, most clienteles could count upon finding advocates for their causes *within* government; bureaucrats, long-tenured members (and staffs) of concerned committees, legislative and administrative ombudsmen, and the like—who came to see their professional and career aspirations as inextricably linked to the interests of their "adopted constituencies"— virtually guaranteed them access, and usually support, inside the federal machinery.[63]

Even these developments would not, to be sure, eliminate all opportunities for lobbyists.[64] In any event, when Grant was president, all of

---

APSR, 63 (1969), 787–807; Harrison W. Fox, Jr., and Susan Webb Hammond, *Congressional Staffs: The Invisible Force in American Lawmaking* (New York, 1977), pp. 15–20; and Michael J. Malbin, *Unelected Representatives: Congressional Staff and the Future of Representative Government* (New York, 1980).

61. Skowronek, *Building a New American State,* part 3; Morton Keller, *Affairs of State: Public Life in Late Nineteenth Century America* (Cambridge, Mass., 1977), pp. 272–75, 313–14; White, *Republican Era,* pp. 131–33, 317–22, 348–58; B. Guy Peters, *The Politics of Bureaucracy: A Comparative Perspective* (New York, 1978), chaps. 2, 4; Guy Benveniste, *The Politics of Expertise* (Berkeley, Calif., 1972).

62. White, *Republican Era,* chaps. 14–16; Skowronek, *Building a New American State,* chap. 6; Rep. Edmund N. Morrill, "Pensions," in *The Republican Party: Its History, Principles, and Politics,* ed. John D. Long (New York, 1888), pp. 122–43; John William Oliver, *History of the Civil War Military Pensions, 1861–1885* (Madison, Wis., 1917), pp. 70–71.

63. Peters, *Politics of Bureaucracy,* chaps. 5–6; Clapham, *Private Patronage and Public Power,* chaps. 1, 9.

64. Obviously, the *number* of lobbyists has grown steadily since the Gilded Age, and no one would consider them powerless. The point, however, is that they face greater competition for and constraints upon their hegemony, and that they operate in ways that are different from those of their late nineteenth-century forebears. Today, for example, most lobbyists spend a greater share of their time with bureaucrats and congressional staffers than with actual senators and Representatives. Also, a larger share of their resources is used in the election process than previously, a development that accelerated

them lay dimly within the future. So lobbying was the only available
resource attuned specifically to the representational needs of clienteles—and to the parallel needs of those who were charged with responding to their demands. A lack of alternatives, then, if nothing else,
meant that lobbyists in the 1870s had tremendous potential power and
influence. But if they were in their heyday, the result was not a "Great
Barbecue" or "Age of Excess," as critics from John W. De Forest to
Richard Hofstadter have alleged. Although the term "lobbyist" may
have been decried or eschewed categorically, those both in and outside
of government sought, and might well have been grateful for, the
agency such individuals provided. Until Americans generally became
acclimated to their modernizing polity, and until officialdom could
develop appropriate mechanisms for coping with its newly assumed
responsibilities, lobbyists filled a variety of indispensable roles. At a
time when active and effective representation was more essential than
ever before, lobbying formed a bridge between particularized publics
and Washington. It served as a counterweight to the potentially paral-
yzing forces of transition and time-lag, enabling a concerned if disor-
ganized citizenry to articulate its demands and an overloaded and
underequipped policy process to hear and respond to at least some of
the messages that were sent its way.

The specific decisions and apparent policy priorities that emerged
under these circumstances often left much to be desired. Many people
unquestionably remained dissatisfied, and idealists of various stripes,
whether contemporary or modern, could find plenty of evidence to
substantiate their critiques of national affairs during the Grant years.
Nonetheless, things could have been worse. Had lobbyists not been on
the scene to mediate between emergent clienteles and the Capitol,
greater confusion, or paralysis, might have ensued. In short, if Congressional Government in the early Gilded Age was to any degree
representative government, it was so because of, not in spite of, lobbying.

---

rapidly in the wake of post-Watergate campaign financing "reforms," passed in 1974,
which liberalized rules for the formation and activities of Political Action Committees
("PACs"). These PACs can operate almost with impunity in campaigns; although they
must report their expenditures, they are not governed by the 1946 Lobby Registration
Act (or by the restrictions on individual campaign contributors).

CHAPTER 4

A Matter of Access:
The System of
Congressional Government

> To introduce a bill properly, to have it referred to the proper
> committee, to see that some member in that committee under-
> stands its merits, to attend to it, to watch it, to have a counsel to
> go and advocate it before the committee, to see that members of
> the committee do not oversleep on the mornings of important
> meetings, to watch for the coming in of the bill to Congress day
> after day, week after week, to have your men on hand a dozen
> times, and to have them as often disappointed; to have one of
> those storms which spring up in the Adriatic of Congress, until
> your men are worried, and worn, and tired, and until they say to
> themselves that they will not go up to the Capitol today,—and
> then to have the bird suddenly flushed, and all your preparations
> brought to naught,—these . . . these are some of the experiences
> of the lobby.
>
> SAM WARD, "King of the Lobby," 1875

It should be obvious by now that conditions in the 1870s Capitol were
hardly ideal for effective conduct of the nation's business. The agenda
was vast and continually expanding. Most members were both institutionally inexperienced and substantively uninformed, with neither staff
nor other indigenous resources to compensate for their inadequacies.
Both formal structures and informal norms combined to produce an
incongruous and debilitating dichotomy between concentration and
diffusion of power.[1] And the constitutionally mandated basis for repre-

1. This dichotomy is discussed in detail in chap. 2, above.

Sam Ward, "King of the Lobby." Drawn by "Spy" (British caricaturist) for
Vanity Fair. Courtesy New York Public Library.

sentation was static, exclusionary, and too often just plain inappropriate to the responsibilities that had to be addressed.

It should also be evident that these circumstances both encouraged and help to explain the rise in lobbying's activism and influence during the Grant years. Some sort of catalyst certainly was needed, as citizens and legislators alike grew increasingly frustrated with the limitations of an overburdened and underequipped federal system. Lobbying, which mediates between clienteles and government officials, constitutes the process through which discrete substantive interests are represented within the public sector. Thus, it could function as the sought-after catalyst—as a bridge to facilitate communication between those with demands and those with authority to respond.

This is not to say, of course, that lobbying was a panacea that single-handedly was responsible for all that was productive in Congressional Government, or that all advocacy was equally effective. A good number, perhaps most, campaigns of influence came to nothing, and some, although fewer than has been alleged, were undeniably corrupt. But lobbying did act as a crucial and sometimes decisive factor in the political and institutional arenas of Washington: it both clarified the internal operations of House and Senate and eased the pressures upon ballot-based representation.

Recognizing the potential in lobbying and understanding how it operated, however, are two entirely different matters that leave many questions unanswered. What, specifically, did lobbying consist of? What roles did lobbyists fill, and what kinds of tactics and strategies did they employ? At what stages in the legislative process, and in respect to what sorts of decisions, was lobbying likely to be most involved? In what ways did the representational functions of lobbyists correspond to, complement, and/or conflict with those of Representatives who were elected? What, basically, was Gilded Age lobbying all about—in concrete and very practical terms? And how and when was it able to alleviate particular systemic weaknesses in the federal sector?

Questions like these will be our principal concern from this point on. And because the issues they raise are revealed most clearly in actual situations, the bulk of the discussion will center on specific cases that exemplify the commonest tasks of 1870s legislative activity. At the same time, though, lobbying is something that cannot exist independently of the officially sanctioned policy system: a system that, as we have seen, operates according to discernible and predictable routines. It should be possible, therefore, to delineate at least some rules and norms that give meaning to lobbying generally—in other words, to construct a broadly applicable model of Congressional Government that incorporates and hence illuminates the participation and implications of the Third House.

Appreciation of lobbying as it really was (and, to a great extent, is still) is easily prejudiced not only by the unflattering image of it of a century ago but, more subtly, by the formal, and ineffectual, regulatory definitions of today. Consider, for example, that the only definitional passages in the 1946 federal statute identify lobbyists not by what they do, but by what they spend.[2] And because neither functions nor objectives are specified, even the types of spending that fall under its rubric are too restrictive, with the most glaring omission unquestionably being that of campaign-related expenditures—a loophole that has widened tremendously with the post-Watergate proliferation of Political Action Committees (PACs).[3] In any event, both lobbyists and legislators now concede that current policy is riddled with escape hatches and is practically useless for either regulatory or definitional purposes.[4]

Legal vagaries are hardly a recent development, as the ambiguities in *Trist v. Child* and the fate of various bills proposed during the mid-1870s, discussed earlier, demonstrate. But permanent legislation, perhaps because it appears so authoritative, has greater potential to mislead. Again, this is nothing new, as Raymond L. Bridgman, an insightful reporter for the *New England Magazine*, made abundantly clear in an early commentary on the first state statute to regulate

2. For the law's text, see "Federal Regulation of Lobbying Act: Title III of the Legislative Reorganization Act of 1946 (Public Law 601, 79th Congress, 2d session, 2 U.S.C. 261–270)," printed for the use of the Office of the Secretary of the Senate (Washington, 1969); see also John F. Kennedy, "Congressional Lobbies: A Chronic Problem Re-examined," *Georgetown Law J.*, 45 (1957), 535–67.

3. Several lobbyists, in interviews conducted prior to passage of the post-Watergate reforms, told me that it would be impossible to effect meaningful correction of abuses until the question of campaign expenditures was addressed; in the succeeding decade, abuses simply worsened. Interviews with James Foristel of the American Medical Association, 24 Jan. 1974; Weldon Barton, National Farmers' Union, 23 Jan. 1974; Clinton Fair, Committee on Political Education, AFL-CIO, 22 Jan. 1974; Mary Gereau, National Treasury Employees' Union (formerly with the National Education Association), 25 Jan. 1974; all in Washington, D.C. See also "PAC Influence Grows," in *Elections '82*, Congressional Quarterly, Inc. (Washington, 1982), pp. 43–61; *Dollar Politics*, 3d ed., Congressional Quarterly, Inc. (Washington, 1982); Edwin M. Epstein, "An Irony of Electoral Reform: The Business PAC Phenomenon," *Regulation*, May/June 1981, pp. 35–41; Fraser/Associates, *The PAC Handbook: Political Action for Business* (Cambridge, 1980).

4. See, for example, virtually all testimony in *Lobbying—Efforts to Influence Government Actions: Hearings before the Committee on Standards of Official Conduct, House of Representatives (94th Congress, 1st session) on H.R. 15 and Related Bills*, Committee Print (Washington, 1976).

lobbying, enacted by Massachusetts in 1890. Bridgman, unlike most observers of his time, believed that lobbying itself was merely a "value-free" intermediary between petitioners and decision makers and that, if corruption existed, it originated with either the "givers" or "takers" in such transactions: "the go-between . . . does not occupy a critical position." Furthermore, he determined that, as far as the Bay State was concerned, most registered lobbyists were "as honest and as legitimate" as could be desired. Nonetheless, Bridgman saw a danger, which came not from the work of agents who had complied with the law, but from unregistered persons he called the "special lobby." This, he asserted, was comprised of "political manipulators and placeholders [who] are difficult to reach and not easy of punishment because of their social, political and business standing." Most important, he concluded, "they are not known as lobbyists—and therein consists the greater part of their danger. The members whom they approach do not know they are hired by the petitioner, [and] supposed that these lobbyists speak to them from reasons of public welfare. . . . It is not dreamed that they are earning a big fee under the cover of a previous good reputation and of an honest occupation."[5]

If we consider Bridgman's analysis in light of what we already know about representation generally, we can see that a usable model for lobbying—as it is, regardless of what it is called—must reflect its three-fold identity as functional, situational, and flexible. Lobbying is functional in two respects. First, it cannot exist in isolation or as an abstraction, but only as a dependent function of the larger policy process; second, it consists of activities, or functions, within the context of that process. Therefore, lobbying is situational, in that the particular roles and responsibilities it assumes are determined by particular circumstances, as are the actors who play those roles and who, hence, operate as lobbyists. So lobbying, both definitionally and in practice, has to remain flexible, with form and agency shaped by context, objective, practitioner, and opportunity.

A few illustrations will amplify these points. Take the matter of letter-writing—specifically, letters of two quite common types. In one, Jones congratulates Smith on his birthday; in the other, Jones expresses his views on currency reform. The fact is that either of these may or may

---

5. Raymond L. Bridgman, "The Lobby," *New England Magazine*, 16 (1897), 151–60; a good summary of early state regulatory efforts, and disparities among them, is in Belle Zeller, "State Regulation of Lobbying," *The Book of the States, 1948–1949* (Chicago, 1948), pp. 124–30.

not constitute lobbying, depending upon a combination of circumstance and intent. And this applies whether or not Jones or Smith is a government official, as the following eight possibilities suggest:

    A. Jones to Citizen Smith.
      1. Birthday greeting from one friend to another.
      2. Birthday greeting for the purpose of reinforcing interest-based contact.
      3. Expression of views on currency as a way of letting off steam.
      4. Expression of views on currency with intent of motivating Smith to take, and act on, a similar public stand.
    B. Jones to Congressman Smith.
      5. Birthday greeting from one friend to another, who just happens to be a legislator.
      6. Birthday greeting as a means of reinforcing personal access to a public official.
      7. Expression of views on currency in order to let off steam.
      8. Expression of views on currency with the intent of influencing Smith's legislative performance in this area.

Each of the even-numbered letters here is an instance of lobbying, for each is written with either a direct or indirect, immediate or long-term, attempt to influence policy. Similarly, a dinner invitation or a gift of wine may be simply an act of sociability or a means of claiming or maintaining a legislator's (or someone else's) attention.

In a similar way, we can see that hiring an agent to advance one's substantive interests is not always hiring a lobbyist. When a person or organization employs a realtor to buy property or a broker to provide insurance, the transaction cannot reasonably be called lobbying, even though it involves client and representative, because it occurs exclusively within the private sector. But when the same person or group engages the same individual to articulate demands before government, the agent becomes a lobbyist.

Context, then, is an essential consideration. Regardless of what is done or who does it, something becomes lobbying when—and only when—it occurs within the policy process with the intent of immediately or eventually influencing that process so as to obtain satisfaction of a clientele's demand(s). Thus, since satisfaction can be provided only by officials (and not directly by ex officio agents), lobbyists perform the role of a "missing link" between those officials and the public they are supposed to serve, thereby—in a legislative setting, at least—strengthening the bond between elected Representatives and their constituents.

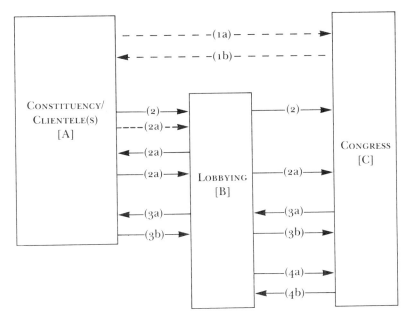

1   unmediated representational relationship
2   initiation of demands
3   policy response/implementation
4a   lobbying groundwork
4b   ACCESS

Figure 1. Lobbying as catalyst: Congressional Government in the early Gilded Age

Figure 1 illustrates the behavioral dimensions of this phenomenon within the arena of Gilded Age Congressional Government. Without lobbying's catalytic input, direct communication between members and citizens tended to be weak and ineffectual, as the broken lines (1a, 1b), denoting paths of unassisted petition and response, are meant to suggest. But when the mediating factor of lobbying is inserted, paths are no longer broken, for communication is clarified and a stronger representational relationship is effected.

Line 2, then, signifies two potential paths along which demands can be articulated. The first of them, (2), parallels the weak and unmediated "1a" except that, here, lobbying intercedes to focus and amplify the message by transforming scattered or isolated constituency members into substantively ordered clientele(s). Such assistance can benefit either individuals or groups—either, for example, a solitary applicant for a patent, whose case might otherwise be buried amid hundreds of similar ones, or a cohort of civil service reformers who, because of their dispersal in varied and widely separated locales, are unable to dominate any legislative district.

At times, however, preliminary efforts had to be made before demands could be brought all the way to Congress. This is when a more circuitous route, indicated by line 2a (A − →B→A→B→C), could come into play. When a clientele had a problem, but no idea what could be done to solve it, its demand was likely to reach the lobbyist in a relatively unformed condition (A − →B). There, however, it could be clarified and, perhaps, united with similar demands originating among other concerned members of the public. Once the agent's plan of action was presented to the interested party (or parties, but still a single clientele) and agreed to (B→A, A→B), the petition could be sent along to Washington (B→C). Although the product of this process would arrive at the Capitol looking just like one that came directly, it obviously had a distinct provenance. A few instances of such activity are discussed below, most notably in connection with the "Claims Agents Act" of 1879 and the evolution of railroads' "clientele consciousness."

None of this means anything, though, unless it leads to a response (3a, 3b). And even satisfaction requires mediation to be effective. Consider, for example, the 1862 Pension Act, which authorized compensation to soldiers' widows, among others. That legislation would do a destitute widow no good unless she was aware of the law—which is where a mediator could serve to bridge the gap between officialdom and potential beneficiary (C→B→A). In this case, however—and it was not unique—awareness was not enough. For the procedure involved in applying for a pension was complex and highly technical. In order to obtain her benefits, the widow needed more assistance for her cause: again, an agent's aid and advocacy (A→B→C). Thus, policy implementation, particularly in distributive matters, was a two-tiered process (C→B→A, A→B→C), and a catalyst could be helpful on both levels.

Of course, not every agent was equally adept, and productivity required the presence of an *effective* lobbyist. This is where the fourth path came in, and it is the one to which most of the current chapter will be devoted—although it does not directly involve clienteles at all. For this was the route by which lobbyists acquired, reinforced, and maintained the most critical prerequisite to competence: access to the world of Congressional Government. To be sure, other qualities were useful: expertise in specific policy areas, theoretical knowledge of how the system worked, occupational tenure, and so on. But none of these would do much good if the lobbyist could not get to those in power—to officials, usually legislators, with resources to provide tangible responses to clienteles' needs. And this normally was the prerogative only of agents who carefully established and nurtured direct relationships with those in positions especially relevant to the interests of their clients. To do so was not easy; indeed, just a handful of individuals would become sufficiently versed in the business to develop truly professional stature. Nevertheless, some claim to access was essential for anybody who sought to represent substantive interests and who tried to exercise even occasional or limited influence over policy. It was, in short, the lobbyist's "bottom line" within the system—the key to an effective role in Congressional Government.

Access, like the representational efficacy it facilitated, does not lend itself to simple definition or measurement. For one thing, it was (and is) exhaustible and unstable. Once secured, it might be spent quickly or dissipated rashly, and lobbyists who wanted to maintain their influence had to work continuously to replenish it. Access also, for the most part, was specific and nontransferable. Outsiders with one member's ear could not count thereby on reaching his colleagues, while those with credibility in particular policy areas did not automatically enjoy the same in others. No wonder that such a commodity was seen as fragile and precious, and that a sizable amount of all agents' energies went into its cultivation. Sometimes this meant planting seeds that would not bear fruit for years. And by the time they did—that is, by the time they actually could be used in behalf of a clientele—their roots might be nearly imperceptible. Thus, as we shall see when we dig beneath the surface, part of what facilitated access doubtless will have to remain buried, while some of the rest may seem only tangentially relevant to traditional notions of lobbying, representation, or the legislative process. Additionally, we will discover great behavioral variation, depending on circumstance, personalities, and serendipity. The result, then—with one exception—will not consist of universally valid or ironclad laws that apply wherever access is concerned.[6]

The exception is important, though, and one that, however self-

---

6. "Definition of what the job of lobbying requires is by no means clear. The tasks not only vary from lobbyist to lobbyist but also among the working days of any given lobbyist. . . . The most general way to state the nature of the lobbyist's job is to note that he must in some way communicate with governmental decision-makers." Lester Milbrath, *The Washington Lobbyists* (Chicago, 1963), p. 115.

evident it may appear, bears critically upon how we envision both representation generally and the representation of clienteles in particular. It is this: the persons with greatest potential for securing access were those already within the system, that is, members of Congress themselves. Thus, clienteles that found elected advocates already in place and, to a somewhat lesser degree, outside agents who could identify insiders willing to work cooperatively with them generally had a tremendous edge over those without this base.

Not all congressmen were equally valuable, of course; novices, backbenchers, and those out of favor with the leadership naturally had less clout among their fellows than long-tenured professionals, recognized policy experts, those on significant committees, and so on. But this was true whether they were performing their regular duties or speaking for "assumed constituencies," or clienteles. Native Americans and those concerned over their welfare, for example, had at least two member-lobbyists during the mid-1870s: Joseph Rainey, Republican of South Carolina, and Wisconsin Independent George W. Cate. Rainey, however, was black and Cate was a powerless maverick who, if he was known for anything, was thought of as a knee-jerk sympathizer for causes most others wanted to ignore. Not until powerhouses like William B. Allison and Henry L. Dawes became active in this area would House and Senate start to take it seriously.[7] Similarly, former Oberlin professor James Monroe and his Amherst counterpart, Julius H. Seelye, both felt deeply about, and spoke out in behalf of, federal aid to education. Yet the impetus for real action came, not from them, but from James A. Garfield and George Frisbie Hoar—who to be sure had impeccable credentials in the field but who also, and more crucially, enjoyed broad-based respect and influence among their peers.[8]

Still, even a Cate or Seelye had access to more tangible resources than agents operating entirely from without. They could speak on the floor (and get remarks printed by the government), they could introduce bills, and they had numerous opportunities for informal discourse with their fellows, as well as the potential—however unrealized in these cases—to grow eventually into legislative leaders. So while those with

7. On Cate, see *BDAC*, p. 674, and bills such as the following, all from the 44th Congress: H.R. 1296, 1297, 1528, 1529, 2099, 2535, 3569; on Rainey, see William Horatio Barnes, *The American Government: Biographies of Members of the Forty-Third Congress*, 3 vols. (New York, 1874), 2:273–74. See also Loring B. Priest, *Uncle Sam's Stepchildren: The Reformation of United States Indian Policy, 1865–1887* (New York, 1969).

8. On Seelye, see *BDAC*, p. 1579 [Seelye also was an advocate for Indians, e.g., H.R. 3360, 3591, 3593, all 44th Cong.]; on Monroe, see Barnes, *Biographies*, 3:47–48; for Garfield and Hoar, see chap. 3, n. 38, above.

business before the government might hope to find already well-placed and powerful allies to plead their cause, only the least sophisticated and assertive would give up if friends like that did not come ready-made. Shrewd petitioners—and shrewd agents—appreciated that, instead of trusting solely to luck, there was a lot they could do to improve the chances of generating new sources of advocacy from within, and of enhancing the effectiveness of what was there.

But before a well-disposed legislator could be well situated, he had to get to Washington in the first place. So in the Gilded Age, as now, citizens campaigned in behalf of candidates who, if elected, might reasonably be expected to promote their interests. Veterans seeking pensions tended to vote for other veterans, industrialists generally supported one of their own, farmers were attracted to nominees with experience behind a plow, and temperance groups were naturally drawn to aspirants for office who, like themselves, had "taken the pledge." It is in this context that Texas & Pacific stockholder James Throckmorton's promises to lobby for the line, John P. Jones of Nevada's proud espousal of silver, and protectionist "Pig Iron" Kelley's refusal to disavow his nickname ought to be understood.[9] As these men would argue, and not entirely without justification, their openly avowed identification with economic clienteles was really little different—or no less legitimate—than that of Generals Garfield, John A. Logan, and Benjamin Butler with their former comrades-in-arms, black members' renowned friendship (and that of their allies, like Butler) for the freedmen, or the less immediately concerned boosterism of New York's S. S. Cox for the well-being of America's postal workers.[10] As Ways & Means chairman Henry Dawes once queried, implicitly in defense of his own ties to New England's textile mills: "Shall the right of a member to vote upon a duty on cotton goods be challenged because he happens to be a cotton manufacturer? If so, the cotton-raiser, the sugar-maker,

9. On Throckmorton, see Claude Elliott, *Leathercoat: The Life History of a Texas Patriot* (San Antonio, 1938), pp. 222–28, and chap. 3, above. On Jones, see *DAB*, 10:188–89. On Kelley, see *DAB*, 10:300; Barnes, *Biographies*, 2:179–80; and *Memorial Addresses on the Life and Character of William D. Kelley, A Representative from Pennsylvania*, 51st Cong., 1st sess., Hse. Misc. Doc. No. 229 (Washington, 1890).

10. Mary R. Dearing, *Veterans in Politics: The Story of the GAR* (Baton Rouge, 1952); regarding Butler, see William E. Isbell to Butler, 21 Jan. 1874, Butler to W. S. McFarlane and Butler to Mrs. E. A. Stevens, 18 Apr. 1876; William Brown to Butler, 6 Jan. 1874; and Leroy C. Johnson to Butler, 3 Jan. 1874, all Butler Papers, L.C. Garfield was president of the Washington-based "Veterans' National Committee," whose by-laws are in Garfield Papers, L.C., filed under 25 Mar. 1876. Emma Lou Thornbrough, *Black Reconstructionists* (Englewood Cliffs, N.J., 1972); David Lindsey, *"Sunset" Cox: Irrepressible Democrat* (Detroit, 1959), p. 257.

the farmer, and every gentleman in this house may have such a personal interest in a . . . bill that no one can vote for it." To this, Speaker Blaine added in concurrence, "One can go through the whole round of business and find on this floor gentlemen who, in common with many citizens outside of this House, have an interest in questions before this House. But they do not have that interest separate and distinct from a class, and, within the meaning of the rule, distinct from the public interest."[11]

None of this should be considered necessarily unethical—although of course it may have been in certain cases. For both participants in and students of legislative politics have long recognized that it is far more effective to encourage the natural backers of a cause than it is to convince waverers or convert opponents.[12] Thus, there are very few instances in the Grant years, or any other era, of members who served a clientele solely because of campaign contributions or similar incentives; those who might seem to have been "in the pocket" of particular interests were likely just to be following their own previously established (and publicly articulated) inclinations.[13] Such overt sympathies might, understandably, attract pecuniary and other forms of support at election time, but subsequent behavior should not inevitably be regarded as mere fulfillment of a *quid pro quo*. In fact, those who tried to buy spokesmen were not infrequently disappointed with their purchases.[14] Most astute outsiders tended to eschew this approach, preferring instead to ensure the continued tenure of proven allies and to assist those who were promising but quiescent. Then lobbyists' attention could be directed more efficiently toward placing them where they could do the most good: in the leadership or on appropriate committees.[15] In any event, both electoral and organizational strategies for the

11. DeAlva S. Alexander, *History and Procedure of the House of Representatives* (Boston, 1916), pp. 146–47.

12. Malcolm Jewell and Samuel Patterson, *The Legislative Process in the United States* (New York, 1966), pp. 297–98.

13. See discussion of adopted constituencies, above; and George B. Galloway, *The Legislative Process in Congress* (New York, 1953), pp. 509–10; Ralph K. Huitt, "A Case Study in Senate Norms," in *Legislative Behavior: A Reader in Theory and Research*, ed. John C. Wahlke and Heinz Eulau (Glencoe, Ill., 1959), p. 258.

14. See, e.g., Chap. 3 at n. 36, above; Jay Gould to William E. Chandler, 16 Dec. 1874, Chandler Papers, L.C.; Mark Hopkins to Collis P. Huntington, 20 Feb. 1875, in *Letters from Mark Hopkins . . . to Collis P. Huntington. . . .* (New York, 1891), pp. 19–20; and Collis P. Huntington to Leland Stanford, 16 May 1874, 1 June 1874, and Huntington to Hopkins, 19 Nov. 1875, in *Letters from Collis P. Huntington to Mark Hopkins, Leland Stanford. . .* , 3 vols. (New York, 1894), 3:131, 139, 409–10 (latter 2 vols. both privately printed and at the Henry E. Huntington Library, San Marino, California).

15. See chap. 5, below, and Richard E. Fenno, *Congressmen in Committees* (Boston, 1973), pp. 38–39.

inside track demanded campaigns for access that had to begin long before Congress convened.

Other methods of obtaining access were equally dependent on preliminary groundwork, including those based on friendship, trust, public opinion, and professional expertise and reliability. David Rothman, for instance, has documented many friendship-based lobbying campaigns in the late nineteenth-century Senate, in which professional agents would arrange for dozens of individuals to approach particular members they knew personally. Perhaps because this strategy seemed so often to be successful, it was vulnerable to heavy criticism or censure if discovered; both Justice Swayne's opinion in *Trist v. Child* and Bridgman's attack on the "special lobby" exemplify such reactions.[16] Nonetheless, obtaining access through friends remained a popular tactic—and may have been more common in the larger and more anonymous House than it was in the other body. Thus, A.Y. Poppleton once advised railroad attorney J. Sterling Morton to request Republican Representative Jay Hubbell, a "Chi Psi—whom you must have known well," to intercede with another Michigander who chaired a Pacific Railroads subcommittee that was considering possibly harmful legislation: "I asked Dr. Miller," wrote Poppleton, "to suggest to you that you write Hubbell and get him on personal grounds, to interfere with [Rep. William B.] Williams and prevent him . . . from acting adversely to us on 'terminus.'" For, he concluded, "I think Hubbell would help us if asked to by yourself & Lyman Richardson." Similarly, E. R. Robertson told New York *World* editor Manton Marble that the protectionist tendencies of their fellow Manhattan Club member Abram S. Hewitt (D-N.Y.) would "disappear if he is given a seat alongside of [S. S.] Cox, and is treated in a kindly way. . . . a little reflection & conversation with Cox as well as with yourself & myself would soon dissipate the bit of fog which has gotten into a mind on most subjects very clear."[17]

Such intimate access was, of course, primarily an option for elites. And even they, as the Morton incident reveals, could not count on having friends in precisely the right places. A more prevalent approach, therefore, was through letters of introduction—in which someone who wanted to meet with, or write to, a decision maker would get one, or several, endorsements from persons the official knew or was known to respect. These documents, naturally, were not all equally valuable. Most public figures in the Grant years developed sensitive

16. *Trist v. Child,* 21 Wallace (1875), 441–453, and chap. 1, above; Bridgman, "The Lobby."

17. Poppletion to Morton, 16 Mar. 1874, Morton Family Papers, Chicago Historical Society; Robinson to Marble, Election Day 1874, Marble Papers, L.C.

antennae to pick up subtle signals, and learned quickly to read between the lines.[18] A perfunctory note might be merely a meaningless courtesy, particularly if its author was understood to be incapable of refusing such requests. As Mississippi governor Adelbert Ames confessed to his father-in-law, Benjamin Butler, "I have yielded to the solicitations of friends (?) and given them letters of introduction to you. It is easier for me to do so than to decline," he admitted, even though "those who are the most persistent in asking are as a rule the least deserving." So, he ended wearily, Butler should feel in no way compelled to respond. A Bay State colleague of Butler's, meanwhile, developed a code whereby recipients of his endorsements could easily winnow the wheat from the chaff. According to George F. Hoar, James Buffington was a soft-hearted man who hated to say no to anyone, especially constitutents seeking patronage. Consequently, all who asked got letters of recommendation, but "he had an understanding with the appointing clerks that if he wrote his name Buffington with the g he desired that the man should be appointed, but if he wrote it Buffinton without the g he did not wish to be taken seriously."[19]

Even a sophisticated pro like James G. Blaine might sometimes acquiesce to obscure requests for endorsements—one of which eventually found its way to Mark Twain. When *The Gilded Age*'s author could not resist asking why the Speaker had succumbed, Blaine replied with great glee—and wit that rivaled his correspondent's—that "it does my heart good to know that Hartford is getting its share" of the "innumerable caravan of dead beats whose headquarters are in Washington. . . . Your evident impatience under the affliction," he continued, "show[s] how ill-fitted you would be for the stern duties of a Representative in Congress." And he expressed his ardent hope that, if nothing else, the satirist and his friends might acquire "a newer, keener, fresher appreciation of the trials and troubles, the beggars, the bores, the swindlers, and the scalawags wherewith the average Congressman is evermore afflicted."[20] Yet the eagerness with which even meaningless introduc-

18. For a variety of (unsuccessful) approaches, see Mrs. R. A. Minor to James G. Blaine, 10 Dec. 1873, Blaine Papers, L.C.; Rev. John W. Brown to Sen. Thomas F. Bayard (D-Del.), 14 Jan. 1874, Bayard Papers, L.C.; letter from Stephen R. Sweet, 6 Jan. 1876, forwarded to George F. Hoar by W. H. Baker (R-N.Y.), George F. Hoar Papers, Massachusetts Historical Society, Boston; Leroy C. Johnson to Benjamin F. Butler, 3 Jan. 1876, and Butler to Johnson, 8 Jan. 1876, Butler Papers.

19. Ames to Butler, 17 Apr. 1874, Butler Papers; George F. Hoar, *Autobiography of Seventy Years*, 2 vols. (New York, 1903), 1:227–28.

20. Samuel Clemens [Mark Twain] to Blaine, 7 Oct. 1875; Blaine to Clemens, 9 Oct. 1875; Clemens to Blaine, 11 Oct. 1875 (enclosing clipping of a letter by Clemens from the Hartford *Courant* on this subject); all Blaine Papers.

tions were pursued suggests the benefits that might accrue from really legitimate ones. For in an arena where "reputation" and "contacts" were negotiable commodities, knowing the right people could indeed open the door of access.[21]

Still another entrée to Congressional Government consisted of inciting or, perhaps more accurately, seeming to incite a climate of "favorable public opinion." The objective was to create the impression that a particular clientele's demand was also the will of the people—either nationally or within selected states or districts. Occasionally, of course, intense popular sentiment developed spontaneously; the broad support for pensions during and after the Civil War, and the uproar demanding repeal of the 1873 Salary Grab, are two cases in point. But as these examples suggest, such collective action was likely to emerge naturally only when widely publicized issues, usually with high emotional appeal, were at stake.[22] At most other times, citizen participation had to be orchestrated, often by professional agents (see Figure 2).

Mass lobbies, unlike spontaneous movements, were the Gilded Age forerunners of twentieth-century interest groups. Not all of them were formally organized, but when policy questions relevant to their interests came up—often in response to initiatives by their leaders—concerned parties were mobilized. They wrote letters, sometimes from prescribed texts; signed petitions, frequently appended to standardized, printed forms; confronted their own congressmen personally; and so on.[23] The entire thing would be arranged so that members' principal contact would be with their own constituents, to minimize chances of campaigns being labeled as the instruments of "outside

21. Even knowing a legislator personally could not, of course, guarantee direct access; I found countless letters bearing the legend "private" or "confidential" in nearly every collection of congressional correspondence—almost all bearing signs of having been screened by secretaries or aides. One of these (with screening note) asked a common question: "How can a letter be addressed to you so to be read by you alone, instead of a private secretary?" Anna Deerfield to Benjamin F. Butler, 28 May 1874, Butler Papers. Novice legislators and nonvoting delegates also had access problems in getting to their powerful colleagues; for how one man who fell into both categories surmounted the difficulty, see Oscar Doane Lambert, *Stephen Benton Elkins* (Pittsburgh, 1955), pp. 41–42.

22. For two accounts of such spontaneous agitation, see L. White Busbey, *Uncle Joe Cannon: The Story of a Pioneer American* (New York, 1927), p. 117; Ari Hoogenboom, "Spoilsmen and Reformers: Civil Service Reform and Public Morality," in *The Gilded Age: A Reappraisal*, ed. H. Wayne Morgan (Syracuse, 1963), pp. 70–74.

23. The best collection of relevant documents on such campaigns is in the Congressional Petition File, Legislative and Judicial Division, National Archives, Washington.

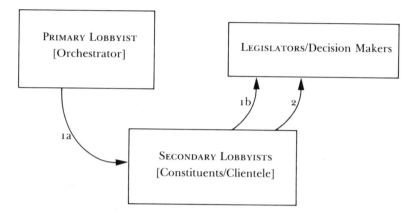

1a–1b: path perceived by primary lobbyist.
2: path perceived by decision makers.

Figure 2. Grass-roots campaigns: the path of indirect lobbying

influence" or "special interests."[24] One of the best orchestrated of these
efforts during the Grant years was put together in 1874 by the embryonic American Medical Association, organized even then to the
county level; it included several printed memorials, locally circulated
(but uniform) petitions, and fact sheets in behalf of legislation to end
discrimination against physicians in the Army Medical Corps. Temperance and veterans' groups were other pioneers of this strategy; only
the floods of absolutely identical petitions, sent to the Capitol from all
over the country, gave away that these were not what they seemed to be:
unrelated, spontaneous manifestations from the grass roots.[25]

Whether they were spontaneous or planned, however, campaigns of
popular pressure depended heavily upon the press, many of whose
most prominent Gilded Age practitioners ranked as well among the
nation's leading lobbyists. Late nineteenth-century media were highly
politicized; the majority of periodicals were overtly partisan and the
rest, although nominally "independent," were hardly apolitical. In an
America that, during the 1870s, boasted 4500 newspapers, virtually

24. David J. Rothman, *Politics and Power: The United States Senate, 1869–1901*
(Cambridge, 1966), pp. 198, 205; see also Carl Schurz to Manton Marble, 1 Feb. 1874,
Marble Papers.

25. File No. 43A-H10.4, Military Affairs Committee (House), Petition File, 43d Cong.;
see also File No. 43A-J7.1, Invalid Pensions Committee (House), and (on temperance
issues) Files Nos. 43A-H8.1, 43A-H8.4, Judiciary Committee (House), Petition Files, 43d
Cong.

every public figure had at least a couple he could safely regard as "his," and no town of 1000 was likely to be without a minimum of two distinctive weeklies.[26]

The press provided vital links between officeholders and the public. It printed texts or lengthy excerpts of presidential messages, congressional debates, and campaign speeches. Since copyright restrictions were loose or nonexistent, articles, especially from big city papers, reappeared all over the country. Allegations and rumors circulated widely, as did facts and opinions, as journalists sought to let the voters know what their Representatives were up to—and, in turn, to let those in power know what folks back home presumably were thinking. Such information, biased as it might have been, was vital to both politicians and public at a time when national legislators might be absent from their districts for months at a stretch. Indeed, it would be difficult to overestimate the media's political import during the Age of Grant— when it was neither accidental nor incongruous that the General's 1872 opponent topped the masthead of the New York *Tribune*.[27]

Media influence was manifest in diverse ways within the Capitol itself. Twenty-four members of the Forty-third House alone, including Speaker Blaine, and an equal number in the Forty-fourth were themselves former editors or publishers.[28] Some reporters, most notably Ben: Perley Poore, served simultaneously as committee or department clerks, while others, such as Philadelphia newsman Uriah H. Painter, moonlighted as corporate lobbyists. But some of the most powerful press figures never held jobs in Washington, although their presence was felt strongly nonetheless. Horace Greeley was one, of course, as was editor Manton Marble of the New York *World:* leader of "Swallowtail" Democracy, adviser to Samuel Tilden, principal author of his party's 1876 national platform, well-known and influential proponent of hard

26. Frank Luther Mott, *American Journalism: A History of Newspapers in the United States,* 3d ed. (New York, 1962), pp. 389–90, 396, 404–5; see also Douglass Cater, *The Fourth Branch of Government* (Boston, 1959).

27. One account of journalists' influence on the Liberal Republican movement generally is in Joseph F. Wall, *Henry Watterson, Reconstructed Rebel* (New York, 1956). Some good examples of the diffusion of commentary in the absence of strict copyright laws are in the clipping scrapbooks, Blaine Papers. See also: Mott, *American Journalism,* and Leon Burr Richardson, *William E. Chandler, Republican* (New York, 1940), pp. 89, 168; C. O. B. Bryant (Associated Press) to Jeremiah S. Black, 22 Oct. 1874, Black Family Papers, L.C.; William P. Kellogg to Benjamin F. Butler, 20 Feb. 1874, Butler Papers.

28. Figures compiled from data in the *BDAC*. In addition, some members had relatives who worked as journalists; the most remarkable, perhaps, was Rebecca Latimer (Mrs. William H.) Felton of Georgia; see R. L. Felton, *My Memoirs of Georgia Politics* (Atlanta, 1911), and below.

money and free trade, and (as we shall see in Chapter 5) a potent, perhaps controlling force behind the Speakership of Michael C. Kerr.[29] Others with clout included Charles Dana (New York *Sun*), Whitelaw Reid (New York *Tribune*), Henry Watterson (*Louisville Courier-Journal* and an appointed member of the Forty-fourth House), Joseph Medill (Chicago *Tribune*), Murat Halstead (Cincinnati *Commercial*), Henry Grady (Atlanta *Constitution*), and Samuel Bowles II (Springfield, Massachusetts, *Republican*).[30] Magazines, meanwhile, contributed Henry Adams *(North American Review)*, William Dean Howells *(Atlantic Monthly)*, and Edwin L. Godkin *(Nation)*, not to mention Thomas Nast and his rival cartoonists, such as those in *Frank Leslie's Weekly*.[31]

Besides partisan organs, the Gilded Age was an era of proliferating "special interest" periodicals. These were remarkably diverse, ranging from temperance and religious tracts, to trade association journals, to foreign language papers, to Susan B. Anthony's *Revolution*, to *Moore's Rural New Yorker*, to veterans' newsletters like the *Soldier's Advocate* and George Lemon's *National Tribune*. Many of the printed petitions for orchestrated campaigns came from these sources; through their pages, readers were kept informed about how government might affect their lives and what they might do to encourage or stop it. Such organs were crucial to the evolution of "clientele consciousness," as Chapter 7 will demonstrate. Their influence was profound, and the shrewdest entrepreneurs and agents of the seventies showed no reluctance to exploit their potential.[32]

29. On moonlighting journalists, see the memoirs of the most successful one, Ben: Perley Poore, *Perley's Reminiscences of Sixty Years in the National Metropolis*, 2 vols. (Philadelphia, 1886–87). One of the earliest measures to restrict the activities of lobbyists was an 1852 House rule prohibiting congressional press credentials to any journalist "who shall be employed as an agent to prosecute any claim pending before Congress": Kennedy, "Congressional Lobbies," 529–40. George T. McJimsey, *Genteel Partisan, Manton Marble* (Ames, Iowa, 1971); Marble Papers; chap. 5, below; Glyndon G. Van Deusen, *Horace Greeley: Nineteenth-Century Crusader* (Philadelphia, 1953).

30. See biographies of these, and similar, individuals; Wall, *Watterson*, p. x; Mott, *American Journalism*, esp. pp. 360–459.

31. See relevant magazines, and Frank Luther Mott, *A History of American Magazines, 1865–1885* (Cambridge, 1938).

32. Both volumes of Huntington correspondence, cited above in n. 14, for example, were filled with letters on his, and rival magnates', efforts to use the press to advance their corporations' causes; one instance by the Texas & Pacific, consisting of a large compilation of favorable press notices, is *The Press and the People on the Importance of a Southern Line Railway to the Pacific and in Favor of Aid to the Texas and Pacific Railway Co.* (Philadelphia, 1875); see also plan "to manufacture in the minds of committee men and of Congressmen a proper appreciation of the claims of Chicago. . . . agitation is of great importance in that matter & [the Board] will take steps to enlist the press in its favor," draft of statement included in Directors' documents for 7–8 Feb. 1876, Chicago Board of Trade Papers, University of Illinois—Chicago Circle.

Because of journalists' openness in avowing their partisanship, and widespread awareness of what the media were all about, only the most naive voters and officeholders were vulnerable to outright deception.[33] Most took what they read with a grain of salt—but, nonetheless, read they did. For periodicals were the only widely available sources of information and feedback. It was from daily papers, for example, that most citizens first learned of the 1873 Salary Grab, and those same papers subsequently let Washington know of the nearly universal outrage with which constituents responded to the measure. Between legislative sessions, many members used the papers as vehicles to respond to criticism, justify their behavior, boast of opposition to the bill, or announce intentions to give the money back. Congressmen obviously had other means of learning where the electorate stood: correspondence, memorials, and so on. Yet most of these communications would not have occurred without the initial journalistic coverage, and follow-up articles on the mail being generated enhanced its persuasive impact even further. In circumstances of this sort, then, the press facilitated access in two directions, from clienteles or constituents to decision makers—by orchestrating grass-roots sentiment—and vice versa. It served, in short, as the catalytic agent that lobbying was really all about. And that access and responsiveness did ensue is demonstrated in congressmen's diaries, autobiographies, extant correspondence, and events in the Capitol themselves. As James A. Garfield wrote after the Forty-third House's first full day of deliberation: "We witnessed the humiliating spectacle of twenty-five different members rushing in with a bill to repeal the salary clause when everybody knew that one was enough. Of course this was done merely to exhibit to the public eye an appearance of zeal."[34]

When there was a spontaneous popular consensus, formal lobbying usually was unnecessary. But only a handful of issues were ever controversial or spectacular enough to attract widespread attention; most

33. "People are vastly more intelligent than they were twenty years ago—the newspapers, far beyond books, have made them so—and the readers draw inferences by rapidly progressive trains of thought as readily as locomotives draw trains of cars"; Philip Ripley (of the *American Cyclopaedia*) to Manton Marble, 3 Apr. 1876, Marble Papers.

34. George F. Hoar began a response to an inquiry on the Salary Grab from the publisher of the Worcester, Mass., *Evening Gazette* and *Aegis Gazette* by stating, "I do not think it desirable to be constantly or frequently making explanations of the votes which I give even when the votes excite earnest public criticism"—and then sent a thirteen-page response! Charles H. Doe to Hoar, 29 Dec. 1873, and Hoar to Doe, 30 Dec. 1873, Hoar Papers. On Garfield, see James D. Norris and A. H. Shaffer, eds., *Politics and Patronage in the Gilded Age: The Correspondence of James A. Garfield and Charles E. Henry* (Madison, Wis., 1970), esp. p. 46; *The Diary of James A. Garfield*, ed. Harry James Brown and F. D. Williams, 4 vols. (East Lansing, 1967–81), 2:254 (4 Dec. 1873).

played to smaller audiences and were interesting only to a few clienteles. It was these that required concerted advocacy to catch the congressional eye—and rarely was it feasible or credible to plan a campaign of grass-roots activism.

Some of the more typical, but less sexy, matters had internal advocates in place—perhaps because of foundations laid by professional agents at the organizational stages of congressional life. If so, a measure of access could be assumed. But such in-House lobbyists tended to exist only for clienteles that dealt regularly with government—railroads, veterans, freedmen, and the like—and as clientele-collectives more than as individuals. They were unlikely to be on hand—and it would have been unrealistic, as well as inefficient, to develop them—for short-term or one-shot petitioners. This category, of course, included not only minor and less consistently agitated economic and social interests, but also those masses of individuals seeking patronage or relief through private legislation. And these were the matters that comprised the bulk of Gilded Age congressional business.

It was with these lesser (or, at least, less publicized) and essentially distributive questions that much basic, access-oriented lobbying necessarily was concerned. For unlike big or controversial issues, demands like these most clearly needed help in calling attention to themselves. Without explicit advocacy on their behalf, it was possible if not probable that decision makers could remain unconcerned or ignorant of their existence. Generally, then, the intensity of lobbying that was necessary to secure attention to a demand was inversely proportional to its "natural" access: through popular consensus, notoriety, centrality to the national interest, and so on.

Figure 3 roughly illustrates this principle. Point "A" on the diagonal represents the approximate locus of a very popular, consensual demand, like that impelling passage of the first Civil War pensions in 1862. Point "B" denotes a policy with slightly less public appeal, such as the Bounty Bill or other more expansive veterans' benefits.[35] "C" might be a matter of general public interest, but might lack sizable, activated support: the 1872 Education Act, or authorization to complete construction of the Washington Monument. Finally, "D" and "E" indicate highly specialized or obscure distributive measures—particular private relief bills, authorizations for new post offices and bridges, other local

35. For such proposals, see William H. Glasson, *Federal Military Pensions in the United States* (New York, 1918), esp. pp. 165–66; and chap. 7, below.

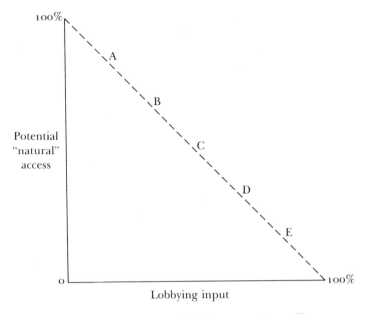

Figure 3. Intensity ratio: lobbying versus "natural" access

improvements, specific commodity tariffs, and so on. For these, the contribution of lobbying to the procurement of access had to be very great, indeed.

This model should help to explain why money and lobbying so often seem to go together, especially in the Gilded Age—even though the right of petition is constitutionally an equal right of all. Establishing access, particularly if one's demand was individual and basically indistinguishable from hordes of others, was time-consuming, debilitating, and practically impossible unless someone was continuously on the scene to oversee it. Obviously, one's chances were improved if one could afford to hire an advocate—and the better the advocate's record was, the higher his or her fees (and the larger his or her commitments) were likely to be. Consider, for example, the situation of the average applicant for a pension during the Forty-third Congress, when 2666 private (of 4891) bills were introduced, and just 441 (16.6 percent) were enacted. Imagine the dilemma of the eleven Invalid Pension Committee members, who were without time, staff, or other resources to investigate such matters as merit; remember, too, the contention among all committees for space on the legislative calendar. Thus, our would-be pensioner was competing for attention, not only with hundreds of others who had similar demands, but with the myriad clienteles of every sort who looked to Congress for satisfaction.[36]

We will see later how this conundrum was resolved, for veterans and their dependents in particular. But that resolution did not occur until the late 1870s, after more than a decade of widespread disappointment and suffering. This frustration was not caused by deliberate neglect, unconcern, or mercenary malice, but by inadequacy of access to an overloaded system, and by the absence of what in the end would lead to change: coordinated grass-roots pressure. Persistent and skillful lobbying could help in the interim, of course—but how many ordinary claimants could afford it?

The fact is that, indigent and desperate though they were, hundreds of relief-seeking citizens did hire lobbyists. Extant congressional correspondence is full of letters from such agents, many perfunctory, but a sizable percentage evincing serious efforts at advocacy. Just as common, however, were letters from constituents—equally sincere in complaints about the failures or incompetence of their agents, some of whom had been on retainer for years without accomplishing anything for their clients.

What was going on? There is no question that many who set up offices in Washington were well intentioned, but others sought to take advantage of naive petitioners from the hinterlands. Agents, then as now, were unlicensed and subject to no code of standards. Some were attorneys; others, according to their own letterheads, combined their advocacy with such incongruous trades as haberdashery and shoe repair. Nothing in principle, of course, prevents a skillful cobbler from also being a skillful lobbyist, but such a combination must be rare.[37]

Lobbying, then, like representation generally, was not an undifferen-

36. Figures based on data in Index to *Hse. J.,* 43d Cong., 1st sess., 1627–1762, and 2d sess., 828–73; and George B. Galloway, *History of the House of Representatives* (New York, 1962), p. 304; also chap. 7, below.

37. S. C. Corbin, claims agent and, according to his letterhead, "Dealer in Leather, Boots, and Shoes," to William B. Allison (R-Iowa), 10 Jan. 1877; William B. Allison Papers, Iowa State Dept. of History & Archives, Des Moines. Quality control, of course, was a principal motivation behind the Hoar Resolution and George Boutwell's attempt to establish a "Bar" of Congress (see chap. 1, above). Lack of quality control, meanwhile, made the villainous lobbyist a popular antagonist in Gilded Age political novels, e.g., Henry Adams, *Democracy, An American Novel;* John William De Forest, *Playing the Mischief* (1875; State College, Pa., 1961), and *Justine's Lovers* (New York, 1878); see also Edward Winslow Martin [James Dabney McCabe], *Behind the Scenes in Washington* (Philadelphia, 1873), chap. 1; and Mary Clemmer Ames, *Ten Years in Washington: Life and Scenes in the National Capital* (Hartford, 1875), esp. chap. 12 (on a category of unscrupulous female agent whom she calls "A Dragon of a Woman, A Lady Who is Feared if not Respected").

tiated commodity. Quality was crucial, particularly when competition for attention was heavy or when the potential for natural access was negligible. But what made an effective lobbyist? For an answer, we have to turn to our original model, and especially to its bottom line, that is, the path of professionalization: the inside track of access to Congressional Government.

The "professional" lobbyist—or Entrepreneur, as we shall call him—shared many characteristics with his elected counterparts in the business of representation. Both were atypical in their spheres. Both regarded their vocations as full-time pursuits, both spent time paying dues before establishing their influence, and both could boast of strategic and institutional expertise that equaled or surpassed their command of substance. The Entrepreneur, like the legislative insider, understood the larger governmental and political system in which he operated; his skills, therefore, were readily transferable from one policy area to another—and almost surely were more diverse and highly developed than those of all except a handful of congressmen. Thus, as V. O. Key could say about lobbyists in mid-twentieth-century state legislatures (an arena that bore a striking resemblance to the 1870s House): "Their tenure is likely to be longer than that of many legislators; and in the course of their service they gain [legislators'] confidence and respect." And, Key added, "government may be so inadequately staffed and the lobbyist so well backstopped . . . that he comes to exert an influence based on a not disinterested competence."[38]

Because Entrepreneurs were so few during the Gilded Age, their power was vastly disproportionate to their number. Consider, for example, William E. Chandler. Just thirty-eight years old when Grant's second administration began, the New Hampshire Republican already had been Speaker of his state's legislature, solicitor and judge advocate general for the U.S. Navy Department, and first assistant secretary of the Treasury. During the mid-1870s he was executive secretary of the G.O.P. National Committee—service that included a pivotal role in resolution of Hayes's presidential bid—and, later, he would hold the Naval portfolio in Chester Arthur's cabinet and serve fifteen years in the Senate. Yet Chandler's most usual occupation, often pursued concurrently with others, was as "Capitol counsel" for a wide variety of employers who knew about and respected his proficiency. As one man who sought his services in 1875 declared, "He is one of the best men in Washington and we must have his co-operation." And Grenville M.

38. V. O. Key, *Politics, Parties, & Pressure Groups*, 5th ed. (New York, 1964), p. 132.

William E. Chandler. Courtesy Library of Congress, Division of Prints and Photographs.

Dodge, himself an Entrepreneur of nearly comparable skills, told the Union Pacific Railroad's directors that "they [could not] get along in Washington without [him]."[39]

Chandler's command of advocacy is suggested by a partial list of his clients during the Grant years: Jay Cooke and his banking house, before and during the Panic of 1873; the Washington Market Company, seeking a federal bill of incorporation; shipbuilder John Roach; shipping and telegraph magnate Thomas T. Eckert; promoters of the Gatling gun; various diplomats, including Minister to Spain Daniel E. Sickles, who was discredited by his performance during the *Virginius* affair and whose resignation Chandler negotiated; Louisiana Republicans William P. Kellogg and P. B. S. Pinchback, in their drawn-out electoral contests, and other southern elected and appointed officials who were buffeted by the shifting winds of Reconstruction; and dozens of individual job- and claims-seekers.[40] Some members of Congress themselves asked him to lobby for their appointment to particular House committees; many sought his advice on how to deal with matters under their jurisdiction once they got there.[41] But Chandler's most remunerative and faithful clientele came from within the railroad industry, his subsequent opposition to transportation trusts as a Progressive senator notwithstanding. In 1874 alone, he held retainers from at least four lines: Union Pacific, Texas & Pacific, Kansas Pacific, and Arkansas Valley. What may be most remarkable is that officials of a minimum of three of these companies knew of his retainers from others; since disputes among them occurred frequently, if not inevitably, their willingness to employ him was potent testimony indeed to both his discretion and his prowess.[42]

39. *BDAC*, p. 860; Richardson, *Chandler*, esp. p. 163; Rothman, *Politics and Power*, pp. 166–68, 193; S. Anable to "his brother," 8 Oct. 1875, and Dodge to Chandler, 26 Dec. 1875. Chandler Papers, L.C.

40. An incomplete but representative sample of correspondence includes Jay Cooke to WEC, 6 Oct. and 16 Dec. 1873; John Roach to WEC, 27 June 1874; Thomas T. Eckert to WEC, 22 Jan. 1874; D. E. Sickles to WEC, 23 July 1873; P. S. Post (U.S. Consul at Vienna) to WEC, 4 May 1874; W. P. Kellogg to WEC, 22 and 23 Apr. and 17 Dec. 1873; Sen. W. E. Spencer (R-Ala.) to WEC, 16 Feb. 1873; and A. A. Knight (collector of customs, Florida) to WEC, 12 July 1873 (all in Chandler Papers, L.C.). A much fuller collection of his correspondence on patronage and private legislation is in the William E. Chandler Papers, New Hampshire Historical Society, Concord.

41. William Lawrence (R-Ohio) to WEC, 7 Nov. 1873; H. H. Starkweather (R-Conn.) to WEC, 17 Nov. 1873; Sen. W. E. Spencer to WEC, 24 Jan. 1874; James S. Negley (R-Pa.) to WEC, 19 Oct. 1874; J. H. Platt (R-Va.) to WEC, 21 Feb. 1875; W. P. Frye (R-Me.) to WEC, 25 Apr. 1876; L. Crounse (R-Neb.) to WEC, 12 July 1876; Sen. S. A. Dorsey (R-Ark.) to WEC, 30 May 1876 (all in Chandler Papers, L.C.).

42. J. C. Reiff to WEC, 22 June 1874 (Arkansas Valley); Robert E. Carr to WEC, 7, 12,

Chandler was at the pinnacle of his profession, but a handful of others were not far behind and kept equally busy when they wanted to. In an era when the average Representative served just one or two terms, a "parliamentary practitioner" with ten years' experience in the capital almost surely understood machinations on the Hill a good deal better than most of the members he hoped to influence. Naive first-termers might be taken in by the unskilled or unscrupulous—novels like De Forest's *Honest John Vane* were based on such a premise—but backbenchers were unlikely to have the clout to accomplish what a petitioning interest needed. Experienced members, on the other hand, including those in the leadership, tended to prefer dealing with advocates whom they had come to know and trust. And after long periods of working together—in an arena where, even today, people who remain for seven or eight years are thought of as old-timers—it was not uncommon for deep respect and even close personal friendships to evolve between bastions of power in the First and Third Houses.[43]

An Entrepreneur's ties to leadership enhanced the efficiency of his advocacy, not simply the quality of his contacts. For the House was a hierarchical institution—a pyramid, really, in which power was diffused as it descended through the various levels (Figure 4). Those at the peak, most notably the Speaker, allocated authority among those underneath, thereby exercising considerable sway over both personnel and the agenda. It is easy to see why it could be so crucial to have access to the top—from which influence, as well as institutional authority, could be trickled down. One who had the Speaker's ear could make suggestions, for instance, about the composition and chairmen of committees, especially those likely to have jurisdiction over the interests of one's usual clients. And a sympathetic committee, with a chairman whose place was partly a product of an Entrepreneur's solicitousness, was probably not going to be averse to listening to him later on. Compare

18 Mar. 1874 (Kansas Pacific); Thomas A. Scott to WEC, 12 Dec. 1873 and 14 June 1874 (Texas & Pacific); almost daily communication with Jay Gould, UPRR President, beginning with Gould to WEC, 4 Jan. 1874 (all in Chandler Papers, L.C.); Richardson, *Chandler*, chap. 6 and passim; and chap. 7, below.

43. Chandler's friendship with James G. Blaine, for instance, is documented in Richardson, *Chandler*, pp. 173–74; Gail Hamilton [Mary Abigail Dodge], *Biography of James G. Blaine* (Norwich, Conn., 1895), pp. 365–70; Walker Blaine to Mrs. J. G. Blaine, 19 Feb. 1877, Blaine Papers. For information on two other Entrepreneurs, see Stanley P. Hirshson, *Grenville M. Dodge: Soldier, Politician, Railroad Pioneer* (Bloomington, Ind., 1967); Jacob R. Perkins, *Trails, Rails, and War: The Life of General G. M. Dodge* (Indianapolis, 1929); Grenville M. Dodge Papers, Iowa State Dept. of History & Archives, Des Moines; Thomas, *Ward*, esp. p. 351; Maude Howe Elliott, *Uncle Sam Ward and His Circle* (New York, 1938), esp. pp. 497–98, 561–68.

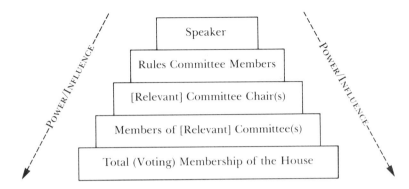

Figure 4. Power in the House: the prismatic diffusion of influence

this situation to that of the lesser agent, whose entrée into the pyramid was someplace much closer to the bottom, and the value of ground-work—sometimes years in evolving, and sometimes a product of rela-tionships and services that bore little overt connection to legislation—ought to be easy to appreciate. Stated simply, it is easier to work with a handful of congressmen at the upper echelons than with the House membership at large. And Entrepreneurs, compared to the majority of lobbyists, were much better equipped to make the long-term invest-ments that access to the pinnacle required.

Men like Chandler, Grenville Dodge, and self-proclaimed "King of the Lobby" Samuel Ward were exceptional in their understanding of the delicate balance, and difference, between social connections and respect derived from professional reliability. All had close friends among the Capitol's leaders; all, and particularly "Uncle Sam," were renowned for their opulent entertaining. But Ward, like any profes-sional, never forgot his main objective, which was to win and to retain for himself the sorts of contacts and comrades who would come in handy later. Thus, Ward and the others were careful to be as scru-pulous and dependable in their more explicit lobbying as in their entertaining.[44] When they undertook to represent clients, they did so openly and, to the greatest extent possible, could be relied upon to be informed thoroughly about the issues in the cases they accepted. Legis-lators, therefore, aware as they were of the agents' interests, knew as well that they could count on the substantive accuracy of what they were told. Further, they knew that with such agents access was a two-way

44. Beverly W. Smith, Jr., "All-Time Champ of the Lobbyists," *Saturday Evening Post,* 23 Dec. 1950, 53–55; Thomas, *Ward,* pp. 342, 339–40; Elliott, *Ward,* p. 459.

street: they could approach the Entrepreneurs, for business or pleasure, even when they had no cases pending. For effective lobbyists
could not appear solely as fair-weather friends. And so the relationships that evolved were based on *mutual* respect, accountability,
dependency, and trust. On such foundations—social and substantive—
rested the Entrepreneurs' continued assurance that they would get at
least an initial hearing from decision makers. And that, of course,
rendered them continuously more proficient and productive.[45]

Indeed similar ground rules applied to all lobbyists, and not just to
Entrepreneurs. Most, in fact, were specialists, who therefore could
concentrate their efforts and energies on officials within particular
jurisdictions. For some, such as district or state patronage bosses, the
relevant spheres might consist exclusively of individual members or
delegations. Claims agents and patent attorneys worked primarily with
specific committees and their bureaucratic counterparts, who shared
authority over the distributive outputs that their kinds of clients
sought.[46] There were single issue advocates of other sorts, too: proponents of discretionary matters like aid to education, abolition of capital
punishment, and expanding civil rights for women.[47] But while spe-

45. Galloway, *Legislative Process*, p. 491; Lewis Anthony Dexter, *The Sociology and Politics of Congress* (Chicago, 1969), p. 5. Some Entrepreneurs, such as G. M. Dodge on railroad matters, also qualified as experts, e.g., Dodge to Rep. George W. McCrary (R-Iowa), 22 May 1876, Dodge Papers. Expertise and reliability were the bases for David Wells's influence on free trade and specie; David Earl Robbins, "The Congressional Career of William Ralls Morrison" (Ph.D. diss., University of Illinois, 1963), pp. 65–66; Albert V. House, "The Political Career of Samuel Jackson Randall" (Ph.D. diss., University of Wisconsin–Madison, 1934), p. 272; August Belmont to Wells, 29 Jan. 1878, David A. Wells Papers (Weinstein Notes). Other examples of expertise-based lobbying include C. V. Riley (Office of the State Entomologist, St. Louis, Mo.) to William B. Allison, 12 Dec. 1876 (on locust control bill); Washington Townsend (R-Pa.) to M. Warner, enclosing communications from the National Education Association (instructing Warner to see George F. Hoar and L. Q. C. Lamar of the Education & Labor Committee), 23 Dec. 1875, and Andrew D. White (president, Cornell University) to Hoar, 20 Dec. 1873 and 12 June 1874, Hoar Papers; Ari J. Hoogenboom, "Thomas A. Jenckes and Civil Service Reform," *MVHR*, 47 (1961), 636–58; and Glasson, *Federal Military Pensions*, pp. 136–37. For general discussions, see John G. Sproat, *"The Best Men": Liberal Reformers in the Gilded Age* (New York, 1968), pp. 72–75, 257ff.; Burton J. Bledstein, *The Culture of Professionalism: The Middle Class and the Development of Higher Education in America* (New York, 1976), pp. 122–23.

46. For information on two important bosses, see Norris and Shaffer, *Politics and Patronage*, and Chandler Papers, NHHS; see also chap. 6, below. Of course, the most prominent and successful patronage boss doubtless was Chester A. Arthur, collector of the Port of New York, who went directly from there to the vice-presidency—and presidency; Thomas C. Reeves, *Gentleman Boss: The Life of Chester A. Arthur* (New York, 1975). On claims agents and others connected with private legislation, see chap. 7, below.

47. George F. Hoar, an eclectic reformer, was a particularly frequent recipient of

cialists could focus on narrower sectors of the legislature than did Entrepreneurs, they could not disregard laying foundations for access, the basic prerequisite to success. Thus, the best of them, much like the elite, were active throughout the legislative process: from elections, to the politics of institutional organization, to agenda setting, committee work, and floor votes. Here, as always, lobbying coexisted with the entirety of Gilded Age Congressional Government.

What, then, if anything, can we discern about the kind and degree of lobbyists' influence? Although previous observers have arrived at various answers, the majority seems to go along with Matthew Josephson and Richard Hofstadter in attributing tremendous power to the "spoilsmen."[48] David Rothman, meanwhile, whose study of the late nineteenth-century Senate in some ways parallels this one of the House, agrees with the consensus and gives evidence to substantiate his position. About the roles of lobbyists in the upper chamber, Rothman writes: "Agents typically answered the inquiries of interested senators, explaining the various proposals on the calendar and clarifying the pertinent but dull details of intricate bills. With regularity, they supplied information [and helped] members of Congress to understand the increasingly technical legislation that came before [them]." So, he believed, "lobbyists became the experts in an era of specialization. . . . As *amicus curiae*, welcomed assistants, lobbyists achieved influence in the legislative process."[49]

The staff functions of lobbyists which Rothman explicitly emphasizes were, if anything, more decisive in the House than in the Senate. It was not unusual, after all, for members to receive fifty to one hundred letters a week, which had to be read, processed, and answered—by hand, as the typewriter was not yet in common usage. Since only chairmen of major committees and the Speaker had offices in the

---

letters from single-issue lobbyists: W. G. Eliot (Washington University, St. Louis) to Hoar, 8 May 1876 (in opposition to H.R. 2440, for "the regulation of social evils"); Francis E. Abbott to Hoar, 10 May 1876 (on religious freedom and opposition to "Blue Laws"); Henry Blackwell (co-editor of the *Woman's Journal*, husband of Lucy Stone, and official of the American Woman Suffrage Association) to Hoar, 26 Sept. 1873, 16 Dec. 1873, 2 May 1874 (all in Hoar Papers). On abolition of capital punishment, see Marion H. Bovee to W. B. Allison, 19 May 1875, 9 Nov. 1875, 20 Apr. 1875, Allison Papers; Bovee to Nathaniel P. Banks, 7 Jan. 1876, Banks Papers, L.C.; and Marion H. Bovee Papers, Henry E. Huntington Library, San Marino, California.

48. Richard Hofstadter, "The Spoilsmen: An Age of Cynicism," in *The American Political Tradition and the Men Who Made It* (New York, 1948), pp. 164–85; Matthew Josephson, *The Politicos, 1865–1896* (New York, 1938); and chap. 1, above.

49. Rothman, *Politics and Power*, pp. 203–4.

Capitol and (albeit often part-time) clerks at their disposal, most legislators had to do their own work; and whether they did it at home or at
their desks on the chamber floor, they were beset by distractions.[50]

Some members, to be sure, came up with ingenious solutions to such
problems. James Garfield prevailed on recipients of his patronage to
provide him with gratuitous secretarial help. A few others, like William
W. Phelps (R-N.J.), had personal fortunes with which they could hire
stenographers and clerks. Some could depend on help from family
members. The wife of William Morrison (D-Ill.), for example, "took a
direct share in his political work, studied political questions, [and]
attended to his correspondence;" Sam Randall's daughter—"his greatest help and surest resource"—seems to have worked as a nineteenth-
century equivalent to the modern legislative assistant.[51] And then there
was the extraordinary case of the wife of William H. Felton (D-Ga.),
surely among the most impressive ex officio aides of this, or any, era. A
college graduate and former teacher, Rebecca Felton pursued an independent and successful career as journalist and author, all the while
"assisting her husband in all needed ways, and doing the work now
delegated to clerks. In the words of Hon. Alexander H. Stephens, 'no
congressman ever had or could have had a better help'"; in 1922, at the
age of eighty-seven, this ardent suffragist and Progressive reformer
would become the first female U.S. senator![52]

For most members, however—including those above—the absence of
staff was a very real obstacle, and Rothman is correct in arguing that
lobbyists often helped to ameliorate the overload. But in the end,
Rothman fails to acknowledge the importance of both substantive and
social favors. While such devices to ensure access (as Rothman rightly
observes) could not alone guarantee that lobbyists would obtain favorable policy outcomes, to consider only outcomes and to find no clear or
obvious connection between them and explicit lobbying misses a good
deal of the point.[53] To begin with, much lobbying is *de*fensive: aimed at
keeping things off the agenda, rather than putting them on. Some of

50. Alexander, *History of the House*, p. 243 and passim.
51. Margaret Leech and Harry J. Brown, *The Garfield Orbit* (New York, 1978),
pp. 181–82; Allan Peskin, *Garfield* (Canton, Ohio, 1978), pp. 433, 549–50; Hugh M.
Herrick, *William Walter Phelps: His Life and Public Services* (New York, 1904), p. 55;
Franklin D. Scott, "The Political Career of William R. Morrison," Illinois State Historical
Society *Transactions*, 33 (1926), 136; *Nat. Cyc.*, 3:58 (Randall).
52. Felton, *Memoirs; Nat. Cyc.*, 13:410; *DAB*, 6:319–20; *BDAC*, p. 880.
53. Rothman, *Politics and Power*, p. 192; Samuel J. Randall to Sam Ward, 12 Jan. 1876,
and Ward to Randall, 19 Jan. 1876, Samuel J. Randall Papers, Van Pelt Library, University
of Pennsylvania.

the most aggressive campaigns were and are mounted simply to maintain the status quo, or to permit events to take their natural course, without interference of any kind. At least one modern lobbyist has said that her job "might best be described as 'treading water'—or frantically running harder and harder just to stay where I am." In one case from the 1870s, agents of several railroads fought persistently to keep the government from renewing an assortment of mechanical patents held by other interests. And the correspondence of every member contained countless letters pleading with them to try to "kill" measures detrimental to the welfare of their authors' clients.[54] But if these bills did not pass, who can tell whether defensive tactics were responsible, or whether they were doomed for other reasons? How does one assess, or even always detect, these sorts of negative findings?

Furthermore, the preponderance of lobbyists' energies was devoted to awakening and strengthening the commitment of those already supporting their positions, rather than to persuading waverers or winning converts. Again, how can a review of roll calls or similar data reveal whether a "friend of the freedmen" voted for the 1875 Civil Rights Act because he was lobbied or because he was inclined to do so anyway? Indeed, he might even have opposed the law, believing it not forceful enough. Ex post facto motivational analysis—examining effects and, from them, trying to intuit causes—is both inadequate and misleading, particularly with application to something as complex and nuance-ridden as lobbying.[55]

Finally, we should remember that lobbying—especially when it comes to discretionary or controversial issues—is almost never one-sided. Advocates appear on both (or many) sides, not more than one of which can be satisfied. Hence, can outcomes in circumstances like these be evaluated as victories or defeats for "the lobby"? The answer, obviously, depends on one's perspective, and not merely on empirical observation.

Add to these problems the knowledge that most policy making is incremental and distributive, rather than broadly innovative, and the

---

54. Mary Gereau, interview with the author, 25 Jan. 1974; J. A. Potter to James A. Garfield, 23 Mar. 1876, and J. Armstrong to Garfield, 30 Jan. 1874, Garfield Papers; B. C. Cook to J. M. Walker, 16 Jan. 1874, CBQ Railroad Archives, Newberry Library, Chicago; J. M. Denison to J. H. Raymond, 18 and 23 Dec. 1876, 29 Jan. 1877, Denison to Rep. Abram S. Hewitt (D-N.Y.), 23 Dec. 1876, and Hewitt to William K. Ackerman, 28 Jan. 1876, Illinois Central Railroad Archives, Newberry Library, Chicago.

55. "Of course no man can change without being charged with being purchased, and unless someone gets sick or dies, there must be a compromise"; Jacob Rich (pension agent) to William B. Allison, 14 Jan. 1874, Allison Papers.

chance of finding many occasions when lobbyists (or any other group) are single-handedly responsible for major changes evaporates almost entirely. This was especially true in the early Gilded Age, that time of "small contests, on little points." Yet this was also the era when the Third House allegedly enjoyed its most pervasive influence. Can these perceptions be reconciled? Do they need to be?—are they, in fact, contradictory? The contention here is, clearly, that they are not.

It was precisely because of the preponderance of "small contests, on little points" that lobbying did make a difference. In a universe of options, none seeming particularly essential or critical, advocates for certain clienteles enabled some demands to be set apart and distinguished from the mass.[56] At a time when institutional weaknesses typically prohibited legislators from rationally ordering their own business, lobbyists, by calling attention to some measures and not to others, provided decision makers with direction, helping them to set an agenda and to give some semblance of priorities to their deliberations. Sympathetic officials were kept informed as to which of the thousands of policy options mattered most to those whose interests were espoused.[57] House members who lacked procedural or substantive expertise were given support and guidance from persons who had stakes in facilitating the process; experienced congressmen who knew what they were doing worked *with* lobbyists, joining in what often became common cause to enable the system to function more smoothly.

Thus, lobbying had an impact—indeed, several effects—throughout the entire legislative system. Lobbyists were not disinterested in outcomes, but the significance of their efforts frequently exceeded their particular purposes and transcended direct policy payoffs. Even deferral of immediate policy goals could have profound institutional and political implications, regardless of lobbyists' or legislators' intentions. For in the course of laying groundwork for the future in specific campaigns of promotion and persuasion, clienteles' representatives helped make sense out of the confusion in which constituencies' representatives had to operate. They helped in innumerable ways to untangle the spider web of Congressional Government.

56. Thus, David R. Dillon (banker, Savannah, Ga.) wrote to John Cassell (Butler's secretary): "Edmunds, Frelinghuysen, & Judge Wright, Senators promised to assist me. Do me the favor of calling the Gen's attention to this and get the Genl to look after the *bill*. As he can explain the object of the bill and it may refresh the *Senators memory*. . ."; 30 May 1874, Butler Papers.

57. For example, Spencer F. Baird, U.S. Commissioner of Fish and Fisheries, wrote to James G. Blaine about a bill "of some importance to your State," and asked Blaine to intervene; Baird to Blaine, 2 Feb. 1876, Blaine Papers.

CHAPTER 5

"Setting Up House": Lobbying and the Politics of Organization

> The construction of committees, having regard for harmony and
> the effect upon legislation as a whole, requires much patience,
> rare skill, and a thorough knowledge of the views and fitness of
> members. There must also be more or less bargaining.
>
> REP. DEALVA S. ALEXANDER

We have seen that access is the key to affecting outcomes in Congressional Government. We have also seen that power is concentrated at the top of the House's pyramidal structure; both the agenda's overall tone and the substance of particular decisions are determined by institutional and committee leaders, and not by the membership at large. Advocates with access to Speakers and chairmen, therefore, are able to conduct preemptive and more focused campaigns of persuasion than their less privileged colleagues. In short, the efficiency and potential impact of lobbying depend heavily upon where they enter into the decision-making process. So it should come as no surprise that organizational matters have always been among lobbyists' fundamental concerns—and that much of the shrewdest and most aggressive pressure in the Grant years was directed toward "setting up House."[1]

1. An expanded version of this argument is in Margaret Susan Thompson, "Outsiders on the Inside Track: Lobbying and Committee Construction in the Gilded Age House of Representatives," unpublished paper delivered before the Organization of American Historians, Detroit, 1981.

Indeed, circumstances in the seventies both improved the chances of outsiders affecting speakership selection and committee construction and enhanced the benefits that might accrue from such successes. High turnover rates on the House rosters prevented both entrenched and potential leaders from developing personal familiarity with all their colleagues before a session began; they had to rely on others, therefore, to provide information on novices, and to generate and bolster support in advance of party nominating caucuses. The diversity of policy positions among Democrats and Republicans alike, meanwhile, on matters such as currency, tariffs, subsidies, and retrenchment, meant that the politics of setting up House went on relentlessly, regardless of which group was in control. At the same time, both the size and number of House committees were expanding, thereby enlarging the job of composing them. And paralleling this was a fuller and more complex federal agenda, as well as more numerous clienteles (and, of course, their agents) directly interested in legislative outcomes. So the payoff for obtaining appointments that might ensure sympathetic consideration of one's business grew correspondingly greater.

In short, if lobbying did not start long before Congress convened, it might not get under way at all. This was especially true when the Speakership was up for grabs, but even an entrenched incumbent, like James G. Blaine in 1873, was not exempt from lobbyists' overtures and petitions. Journalists throughout the country began to speculate about organizational prospects just as soon as federal election results were known, while skillful Entrepreneurs, such as William E. Chandler and Grenville M. Dodge, routinely made it their business to arrive in Washington—with henchmen—weeks before the House was due to meet. As Lauros McConachie, perhaps the Gilded Age's most insightful contemporary analyst, once remarked: "The practical relations of an American and his committees may be studied from the standpoints of his influence, first, in determining their composition, and [only] second in directing their action.[2] Consideration of events throughout the 1870s, particularly the contrasts and similarities in the experiences of Speakers Blaine, Kerr, and Randall, will validate and illuminate McConachie's astuteness.

2. Arrivals of Dodge and Chandler: addresses on relevant correspondence in William E. Chandler Papers, L.C., and Grenville M. Dodge Papers, Iowa State Dept. of History & Archives, Des Moines. Lauros G. McConachie, *Congressional Committees: A Study of the Origins and Development of Our National and Local Legislative Methods* (1898; New York, 1973), p. 44.

Any Speaker, merely by virtue of his office, wields considerable clout over House personnel and performance. And true as this may be today, it was even truer in the late nineteenth century. Mary P. Follett described him in 1896 as "the central figure of our actual system of government"; Godlove S. Orth (R-Ind.), a veteran of the seventies and himself an aspirant to leadership, called him "a one-man power of far reaching influence" and declared that "the career of every member is in [his] control." Several factors explain these and similar assessments. Speakers presided over floor activities, granting and denying recognition to colleagues and their contending views; through shrewd use of parliamentary procedure—and sometimes by sheer force of will—they could determine not only the course of current debate, but also precedents for the future. When ties occurred during teller votes, their ballots could break the deadlock; in the more common circumstance of close voice votes, their ears would judge which side had shouted louder.[3]

Off the floor a Speaker's hegemony was, if anything, even greater. From 1858 until the overthrow of "Czar" Joseph Cannon in 1911, he served concurrently as chairman of the potent Rules Committee, which had exclusive privilege, as Speaker Randall asserted, to "report at any time . . . as to the manner of conducting the business of the House."[4] This meant, among other things, authority over the order and content of the legislative calendars. But most important was the presiding officer's exclusive control over House appointments, especially to committees, where much of the real power over policy and distribution was routinely and decisively relegated.

The perquisites of the chair, both within and outside the chamber, remained constant regardless of who might be sitting in it. So it was always advantageous to those with business before the House to have access to its occupant—which is why his selection always involved the representatives of clienteles, as well as those elected at the polls. When the outcome was predetermined—when, for instance, a virtually unassailable incumbent was in place—the influence that could be exerted

---

3. See chap. 2, above, and DeAlva S. Alexander, *History and Procedure of the House of Representatives* (Boston, 1916), chaps. 4–5; Mary P. Follett, *The Speaker of the House of Representatives* (New York, 1896), chaps. 4–10; Albert V. House, "The Contributions of Samuel J. Randall to the Rules of the National House of Representatives," *APSR*, 29 (1935), 837–41.

4. McConachie, *Congressional Committees*, p. 195; Follett, *Speaker*, pp. 274–78; Lewis J. Lapham, "Party Leadership and the House Committee on Rules" (Ph.D. diss., Harvard University, 1953).

was minimal and was likely to have subsequent committee configurations as its real, if indirect, target. Even in that connection, however, lobbying was not generally too successful, as events surrounding James G. Blaine's third Speakership election, at the outset of the Forty-third Congress, reveal clearly and as we will see a bit later. But when there was competition for the gavel—a far commoner circumstance in the nineteenth century—the result was greater fluidity and greater opportunity for aggressive participation by outsiders. Three episodes of the 1870s, all involving Samuel J. Randall of Pennsylvania, illustrate this: his unsuccessful battle with Michael C. Kerr (D-Ind.) in 1875, his assumption of the office upon the Hoosier's death just nine months later, and his victorious struggle for a full term at the helm in 1877. A close look at what happened, especially in 1875, is highly instructive as to the "whys and hows" of lobbyists' roles in setting up House—in selecting the hands into which power would fall and the ends to which that power could be used.[5]

Elections in 1874 had resulted in the first non-Republican-controlled House since 1859. The overriding issues had been corruption and Reconstruction, and popular disillusionment with these two phases of so-called "Grantism" was a primary factor in Republican defeat. Democracy's success had implications both for legislative policy and for presidential politics two years hence. In neither case could a prediction be made with any certainty; the programmatic cast of Gilded Age parties was far from clearly drawn, and both the G.O.P. and its opposition contained diverse candidates with aspirations to direct the course of history. No wonder, then, that avid partisans and public alike were deeply interested in the outcome of the congressional caucuses, scheduled for early December 1875. Whatever else ensued, the result would be a Speaker whose identity would be scrutinized for clues to Democrats' probable agenda and their centennial year strategy.[6]

5. Some earlier versions of the analysis that follows include more extensive references and notes. See Margaret Susan Thompson, "The 'Spider Web': Congress and Lobbying in the Age of Grant" (Ph.D. diss., University of Wisconsin–Madison, 1979), chap. 7; "Priorities and Legislative Politics: Agenda-Setting in the Reconstruction Congress," unpublished paper presented before the Organization of American Historians, Boston, 1975; "Outsiders on the Inside Track." The first of these three episodes is also discussed in Albert V. House, "The Speakership Contest of 1875: Democratic Response to Power," *JAH*, 52 (1965), 252–74. House's perspective and several of his conclusions differ from those here.

6. A. V. House, "Speakership Contest," 253–54; Follett, *Speaker*, pp. 109–10; M. C. Kerr to J. G. Blaine, 21 Nov. 1874, and Robert Schenck to Blaine, 18 Dec. 1874, James G. Blaine Papers, L.C.; Washington Townsend to George F. Hoar, 6 Nov. 1875, George F. Hoar Papers, Massachusetts Historical Society, Boston; on parties, chap. 2, above.

From the outset, the new majority suffered no shortage of hopefuls. New York alone produced two: Samuel S. Cox and Fernando Wood. Cox, a former journalist and a Representative from Ohio during the 1850s and 1860s, had been gerrymandered out of his district and had moved to Gotham, where he quickly aligned himself with the city's genteel "Swallowtail" Democracy. Its support helped return him to the House in 1869, and, except for a brief stint as Cleveland's Minister to Turkey, he would remain a Representative until his death in 1889. Personally popular with members on both sides of the aisle, Cox was an able parliamentarian, and consistent opposition to jobbery, including the 1873 Salary Grab, was one of his biggest assets. But Cox suffered from three handicaps. First, he was too overtly eager for the honor of the Chair at a time when political etiquette demanded a facade of reserve, no matter how ardent or justifiable one's ambition might be. Second, despite his intelligence and know-how, Cox's ebullient good nature and witty speeches gave him a reputation for frivolity and engendered suspicion that he was basically a lightweight. Thus, a minority member of a panel Cox chaired once confided to a colleague: "As I am on his committee I will hear some good jokes if I do not learn a great deal of finance from 'his Presidency.' "[7]

Third, Cox could not secure the united support of his own delegation. To begin with, there was his persistent opposition to Governor Samuel J. Tilden's presidential aspirations, which eventually would lead to Cox's estrangement from the Swallowtails, including New York *World* editor and Tilden intimate Manton Marble.[8] And then there was the matter of Fernando Wood, who also wanted to be Speaker. Wood, former mayor of New York and a ten-year House veteran, would continue to serve in the House until his death in 1881. He had been the Democratic caucus's nominee for the Chair in 1873 and, largely thanks to that, had been appointed by Blaine to a Ways & Means vacancy that Cox had also desired. Wood was a man of unquestioned ability and was

7. Basic data on Cox from *BDAC*, pp. 745–46. David Lindsey, *"Sunset" Cox: Irrepressible Democrat* (Detroit, 1959); George T. McJimsey, *Genteel Partisan: Manton Marble, 1834–1917* (Ames, Iowa, 1971), pp. 108–10; Henry Watterson, *History of the Manhattan Club* (New York, 1915), chap. 1; Cox to Marble, 12 Nov. 1874, 27 May 1875, Marble Papers; Samuel J. Randall to Chauncey F. Black, 15 Sept. 1876, Black Family Papers, L.C.; Washington Townsend to George F. Hoar, 23 Dec. 1875, Hoar Papers.

8. S. S. Cox to Manton Marble, 27 May 1875, Marble Papers; Joseph F. Wall, *Henry Watterson, Reconstructed Rebel* (New York, 1956), pp. 131–32; speeches by Amos J. Cummings (D-N.Y.) and James O'Donnell (R-Mich.) in *Memorial Addresses on the Life and Character of Samuel Sullivan Cox, a Representative from New York* (Washington, 1890), pp. 21, 139.

Speaker Michael C. Kerr, Democrat, Indiana. Courtesy Library of Congress, Division of Prints and Photographs.

among his party's most astute floor leaders. Still, his early (albeit terminated) involvement with Tammany—especially in light of recent exposures of fraud in the administration of Boss William Tweed—and public awareness of his "Copperheadism" during the War left him with what journalist Ben: Perley Poore called an "unsavory reputation."[9] Given his party's desperate desire to bury the bloody shirt and to assert itself as a clean alternative to the "Grantism" of the G.O.P., the odds against him were overwhelming.

The two New Yorkers were probably the strongest contenders among the long-shot candidates, a group that also included Ohio's Henry Banning and Milton Sayler, Indiana's William S. Holman, and even, in the minds of some, former Vice-President of the Confederacy Alexander Stephens. None could himself be chosen, although several had sufficient leverage to help determine the eventual victor.[10] But any realistic assessment of the situation revealed only two men who would be considered seriously: Michael C. Kerr of Indiana and Pennsylvania's Samuel J. Randall.

Although Kerr was a westerner, he was "as firm in his belief in the moral and economic virtues of hard money as the veriest Bourbon" and more clearly reflected the views of eastern Swallowtail Democracy than his Pennsylvania rival; according to a letter he wrote in 1874, it was his desire to effect monetary policy and to promote free trade that persuaded him to run for the Speakership. Kerr defended these positions with an "inflexible purpose. . . . His was truly a firmness that would have led him to a martyr's stake." Indeed, inflexibility was easily the most notable dimension of his character—when he died, eulogists would recall his "rigid exterior," "austerity," and lack of wit or humor. One admirer would describe him as "cold, reserved, and unsympathetic," while another saw him as "a man apparently so uncongenial and cold. . . . Reason and conscience were his religion."[11]

9. Basic data on Wood from *BDAC*, p. 1843. Samuel Augustus Pleasants, *Fernando Wood of New York* (New York, 1948); *DAB*, 20:456–57; *Nat. Cyc.*, 3:207–8; Ben: Perley Poore, *Perley's Reminiscences of Sixty Years in the National Metropolis*, 2 vols. (Philadelphia, 1886–87), 2:214; S. S. Cox to J. G. Blaine, 5 Nov. 1873, Wood to Blaine, 11 Nov. 1873, and Blaine to Cox, Dec. 1873 (draft), Blaine Papers.

10. A. V. House, "Speakership Contest," 255–56.

11. William G. Carlton, "The Money Question in Indiana Politics, 1865–1890," *Indiana Mag. of Hist.*, 42 (1946), 123–24; A. V. House, "Speakership Contest," 257; M. C. Kerr to Manton Marble, 4 Dec. 1874, Marble Papers; remarks by William S. Haymond (D-Ind.), J. Proctor Knott (R-Ky.), S. S. Cox (D-N.Y.), and James Monroe (R-Ohio) in *Memorial Addresses on the Life and Character of Michael Crawford Kerr (Speaker of the House of Representatives of the United States). . . .* (Washington, 1877), pp. 15, 18, 31, 37, 55 [hereafter, *Kerr Eulogies*].

Yet in the context of the times, these traits actually were viewed as points in Kerr's favor; when corruption was perceived as running rampant, it was advantageous to be seen as "unpolitical." Hence, when Pennsylvania's William D. Kelley said of Kerr that "he seemed to me to have little special fitness for public life," he meant it as a compliment. The Hoosier's clean image also was enhanced by his consistent record of hostility to jobbery, subsidies, land grants, and other programs allegedly beneficial to so-called special interests.[12]

A final point in Kerr's favor was his reputation as an outspoken and sincere friend of the South. Prior to his defeat in the 1872 election, he had been one of the most outspoken northern critics of Republican Reconstruction, basing his position both on a desire to "heal the wounds of war" and on a strong commitment to states' rights, for which his expertise as a constitutional lawyer enabled him to argue quite effectively. As a contender for the leadership of a majority that would contain at least forty-six Confederate veterans, comprising 53 percent of Southern caucus members and 27 percent of the total, this record would surely be an asset.[13]

On the other hand, two factors were potentially detrimental to his candidacy. First, he had been absent from the Forty-third House, and thus removed from the Capitol and national spotlight for the two years preceding the Speakership contest. Second, and potentially more damaging, was the question of his health. Kerr suffered from an acute case of consumption, of which his caucus colleagues were aware, that left him weak and often entirely incapacitated.[14] The disease even-

12. *Kerr Eulogies*, p. 10, also pp. 7, 14, 26, 29, 32, 37; William Wesley Woollen, "Michael Crawford Kerr," in *Biographical and Historical Sketches of Early Indiana* (Indianapolis, 1883), p. 343.

13. In 1872 Kerr ran for Representative at large, instead of from his old district (where he ran again in 1874): *Kerr Eulogies*, p. 5. On southern sympathies, see Albert V. House, "Northern Congressional Democrats as Defenders of the South during Reconstruction," *J. of Southern Hist.*, 6 (1940), 46–71; Matilda Gresham, *Life of Walter Quintin Gresham, 1832–1895*, 2 vols. (Chicago, 1919), 1:333–38, 432–33; "Record of the Democratic Speaker," *The Republic*, 6 (1876), 104–17; Beverley Tucker to Samuel J. Randall, 1 and 16 Apr., 3 May, 7 July 1875, Samuel J. Randall Papers, Van Pelt Library, University of Pennsylvania. Figures on Confederate Army veterans from data in *BDAC;* see also "Confederate Leaders in the Forty-Fourth Congress," *The Republic*, 6 (1876), 252–59; on Kerr as constitutional lawyer, see *The Diary of James A. Garfield*, ed. Harry James Brown and F. D. Williams, 4 vols. (East Lansing, 1967–81), 3:14, 15.

14. On Kerr's illness and his and his colleagues' knowledge of it, see *Kerr Eulogies*, esp. pp. 10, 15, 23–24, 13; Woollen, "Kerr," pp. 336–37. At least one member eventually voted for Randall largely because of Kerr's health: "Kerr is a man whose appearance voice &c show he is unable to discharge its duties. He looks to me, like a dying man that is—like one in whom consumption had fixed its grasp—and he cannot control this House." John Randolph Tucker (D-Va.) to Henry St. George Tucker, 7 Dec. 1875, Tucker Family Papers, Southern History Collection, University of North Carolina Library, Chapel Hill.

tually would kill him, in August 1876—and so would give Kerr the dubious distinction of being the first Speaker to die in office.

Samuel Randall, in contrast, was vigorous, at the peak of his capacities, and at the halfway point of what would be a practically unprecedented, uninterrupted twenty-seven year House career. Insiders had long regarded him as a strongman, but the Pennsylvanian first came into the public eye during the waning hours of the Forty-third Congress, when he led Democracy's successful fights to emasculate the Civil Rights Act and to defeat a force bill introduced by John Coburn (R-Ind.). This performance caused men like New York *Sun* editor Charles A. Dana, who already had admitted a private preference for Kerr, to express appreciation for the "extraordinary services [Randall] rendered at the end of the recent session," and to say he "was astonished at as well as gratified by the talent and capacity for leadership which he then evinced." The same efforts, and his promotion of amnesty for former Rebels, also resulted in his recognition as a "true friend of the South and its people"; as William H. Blount (D-Ga.) would recall in 1890: "The force bill never became a law, the civil rights was declared unconstitutional by the Supreme Court, the sky brightened in the Southern land, and henceforward the name of SAMUEL J. RANDALL was revered and loved at her every hearthstone."[15]

But if Randall and Kerr held similar views on Southern affairs, they were less compatible in other areas. Unlike the firmly monometalist Hoosier, the Pennsylvanian seemed to care little about currency; his ideas on specie could only be described as hazy. He did believe strongly in retrenchment, however, that Gilded Age catch-all for reduction of government spending. And he had a record of being "anti-bank," although it was probably more reflective of his working-class Philadelphia constituency and his outspoken Jacksonian father than of any independent thinking on the subject.[16] His most developed economic principle, and his most decided dispute with Kerr, was over the matter

15. Basic data on Randall from *BDAC*, pp. 1496–97. A. V. House, "Northern Congressional Democrats"; James G. Blaine, *Twenty Years in Congress: From Lincoln to Garfield*, 2 vols. (Norwich, Conn., 1886), 2:554–55; James Ford Rhodes, *History of the United States from the Compromise of 1850 to the Final Restoration of Home Rule at the South in 1877*, 7 vols. (New York, 1906), 7:177–78; Charles A. Dana to Chauncey F. Black, 23 Mar. 1875, Black Papers; remarks by W. McAdoo (D-N.J.) and Blount in *Memorial Addresses on the Life and Character of Samuel Jackson Randall, a Representative from Pennsylvania* (Washington, 1891), pp. 103, 46, also pp. 27, 61–63, 74, 107 [hereafter, *Randall Eulogies*]; Albert V. House, "The Political Career of Samuel Jackson Randall" (Ph.D. diss., University of Wisconsin –Madison, 1934), p. 58.

16. Albert V. House, "Men, Morals, and Manipulation in the Pennsylvania Democracy of 1875," *Pennsylvania History*, 23 (1956), 262, and "Randall," p. 63; *Randall Eulogies*, pp. 52, 1–2.

S₁ ᵢker Samuel J. Randall, Democrat, Pennsylvania. Courtesy Library of Congress, Division of Prints and Photographs.

of tariffs. Randall espoused a protectionism on which he was "immov-able"; as he once said in debate: "I am an American, and therefore I am a protectionist."[17] These positions enabled him to work congenially on revenue and trade policy with many Half-Breeds in the G.O.P. Yet that, despite his effective performance as floor leader, created some doubt about his ability to function as a sufficiently partisan Speaker, should he be elected.[18]

Concerning that amorphous but politically sensitive matter, "re-form," the Keystone Stater's record was good, if more ambiguous than that of his most formidable challenger. The lack of clarity was due principally to the temper of the times—in an age when "politician" was almost as epithetic as "lobbyist," Randall was an unabashed public man. It was alleged—and convincingly, to those who wanted to be con-vinced—that the congressman enjoyed a fair degree of intimacy with certain "gentlemen of the lobby"; indeed, he made no secret of his friendship with Sam Ward, while his brother Robert was a sometime partner of the "King of the Lobby" and broker for Texas & Pacific Railroad financiers. Yet Randall could say truthfully to a confidant in 1875 that "I know of no public act of mine which I fear to have fully ventilated nor is there such," and a supporter of his 1874 House race could assert: "It was well known . . . that he would not have money raised in his behalf. He said he wished to return to Congress free, not hampered, as he has."[19] Moreover, he had spent the summer of 1875 in an indisputably clean endeavor: an attack upon and victory over the

17. On "immovability," see remarks by W. S. Holman (D-Ind.), Randall's floor state-ment quoted by L. E. McComas (R-Md.), in *Randall Eulogies*, pp. 110–11, 51 (see also pp. 1–17, 69, 83); Frank B. Evans, *Pennsylvania Politics, 1872–1877: A Study in Political Leadership* (Harrisburg, 1966), pp. 275, 327–28.

18. A. V. House, "Randall," p. 12; undated clipping (eulogy) from the *Nation*, with handwritten concurring comments by J. Randolph Tucker on Randall's "false" tariff views, in Scrapbook No. 9, Tucker Family Papers; see also two letters from Blaine to Randall: (1) "I see they have tried to hurt you by alleging that the repub. prefer you—that wont work. Hope to see you Saturday next, but probably it is as well not to have it known that I am visiting you" (28 Nov. 1875); (2) "If we would elect a Republican I should be glad—but as we cannot I hope you will get it. Perhaps there is no way I can aid you except by good wishes—but I shall not harm you by advocacy" (8 Oct. 1877); Randall Papers. See also *Garfield Diary*, 3:534.

19. Follett, *Speaker*, p. 111; Alexander, *History*, pp. 69–70; A. V. House, "Speakership Contest," p. 259; but see also A. V. House, "Randall," p. 65; Ward to Randall, 29 Jan. and 5 Dec. 1875, Randall Papers. Information on Robert Randall from a clipping (source unknown) entitled "Mr. Randall's Brother," in Fernando Wood to Randall, 1 Oct. 1877, Randall Papers; and Virginia H. Taylor, *The Franco-Texan Land Company* (Austin, 1969), p. 92; Randall to C. F. Black, 25 Sept. 1875, Sally Jones to Charles A. Dana, 30 Nov. 1875, Black Papers.

potent "Treasury Ring," headed by U.S. Senator William A. Wallace and backed by moguls like Jay Gould, which long had controlled his state's Democratic politics; although the *Sun*'s Dana might express "vague rumblings" of concern about the Pennsylvanian's probity, even he had to praise that tour de force.[20]

On the other hand, Randall suffered from his association with the 1873 Salary Grab, which he not only voted for and accepted the benefits of, but also defended; as he said in the House: "I have declared to the country and to my constituents that I believed I have earned $7,500 a year since I have been in this Congress, and that I could not live here for less with my family with any sort of decency." This episode was rehashed relentlessly in newspapers hostile to Randall's candidacy, and, just before the 1875 caucus, the New York *Times* reported that some of his colleagues, otherwise favorably disposed, would oppose him because "we cannot afford to encounter the constant newspaper cry about this salary business [or] to be continually on the defensive because of the Speaker we elect."[21]

Still, the Grab, albeit controversial, was not illegal—and Randall was hardly alone in the stand he took. And apart from the routinely unsubstantiated mudslinging that most officeholders have to endure, his name was linked specifically with impropriety only once, in 1879, long after events recounted here, and ended with his complete exoneration. This was a record that few of his equally prominent contemporaries, including Kerr, were able to surpass. Thus, one eulogist wrote, "He was . . . above reproach. He lived through the days of jobbery and corruption; he came out with garments pure and spotless." Richard Vaux, who replaced him in the House, stated that "schemes, jobs, covert efforts to secure public plunder by legislation, were neither countenanced nor encouraged. . . . His integrity was one of the powers that gave him his influence." Indeed, Vaux capped his assessment conclusively by declaring that Randall, without a doubt, was "the enemy of the lobbyist."[22]

20. A. V. House, "Men, Morals, and Manipulation," esp. pp. 260, 263; Evans, *Pennsylvania Politics*, chap. 6.

21. *Cong. Globe*, 42d Cong., 3d sess., p. 2102; *Times* quoted in A. V. House, "Randall," p. 63. Kerr accepted the pay raise and then begged his friends to tell him what to do in the face of criticism; various New York Swallowtails offered to loan him $2000 if he repaid the bonus (which he did in late May 1877); Ivory Chamberlain to Marble, Apr. 1873 (enclosing Kerr to J. S. Moore, 18 Apr. 1873), and Kerr to Marble, 7 July 1873, Marble Papers, A. V. House, "Speakership Contest," p. 258.

22. The Randall incident is summarized in Follett, *Speaker*, p. 111; see also *Hse. Jnl.* 45th Cong., 3d sess., pp. 541, 671–74. In 1876 Kerr was exonerated of allegedly having accepted a $500 bribe in 1866 to secure an army appointment; *Hse. Jnl.*, 44th Cong., 1st sess., pp. 1098–1100; see also *Kerr Eulogies*, pp. 7, 41–43; *Randall Eulogies*, pp. 29, 38, 53.

Currency, tariffs, Southern policy, and corruption: these were the main issues that would shape the 1875 contest. On only one, tariffs, did Kerr and Randall offer sharply contrasting records, which would have some small bearing on the outcome. But protectionism was not so crucial then as it would become in the following decade, and, in any event, a free trade stance was not yet part of the litmus test for Democratic orthodoxy.[23] Meanwhile, the campaign would center on those other matters where distinctions were relatively blurred, and on the candidates' personalities—never a negligible factor in politics, and certainly not so in 1875. Indeed, given the similarities in substance between the Hoosier and the Pennsylvanian, image and style, both apparent and actual, turned out to be extremely important. At the very least, they explain the coalition of outsiders that developed behind Kerr (and, implicitly, against Randall), as well as the strategies both sides employed in attempting to woo members of the caucus.

Wooing members was no simple task, especially before the Forty-fourth Congress. For of the 173 Democrats who would convene in Washington on December 6, two-thirds would be Capitol novices. Only forty-nine could have known Randall during previous terms in the House, and a mere sixteen had served with Kerr (who, again, had been absent from the Forty-third). Both hopefuls, then, were strangers to the vast majority of participants, who in turn had to familiarize themselves with the leaders before deciding which one to back. The result was intensive lobbying in two directions—from Kerr and Randall to their future colleagues, and back again—so that whoever was chosen would have the information necessary to construct his committees. This task would devolve immediately upon the victor, so both of the contestants had to prepare for that contingency at the same time that they were campaigning for office.[24] Not surprisingly, therefore, agitation in behalf of the favorites began almost immediately after election day. By late November 1874 both Kerr and Randall, as well as some of the long shots, had support teams operating around the country. And their efforts—reinforced by public and private rumors, intelligence-gathering, and bargains—would persist unabated until Congress convened thirteen months later.[25]

23. A. V. House, "Speakership Contest," p. 259, and "Randall," p. 63; chap 2, above.

24. Figures calculated from data in *BDAC* and *Hse. Jnl.*, 44th Cong., 1st sess., pp. 9–10; Kerr announced his appointments on 20 Dec. just two weeks after being elected Speaker: *Hse. Jnl.*, 44th Cong., 1st sess., pp. 84–89.

25. Randall's campaign is documented extensively (over 100 letters) in the Randall Papers. Kerr's activities are more difficult to trace, as there is no extant collection of Kerr Papers and virtually no research has been done on him (he is not, for example, even

The front-runners attracted most attention, of course, and each was aided in his cause by persons of national prominence, as well as those known mainly to political insiders. Randall's team was headed by his close friend Chauncey F. Black of York, a journalist to whom Dana once offered the editorship of the *Sun* and who later would be Pennsylvania's lieutenant governor. Also involved was Chauncey's father, former U.S. attorney general and secretary of state Jeremiah S. Black, whose extensive acquaintance with leading Southerners was especially appreciated by the candidate. Aiding the Blacks were several journalists and Keystone State luminaries who had helped in the Treasury Ring affair: W. B. Reed and J. W. Cooper of the New York *World* and A. M. Gibson of the *Sun*, former Philadelphia mayor Richard Vaux, former U.S. senator Charles Buckalew, and the son and namesake of former vice-president George M. Dallas. Finally, Randall had the somewhat mixed blessing of the self-starting Virginia enthusiast Beverley Tucker, brother of new Representative John Randolph Tucker and son of Henry St. George Tucker: one of the less distinguished hybrids from several of the Old Dominion's most distinguished family trees, and a sometime lobbyist for the Texas Pacific Railroad who proclaimed himself Sam's "Southern director." Thanks to him, and despite a consistent record of anti-T&P behavior, Randall would be embarrassed by and would suffer tremendously from allegations that he was the "Railroad's man."[26]

---

included in the *DAB*). The largest concentration of source materials is in the Marble Papers, which include a score or so of Kerr letters from 1875; Kerr's activities are also discussed by other Marble correspondents, notably Sidney Webster and David Wells; additional background is in Kerr to Samuel L. M. Barlow, 15 Sept. 1871, 19 Jan. 1872, and 11 Apr. 1873, Samuel L. M. Barlow Papers, Henry E. Huntington Library, San Marino, California. Organizational activities by Cox documented in Cox to Marble, 12 Nov. and 31[?] Dec. 1874, 27 May 1875, Marble Papers, and Cox to Sen. Thomas F. Bayard (D-Del.), 20 Nov. 1874, Thomas F. Bayard Papers, L.C.

26. Randall to C. F. Black, 17, 18, 24 Aug. 1875, Chauncey to Jeremiah S. Black, 11 July 1875, Black Papers; numerous letters from all other Randall team members in the Randall Papers. Tucker volunteered his services to Randall on 8 Jan. 1875; letters to Randall of 9 Mar. and 1 Apr. 1875 document Scott's dropping him from the T&P payroll (Randall Papers). House regarded Tucker as helpful to Randall ("Speakership Contest," pp. 262–63), but there is evidence to the contrary. Tucker's advocacy did not even sway his own brother: John Randolph Tucker voted for Randall at the last minute only because of fear for Kerr's health; Beverley Tucker to Randall, 1 and 16 Apr. 1875, Randall Papers; J. R. Tucker to Henry St. George Tucker, 7 Dec. 1875, and John L. Marye to J. R. Tucker, 16 Dec. 1874 (see also Beverley Tucker to J. R. Tucker, 4 Sept. 1877), Tucker Papers. Furthermore, Tucker's support of Randall seems to provide the best basis for the rumor that Randall was "Scott's man"—a charge expressed explicitly in C. Vann Woodward, *Reunion and Reaction: The Compromise of 1877 and the End of Reconstruction* (1951; Garden

Given Kerr's currency and tarriff positions, it was inevitable that he would be favored by the "genteel partisans" of Swallowtail and Bourbon Democracy. Many of these resided in New York, where they comprised the exclusive Manhattan Club; among its members who worked actively for Kerr were the *World's* Manton Marble, corporate magnates like Sidney Webster and Samuel L. M. Barlow, and ex–Democratic national party chairman and investment banker August Belmont. Also in the Hoosier's camp were champions of free trade like David Wells and J. S. Moore. And so was Charles Dana of the New York *Sun,* although his concomitant respect for Randall inhibited him from as great a devotion to Kerr's cause as the others entertained.[27]

Both teams conducted tactically similar campaigns, consisting of voluminous correspondence, extensive travel, manufactured manifestations of "grass-roots" enthusiasm, and so on—aimed at attracting publicity for the officially uninvolved candidates and winning caucus support for their respective aspirations. And both were successful in their groundwork, at least to the extent that, together, they preempted the field. By the time Congress convened, only the eternally optimistic "Sunset" Cox harbored any illusions that someone other than Kerr or Randall might be chosen. Yet even on the eve of balloting, almost nobody was rash enough to predict the outcome; each side claimed publicly that it had the votes, but privately admitted it was too close to call.

Given the far from antithetical records and espoused policy positions of the two front-runners, it is not entirely frivolous to wonder just what the fuss was all about. Was power or ambition the key issue in 1874— and, if so, whose; was it mainly a question of personalities? To put it another way, why did the race inspire the intense commitments and efforts of so many lobbyists? Did the outcome really matter, in substantive terms? Would it make any difference to the course of Congressional Government—or anything else?

City, N.Y., 1956), pp. 102–3, and reiterated (citing Woodward as source) in subsequent scholarship: e.g., Terry L. Seip, *The South Returns to Congress: Men, Economic Measures, and Intersectional Relationships, 1868–1879* (Baton Rouge, 1983), pp. 283–84; see further discussion of this below.

27. McJimsey, *Genteel Partisan,* pp. 172–74; David Earl Robbins, "The Congressional Career of William Ralls Morrison" (Ph.D. diss., University of Illinois–Champaign-Urbana, 1963), p. 56; A. V. House, "Speakership Contest," p. 269; M. C. Kerr to J. S. Moore, 17 Nov. 1874, August Belmont to Marble, c. 1 Feb. 1875, David Wells to Marble, 6 Feb., 27 Sept., 18 Oct., 24 Nov. 1875, and Thomas Holland to Marble, 27 Sept. 1875, Marble Papers; Randall to C. F. Black, 27 Nov. 1875, Black Papers.

The outcome did matter, in ways demonstrable by intent, if not implementation. Kerr, the winner in 1875, lived for just nine months after the caucus, but actively wielded the gavel even more briefly; by March 1876, he was spending most of his time at Rockbridge Alum Springs, Virginia (where he would die), and various colleagues presided in rotation over deliberations on the floor. Still, the tubercular Hoosier managed to stay in town long enough to form committees that clearly reflected his—or his backers'—policy objectives. Furthermore, he was succeeded by Randall, his erstwhile rival, who thus could make assignments of his own. And he did so in a House (the Forty-fifth) that, unlike almost all in contemporary memory, contained a nonfreshman majority. Both men, therefore, had unusually similar raw material to work with, which enhances the validity of comparisons between them, as does the substantial number of key members whom Randall could either keep where Kerr had put them or replace with men of his own. Comparison reveals that substantive differences, however limited, between the two leaders were reflected in their decisions. It also illuminates the agenda(s), both hidden and openly espoused, of Kerr's main backers: the rationales behind their efforts toward getting him elected, at least some of which warrant a bit of scrutiny.

Kerr's most aggressive supporter was Manton Marble, whose behavior—before, during, and after the Speakership contest—and motives, in all their complexity, point to the competition's high stakes. Just forty years old in 1874, this multitalented man was one of the leading personages of his time: editor and publisher of the New York *World,* perhaps Democracy's foremost daily; confidant of and mentor to Samuel J. Tilden; co-founder of the Manhattan Club, Swallowtail Gotham's answer to the Republican Union League; genteel literary critic; scribbler of racy limericks; and internationally recognized authority on hard currency and free trade. Not one to run for office himself, Marble preferred instead to determine and dominate those who did—a strategy that served him remarkably well.[28] Indeed, had Tilden's claim to the presidency been upheld, and had Kerr lived to stay at the House's helm, by 1877 Marble arguably would have been the single most powerful figure in Washington. He appreciated and could practically taste such prospective hegemony as the Forty-fourth Congress drew near, which explains a good part of his year-long devotion to the cause of a tubercular Hoosier, whose success would set strong

28. General background on Marble is in McJimsey, *Genteel Partisan,* and in the Marble Papers (in which limericks are found); see also Watterson, *Manhattan Club.*

Manton Marble, Editor, New York *World*. From *Harper's Weekly*, volume 14.

philosophical precedent for a national nominee of Tilden's stripe. But other factors, both personal and political, were at play here, too, not least of which was Marble's continued control of the *World*. The editor's ability to maintain that control depended on a number of contingencies, among them a cooperative—or malleable—man at the congressional podium, for reasons that will become apparent shortly. At any rate, the ailing, naive, and vulnerable Kerr was ideally suited to those purposes. For if he appeared to be endowed with "a firmness that would have led him to a martyr's stake" over matters of principle, he also could be relied on to beg "trusted friends" for guidance over seemingly less fundamental questions. Thus, while it was important that the Indianan, like Tilden, shared most of his best benefactor's views, especially in the realm of economics, his candidacy's attractiveness was enhanced considerably by the opportunities it offered for manipulation.[29]

Marble was too shrewd to underestimate the connection between his own clout and his role at the *World*. That paper, however, even if secure in its preeminence as a party organ, was constantly in danger of going under, despite repeated infusions of funds from the likes of Tilden and S. L. M. Barlow. By 1875 its owner-editor was desperate, and, after a final futile appeal to August Belmont and one more $7000 bailout from the governor, started searching for a buyer. Eventually he found one in fellow-Swallowtail William Henry Hurlbert. But Hurlbert's principal associate in the venture was railroad magnate Thomas A. Scott, president of the Pennsylvania and (more pertinent) of the Texas & Pacific, which was in the middle of a decade-long—and ultimately unsuccessful—effort to obtain congressional subsidy. According to the arrangement Marble reached with his purchasers, he was to receive $100,000 in cash and $150,000 in railroad bonds. But the contract also stipulated that Scott would pay an additional $100,000 "within thirty days after the adoption by the Congress of the United States of any bill or bills securing the endorsement by the United States Government of the Texas Pacific R.R. . . . or any other practical guaranty in subsidy to said road."[30] Naturally, this contingency was attractive, but such legisla-

---

29. *Kerr Eulogies*, p. 55; on Marble's craving for power, see McJimsey, *Genteel Partisan;* and Wall, *Henry Watterson*, p. 136.

30. McJimsey, *Genteel Partisan*, pp. 180–83; Alexander C. Flick, *Samuel Jones Tilden: A Study in Political Sagacity* (New York, 1939), pp. 142, 175; August Belmont to Marble, 30 June and 11 Sept. 1875, Marble to Belmont, 30 June and 11 Sept. 1875, N. D. Bangs to Marble, 16 July 1875, Marble to Sidney Webster, 21 Apr. 1876, Scott to Hurlbert, 12 and 19 Feb. 1876, Hurlbert to Marble, 15, 16, 17, 18 Feb., 8 Mar., 19 Apr. 1876, and contract details in undated memo by Hurlbert (with additions by Barlow), Marble Papers.

tion required approval by the House. And if the House were led by someone under Marble's control, its chances not only of securing a place on the floor agenda but also of obtaining a favorable report from a sympathetically constructed Pacific Railroads Committee would doubtless be enhanced considerably.

The T&P's subsidy was one of the most complex, explosive, and pivotal issues of the 1875 Speakership race.[31] On the one hand, both Kerr and Randall were firmly on record as opposing jobbery, a position favored, at least in principle, by most Democrats outside the former Confederacy. On the other hand, most Southerners elected to the Forty-fourth favored government aid to the Texas Pacific; to them, it was an internal improvement necessitated by the exigencies of the region's post–Civil War economic recovery. For much of the South, therefore—from which there were eighty-six Democrats, or 48.3 percent of the caucus—a would-be Speaker's sympathies required stronger proof than his ability to whistle Dixie. In practical terms, the T&P mattered more than tarrifs, currency, or abstract reformism to most of the Southern members.[32]

At least one of Sam Randall's supporters was painfully aware of this. Virginia's Beverley Tucker, the sometime lobbyist for Scott's proposed western line who wanted Randall to be Speaker in spite of his anti-subsidy position, wrote frequently to his standard-bearer about how that attitude was hurting his prospects for leadership. Referring to a roll call from the preceding session, he said that members from the Old Confederacy suspected that "the vote you gave *against* even considering the Texas Pacific Railway bill, may be an indication of your uncompromising opposition, not only to *it,* but to all other measures for the promotion of the *material* prosperity of the South & South West." They feared, he repeated, "that such opposition, may endanger, if you are elected Speaker, the composition of committees pronouncedly op-

31. There is no history specifically of the Texas & Pacific, but see Stuart Daggett, *Chapters on the History of the Southern Pacific* (1922; New York, 1966), chap. 12; Lewis Lesley, "A Southern Transcontinental Railroad into California: Texas and Pacific vs. Southern Pacific, 1865–1885," *Pacific Hist. Rev.,* 5 (1936), 52–60; Robert E. Riegel, *The Story of the Western Railroads* (New York, 1926), chaps. 8, 12; *Letters from Collis P. Huntington to Mark Hopkins, Leland Stanford, Charles Crocker and D. D. Colton,* 3 vols. (New York, 1894), vol. 3 (privately printed; located at the Huntington Library); *Hse. Rpts.,* 44th Cong., 2d sess., No. 139, and 45th Cong., 2d sess., No. 619; Seip, *South Returns to Congress,* chap. 7; and relevant manuscript collections, especially William E. Chandler Papers, L.C., and Grenville M. Dodge Papers, Iowa State Dept. of History & Archives, Des Moines.

32. A. V. House, "Speakership Contest," and "Northern Congressional Democrats"; Seip, *South Returns to Congress,* esp. chap. 7.

Thomas A. Scott, President, Texas & Pacific Railroad. Courtesy Library of Congress, Division of Prints and Photographs.

posed to the granting of Govt. Aid to some of these measures, to which *every newly elected* member feels himself committed." Further, he complained, Thomas A. Scott was so angry at Randall that he dropped Tucker from his payroll in retaliation for Tucker's efforts on the Pennsylvanian's behalf.[33]

It would be inaccurate to portray Kerr as a willing instrument of the Texas Pacific interests; his frequent, explicit, and apparently sincere pronouncements against "jobbery" preclude that. Yet regardless of some historians' assertions to the contrary, it is clear that the Indianan was this Road's favored candidate, that officials of other lines also saw him as better disposed toward their industry, and that, within the South, he was promoted and perceived as more sympathetic to subsidy.[34] It is equally true, however, that allegations of a Scott preference for Randall appeared in the Northern press during the week before Congress opened, originating in the *World* and New York *Sun*.[35] Marble, of course—in the preliminary stages of negotiating to sell his paper—was largely responsible for that last-minute media blitz.

Briefly, then, the pro-Kerr campaign motives can be summarized as follows. While the orchestrators, mainly Swallowtails from New York's Manhattan Club and most notably Manton Marble, were deeply concerned about free trade and currency, they appreciated that emphasiz-

33. Tucker to Randall, 9 Mar. and 1 Apr. 1875, Randall Papers.

34. On presentation of Kerr, see various letters of Tucker to Randall, already cited, Randall Papers. On preference of Collis P. Huntington (president, Central and Southern Pacific Railroads) for Kerr and opposition to Randall, see Huntington to Mark Hopkins, 4 Dec. 1875; in *Letters from Collis P. Huntington*, 3:420. The historiographic consensus on Scott's alleged preference for Randall is traceable to Woodward: "In the race for speakership in December 1875, Scott had swung his support to Samuel J. Randall of Pennsylvania"; *Reunion and Reaction*, pp. 102–3. This assertion appears with no substantiation or documentation, but is followed by rather remarkable selective quotation to sustain the charge; Woodward gives part of Randall's cynical letter to Chauncey Black of 5 Dec. 1875 (quoted below and cited in n. 39)—but *without* the essential last sentence! Finally, this statement appears: "Actually [Randall] was known to oppose subsidies, and the South was doubtful of him. He was elected speaker on the opening of Congress in December 1876, after Kerr's death, but it is questionable that Scott expected any great advantage from Randall's speakership." Obviously none of this hangs together, but this nonetheless has been cited repeatedly and, exclusively in much subsequent scholarship to perpetuate the pro-Scott judgment of Randall: e.g., McJimsey, *Genteel Partisan*, p. 180; David Lavender, *The Great Persuader* [biography of C. P. Huntington] (New York, 1970), pp. 310–11. Most recently, Terry Seip comes to a similar conclusion, based partly on the false optimism in several of Tucker's letters to Randall and a few other data (such as newspaper commentaries) solely from the months *before* the contest, but also in large part on Woodward's incomplete quotation of the Black letter to Randall: *South Returns to Congress*, pp. 255, 283–84.

35. New York *World*, 1 Dec. 1875; New York *Sun*, 27 Nov. 1875.

ing these positions might alienate at least as many Democrats as it might win.[36] Consequently, while they did not ignore these subjects in appropriate quarters, they stressed their candidate's orthodoxy on the period's more fiery or emotional concerns—statesmanship and reformism, sympathy for the beleaguered South, anti-jobbery, and so on—as well as the groundwork such a paragon could lay in anticipation of 1876. The occasion did not, of course, require proof of their man's actual beliefs or intended behavior. His operatives simply had to present a case, regardless of accuracy, sufficient to persuade a caucus majority to go for him instead of Randall. It helped, too, that so few legislators knew the contenders personally; the parvenus in particular were fertile ground for the planting of unsubstantiated allegations.

Different arguments, moreover, could be used on different targets. Thus, Northerners heard mainly about Kerr's record of opposing subsidies, of his repudiation of the Salary Grab, and of the fact that he put "principle before physical comfort" by running for Speaker despite his frailty.[37] Among Southerners, meanwhile, it was quietly circulated, probably without the candidate's knowledge, that Kerr was willing to express friendship for Dixie in more than rhetorical terms: that he would be likelier than the more "political" Pennsylvanian to advance the cause of the Texas Pacific. Tom Scott himself assisted in this particular drive, most concretely during a "National Railroad Convention" that he staged in St. Louis less than two weeks before the opening of Congress—a thinly disguised promotional endeavor attended by several undecided legislators.[38]

Marble, Scott, and their cohorts clearly did their jobs well, for on December 6, 1875, the Forty-fourth Congress elected Michael C. Kerr as its Speaker. Randall certainly gave Kerr's political friends much of the credit for the outcome. He believed absolutely that the *World's* and *Sun's* last-minute allegations that he had "made a deal" with Scott, combined with their simultaneous endorsements of Kerr, cost him at least fifteen formerly pledged votes from New York, Ohio, and North Carolina (one of the few Southern states unaffected directly by the proposed railroad). On the other hand, he noted cynically, Kerr's strat-

36. Kerr to Marble, 28 Nov. 1875 (Marble Papers), acknowledges that his position, if publicized, would hurt him in the West; see also *Kerr Eulogies*, pp. 4–5, 26; Carlton, "Money Question in Indiana Politics," 123–34, and "Why Was the Democratic Party in Indiana a Radical Party, 1865–1890?" *Ind. Mag. of Hist.*, 42 (1946), 207–28.

37. But see n. 21, above, on Kerr's actual behavior during the Grab.

38. *Proceedings of the National Railroad Convention at St. Louis, Mo., November 23 and 24, 1875, In Regard to the Construction of the TEXAS AND PACIFIC RAILWAY. . . .* (St. Louis, 1875).

egists were equally successful in preventing the rumors from carrying weight with any members who did back the T&P. As he told Chauncey Black just after the caucus, "The charge that Scott wanted me—had its effect. The energy of his friendship is shown by the votes—of Louisiana—Tennessee & Missouri in our Caucus. The three States which have within their limits the three forks of the route—at Eastern End. In these—States—I received two votes. . . ."[39]

On the day after his elevation to the Speakership, Michael C. Kerr wrote Manton Marble: "[I] would exceedingly like to consult with you about many matters of public concern. But now, and specially, I want your advice about the fittest person for chairman of Ways & Means. Of course I cannot appoint Mr. Randall. Both Cox & Wood are anxious to get the place. You know them both and their qualifications. What do you advise? Can't you take an hour," he pleaded, "& write me many suggestions touching matters here? I will most gladly & thankfully receive any such suggestions from you. A thousand thanks," he concluded, "for the kindness of the World and for your personal kindnesses towards me." Subsequent correspondence shows that the editor went even further than his harassed petitioner requested. Within a few days he arrived in the capital, to be helpful—and heeded—in the entire process of constructing committees.[40]

The House had forty-seven standing panels at the time, and it would be impossible here to analyze them all specifically. Instead, we shall focus on those that related most directly to the issues in the campaign and those that most concerned the pro-Kerr lobbyists: Pacific Railroads, Banking & Currency, the several committees directly pertinent to Southern interests, and Ways & Means. Since Kerr started with the tariff committee, we shall, too; it merits attention both for its institutional significance and for what it demonstrated about Marble's influence. It was always, as one contemporary congressman remarked, extremely important, since "by courtesy the chairman . . . has been nominally the leader of the House" (a contention confirmed by the statistical analysis presented earlier).[41] But in 1875 choosing a chairman also had profound programmatic implications, especially since Kerr and Randall differed more on tariffs than on any other substantive issue. Further, the Speaker's decision bore directly on the upcoming presidential race, for a decidedly reductionist revenue panel,

39. Randall to Black, 5 Dec. 1875, Black Papers; *Hse. Jnl.*, 44th Cong., 1st sess., pp. 9–10.

40. Kerr to Marble, 7 and 13 Dec. 1875, Marble Papers.

41. *Randall Eulogies*, pp. 107–8; statistics in chap. 2, above.

particularly if it achieved some success in revising schedules, would surely help the chances of someone like Tilden.

Not surprisingly, speculation was rampant as to who would be named. Despite the evidence of Kerr's letter, Fernando Wood—a House party leader, but at least as ardent a protectionist as Randall—was never seriously in the running. Fellow New Yorker S. S. Cox, even though neither Kerr nor Marble wanted him, was a more likely candidate. One Washington observer even reported that "Sunset" was slated for the job; he shared the Speaker's free trade philosophy, after all, and the first ballot support he gave Kerr in the caucus provided the Hoosier's winning margin. Marble's biographer has suggested that a desire to prevent "dissension" within Empire State Democracy might have been decisive in confirming the editor's opposition; Cox's adamant hostility to Tilden, as well as the Wood rivalry, reinforce that assessment.[42]

Virtually no one at the time correctly predicted the member who actually got tapped for the post. Indeed, more than one newspaper, in announcing the appointment of William Ralls Morrison, headlined their stories: WHO THE HELL IS MORRISON? Morrison, of Waterloo, Illinois, would later achieve some renown as chairman of the Interstate Commerce Commission. In 1875, however, his name was hardly a household word. James Garfield noted in his diary that "the Chairman . . . has made no mark in Congress and his appointment is a great surprise"; another Republican wrote to a colleague that he had "sat all last Congress with Morrison, in the House, and when his name was announced I did not know there was such a man."[43] But it is certain that he had come to Marble's attention, and that the free trade community generally was familiar with his performance in the Forty-third. Nearly a year before the caucus, David Wells had written to the *World* editor about a bill that Morrison had introduced as an alternative to the majority's protectionist one, which he thought the paper should publicize. Thus, Morrison's reductionist credentials were well established in the circles that mattered. And with his designation, the Swallowtail's continued influence was virtually assured, for the chairman retained

42. Kerr to Marble, 16 Dec. 1875, Marble Papers; A. M. Gibson to C. F. Black, 23 Dec. 1875, Black Papers; McJimsey, *Genteel Partisan*, p. 173.

43. Franklin D. Scott, "The Political Career of William R. Morrison," Illinois State Historical Society *Transactions*, 33 (1926), 149; *Garfield Diary*, 3:204; Washington Townsend to George F. Hoar, 23 Dec. 1875, George F. Hoar Papers, Massachusetts Historical Society, Boston.

both Wells and J. S. Moore as "consultants" in drafting tariff legislation.[44]

That Marble was responsible for the decision, and that others were aware of the weight his word carried with the presiding officer, is abundantly clear. To begin with, Kerr brought the future chairman to the editor's temporary Washington headquarters, seemingly in response to a request from his patron to let him look the man over. Then on December 15, New York's Hiram Calkins wrote to Marble on behalf of Wood's aspirations to the post, and asked that he use his influence with the Speaker to advance Wood's chances. Marble's response—that Ways & Means was already determined and that Wood was not to get it—was obviously not what Calkins wanted to hear, but he accepted Marble's statement as conclusive: "Your note received this morning. It satisfies me that there is no use of my going to Washington to help Wood." Yet this exchange was completed two days before Kerr wrote to Marble announcing that he had "definitely decided" not to make Wood chairman of the panel.[45]

In fact, Ways & Means generally had a decidedly free trade cast in the Forty-fourth. Only one identifiable Democratic protectionist, Wood, was on it, and he was kept relatively powerless and felt perpetually frustrated. Two of the remaining majority members were well known for their hostility to high tariffs. One was John Hancock of Texas. The other was J. Randolph Tucker, a future Ways & Means chairman, who "vigorously opposed" such rates. The minority was mixed, but definitely more "liberal" than the Republican party as a whole. Its two protectionists were former Speaker James G. Blaine, who left within months for the Senate, and the extremist William D. ("Pig Iron") Kelley. Yet it also had Garfield, whose record was ambiguous but who once had said that "as a mere doctrine of abstract theory the doctrine of Free Trade was the true doctrine"; and Horatio Burchard of Illinois, a reductionist who had served compatibly with Kerr on Ways & Means during the Forty-second.[46]

44. Wells to Marble, 6 Feb. 1875, J. S. Moore to Marble, 8 Jan. 1876, and "O.R."[?] to Marble, 3 Feb. 1876, Marble Papers; McJimsey, *Genteel Partisan*, p. 174; Scott, "Morrison," pp. 149ff.; Robbins, "Morrison," pp. 45–60.

45. Kerr to Marble, 13 Dec. 1875, Calkins to Marble, 15 and 16 Dec. 1875, and Kerr to Marble, 18 Dec. 1875, Marble Papers.

46. "O.R." [?] to Marble, 3 Feb. 1876, Marble Papers; on Hancock, *DAB*, 8:220; on Tucker, *DAB*, 19:35, and *Nat. Cyc.*, 7:487; on Kelley, *DAB*, 299–300, and *Memorial Addresses on the Life and Character of William D. Kelley, a Representative from Pennsylvania*

Thus, insofar as the tariff was concerned, Kerr delivered on his campaign promises and followed the specific directions of the benefactors who had helped him in the contest. And the same could be said for currency. Cox's position on the issue was as "hard" as Marble's and the Speaker's; writing to the editor a few years earlier, he had boasted (with some hyperbole): "I am the only one, on our side, who has persistently fought for resumption, by speech & vote, in Committee & out." Consequently, selection of him to head Banking & Currency was appropriately in accord with Swallowtail principles. The ranking majority member, meanwhile, was Henry Payne, a firm specie man who had fought passionately against his state party's adoption of the "heretical" inflationist platform that became known as the "Ohio Idea." Also on Banking was Louisiana's Randall L. Gibson, who "was opposed to the Greenback craze in the late seventies and early eighties" and who, after his elevation to the Senate in 1882, "although the Louisiana legislature passed a resolution instructing him to support 'rag money' measures. . . refused to be bound by these instructions." Obviously, he embodied the right views, as did most of the panel's other members; Garfield was correct when he wrote that "democracy started out with strong declarations in favor of a sound currency saying that they would show that they were hard money men and sounder than the Republicans on that question. The election of Kerr was a triumph of the hard money wing of that party—the appointment of his Committee was in the same line of policy."[47]

Kerr's designations to such committees, then, stressed "low tariff and hard-money views . . . two of the basic tenets of Bourbon political religion."[48] Assuming that the campaign positions of both 1875 frontrunners were credible, then we should expect Randall's behavior to have been measurably dissimilar. This is borne out by events in 1877. The pro-tariff Wood became chairman of Ways & Means, while Morrison was demoted to Public Lands. "Pig Iron" Kelley stayed on to sustain the new Speaker's principles for the minority, while protec-

(Washington, 1890); on Blaine, Edward Stanwood, *American Tariff Controversies in the Nineteenth Century*, 2 vols. (Boston, 1903), 2:178–90; Garfield quote (and assessment of his record as "ambiguous") is from Allan Peskin, *Garfield* (Kent, Ohio, 1978), p. 265; on Burchard, William Horatio Barnes, *The American Government: Biographies of Members of the Forty-Third Congress*, 3 vols. (New York, 1874), 3:147–48, and Burchard's remarks in *Kerr Eulogies*, p. 26.

47. Cox to Marble, 13 Oct. 1873, and Kerr to Marble, 18 Dec. 1875, Marble Papers; McJimsey, *Genteel Partisan*, p. 174; *DAB*, 7:257; Garfield to Hayes, 2 Mar. 1876, Rutherford B. Hayes Papers, Hayes Library, Fremont, Ohio.

48. A. V. House, "Speakership Contest," p. 266.

tionism's strength on both sides of the party line was reinforced by a number of newcomers. These included Gibson, late of Banking & Currency, from sugar-producing Louisiana; New York's William W. Phelps; and Massachusetts's iconoclastic Nathaniel P. Banks, who told one industrialist, "It will give me great pleasure to receive from you suggestions in regard to [tariff] provisions which you and your friends may think important," and who won praise from the chief lobbyist of the National Association of Wool Manufacturers for the "high service which you rendered to our cause."[49] Thus, the worst fears of free traders were realized; the Speaker's identity did matter.

Randall's ascension also changed the face of Banking & Currency. The Philadelphia *Inquirer* declared his panel to be "a soft committee in favor of the repeal of the Resumption act and the remonetization of silver." Cox was removed as chairman and put instead at the helm of the lowly Joint Committee on the Library; he was replaced by Missouri's Aylett H. Buckner. Buckner, though a banker himself, was more flexible on currency than Cox had been; moreover, as a former state commissioner of banking, he had revealed decided antipathy toward the national banking establishment in which many of Kerr's Swallowtails were prominent. Again, the Bourbons were disappointed by Randall's actions and felt confirmed in their 1875 assessment of him as the candidate of "inflationist lunatics."[50]

During the contest of that year, both Kerr and Randall had campaigned as advocates of retrenchment, and their respective Appropriations Committees were similarly conservative—hardly a surprise, since Randall had chaired the panel under his adversary. But if spending generally had not been an issue, its infamous sibling "jobbery" most certainly was, especially in the context of alleged collusion with Tom Scott and the Texas Pacific. Speculation as to the composition of Kerr's committee began as soon as the caucus ended. On December 14, it appeared that Lucius Q. C. Lamar of Mississippi—"devotedly interested" in Scott's line—would chair it; the complete roster was announced December 20. On the 22d Randall reported to Chauncey Black that "The friends of T&P RR claim eleven members of Com[mittee]"; the next day, he added, "The arrangement of committees is bad—very bad. . . . Pacific Railroad ticket—10 out of 13 on it are their

49. Scott, "Morrison," pp. 147–48; *Nat. Cyc.,* 1:297, 7:451; Fred Harvey Harrington, *Fighting Politician: Major General N. P. Banks* (Philadelphia, 1948), p. 207.

50. Philadelphia *Inquirer,* 30 Oct. 1877; Barnes, *Biographies,* 3:191–92; the phrase "inflationist lunatics" is from David Wells to Marble, 18 Oct. 1875, Marble Papers.

friends. Bargain & sale written all over." Aside from Lamar its members included the T&P's part owner and former state lobbyist James W. Throckmorton, the man whom Grenville M. Dodge, Scott's chief man in Washington, once called "more valuable to us than any man we have . . . devoted to our interests." Indeed, Dodge agreed with Randall's assessment of the entire panel, exclaiming in early January that it was a "good one; much better than I expected." Collis P. Huntington, meanwhile—head of the rival Southern Pacific and Scott's most aggressive intraindustrial foe—declared himself "disappointed" in the outcome, claiming that not one of the members *his* lobbyist had suggested was included on the final roster.[51]

Two years later, under Randall, the Pacific Railroad Committee was less favorably constituted, at least from the T&P's perspective. Beverley Tucker, apparently back on Scott's payroll because of his access to the Speaker and headquartered in Washington, complained in a letter to the Pennsylvanian that "while I never to mortal man averred that you were in favour of the Texas Pacific Bill, *per se,* I have always expressed my confident belief, to its friends, that if chosen Speaker you would, at least, give it a majority of one, including a Chairman *friendly* to it. This Mr. Kerr gave us."[52] And the Virginian's overall evaluation remained justified, despite an ironic and unpredicted turn of events that owed nothing to his efforts or influence, which culminated on October 30, the very day he dispatched his criticism to the Capitol. Randall's choice for chairman was New York's Clarkson Potter, who shared the leader's opposition to a T&P subsidy but who also—unbeknownst to Randall— held stock in another line seeking federal assistance. Because of this apparent conflict of interest, Potter felt obliged to resign from Pacific Railroads, at which point House rules required automatic promotion of the second-ranking majority member. This, however, was none other than James Throckmorton, a personal friend of the Speaker but too intimately tied to Scott's corporation for the leader to be happy about his impending ascension. Consequently, Randall petitioned the Rules Committee to change the applicable policy. But the committee, out of

51. A. M. Gibson to C. F. Black, 14 Dec. 1875, and Randall to Black, 22 and 23 Dec. 1875, Black Papers; draft of letter from G. M. Dodge to Tom Scott, Nov. 1872, and Dodge to Throckmorton, 5 Jan. 1876, Dodge Papers; on Lamar, see *Nat. Cyc.*, 1:37; for Throckmorton, see Claude Elliott, *Leathercoat: The Life History of a Texas Patriot* (San Antonio, 1938); for Huntington, see Huntington to David Colton, 22 Dec. 1875, in *Letters of Collis P. Huntington*, 3:432; see also Seip, *South Returns to Congress*, chap. 7.
    52. Tucker to Randall, 30 Oct. 1877, Randall Papers.

concern over setting an unwise general precedent, refused to act favorably on his request.[53]

Even with Throckmorton at the helm, the panel's roster was so stacked against the T&P that Dodge, its principal agent, left abruptly for an extended European tour.[54] Neither he nor Tucker had managed to move the Speaker, although Scott had explicitly urged them to try, once he realized that Randall's victory was inevitable. The Pennsylvanian was furious and, if anything, intensified his anti-subsidy stand; as he told Chauncey Black: "If everybody in Texas & Pacific are for me— then they are so without promises of any sort. . . . One thing is certain," he continued, "they are all of opinion I am sure to win & I think that controls or forces their action. . . . It is not true," he insisted, "that I ever authorized any one to communicate to Col. S[cott] a ray of hope— that I would give the least support or countenance to his subsidy. . . . I stand today where I have stood for fourteen years. . . . I have never been and am not now & never will be their willing, persuaded or interested tool. . . . I once lost speakership because I could not compete with the modes adopted of reaching its attainment—I can afford to lose it again but I will never forfeit my views grounded in principle."[55] And, apparently, he never did "forfeit" his views; in 1879, largely because "Randall's lobby support had deserted him due to his anti-subsidy record during the Forty-fifth," a serious, but unsuccessful, Southern challenge was mounted to his reelection to the Speakership.[56]

Kerr clearly had been more amenable to the T&P than Randall; in this respect, Southerners and Swallowtails alike were justified in their backing of the Hoosier. But what of the more general question of "Southern sympathy"? Both contenders had asserted deep friendship in 1875, but given Dixie's overall caucus vote, the arguments in favor of Kentucky-born Kerr seems to have been more persuasive. In any event, when he announced his committees, a great deal of "instant analysis" was devoted to his placement of Southerners. A. M. Gibson, an erstwhile Randall man, saw the roster and thought it was "very bad," noting

53. Potter to Randall, 29 Oct. 1877, and Randall to Potter, 30 Oct. 1877, Randall Papers. In his letter of 5 Dec. 1875 to Chauncey Black, Randall noted that his "dear personal friend" Throckmorton had voted for him in the caucus; Black Papers. Information on Rules Committee incident in *Garfield Diary*, 3:547–48.

54. Stanley P. Hirshson, *Grenville M. Dodge: Soldier, Politician, Railroad Pioneer* (Bloomington, Ind., 1967), p. 206.

55. Randall to Black, 13 May and 14 Aug. 1877, Black Papers.

56. A. V. House, "Randall," p. 115.

that "Penna was slaughtered," and concluding that "Ky Ohio—Mo & Ills bore off nearly everything." His was one of the more geographically accurate of early reports. Lobbyist Grenville Dodge confided that the lists "are a surprise to me," and observed that "it is a very judicious make up for the west and south, but I don't know how the east will take it." Most Republicans, meanwhile, regardless of where they were from, were "horrified" by what they saw. The strictly partisan *Republic* denounced the roster as "in the worse[sic] traditions of *ante bellum* Democratic management. . . . They are 'fearfully and wonderfully made,' . . . It is a profound abyss, into which only Southern and sectional rays seem to penetrate." Garfield agreed, calling the slate "the old Southern Rule returning with a vengeance." The Ohioan complained that "out of the 34 most important Committees the Chairmen of 21 were made from the late Slave States." In fact, that number encompassed nearly all the chairmanships that such congressmen got and no one, including a calmer Garfield, would have classified those like Railways & Canals or Expenditures in the Post Office Department as "important." Still, consensus had it that the South had come out very well, and that Dixie's Representatives had been acting in their own best interests when they cast their caucus ballots for Kerr.[57]

Two years later the response to Randall's constructions was more subdued—perhaps because, after Hayes's assumption of the presidency, agitation over Reconstruction was substantially dissipated. Rumors die slowly, however, and it should be remembered that the most concrete opposition to the Pennsylvanian's election in 1877 had come—as it would again in 1879—from a bloc of aggressive Southerners.[58] But the Speaker's actions belied the charge that he would "betray" the South, during his first term or after.

A comparison of appointments made by Kerr and Randall shows that, where the South was concerned, there was virtually no difference between them (Table 14). Of course, given the larger pool of nonfreshmen at Randall's disposal, his lists might have been slightly more favorable to the region than they were. But there is reason to suspect that Randall's rewards to Dixie would have been greater had there been no organized opposition to his candidacies; as a biographer explained,

57. A. M. Gibson to C. F. Black, 23 Dec. 1875, Black Papers; Grenville Dodge to Sen. William B. Allison (R-Iowa), 21 Dec. 1875, William B. Allison Papers, Iowa State Dept. of History & Archives, Des Moines; "The Democratic Speaker and the House Committees," *The Republic,* 6 (1876), 98; *Garfield Diary,* 3:204.
58. A. V. House, "Randall," pp. 113–14; J. Randolph Tucker to his wife, 18 Oct. 1877, and to Harry St. G. Tucker, 15 Oct. 1877, Tucker Papers.

Table 14. The Southern membership of committees, 44th and 45th Houses

	44th House	*45th House*
Total House membership	293	293
Southern membership[a]	*105 (35.9% of total)*	*105 (35.9% of total)*
Committees		
Total	47	47
Chaired by South	24 (51.1% of total)	25 (53.2% of total)
"Major & Southern interest"[b]	12 (25.5% of total)	12 (25.5% of total)
Chaired by South	7 (58.3% of category)	8 (66.7% of category)
Allocative[c]	7 (14.9% of total)	7 (14.9% of total)
Chaired by South	5 (71.4% of category)	4 (57.1% of category)
Remainder	28 (59.6% of total)	28 (59.6% of total)
Chaired by South	12 (42.8% of category)	13 (46.4% of category)
Committee slots		
Total	429	453
Held by South	159 (37.1% of total)	185 (40.8% of total)
"Major & Southern interest"[b]	128 (29.8% of total)	128 (28.3% of total)
Held by South	46 (35.9% of category)	47 (36.7% of category)
Allocative[c]	77 (18.0% of total)	77 (17.0% of total)
Held by South	32 (41.6% of category)	33 (42.9% of category)
Remainder	224 (52.2% of total)	248 (54.7% of total)
Held by South	81 (36.2% of category)	105 (42.3% of category)

Sources: Congressional Directories, 44th and 45th Congresses (1st sess.).
[a] Includes all former slave states, except Delaware: Alabama, Arkansas, Florida, Georgia, Kentucky, Louisiana, Maryland, Mississippi, Missouri, North Carolina, South Carolina, Tennessee, Texas, Virginia, and West Virginia.
[b] Includes Ways & Means, Appropriations, Rules, Banking & Currency, Commerce, Naval Affairs, Military Affairs, Elections, Judiciary, Foreign Affairs, Pacific Railroads, Improvements on the Mississippi Levees.
[c] Includes Claims, War Claims, Invalid Pensions, Revolutionary Pensions, Private Land Claims, Patents, Post Offices & Post Roads.

"he shrewdly distributed his chairmanships only to those Southerners who had worked faithfully for him."[59] What may be more surprising is that *neither* Speaker seemed to have translated his avowed friendship for the South into empirically detectable terms, contemporary reactions to Kerr notwithstanding. In neither chairs nor other prestigious assignments—even when they are augmented by the inclusion of three committees of particular interest to the South (Elections, Mississippi Levees, and Pacific Railroads)—was Dixie overrepresented. The only

59. A. V. House, "Northern Congressional Democrats," p. 67; Frank Morey (R-La.) to Randall, 12 May 1875, Randall Papers.

noticeable exception was in the case of both men's allocative panels. But even there, Kerr and Randall each gave the chairs and most seats to Northerners on the two that were mostly directly concerned with Civil War–related demands: War Claims and Invalid Pensions.

Circumstances in 1875 and, to a lesser extent, 1877, were typical of the mid-nineteenth century, with its frequent changes in legislative majorities and consequent competitions for leadership. But there were moments of stability, even in the seventies, when both Congress and the Speakership stayed in the same hands, and when, therefore, both were less vulnerable to influence and alteration by lobbyists. We saw how Randall, as early as 1877, could afford to ignore Tom Scott's attempts to win him over; two years later, although some Southerners continued to oppose him—again, as in 1875, with some lukewarm cooperation from Scott—even the New York Swallowtails by then had bowed to the inevitable and grudgingly endorsed the incumbent.[60]

Yet no Speaker, no matter how well established or secure his position, was entirely immune to lobbyists' efforts to assist him in setting up House. Both Randall and James G. Blaine, in their later terms, received a good deal of mail regarding assignments; the otherwise sparse Blaine Papers contain over two dozen such letters for 1873, while Randall's include over a hundred for 1877. And given the high turnover every two years of both legislative and committee members, outsiders were never without hope of organizational influence, particularly when it came to the placement of freshmen. But comparison of these communications with subsequent committee rosters discloses little congruence between petitions and actual appointments, regardless of the writers' knowledgeability, stature, political persuasion, or degree of intimacy with either the presiding officer or the men they were promoting. In fact, cases where congressmen were put into the sought-after slots were so few, and so collectively dissimilar, that with some notable exceptions they probably reflect nothing more than mere coincidence.[61]

Some elements in Blaine's 1873 experience, however, indicate that even an entrenched incumbent might be susceptible to certain forms of agitation. For while lobbyists knew that they had no chance of thwarting

60. A. V. House, "Randall," p. 115.

61. Evidence for this conclusion, too tedious to replicate here, is comparison of letters in the Blaine and Randall Papers with committee lists in the *Cong. Rec.*, 43d and 44th Congs.

the Speaker's reelection, they also were aware of his vulnerability on another level: that of presidential politics. It was no secret that the Maine Republican aspired to his party's endorsement in 1876, and that reelection to the Chair without intrapartisan dissent would strengthen his position considerably. Backers of other G.O.P. hopefuls, therefore, saw the Speakership caucus as an opportunity to create suggestions of controversy, which might garner publicity or open doors for alternative nominees. That was the principal motivation, for instance, behind the chimerical "boomlet" on behalf of Indiana's Godlove S. Orth. Instigated by the Indianapolis *Journal*, it was revealed to be part of a campaign to promote Senator Oliver P. Morton to the presidency. Even Orth, who was not without leadership ambitions, refused to lend it credence: in a note to Blaine, accompanying a *Journal* clipping, he wrote in jest, "I submit to you, in all the sober-seriousness at my command, whether in view of the enclosed . . . it is not about time for you to become alarmed about the future?"[62] Similarly, the name of William A. Wheeler was put forward by some anti-Blaine politicos in New York, presumably fans of the Speaker's arch-enemy Roscoe Conkling; the future vice-president, meanwhile, like his Hoosier colleague, declined to run and informed Blaine directly that he repudiated the effort.[63]

Such activities were heavy-handed, easily exposed, and ultimately ineffective. But two other lobbying ventures were more significant and potentially more productive. The first had to do with the fates of Blaine's two principal floor lieutenants, Henry L. Dawes (R-Mass.), chairman of Ways & Means, and head of Appropriations James A. Garfield. The second, reminiscent of the "Southern" issue of 1875, concerned allegations of bias against western interests and members.

The former controversy arose in response to exposure of Credit Mobilier, which, along with the Salary Grab, had cast a decided pall over the preceding session.[64] An outraged public, encouraged by certain agents of the press, began to demand that Speaker Blaine remove

62. Orth to Blaine, 21 Oct. 1873 (clipping from *Daily Courier*, 20 Oct. 1873); see also clippings from the St. Louis *Daily Globe*, 23 and 25 Oct. 1873, and New York *Sun*, 24 Oct. 1873, the last of which reported the connection between Orth and Morton's presidential aspirations, and noted the role of the Indianapolis *Journal*, which Morton "controlled," in the whole affair; all in a scrapbook of clippings [hereafter "Blaine Scrapbook"], Blaine Papers.

63. Wheeler to Blaine, 2 Oct. 1873; clippings from the Chicago *Times*, 19 Oct. 1873, and Washington, D.C., *Republican*, 27 Oct. 1873, "Blaine Scrapbook," Blaine Papers; see also *DAB*, 20:57.

64. See chap. 1, above.

all those implicated in either incident from positions of authority in the House. Attention focused especially on Dawes and Garfield, who were both prominent and, as insiders knew, the ablest and most important of Blaine's floor leaders.

Of the two men under attack, Garfield's plight was more serious because of his misconstrued connection with the Salary Grab, as well as with Credit Mobilier. The Ohioan had never favored the pay raise and, indeed, had fought strenuously against it in committee, on the floor, and in conference with the Senate. But because he chaired the panel in which the offending legislation originated, Garfield suffered from the full force of reaction to it, despite his loud and persistent denials of culpability, his declaration that he "was compelled to choose between signing the [conference] report and running the risk of bringing on an extra session of Congress," and the fact that he was the first member to return his bonus to the U.S. Treasury. Implication can be more injurious and harder to refute than truth; the charges that Garfield was a leading "Grabber" were more persuasive to some than his numerous attempts to discuss the facts.[65]

The Philadelphia *Evening Star* was one of many papers that urged Blaine to repudiate both Dawes and Garfield, especially if he wanted to be president. And there is no question that the Speaker, aspiring to nomination by a party stigmatized with the burden of "Grantism" took the matter seriously. The otherwise small Blaine Collection at the Library of Congress contains a scrapbook filled with clippings on the controversies of 1873, suggesting not only the tenor of national opinion but also the man from Maine's preoccupation with it. Of course the press, as is common in such cases, was divided in the positions it espoused. Many journalists, to be sure, sided with the *Evening Star*. But others took stands like that of the Cleveland *Leader*, urging the Speaker with some ambivalence not to "actively join hands" with "tainted" members, while noting simultaneously that removal of Garfield and Dawes would deprive the country of their experience and wisdom. And the Chicago *Tribune*, in an article widely disseminated among Republican organs, queried: "Why should Mr. Blaine be expected to punish Congressmen for their political sins?" and denounced the cry for him to "play executioner."[66]

---

65. *Cong. Globe*, 42d Cong., 3d sess., p. 2101; Peskin, *Garfield*, pp. 354–86.
66. Philadelphia *Evening Star*, 11 Oct. 1873, Cleveland *Leader*, 3 Sept. 1873, Chicago *Tribune*, 22 Nov. 1873, and references to this last in numerous other clippings; "Blaine Scrapbook."

The principal targets of this agitation were as upset by it as the Speaker; both appreciated that popular fury was a potent force and that Blaine could not ignore it entirely. Dawes, in the midst of planning his first Senate campaign, was worried that the uproar would hurt his chances and help those of reform rivals like George Frisbie and Ebenezer Rockwood Hoar.[67] Garfield, meanwhile—a complex and deeply religious intellectual who was moody under the best of circumstances—was sorely wounded by the assaults on his integrity, which he could not understand, and wrote page after page about it in his diary and in letters to close friends. In a letter to Burke A. Hinsdale he blamed his problems almost entirely on "a few newspapers spreading half-truths and innuendos," and said that "public sentiment here [in Washington] is very strongly in my favor." Yet he realized how great was the pressure on the Speaker, and speculated that Dawes and he ultimately would be placed at the heads of less prestigious committees.[68]

In the end, Blaine retained Garfield and Dawes as chairmen of the two top finance panels, telling the Ohioan later that this had been his intention all along.[69] We cannot, of course, ascertain whether or not this was really true, although the effect of declarations like that of the Chicago *Tribune* may have have had their impact, suggesting as they did that the party press would not desert the Maine Republican if he stuck by his prominent colleagues. The expertise argument may also have helped Blaine to make up his mind; had he demoted the two leaders, no men of comparable caliber seemed available to replace them.[70] Further, their personal loyalty, now augmented by gratitude, would have been as hard to replicate as their know-how. Garfield, at least, knew how affected Blaine had been by the newspaper criticism, which persisted long after the assignments were announced. As a result, some biographers of the twentieth president have gone so far as to suggest that obligation toward the former Speaker for resisting the press lobby

67. Blaine to Dawes, 3 July and 20 Aug. 1873, L. M. Clark to Dawes, 20 July 1873, and Charles Allen to Dawes, 2 and 4 Sept. 1873, Henry L. Dawes Papers, L.C.

68. Garfield to Hinsdale, 24 Nov. 1873, Hinsdale to Garfield, 28 Nov. 1873, Garfield to Hinsdale, 10 Dec. 1873, and several other letters from 1873 in *Garfield-Hinsdale Letters: Correspondence between James Abram Garfield and Burke Aaron Hinsdale*, ed. Mary L. Hinsdale (Ann Arbor, 1949), pp. 252–56, 261–62, and passim; see also *Garfield Diary*, 2:237–55, and various letters in the Garfield Papers, L.C.

69. Theodore Clarke Smith, *The Life and Letters of James Abram Garfield*, 2 vols. (New Haven, 1925), 1:563–64.

70. The expertise argument is explicitly made in a letter from the not usually supportive editor of the Springfield, Mass., *Republican*, ending "Forward this with my love to Garfield": Samuel Bowles to David Wells, 3 Nov. 1873, Garfield Papers; see also Bowles to Dawes, 14 Feb. 1874, Dawes Papers.

was a serious motivation for his later designation as Garfield's secretary of state.[71]

Meanwhile, another sector of the press, more preoccupied with regional issues than national scandals, contributed to a discernible change between the committee constructions of 1871 and those two years later. A sizable number of western editors accused Blaine of being insufficiently appreciative of their section's interests, and wanted him to give "a controlling majority to the West on every committee where Western interests are either generally or locally concerned." Accordingly, the St. Louis *Daily Globe* offered members some tactical advice: "We do not hesitate to say that Western members ought to request of Mr. Blaine the control of such committees, and that, if he does not grant it, they ought to unite their votes upon some other man who will."[72] Obviously this movement—which could be construed to apply to the entire committee roster—might affect the Maine Republican's presidential drive quite significantly, since western support was essential to its success.

Once again, truth and charges were not completely congruent. As even some journalists pointed out, particularly in staunchly Republican Iowa, the Speaker had, if anything, favored the West over his native New England and the mid-Atlantic in past assignments, since members from beyond the Alleghenies held a percentage of prestigious chairmanships and seats out of proportion to their number in the House.[73] And, in aggregate terms, the final roster in 1873 was cumulatively less advantageous to the West than that of the preceding session. But there was one important difference, significant enough for the Cleveland *Leader* and other formerly hostile papers to pronounce themselves pleased with the outcome: Blaine chose westerners to head five of the six committees primarily concerned with private legislation.[74]

71. See, for example, Buffalo *Courier*, 11 Dec. 1873, "Blaine Scrapbook"; editor's introduction to chap. 6 in *Garfield-Hinsdale Letters*.

72. Cleveland *Leader*, n.d.; St. Louis *Daily Globe*, 24 Oct. 1873 (quoting concurring opinion from Springfield, Mo., *Patriot*); Washington, D.C., *Evening Star*, 29 Sept. 1873; Boston *Globe*, 23 Sept. 1873; Lafayette, Ind., *Daily Courier*, 27 Sept. 1873. The most commonly mentioned western alternatives were Orth (see above) and Iowa's John A. Kasson, although the *Evening Star* piece contained "reservations" about the latter, saying that the Iowan's wife had left him, allegedly because he was "running around." All in "Blaine's Scrapbook."

73. Note esp. the Des Moines *Iowa State Register*, 14 Sept. 1873, and Dubuque *Daily Times*, 22 Oct. 1873; see also Philadelphia *Evening Star*, 11 Oct. 1873 (all in "Blaine Scrapbook").

74. "The West should appreciate that Blaine has given a controlling majority to the West on every committee where Western interests are either generally or locally involved": Cleveland *Leader*, n.d., "Blaine Scrapbook."

The honor attached to distributive jobs might have been too subtle to be obvious to the general public, but it was appreciated by legislators and savvy journalists. Among other things, it meant that western petitioners for payment of claims and pensions stood better chances of getting their cases reported from committee than other Americans with similar problems. And it located the men who held such places securely within the power structure of the House. As Representative George F. Hoar once wrote: "the Chairmanship of the Committee on Claims was with two or three exceptions the most important position in the House. . . . His opinion carried great weight [and] his judgment became its law in matters within the jurisdiction of his committee."[75]

So, apparently, Blaine satisfied his critics in the western lobby. But there is, on the other hand, no concrete evidence to prove that he acted as he did because of its pressure. The mixed content of the Credit Mobilier/Salary Grab agitation makes this even more difficult to assess. It does appear that Blaine, as a third-term Speaker, was able to shrug off outside influences rather easily. For whatever consideration he gave to any of this lobbying was almost surely due more to its potential bearing on his presidential aspirations than to its ability to threaten his hegemony within the House.

What can we say about lobbying's effects upon organizational politics, and their implications for the subsequent conduct of Congressional Government? At least three conclusions seem justified. First, outsiders were far more able to exert influence when the Speakership was contested than when it was not. Second, and equally important, lobbyists persisted in efforts to help set up House even when the odds against them were high—when, for instance, an entrenched incumbent wielded the gavel. As noted before, failed campaigns, including those whose failure was practically a foregone conclusion, must not be ignored or discounted; among other things, they suggest how great the advantages of success were by instancing the lengths to which lobbyists would go if there were any chance at all to achieve it.

It really mattered, on several levels, whether Kerr or Randall was

---

75. George F. Hoar, *Autobiography of Seventy Years*, 2 vols. (New York, 1903), 1:226. The five committees and their chairmen were: Claims (B. J. Hawley, Ill.), War Claims (W. Lawrence, Ohio), Invalid Pensions (J. M. Rusk, Wis.), Patents (O. D. Conger, Mich.), and Private Land Claims (J. Packard, Ind.); the sixth, Revolutionary Pensions, was chaired by L. D. Shoemaker (Pa.). In addition, Military Affairs, which handled many private bills during this period, was headed by westerner John Coburn (Ind.), *Cong. Dir.*, 43d Cong., 1st sess.

Speaker—as Tom Scott, Manton Marble, Samuel Tilden, Beverley Tucker, and any number of congressmen and clienteles would readily have testified. And decisions Blaine made in 1873 would reverberate throughout the rest of his career. Thus, if anything, the Washington *Capital* that year was guilty of understatement when it declared that "the election of a speaker of the House of Representatives is not so simple a matter as, to the uninstructed in the ways of political life, it may appear." This was especially true during the early Gilded Age, when high turnover and intrapartisan policy disputes meant that the potential for biennial change was great indeed. Organizational decisions, and lobbyists' part in making them, had profound institutional, programmatic, and political ramifications, ramifications that were felt well beyond the duration of any congressional session and well beyond the confines of the Capitol.

CHAPTER 6

The Patronage Game: Lobbying and the Politics of Distribution

> There seems always to be something Alpine about political refor-
> mers. They call a little frostily to one another from peak to peak,
> each very happy on his glacial height, nourishing his ego on an
> air on which the ordinary mortal is fain to choke to death—and
> they are terribly indisposed to come down and foregather with
> the crowds in the valley below, where men give and take, indif-
> ferent to each other's foibles.
>
> ROYAL CORTISSOZ, *The Life of Whitelaw Reid*

Nineteenth-century humorist Artemus Ward once wrote that the
Union Army's hasty retreat from Bull Run was brought on by a rumor
of three openings in the New York Custom House. In 1880, a Texan
allegedly declared at his party's national convention: "What are we here
for if not for the offices?" Apocryphal though they may be, both stories
are credible for what they have to say about Gilded Age politics. For so
far as government was concerned, much of what interested the nation's
people most directly was distributive and intensely personal in nature.[1]

The preceding chapter focused mainly on events leading up to and
ensuing from Michael C. Kerr's election as Speaker on December 6,
1875. It may be assumed that this was the most publicized incident of
the day in Washington, but was it necessarily the most significant?
Perhaps it was, if one were former Representative George Adams of
Kentucky, elected clerk of the House on the strength of a protector's
victory in the battle to wield the gavel—or former Dakota delegate

---

1. James Parton, "The Power of Public Plunder," *NAR*, 133 (1881), 43–64.

M. K. Armstrong, whose corresponding aspirations lost with Samuel Randall. But for many Americans the "real" business of government was taking place away from the chamber floor, and remained basically unaffected by events there. Its domain, as always, was in the Departments, where pensions, claims, and patronage reigned. Thus, that very morning Ohio's Garfield first "went to the Interior Department to secure an appointment for Lester King," and "telegraphed J. Q. Smith asking him to accept Commissionership of Indian Affairs." Only "thence" did he proceed to the Capitol.[2]

We already have seen how, by the late nineteenth century, ombudsmanship had assumed a crucial place in the federal Representative's role; even a cursory glance at correspondence and other sources reveals the awesome burden of such nonlegislative demands. The Grant years, after all, have been called the "Great Barbecue"—at which Representatives were supposed to cook and serve the feast. But, as interested parties found, someone else was often needed to light the coals.

Indeed, it was in implementing this sector of the federal agenda that time-lag probably was most acute and that the contributions of lobbyists, as catalysts who facilitated decision making, might well have been most essential. The legislative workload, especially in respect to patents, patronage, claims, and pensions, had expanded rapidly and prodigiously, without a commensurate increase in institutional capacity to respond. Thus, lobbyists of various kinds became integral parts of the allocative machinery; they called attention to individual claimants, backed competing seekers of jobs, gathered and communicated data, handled paperwork—in short, aided both officials and clienteles in the conduct and routines of Congressional Government.

No brief discussion could possibly cover either the entire range of distributive policy or lobbying's contributions to it. So the emphasis here will be on patronage, one of the seventies' most common allocative tasks. It was both more typical and more revealing than patents, for example, which for the most part were handled forthrightly within the Patent Office, where deference to technical expertise, rather than influence, normally prevailed. Claims and pensions, of course, cannot be similarly dismissed (both—especially pensions—are discussed at length

2. *BDAC*, p. 206; *Hse. J.*, 44th Cong., 1st sess. (6 Dec. 1875), 13–14; M. K. Armstrong to S. J. Randall, 25 Aug. and 15 Dec. 1875, Samuel J. Randall Papers, Van Pelt Library, University of Pennsylvania, Philadelphia; *The Diary of James A. Garfield*, ed. Harry James Brown and F. D. Williams, 4 vols. (East Lansing, 1967–81), 3:194–95 [hereafter, *Garfield Diary*].

in Chapter 7). For although many cases were processed routinely through purely bureaucratic channels, thousands were not; collectively, such matters were highly politicized and very vulnerable to the pressures of lobbying.[3] Keep in mind, therefore, that much of the discussion below could apply equally well to other items on the distributive agenda whose resolution involved competition within and among constituencies.

Patronage is fertile ground for case study. Since the majority of jobs were in the gift of particular legislators, one can trace the entire course of many cases' dispositions, and the impact of lobbying upon them, through the correspondence of single members. And whereas data on most pension and claims agents are scarce, some patronage bosses were notable and, hence, accessible figures.[4] Moreover, the unusually rich collections of materials on Massachusetts Representatives—including those from the Boston area—permit investigation of intradelegational rivalries for offices, which often had considerable political and even substantive implications.[5] Finally, agitation in behalf of federal civil service reform accelerated throughout Grant's tenure, thereby making it an acutely vital and timely issue. And while the tangible results of this campaign were slight during the seventies, the publicity that it engendered both bore upon and illuminated the short-term disposition of jobs.[6]

More than feasibility, however, recommends this focus. Patronage, as

3. Leonard D. White, *The Republican Era, 1869–1901: A Study in Administrative History* (New York, 1958), pp. 208–31; Gustavus A. Weber, *The Patent Office* (Baltimore, 1924); Records of the House Committee on Patents, and Petitions and Memorials referred to the Patent Committee (stored separately), 43d and 44th Congs., Legislative and Judicial Division, National Archives, esp. petition files 43A-F20.1-4, 44A-F25.1-4, 43A-J12.1-2; Mary R. Dearing, *Veterans in Politics: The Story of the G.A.R.* (Baton Rouge, 1952); *Report of the Committee on Expenditures in the Interior Department, Hse. Rpts.,* 43d Cong., 3d sess., no. 189; William Henry Glasson, *History of Military Pension Legislation in the United States* (New York, 1900), esp. chap. 7; John William Oliver, *History of the Civil War Military Pensions, 1861–1885* (Madison, Wis., 1917); Rep. Edmund N. Morrill, "Pensions," in *The Republican Party: Its History, Principles, and Policies,* ed. John D. Long (New York, 1888), pp. 124–43; Mary Clemmer Ames, *Ten Years in Washington: Life and Scenes in the National Capital as a Woman Sees Them* (Hartford, 1876), chaps. 12 and 13.

4. For three Iowa "bosses," see the papers of William Boyd Allison, Samuel J. Kirkwood, and (especially) Grenville M. Dodge, all Iowa Dept. of History & Archives, Des Moines. For the Concord, New Hampshire, "Ring," see the two collections of William E. Chandler Papers, one at the L.C. [hereafter, Chandler-LC] and the other at the New Hampshire Historical Society [hereafter, Chandler-NHHS]. The latter is an especially rich source of examples of patronage.

5. George Frisbie Hoar Papers, Massachusetts Historical Society, Boston; Benjamin F. Butler, Henry L. Dawes, and Nathaniel P. Banks Papers, all L.C. Because of New Hampshire's proximity to Boston, the two Chandler collections are also relevant.

6. Henry W. Bellows, *Civil Service Reform* (New York, 1877); Henry B. Adams, "Civil

the allocative area most completely under congressional jurisdiction, demonstrates most directly the interaction between lobbying and legislative behavior. Besides, the effectiveness of both representation and policy making was affected markedly by the character and quality of officials, as well as by the means of their appointment. And the political consequences of patronage were potentially greater than those of other distributive programs. Passage of a pension bill or successful prosecution of a claim was of interest to few beyond the actual recipient, but the selection of postmasters and heads of major federal installations "mattered" concretely to more of the citizenry at large. Similarly, while a diligent but unproductive congressman could explain to disappointed voters—with some real chance of being believed—that he alone was not responsible for claims and pensions, he could not escape so easily from controversies or disappointments generated by allocations within his particular purview.

The immediacy of concerns and rewards connected with patronage, then, gave it a special salience—as both Representatives and the represented knew well.[7] In few other areas were the obligations of congressmen to constituents manifested more unambiguously, and in few other areas would the responsiveness of that relationship be subjected to such explicit tests. Careerists, whose continued influence depended directly upon repeated reelection, were unfailingly conscious of this, which is why the powerhouses of the Capitol were also among those who took the demands of job disbursement most seriously. Rarely, though, were they left to themselves in executing that responsibility. Both inadvertently and by design, they often found themselves beholden to the agency of lobbying.

Most Americans today know little about their twentieth president except that, shortly after his inauguration, he was assassinated by a

---

Service Reform," _NAR_, 109 (1869), 443–75; George L. Prentiss, _Our National Bane; or, the Dry-Rot in American Politics_ (New York, 1877); Jacob D. Cox, "The Civil Service Reform," _NAR_, 112 (1871); Ari J. Hoogenboom, _Outlawing the Spoils: A History of the Civil Service Reform Movement, 1865–1883_ (Urbana, Ill., 1961), esp. chaps. 5–6, and "Thomas A. Jenckes and Civil Service Reform," _MVHR_, 47 (1961), 636–58; Lionel V. Murphy, "The First Federal Civil Service Commission: 1871–1875," _Public Personnel Rev._, 3 (Jan.–Oct. 1942), 29–39, 218–31, 299–323; Carl Russell Fish, _The Civil Service and the Patronage_ (Cambridge, 1920); White, _Republican Era_, chap. 13.

7. In reference to pensions and claims, for example, L. D. White said: "These special acts, indeed, had become a sort of Congressional patronage," which suggests the appropriateness of actual patronage as the focus for generalizations about distributive policy; White, _Republican Era_, p. 210. On perceived salience, see James D. Norris and A. H. Shaffer, eds., _Politics and Patronage in the Gilded Age: The Correspondence of James A. Garfield and Charles E. Henry_ (Madison, Wis., 1970), pp. ix–xxix [hereafter, _Garfield-Henry Letters_].

"disappointed office-seeker." The more learned may also recall that the Pendleton Act, the first U.S. civil service reform of significant scope and enforceability, was adopted largely as "fitting legacy to our martyred leader." Yet for the bulk of his public career, James A. Garfield was a congressman who worked effectively within the so-called "spoils system"—more critical of it than many of his contemporaries, perhaps, but accepting of it as a fact of life with which he and everyone else simply had to deal. What is more, his endeavors in that area are as well documented as they were extensive.[8] They can, therefore, be used profitably to exemplify the operation and politics of federal patronage within an individual legislative district.

Garfield's diary, for instance, conveys a clear impression of incessant engagement in such affairs—and of attitudes that, although they varied with his moods, nearly always included a strong dose of frustration. Sometimes reflectiveness prevailed, as when the former general and some prominent dinner companions discussed the dilemma of finding a "political motive [that] is an adequate substitute for patronage" in a republic. Garfield regarded this as "the central difficulty that underlies the Civil Service," and could propose no satisfactory solution, but that did not prevent him from considering the problem, or being exasperated with the intrusions that it continuously made into his life. The following litany, recorded intermittently during one week in March 1877, was typical: "My house is beset with office-seekers from morning until night," he complained. "The rush of visitors commenced again . . . [until] I fled from the house for protection against their importunate demands. . . . I am thoroughly disgusted with the pressure for office which knows no limits of modesty or self-restraint. . . . Not less than 75 people called." Finally, he admitted that "one of my reasons for going to Ohio now is to escape the annoyance of the ceaseless repetition of their solicitations."

Still, the congressman usually managed to maintain his sense of humor in face of the never-ending onslaught. Thus, later that same month he mused about the possibilities of "finding a psychological interest in the people who call for aid"—a decision apparently impelled

---

8. Published primary source collections that deal extensively with Garfield's patronage activity include *Garfield-Henry Letters*, *Garfield Diary*, and Mary L. Hinsdale, ed., *Garfield-Hinsdale Letters, Correspondence between James Abram Garfield and Burke Aaron Hinsdale* (Ann Arbor, 1949); see also James A. Garfield Papers, L.C.; and Allan Peskin, *Garfield* (Kent, Ohio, 1978), esp. chaps. 22, 24, and "President Garfield and the Rating Game: An Evaluation of a Brief Administration," *South Atlantic Q.*, 76 (1977), 93–102. For Garfield's views at the time of his election as president, see Garfield to Chandler, 1 Dec. 1880, Chandler-NHHS.

by a petitioner whose appeal, if nothing else, was distinctive: "[He] said if I would get a certain man appointed Chief of the Secret Service, that man could certainly make me Speaker, for he could bring the Know-nothing vote of the House to my support. My informant insisted that the Know-nothing party was still in existence in full blast, lying back like a couchant lion waiting to spring when the time comes. Of course ready to spring if this fellow is made a detective. 'Behold how great a matter a little fire kindleth.' "[9]

Black humor toward "notions of *quid pro quo* [that] were evidently borrowed from a counting room," however, should not be construed as flippancy; Garfield was consistently serious and conscientious about the responsibilities and obligations of patronage. Although occasionally he could be swayed by sentiment—especially toward veterans of his Civil War unit and toward those who appeared to be in desperate financial need—he generally sought for his appointees to meet a threefold standard of competence, public acceptability, and political "soundness," and clearly took pride in the normally high caliber of public servants that the Nineteenth District was able to generate.[10]

But even with good intentions and standards, Garfield rarely found it easy to determine which one of the many aspirants vying for an opening was best qualified. As he noted in an essay for the *Atlantic Monthly:* "It is not possible for any[one] to select, with any degree of intelligence, so vast an army of office-holders without the aid of men who are acquainted with the people of the various sections of the country."[11] In short, like the president and his congressional colleagues, the Ohioan was overrun with demands and undersupplied with the information requisite to their satisfaction—a classic predicament that the lobby-catalyst ought to have been able to help resolve, by serving both as a resource to which members could turn for advice and as a conduit for unsolicited intelligence. This certainly happened in Garfield's case, as many incidents during his long House career demonstrated.

Like many others in the Capitol, Garfield brought an eclectic range of experiences with him into national politics. Although he was only thirty-two when he entered Congress, he already had been a lay preacher, teacher and college president, state legislator, attorney, and

9. *Garfield Diary,* 3:470, 454–59, 464–65.
10. "If I had done as many members of Congress do, that is signed all petitions, I might have escaped censure, but I could not have secured my self respect." Garfield to Henry, 9 Mar. 1870, *Garfield-Henry Letters,* p. 17; contrast this with the behavior of James Buffin(g)ton, in chap. 4, above. On his personal sentiment toward veterans and former students, see Peskin, *Garfield,* p. 551.
11. James A. Garfield, "A Century of Congress," *Atlantic Monthly,* 40 (1877), 60–61.

commander of the locally enlisted Forty-second Volunteers. Not surprisingly, therefore, the Ohioan enjoyed a varied circle of friends and contacts throughout the region that elected him to represent it. As is all too common with long-tenured Washingtonians, however, Garfield gradually lost touch with his roots and, consequently, had to rely increasingly on others for knowledge of local conditions.[12] When a postmastership or other position was vacated, he counted upon his inner circle for guidance.

Two among those on whom the Representative relied deserve particular recognition. One was wealthy businessman Harmon Austin of Warren, a trustee of Western Reserve Eclectic Institute (later Hiram College), chairman of the Trumbull County Republican Committee, and manager of Garfield's campaigns. Austin had been responsible for "Young Jim's" selection as the Eclectic's president in 1857, and had engineered his first nomination to Congress five years later, while the candidate was on active duty with the army. The other was Charles E. Henry of Geauga, a student of Garfield's in the late 1850s and a captain in his Union regiment. Unlike Austin, whose stature and financial security enabled him to regard the congressman as an equal, Henry was obligated to Garfield both for his livelihood and for whatever influence he exercised, something neither man ever forgot or aspired to change. In different but equally significant ways, therefore, Austin and Henry —the loyal but personally undependent peer and the protégé solely and sincerely devoted to the advancement of his patron's interests— were men in whom the future president could have complete confidence, and who could provide essential links between the Representative and the represented.[13]

Garfield's relationships with these associates provide compelling illustrations of the symbiosis that could occur between officials and those who exercised influence over them; those on both sides of such political partnerships stood clearly to benefit from the arrangement. For instance, there seemed to be mutual causality between Henry's promotions and increased responsibilities and Garfield's dependency upon him. As the postal agent proved his mettle, he was rewarded with even

---

12. "I have gradually become weaned from Hiram and can leave it but with few regrets. Fifteen years ago it would have seemed sacrilege to quit the place"; *Garfield Diary,* 3:460 (16 Mar. 1877).

13. On Austin, see Introduction to *Garfield-Henry Letters,* p. xvii; Peskin, *Garfield,* esp. pp. 275–76; Margaret Leech and Harry J. Brown, *The Garfield Orbit* (New York, 1978), esp. pp. 118–21. On Henry, see the same, and Frederick A. Henry, *Captain Henry of Geauga: A Family Chronicle* (Cleveland, 1942); Henry's recognition of his subordinate status is clearly articulated in Henry to Garfield, 2 Feb. 1870, *Garfield-Henry Letters,* p. 15.

better federal offices, and these, in turn, enhanced his political usefulness. Thus, by 1873, Henry was one of three Post Office Department special agents in Ohio, which required him to travel throughout the Nineteenth District—and which, not accidentally, enabled him to inform the congressman "more fully of your friends and enemies what are their plans and what they are doing." As he explained to his patron on September 1: "I will be able to get route agents to report to me of what they hear in politics and give you the report from week to week or day to day if need be." Over time, these expectations were more than realized.

The general took full advantage of the proffered services, both generally and in specific situations. Shortly after Henry's promotion came through, for example, Garfield wrote that he "was getting up a list of friends in the different towns that I might write to if necessary. I shall be glad [to] add to it such names as you may from time to time suggest."[14] Heading the list was Austin, of course, with whom both congressman and captain stayed in touch; on it, too, were other old acquaintances about whose reliability Garfield felt secure. But additional contacts nurtured by Henry quickly came to comprise a network of secondary, or localized, sources, who formed the foundation of a political organization that could be activated in Garfield's interests. Practical control of that machine rested not with the general, however, but rather with those on the scene, whose influence over patronage became an instrument they could wield to enforce local partisan loyalties. As a result, Henry and Austin personally were empowered by their efforts in the legislator's behalf, since their endorsements would be won only by those office-seekers who could persuade them of support for the member. And what better way was there to do that convincingly than to have worked previously for the agents' organization?

Clearly, the relationships between these two men and Garfield were multifaceted, and in many respects appear far removed from what falls easily within the rubric of lobbying. But the very closeness and complexity of their interaction meant that, when either Henry or Austin did assume the task of representing certain clienteles' interests, his

---

14. Henry to Garfield, 1 Sept., 20 and 30 Dec. 1873, 16 June 1874; Garfield to Henry, 14 Dec. 1873, 3 Jan. 1874; *Garfield-Henry Letters*, pp. 58, 68, 73, 77–78, 81–82, 105. [Note: All letters in this volume—either originals or typed copies—can be found in the Garfield Papers; due to the greater accessibility of the published collection, citations for all materials contained in it will be to the book, rather than to the manuscripts.]

access to the congressman was sure and direct, and his advocacy was bound to win a hearing. And as the former general came to depend on their advice and to assume that their information was usually reliable, the two men's influence over decisions he made became ever greater and more frequent. By the time Garfield started his second decade in the House, those constituents who wanted federal jobs were well aware of the benefits that could accrue to them through these agents' intercessory support. Thus, both office-seekers and legislator repeatedly put Austin and Henry in the position of facilitating their dealings with each other. When it came to patronage—however informally it happened and however righteously they might have eschewed the title—Henry and Austin began unmistakably to assume the roles and functions of lobbyists.

The impact and persistence of the agents' authority, of course, derived first from the fact that their intelligence and recommendations were appropriate to Garfield's needs, both explicit and implicit. For example, they knew about and, on the whole, approved of the congressman's desire to make competent appointments—and knew also that they soon would lose his ear if very many they endorsed proved unworthy. Thus, one overall consequence of their lobbying was the maintenance of proficiency in the Nineteenth District's federal civil service. By itself, however, that was not too difficult since, in most cases—particularly after the Panic of 1873—a number of qualified candidates were likely to surface for every opening. Once merit could be assumed, other factors became decisive, including local sentiment and political loyalty. Ultimately, then, it was Austin and Henry's ability to appreciate and satisfy these criteria—in which, they complained, the general himself evinced far too little interest—that accounted for the extensiveness and longevity of their influence. It also played no small role in helping to see Garfield through his crucial 1874 reelection bid, when, despite Credit Mobilier and the Salary Grab and Democracy's statewide ascendance, he emerged with the largest majority among Ohio's G.O.P. House members.[15]

He faced a difficult campaign that year, however, and as late as October, success could not be taken for granted. The biggest trouble spot seemed to be the town of Niles, in Austin's Trumbull County, where one of the incumbent's most vocal and potentially dangerous detractors was Alvin J. Dyer, a repeatedly disappointed candidate for

15. Henry to Garfield, 29 May 1876, *Garfield-Henry Letters*, p. 164; Austin to Garfield, 17 and 22 May 1876, Garfield Papers; Peskin, *Garfield*, p. 383.

postmaster. The occasions of Dyer's rejection, and subsequent contests in Niles and in neighboring Mineral Ridge, were classic examples of distributive decision making as practiced in the Garfield orbit.

Aside from Harmon Austin, the congressman's "firmest and most powerful" friend in Trumbull County had been iron manufacturer Josiah Robbins, Sr., who, in appreciation for his support, was named postmaster of Niles in the late sixties. But the aging former state legislator's health began to fail in the fall of 1873, and on December 11 he died. The vying to replace him started while he was still alive. A letter of December 9 from Henry to the congressman warned that "the Niles P.O. may want a little tender handling before long," and said that the hostile Dyer had bought a newspaper there, which he intended to transform into an opposition organ if he were not awarded the federal job. His chief competitor was the dying incumbent's younger son Charles, who himself was not without flaws: "a sort of boy, good hearted, true, but full of dog and gun, and careless about letting people have access behind his letter case." Thus, as Henry admitted, "neither one would make a model postmaster," and both he and Garfield wished in vain that the more responsible Josiah, Jr., were willing to serve, instead of his errant brother.[16]

Nevertheless, "Charlie" and Dyer comprised the field, and one of them would have to be appointed. Garfield was torn; the Robbins family's loyalty was important to him, but so was the fact that Dyer, despite his threats of journalistic retaliation, had been a "42nd boy." At the last regimental reunion, moreover, the general had promised the supplicant that "if I could consistently help him in any way I should be glad to do so"—although, just an hour after that talk, Captain George Pardee had told him "to beware of Dyer as an Enemy," because Dyer "wasn't going to commit himself to Garfield's future" unless and until the politician "came through." Thus, unsure as to what he should do, the congressman took a characteristic course of action. He wrote to Agent Henry: "I have always acted on the principle of giving a P.O. to the man whom the people want, but if Dyer has joined the Trumbull Co. enemy, I don't feel like helping him and turning away from the Robbins boys who have always stood by me. I have written to Harmon Austin and asked him to go down to Niles and look the field over & let me know the situation. I wish you would write me immediately and give

16. Henry to Garfield, 9 and 20 Dec. 1873, and Garfield to Henry, 14 and 18 Dec. 1873, *Garfield-Henry Letters*, pp. 65, 67, 71, 72, and 49 (note 10); see also Peskin, *Garfield*, pp. 366–68; *Garfield Diary*, 2:164–65 (27–31 Mar. 1873).

me your impression of the case. . . . of [all] this you know better than I."[17] What Garfield really hoped was that both "popular preference" and fitness could prevail; hence, he was particularly eager for the captain to look into Dyer's charges of mismanagement under the senior Robbins. But whatever intelligence and sentiment reached him in this manner would hardly be disinterested; it would come to him only through the catalytic action of his established confidants and intermediaries.

By December 22 the congressman had received a variety of communications on affairs in Niles, including reports from friends like Austin, Henry, and others, and a petition signed by 370 of the town's eligible voters, urging the selection of Robbins. It was this last item that he publicly acknowledged as most persuasive, but it is clear that the others also figured prominently in his decision to favor Charlie. The general clearly was impressed by the repeated allegations of Dyer's political "unsoundness," which later events proved to be quite valid— for Dyer responded immediately to his rejection with a "declaration of War." As a result, a follow-up lobbying campaign got under way, but with the "people" and not the member as its target; the same men who so recently had counseled Garfield now turned to his constituents, to persuade them—with some success, as returns the next fall would prove—that, contrary to charges by Dyer and his supporters, the Representative had acted in the "public interest." While Trumbull County continued to be Garfield's biggest headache in the district, the efforts of Austin, Henry, and those under their leadership were able to counteract Dyer's attempts to cause trouble.[18]

The Niles incident of 1873–74 shows lobbying's potential to clarify otherwise knotty and troublesome representational situations. Garfield's agents—operating from long-evolved foundations of proven reliability—not only could take soundings as to what was going on, but could interpret their findings, transmit diagnoses and prognoses to the man in Washington, and to a great extent decide for him what course of action he should follow. Men like Austin and Henry clearly fulfilled the lobbyist's role as intermediary, facilitating communication in both directions between the policy maker and the public.

Not all cases were quite so amenable to such intercession, however, as was revealed by subsequent events in Niles, less than three years after those described above. Charles Robbins, as Garfield and his advisers

17. Garfield to Henry, 14 Dec. 1873, *Garfield-Henry Letters*, pp. 67–68.

18. Garfield to Henry, 22 Dec. 1873, 3 and 13 Jan. 1874, and Henry to Garfield, 1, 5, 7, 8, 14, 17, and 19 Jan. 1874, *Garfield-Henry Letters*, pp. 73–74, 76–77, 80–90. Most of the January letters from Henry refer in part to efforts of Austin on Garfield's behalf.

had feared, soon proved to be an embarrassment; he apparently was "careless" and, on at least one occasion—justified as jubilant "inflation" over the Republican victory of 1875—had been found conspicuously drunk on duty. Obviously, he had to be removed. A Mr. W. H. Biery expressed some interest in taking over, but did not press his case too strongly; in any event, Josiah Robbins, Jr., now was willing to serve, and quietly was appointed to replace his brother. Within just six months, though, rumors surfaced that Josiah wanted to retire.[19] Once again— and, again, before the incumbent actually stepped down—the vying began anew, with half-a-dozen aspirants striving to succeed him.[20]

This time there were no old friends or "42nd boys" in contention. Yet the very absence of either a clear frontrunner or overt enemy made lobbying all the more necessary. How else was an individual to be chosen from a field of virtually indistinguishable men? Complicating matters further was the matter of timing. In the first place, the Republican National Convention was approaching, with both James G. Blaine and Ohio governor Rutherford B. Hayes eagerly soliciting Garfield's support. Second, an equally complicated and thorny postmastership drive was occurring in the town of Mineral Ridge.

The presidential nomination is obviously outside the scope of this discussion, but, even without that, Garfield had plenty to do. Writing to Henry before either sitting postmaster resigned, he complained: "They are in a first class muddle in both Niles and Mineral Ridge, there being a half dozen candidates in each place." The congressman wanted nothing better than to ignore the two affairs, hoping somehow they would resolve themselves. That, of course, was impossible, so he resorted to his usual technique, declaring that "the people" must decide. But just to make sure that they decided *properly*, he dispatched the captain and Harmon Austin to oversee things.[21]

19. Josiah Robbins to Garfield, 6 Nov. 1875, and W. H. Biery to Garfield, 9 Nov. 1875, Garfield Papers.

20. Letters from would-be postmasters and their supporters were dated as early as 13 May 1876: H. H. Mason (vice-president, Citizens Savings & Loan Association, Niles) to Garfield. Mason declared his candidacy and noted that Wilson Biery and William Jones already were circulating petitions for themselves. Mason complained that he could not submit a long petition himself, since the others had known of the vacancy and started collecting names before he could begin. But in that same day's mail, Garfield also received a petition endorsing Mason, with 100 signatures. Both items in Garfield Papers. From that day forward, the congressman's mail always contained items pertaining to the Niles job. But on 31 May he wrote to Henry, "Josiah Robbins has not yet resigned and of course I shall take no action until I hear from him"; *Garfield-Henry Letters*, p. 164.

21. Referring to both contests, Garfield said, "All the candidates had better agree upon

In both towns, controversy emerged not only over whom to appoint, but also over how it should be done. During the last two weeks of May 1876, Garfield received numerous letters—from Henry and Austin, postmastership candidates and their respective backers, and self-proclaimed "disinterested citizens"—either calling for "endorsement elections" among G.O.P. voters or opposing them on the grounds that none could be held fairly. Some people vacillated. In Mineral Ridge, for instance, virtually all leading contenders went on record at various times both for and against a referendum; one must assume that their minds changed as perceptions of their respective chances shifted. Even Harmon Austin, whose opinions on strategy were explicitly solicited by the general, sent contradictory views within a two-day period.[22] And at the same time, Garfield was hearing from various sources that particular candidates were "true Republicans" and "your friends," while their adversaries were Greeleyites, "carpetbaggers," or other equally disreputable types.[23]

After weeks of such commotion, Garfield ordered the Republican voters of Mineral Ridge to hold an instructional election, and promised to give the job there to whoever won. Accordingly, a name was chosen and sent to Washington, and the controversy seemingly was over. Almost immediately, however, Henry, Austin, and other trusted lieutenants wrote urgently to declare the contest to have been fraudulent, since many who voted—including a large proportion of those backing the winner—were Greenbackers or "closet Democrats." Faced with such

---

an expression by petition, so that I may know what the people want"; Garfield to Henry, 31 May 1876, *Garfield-Henry Letters*, p. 164. The "first class muddle" was exacerbated by one man, William Jones, who was running in *both* towns: L. L. Campbell to Garfield, 10 May 1876; William Jones to Garfield, 12 June 1876; Josiah Robbins to Garfield, 15 May 1876 (all in Garfield Papers).

22. Austin to Garfield, 20 and 22 May 1876; two or more letters to Garfield between 17 and 24 May 1876 from each of the following Mineral Ridge candidates: E. J. Ohls, Joseph Stuart, Thomas J. Moore, J. Y. Pearce; all in Garfield Papers.

23. The following letter, referring to Mineral Ridge, was typical: "Since writing you the 15th endorsing Broth T. J. More for the appointment of P. M. at MR I have come in possession of some material facts which make it necessary that you should be apprised of. Namely He is not sound Politically He is what is known here as a 'GreenBacker.' Mineral Ridge Republicans hate them more than they do the Democrats. And so far as party and especially your self If your humble servant has no show for the place your next best man is Joseph Stuart and if he is appointed we will try to keep him straight until the next Congressional Convention in this district. But do not for a moment think of E. J. Ohl or Jones for they have no Republican Influence to do you or the party any good." J. Y. Pearce to Garfield, 16 May 1876 (spelling, capitalization, and grammar as in the original), Garfield Papers. Note that Pearce is retracting one endorsement, making another, and running for the place himself.

an impasse, the general refused to act and, as a result, the office stayed vacant for quite some time.[24]

Matters in Niles, meanwhile, were so confused that in separate letters Henry endorsed two different men—then admitted he had no idea what was going on, suggested it would be best to ignore his comments, and deferred to the presumably superior judgment of Austin. Austin, in turn, declared that he did not have all the facts, either, alleged that the outgoing Robbins was supporting a Mr. Jones and so he also was "inclined" that way, concluded that "I would let them fight their own battles," and asserted that he really wanted to remain neutral. Robbins, incidentally, did not support Jones in Niles, although he did suggest him for the job at Mineral Ridge; a brother, A. M. Robbins, took a stand regarding Niles, but in behalf of a Mr. H. H. Mason.[25]

If in retrospect this all seems hopelessly chaotic, rest assured that it seemed more so at the time. As Postal Agent J. Y. Pearce remarked on May 25: "Letters and their number is Legion. Chaf [sic] abundant. Can you find any wheat?" Immediately, he made things worse—announcing that a new man, John B. Lewis, was entering the Mineral Ridge race with "a clear record as a Union soldier capable Honest and a faithful Party Record [who] will receive the endorsement of the leading Republicans of the county. Make no endorsement before he has a chance to be heard."[26]

Pearce need not have worried; Garfield had no intention of rushing in where even fools would fear to tread. Instead, he wrote an open letter to editor N. N. Bartlett, which was published in the Trumbull County *Independent* on May 31. And while it specifically mentioned only Niles, we can assume that his views on Mineral Ridge were comparable. "So many different candidates have been recommended that I am quite at a loss to know what the majority of the Republicans desire," he declared. "They ought to settle that question for themselves and not require me to make a choice which would be less apt to give satisfaction than their own determination in the case." Then, after listing alternative methods by which the selection could be accomplished, the

24. There are at least thirty letters in the Garfield Papers that document this prolonged quandary, beginning on 10 May 1876 and continuing through the fall; correspondence is especially heavy during July.

25. Henry to Garfield, 29 May and 25 June 1876, *Garfield-Henry Letters*, pp. 163, 165; Austin to Garfield, 17 May 1876, Josiah Robbins to Garfield, 16 May 1876, and A. M. Robbins to Garfield, 22 May 1876, Garfield Papers.

26. Pearce to Garfield, 25 May 1876, and J. B. Lewis to Garfield, 3 June 1876, Garfield Papers; see also note 23, above.

weary member asked Bartlett to "please show this letter to the leading Republicans and request them for me to determine what course shall be pursued."

When the letter was printed, it was accompanied by an editorial comment to the effect that, amid such muddle, neither elections nor petitions were really feasible, and the congressman himself should make the choice. Bartlett realized that some citizens would be dissatisfied with any selection that ensued; nevertheless, he argued, "if the leading Republicans can not unite and decide here and now what they want in this matter it will very illy become them to find fault with Gen. Garfield for not deciding the matter for them."[27]

The confusion Garfield was confronted with was not of his own invention; rather, it can be seen as resulting not from too many pressures, but from the absence of effective ones. Lobbying was supposed to serve as a bridge between the government and the people. What the examples of Niles and Mineral Ridge suggest is that bridges could collapse—and that even the most reliable agents could fail. But their failures did not, as critics of lobbying have charged, enhance the public's chance to speak up and be heard for itself. Instead, no meaningful messages got through, and responsive representation was impossible.

Events in the two Trumbull County towns typified the "small contests, on little points" that so preoccupied the 1870s Congress. Postmasters mattered both concretely and symbolically to ordinary Americans at the time, especially to those in outlying areas, in no small measure because these were normally the only tangible manifestations of federal authority that they encountered. The selection of such officials, therefore, was an important and highly visible expression of political representation at work, which is why so much effort went into determining and satisfying popular opinion (even if only that of *male* partisans).[28] Constructive lobbying, by facilitating those appointments and promoting their public acceptability, could strengthen considerably the often fragile bond between citizens and those who served them in the Capitol. And when that catalytic mediation broke down so, too, did the quality of representation.

27. Clipping from the *Independent* with "editorial comment," filed under 31 May 1876, Garfield Papers.

28. Garfield, "A Century of Congress," p. 62. Ironically, the "postmaster" being replaced in Mineral Ridge was actually a post*mistress*, Mrs. S. C. Willson. Thus, while a woman could hold the job she could not, according to custom or to Garfield's explicit instructions in the 31 May Trumbull *Independent*, participate in the process of filling it.

Jobs within Garfield's gift, like nearly all those at Representatives' disposal, were local, relatively unremunerative, and without much political or programmatic significance to persons outside the legislative district. But the diplomatic service, Supreme Court, cabinet, and other top administrative posts were another matter. Nominees to join these ranks were designated by the president, and House members took no formal part in approving them. Rather, congressional involvement reposed constitutionally in the Senate, whose "advice and [especially] consent" were required for major appointments to go through. Absolved of official responsibility, Representatives were freed to play other roles—including the roles of lobbyists. In the 1870s, with memories of Tenure of Office and Johnson's impeachment still fresh, and confirmations by no means so automatic as they once had been or would become again, such roles were often far from negligible.

Two cases from Boston provide dramatic, but hardly unique, testimony to the machinations that could ensue from high-stakes patronage politics, as well as to the significance that congressmen could have in determining particular outcomes.[29] At the time of Grant's second inaugural, Massachusetts was a center of the civil service reform movement and—with Boston's Custom House and Navy Yards—a leading beneficiary of the spoils system. It was also home to some of the era's most prominent and powerful politicians: its senators were Charles Sumner and former treasury secretary George S. Boutwell, and its House delegation, diminished temporarily by the absence of Nathaniel P. Banks, included George Frisbie Hoar and his brother, former attorney general Ebenezer Rockwood Hoar; Ways & Means chairman Henry L. Dawes; and presidential confidant Benjamin F. ("Black Ben") Butler. All these men were instrumental in—and (especially in Butler's case) affected by—the events to be recounted here. The Bay State Republican party was riddled with ideological and personality-based factions, as the number and identities of its legislative leaders might suggest. So when Bostonians were considered for major federal offices, some camp or interest was bound to be antagonized; contention was practically inevitable.[30] And that is precisely what occurred when

29. A more extended version of the account that follows is in Margaret S. Thompson, "Ben Butler versus the Brahmins: Patronage and Politics in Early Gilded Age Massachusetts," *New England Q.*, 55 (1982), 163–86.

30. Richard E. Welch, Jr., *George Frisbie Hoar and the Half-Breed Republicans* (Cambridge, 1971), pp. 28–58; George S. Merriam, *The Life and Times of Samuel Bowles*, 2 vols. (New York, 1885), 2:86–109, 264–87; Geoffrey Blodgett, *The Gentle Reformers: Massachusetts Democrats in the Cleveland Era* (Cambridge, 1966); and, for more detail on the various factions, Thompson, "Butler versus the Brahmins," 165–67.

William A. Simmons was named Collector of Customs in 1874 and, two years later, when Richard Henry Dana, Jr., was proposed as minister to the Court of St. James.

The facts in both affairs are relatively straightforward. In January 1874, allies of Representative Benjamin Butler devised a plan whereby incumbent Boston collector Thomas Russell would be named—or led to believe he would be named—minister to Spain, thereby forcing him to resign from the Custom House.[31] His place would go to William A. Simmons, then New England district supervisor of Internal Revenue and a man whom Springfield *Republican* editor Samuel Bowles described as "one of Butler's most serviceable lieutenants. . . .a man of good private life, a church-goer, a Methodist class-leader, but a practiced adept in manipulating the lowest class of voters, and in carrying elections by dubious means."[32] Bowles and other critics accused the "Butlerites" of orchestrating the entire scheme; G.O.P. reformers complained that, by the time they learned of the impending vacancy, Grant was committed to Simmons and refused to consider anyone else. Evidence exists to dispute this charge, but it is true that no alternative candidacies ever were contemplated seriously.[33]

When Simmons's nomination to head the Custom House was announced publicly in mid-February 1874, opposition to it was intense and apparently widespread, at least among the "Best Men" of Boston; among those hostile were seven of the Bay State's eleven-man Republican House delegation, its two Republican senators, nearly all of Boston's business and financial establishment, and majority of the city's newspapers.[34] To complicate matters further, Collector Russell—whose anticipated diplomatic commission had failed to materialize—insisted that he had never stepped down officially and that the effort to unseat

---

31. Most scholars place the initiation of this case in February (e.g., James Ford Rhodes, *History of the United States*, 7 vols. [New York, 1906], 7:23), but the earlier date is documented in William A. Simmons to Edward R. Tinker, 6 Feb. 1874, Dawes Papers.

32. Quoted by Merriam in *Bowles*, 2:265–66.

33. Alternatives were discussed in Simmons to Tinker (note 31, above); see also Sarah Hildreth (Mrs. B. F.) Butler to Blanche Butler Ames, 18 Feb. 1874, in *Chronicles from the Nineteenth Century: Family Letters of Blanche Butler and Adelbert Ames*, ed. Blanche B. Ames, 2 vols. (Clinton, Mass., 1957), 1:653.

34. David Herbert Donald, *Charles Sumner and the Rights of Man* (New York, 1970), pp. 581–82; George F. Hoar, *Autobiography of Seventy Years*, 2 vols. (New York, 1903), 1:210–11; Hans L. Trefousse, *Ben Butler: The South Called Him BEAST!* (New York, 1957), pp. 227–28; *Nation*, 19 and 26 Feb. 1874, pp. 116, 131; Gardiner G. Hubbard to Dawes, 24 Feb. 1874, Dawes Papers; J. H. Goodsell to Butler, 25 Feb. 1874, Butler Papers.

Representative Benjamin F. ("Black Ben") Butler, Republican, Massachusetts. Courtesy Library of Congress, Division of Prints and Photographs.

him was thus illegal. Many of Simmons's foes rallied to the erstwhile incumbent's cause.[35]

Normally the senators' hostility alone would have sufficed to defeat the appointment, since senatorial courtesy implicitly forbade confirmation of anybody opposed by a majority party member from his home state. Because of his repeated disputes with Grant, however, Sumner no longer was regarded as "of the President's party" and either did not invoke such privilege or did so ineffectually. Boutwell, meanwhile, announced on the floor that he would refuse to vote for Simmons but, for reasons never articulated openly, would not appeal to senatorial courtesy.[36]

In any event, when the nomination was considered in the Senate on 26 February, it was defeated, 15–20. But since no quorum was present, there was a second ballot the next day, after a night reportedly filled with arm-twisting and threats of political retaliation. Despite the fact that only one New England senator—Rhode Island's William Sprague—said "aye," Simmons was confirmed, 30–16, with heavy Democratic support.[37]

Exactly two years later, when U.S. minister to Britain Robert Schenck was recalled in disgrace for his participation in a fraudulent mining scheme, the Brahmin Richard Henry Dana, Jr., was proposed as his replacement.[38] Today Dana probably is remembered best as the author of *Two Years before the Mast*, but in his own time he was equally renowned as an authority on international law and as an outspoken reform leader. In the latter capacity he had run for Congress as an independent against Ben Butler in 1868. While Butler achieved a clear electoral majority over Dana and a Democrat, the campaign was un-

---

35. Hubbard to Dawes, 24 Feb. 1874, and Governor William B. Washburn to Dawes, 18 Feb. 1874, Dawes Papers.

36. Both Rhodes and Boutwell said that Sumner did invoke senatorial courtesy; Donald argued that he did not: Rhodes, *History*, 7:23; George S. Boutwell, *Reminiscences of Sixty Years in Public Affairs*, 2 vols. (New York, 1902), 2:283; Donald, *Sumner*, p. 582. Boutwell's attempt to explain his own actions is in *Reminiscences*, 2:283; but see also Ames, *Chronicles*, 1:658.

37. *Sen. Exec. J.*, 43d Cong., 1st sess., 26 and 27 Feb. 1874, pp. 259–60. Evidence of lobbying, particularly among Democrats, is in telegrams to Sen. Thomas F. Bayard (D-Del.) from Michael Doherty and F. O. Prince (secretary, Democratic National Committee), both 27 Feb. 1874, Thomas F. Bayard Papers, L.C.

38. On Schenck, see Allan Nevins, *Hamilton Fish: The Inner History of the Grant Administration* (New York, 1936), pp. 649–54, 814–15; and William S. McFeely, *Grant: A Biography* (New York, 1981), pp. 429–30.

usually vitriolic and left lasting scars and undying enmity between victor and vanquished.[39]

Butler, himself defeated in 1874, was not in the House when Dana's designation was announced. Nonetheless, still rancored over the events of 1868, Butler hurried to Washington and began to lobby against confirmation. Accompanying and assisting him was one William B. Lawrence, who, in the late 1860s, had sued Dana for plagiarism in connection with an edition of Henry Wheaton's *Elements of International Law*. The verdict had been generally favorable to Dana, but the plaintiff continued to insist that the Bostonian was guilty. Butler and Lawrence, in an appearance before the Senate Foreign Relations Committee and elsewhere, revived the plagiarism charge, now augmented by charges of perjury, and generated suspicion in the minds of some previously uncommitted Republicans with the unfounded allegation that Dana had voted for Horace Greeley in the presidential election of 1872.[40] Concurrently Lawrence, a Democrat, lobbied determinedly among the minority, whose members did not believe or care about the Greeley business. Instead, they were reminded of Dana's abolitionist heritage and ardent wartime Unionism; further, they were encouraged to see the present occasion as an election-year opportunity to embarrass Grant and the G.O.P. by defeating the administration's choice. Prompted by Lawrence and other party leaders, like New York *World* editor Manton Marble, Democrats eventually would vote in a bloc against the appointment.[41]

Behind Dana were virtually the same forces that had opposed Simmons, including Senator Boutwell. Sumner had died within two weeks of the 1874 collectorship vote, but the current holder of his seat, Henry L. Dawes, added his endorsement to Dana's nomination. Yet neither

39. Charles Francis Adams II, *Richard Henry Dana: A Biography*, 2 vols. (Boston, 1890), 2:343–49; Samuel Shapiro, *Richard Henry Dana, Jr., 1815–1882* (East Lansing, 1961), pp. 141–53; Benjamin F. Butler, *Butler's Book: A Review of His Legal, Political, and Military Career* (Boston, 1892), pp. 921–22. The *Nation*, regarding this as a classic duel between good and evil, published over twenty articles and editorials on the matter between 1 Oct. and 19 Nov. 1876.

40. Shapiro, *Dana*, p. 166 and chap. 11; Adams, *Dana*, 2:282–327; Roland Worthingham (Boston *Traveller*) to Butler, 29 Mar. 1876, and Butler to Worthingham, 1 Apr. 1876, Butler Papers.

41. Of twenty-eight Senate Democrats, only seven were from former free states, and some of these had definite Copperhead tendencies during the War. Thus Butler's appeal might be expected to be effective with at least 75 percent of the caucus. (Data on members from *BDAC*.) William B. Lawrence to Manton Marble, 6, 23, 25, and 26 Mar. 1874, Manton Marble Papers, L.C.; Adams, *Dana*, 2:368, 374.

Boutwell nor Dawes worked particularly hard in Dana's behalf. They surely were aware, for instance, that for reasons of his own, Foreign Relations chairman Simon Cameron (R-Pa.) had granted a secret hearing to Butler and Lawrence.[42] Neither attempted to stop the session from taking place, however, or to let Dana know of it beforehand.

When the nominee learned of Cameron's action and of his intention to issue an adverse report based on the secret testimony, he was outraged. At that point, his supporters persuaded Cameron to grant the "accused" a hearing so that he might refute the charges levied against him. Despite his advisers' urgings, Dana refused to cooperate, declaring that the committee had been "Butlerized" and that he could not dignify such a proceeding with his presence. As he explained later to his son, he would not countenance "the humiliation of going before such a committee to vindicate my character against charges by Butler,—a great office being the prize!" So, he concluded, "My only course was to refuse to go, and to give the true reason for it to the whole world."[43]

Dana sent an open letter to Senator Boutwell declining the invitation to testify; he closed by saying that "there is nothing in the gift of the government which would induce me to go to Washington and submit a question touching my honor to a committee which has taken the course which has been taken by the Senate Committee on Foreign Affairs [*sic*]." While many reformers hailed this response—Samuel Bowles termed it a gesture by which "Dana did more for his party and for himself . . . than he ever did before in all his life"—Cameron and others were not impressed. On 21 March 1876 the committee unanimously rejected Dana and cited the Boutwell letter as justification. Chairman Cameron accused the would-be diplomat of having "flaunted an insulting letter in their faces" and apparently persuaded his colleagues that the "honor of the United States Senate" demanded the rejection of such a candidate. Two weeks later, on the Senate floor, Dana's nomination was defeated by a vote of 17–30.[44]

---

42. Nevins argued that Cameron's opposition stemmed from the hope that his son, J. Donald ("Don"), would be awarded the mission. When Dana was rejected, Attorney General Edwards Pierrepont was confirmed in his stead, Secretary of War Alphonso Taft became attorney general, and Don Cameron was named secretary of war. Nevins, *Fish*, p. 830; Ellis Paxson Oberholtzer, *A History of the United States since the Civil War*, 5 vols. (New York, 1920), 3:187.

43. Quoted by Adams in *Dana*, 2:370–71.

44. Dana to Boutwell, 16 Mar. 1876, quoted in Adams, *Dana*, 2:372–73; Bowles quoted

Ben Butler, according to friends and foes alike, was the single person most responsible for the senatorial verdicts in both the Simmons and Dana cases. When the former name was submitted, for instance, Mrs. Butler told her daughter, "It is your father's doing"; when the matter was decided, the daughter wrote: "We have all been rejoicing in father's great victory—for I am sure it must be considered such." The *Nation*, representative of Black Ben's detractors, repeatedly tied Simmons's name to his; it stated that "Butler had had him nominated" and that, in the subsequent battle, "Mr. Butler is of course the central figure." After Simmons's confirmation Butler received dozens of congratulatory messages, most containing allusions to "your triumph," "the force which you exhibited," "your appointing W. A. Simmons a Collector," or similar expressions. He also got countless requests for aid in obtaining Custom House employment—a flood that included many petitions from outside his district and that began even before his protégé took office.[45] As for Dana, the *Nation* again recognized Butler's decisive participation, while a friend told Senator Dawes that "[Dana's] defeat will give comfort to those who have sought to place Genl Butler in the Gubernatorial chair." A historian would state succinctly in 1926, "Ben Butler, in whose political retinue the distinguished appointee had never been, organized an opposition and the senators rejected the nomination."[46]

Although Butler's central role in these affairs can be accepted without quarrel, several questions still remain. First, and most easily resolved, how did he go about securing his objectives and why was he tactically more successful than his opponents? Second, why did he exert himself in these matters, and what motivated his adversaries? And third, what were the ramifications of his actions, both for himself and for others who had concerned themselves in the disposition of these cases?

The strategic differences between Butler's two lobbying efforts stemmed mainly from the point at which he entered each campaign. In regard to the collectorship, he knew about the impending vacancy in

in Shapiro, *Dana*, p. 168, see also p. 169; Nevins, *Fish*, p. 830; *Sen. Exec. J.*, 44th Cong., 1st sess. (4 Apr. 1876), 216.

45. Sarah Butler to Blanche B. Ames, 18 Feb. 1874, and Ames to Butler, 4 Mar. 1874, in Ames, *Chronicles*, 1:653–56; *Nation*, 19 and 26 Feb. 1874, pp. 116, 131; letters from W. H. Seaman, H. Blanchard, C. H. Frothingham to Butler, all 28 Feb. 1874, and David H. Jones to Butler, 3 Mar.. 1874, Butler Papers.

46. *Nation*, 16 and 23 Mar., 6 Apr. 1874; Charles W. Clifford to Dawes, 22 Mar. 1876, Dawes Papers; Oberholtzer, *History of the United States*, 3:187.

advance—indeed, was instrumental in creating it; thus, he could approach Grant about a replacement and could secure the nomination for his favorite prior to the incumbent's resignation. Timing was of the essence here. By the time potential competitors were alerted to the forthcoming change, it would be too late for them to influence the president. While some attempt was made to pressure Grant to withdraw Simmons's name, it failed, and opponents were forced into the difficult position of attacking the proposal without having any alternative to offer. In Dana's case, however, Grant and Secretary of State Hamilton Fish apparently decided on their own, with no outside consultation, to submit their nominee's name to the Senate.[47] With Simmons, Butler had been able to indulge in slow and meticulous planning; in 1876 he was faced with an unsatisfactory fait accompli, entered the battle at a much later stage, and had to scramble for an effective strategy.

Nevertheless, once senatorial confirmation rather than just nomination was at stake, the Dana and Simmons campaigns exhibited many similarities on the parts of both Butler and his adversaries. Based upon what can be gleaned from extant correspondence, newspaper coverage, and memoirs, those who opposed Simmons and supported Dana seem to have concentrated on orchestrating what were to strike Washingtonians as spontaneous expressions of "grass-roots" sentiment. Through telegrams, letters, journalistic reports, and so forth, they attempted to create the impression that "Simmons is an insult to all decent men," but that the minister-designate was "a really first-class nomination," "a man of character and reputation," and that "it will be a bad thing for us in Boston if Dana is not confirmed."[48] In neither 1874 nor 1876, however, was there much evidence of direct contact between the Brahmin reform lobbyists and those whom they were trying to influence—a circumstance fully in accord with genteel attitudes both toward the process of lobbying and toward "lusting for office."[49]

Butler, too, was backed by communications from the home front. Some seemed to have arrived gratuitously, whereas others obviously

---

47. Hoar, *Autobiography*, 1:210–11; Nevins, *Fish*, p. 829.

48. On Simmons, see A. W. Beard to Dawes, 19 Feb. 1874, and Edward Atkinson to Dawes, two each on 17 and 19 Feb. 1874, Dawes Papers; Edward Atkinson and O. E. Doolittle to George F. Hoar, both 17 Feb. 1874, and E. T. Raymond to Hoar, 20 Feb. 1874, Hoar Papers. On Dana, see Shapiro, *Dana*, p. 167.

49. Thompson, "Butler versus the Brahmins," 165–67; Geoffrey Blodgett, "Reform Thought and the Genteel Tradition," and Ari Hoogenboom, "Spoilsmen and Reformers: Civil Service Reform and Public Morality," in *The Gilded Age: A Reappraisal*, ed. H. Wayne

resulted from concerted agitation by Black Ben's faithful Boston lieutenants. Among the latter were petitions from veterans and workingmen, as well as politicians; the pro-Simmons forces used them as
evidence that they represented the "real" popular sentiment, whereas
the opposition was composed of "self-styled respectable old fogies,"
"Yankee aristocrats," and "anti-office-seeking office-seekers and their
ruffianly newspapers." Similar impressions were cultivated two years
later.[50]

Yet what most distinguished Butler's lobbying from that of his unsuccessful foes, and doubtless contributed materially to his victories, was
the personal elements in it. There was, to begin with, his physical
presence in Washington, even on the floor of the Senate. As one
historian has described his efforts for Simmons: "he 'walked the lobbies, puffing and snorting like a healthy sea lion,' cornering a friend
here, whispering to a Senator there, until the full chamber, badgered,
wheedled, brought into line by his incredible exertions, voted to confirm." More specifically, his pleas to individual members were expressed in terms of friendship for and obligation to him. Thus, he
asked Carpetbag senator and former general George E. Spencer (R-
Ala.) to "see [Arkansas Republican Senators] Clayton and Dorsey for
me and say to them that I will take it as a personal favor if they will
interpose between me and my opponent for many years, Mr. Dana." A
similar appeal to black senator Blanche K. Bruce (R-Miss.) invoked
memories of Butler's long-standing loyalty to the freedmen. Bruce
responded that, because of the request, "I shall certainly vote against
his confirmation"; Spencer was absent on the day of balloting, but the
Arkansans also voted in the negative.[51]

Answers to the second and third questions on the Boston episodes—
why Butler and others cared so intensely about these appointments and

Morgan (Syracuse, 1970), pp. 55–109; John G. Sproat, *"The Best Men": Liberal Reformers in
the Gilded Age* (New York, 1968), chap. 9.

50. Letters to Butler from W. H. Seaman, H. Blanchard, Samuel Norwood ("and
many others"), and George Gorham (secretary of the U.S. Senate), all 28 Feb. 1874, and
from Thomas B. Van Buren, 2 Mar. 1874; petitions contained or referred to in J. Ladd to
Butler, 20 Feb. 1874, Andrew J. Baily (Mass. State Senate) to Butler, 19 Feb. 1874, J. H.
Chadwick to Butler, 21 Feb. 1874, and G. F. Sargent to M. A. Clancey (Butler's secretary),
21 Feb. 1874, Butler Papers.

51. Trefousse, *Butler*, p. 228; Butler to Spencer, Butler to Bruce, and Butler to Sen.
Roscoe Conkling (R-N.Y.), all 21 Mar. 1876 (Conkling, however, voted to confirm), and
Bruce to Butler, 22 Mar. 1876, Butler Papers; votes from *Sen. Exec. J.*, 44th Cong., 1st
sess. (4 Apr. 1876), 216.

what the ramifications of their outcomes were—reflect clearly the differences between the two cases. To put it simply, the collectorship was an office of extremely tangible significance to a large and diverse number of people. In contrast, disposition of the British Ministry mattered to few beyond its recipient; its significance was primarily symbolic.

To understand why the Simmons affair excited so much interest, one must appreciate both the political and economic importance of the Gilded Age Custom House. The Boston collectorship was "the juiciest patronage plum in New England," holding rein over more than a quarter of a million dollars in salaries.[52] But control over hundreds of jobs was only one part of the collector's power; he also determined the "assessments" levied on his employees—the technically illegal but long-exacted contributions that grateful workers "donated" to those to whom they owed their livelihoods. The sum involved normally was between 2 and 6 percent of annual earnings, but actual amounts could run higher. Proceeds usually went to the dominant party, although in factionalized states like Massachusetts, individual politicians might receive them.[53] In addition, the collector determined the rigor with which commercial regulations would be enforced through his oversight of the moiety system, which was supposed to promote compliance with customs laws by authorizing rewards to those who informed on lawbreakers. Actually, the system encouraged bribery and profiteering by officials, and public outrage over alleged jobbery and corruption led to the abolition of moieties in 1874—after Simmons's confirmation. Meanwhile Simmons's candidacy was considered in an atmosphere charged with this potent issue, a charge intensified by the aspirant's well-known comradeship with Ben Butler.[54]

Obviously, the people to whom a collectorship mattered were numerous and diverse: businessmen engaged in affected commerce, congressmen who wanted patronage to dispense and citizens who wanted

52. Blodgett, *Gentle Reformers*, p. 57; "The Boston Collectorship," *Nation*, 26 Feb. 1874, pp. 134–35.

53. Thomas C. Reeves, "Chester A. Arthur and Campaign Assessments in the Election of 1880," *The Historian*, 31 (1969), 573–82; Leon Burr Richardson, *William E. Chandler, Republican* (New York, 1940), pp. 91–103, 164–67; E. A. Rollins to Chandler, 27 Jan. and 8 Feb. 1874, and Daniel Hill to Chandler, 26 Jan. 1874, Chandler-NHHS.

54. On moieties (initiated in 1789), see White, *Republican Era*, pp. 123–26; *Evidence before the Committee on Ways and Means Relative to Moieties and Customs-Revenue Laws*, Hse. Misc. Doc. 264, 43d Cong., 1st sess. (1874).

to receive it, and any politicians who cared about assessments and about the clout attached to the man who directed them. In addition, reformers, especially civil service reformers, concentrated much attention—and wrath—upon the position; they regarded the head of the Custom House as "the symbol of the Spoilsman, running a political machine, sacrificing the needs of the community as a whole to the selfish end of practical politics."[55]

Patronage, of course, was a potent weapon in the development and maintenance of a loyal political following. But in an urban setting like Boston, hard hit by reverberations of the Panic of 1873, access to the public employment rolls was a matter of real economic significance as well. It was an accepted fact of life that "friends" of the collector, and of his patron, would enjoy preferential treatment both in the original disposition of jobs and in their retention, when circumstances demanded cutbacks in the Custom House's labor force. At a time of hardship and retrenchment, the identity of the man who headed a major federal installation was therefore especially critical.

It is easy to document how Simmons played the game by examining how he applied his "hire and fire" policy and how he explained it to different correspondents. Even before his confirmation, he wrote to a crony that, if appointed, "the interests of our friends shall be thoroughly looked after"; in context, it is clear that he was referring specifically to Butler and Dawes. Within two months of his ascension to power, he was proving his loyalty, as he informed his patron: "We have got in the Appraisers Dept a *strong vicious Anti-Butler* man who is Examiner of Drugs. . . .We want to get rid of him *now*." In an only slightly less cordial vein, he would reassure a sympathetic Nathaniel P. Banks, after his return to the federal House, that an ordered reduction in force would "fall as lightly upon your Dist. as possible, and only one man there will go." In striking contrast to these statements were the declarations of "unavoidable cuts" and "impartial application" which the collector offered to adversaries; thus, he was exceedingly polite but unresponsive to Butler's congressional foes when they remonstrated on behalf of their dismissed constituents.[56]

55. William J. Hartman, "Politics and Patronage: The New York Custom House, 1852–1902" (Ph.D. diss., Columbia University, 1952), pp. 18–19.

56. Simmons to Edward R. Tinker, 6 Feb. 1874, Dawes Papers; Simmons to Butler, 23 Apr. 1874, Butler Papers; Simmons to Banks, 21 Dec. 1876, Banks Papers; on treatment of a Butler foe, see Simmons to Luke P. Poland (R-Vt.), 12 June 1874, Butler Papers, and Howard P. Nash, Jr., *Stormy Petrel: The Life and Times of General Benjamin F. Butler, 1818–1893* (Rutherford, N.J., 1969), p. 254.

The direct ramifications of a collectorship appointment by now should be apparent. In the Massachusetts case of 1874, however, political implications went well beyond the allocation of jobs. Consequences for statewide elections were at least as important. For besides its recurrence in Butler's several quests for the governorship, aftershock from the Simmons and Dana affairs would reverberate through at least three successive Bay State senatorial battles.

At the time of the collector's nomination, Butler boasted in the lobby of the House that "I have a hold over Grant . . . and he dares not withdraw Simmons' name." Recalling the episode nearly thirty years later, Senator George F. Hoar agreed that there had been such a "hold" but that he believed it resulted from the president's overestimation of the extent of Butler's clout at home.[57] In fact, Massachusetts Republicanism was extremely factionalized; Hoar, a representative in 1874, and his brother Ebenezer Rockwood were leaders of its sizable and aggressively anti-Butler "reform" contingent.

Both the Hoars and Butler were completely unreserved in their expressions of antipathy toward each other. They were antagonists in a rivalry with roots going back to 1852, which would persist in the minds of their respective loyalists even after the principals' deaths.[58] Yet intense and widespread as this internecine hostility was, it never encompassed all party members in the state. A critical number of unaligned individuals, several with their own faithful personal followings, refused to be absorbed into either of the dominant camps. Although they rarely acted in concert, the neutrals, who included powerhouses like Henry L. Dawes, George Boutwell, and, intermittently, Nathaniel Banks, could cast decisive votes in closely contested elections. Therefore, such men were courted assiduously by Butlerites and reformers; bargains, both explicit and implicit, often resulted from these machinations.

Such a bargain obviously was in effect during the contest to replace Senator Charles Sumner, whose term would expire in 1875. Sumner was a founder of the Republican party and probably the most eminent spokesman of its radical reformist wing. But he was notoriously arrogant, and his continued tenure was threatened by repeated and costly

57. Moorfield Storey and E. W. Emerson, *Ebenezer Rockwood Hoar: A Memoir* (Boston, 1911), pp. 255–56; Hoar, *Autobiography*, 1:362; Rhodes, *History*, 7:24; Nash, *Stormy Petrel*, pp. 16, 250; William D. Mallam, "The Grant-Butler Relationship," *MVHR*, 41 (1954), 259–76.

58. Hoar, *Autobiography*, 1:329–63; Butler, *Butler's Book*, pp. 925–56; Nash, *Stormy Petrel*, p. 44; Welch, *Hoar*, pp. 2, 44.

Representative George Frisbie Hoar, Republican, Massachusetts. Courtesy Library of Congress, Division of Prints and Photographs.

disputes with President Grant, which earned for the senator the enmity of both party regulars and Butlerites.[59] Among the candidates who hoped to unseat him were E. Rockwood Hoar, Henry L. Dawes, and Charles Francis Adams. Then on 10 March 1874—scarcely two weeks after Simmons's confirmation—Charles Sumner died. Suddenly the timetable for his replacement was accelerated, and circumstances surrounding the Custom House affair, particularly the conspicuously silent role of Henry Dawes, became an inextricable part of what ensued.

To put it bluntly, it is clear that Dawes and Butler had made a deal; the former would not oppose Simmons and the latter would cast his weight appropriately in the upcoming senatorial race.[60] Documentation for this charge is abundant. (1) Simmons wrote a letter, dated 6 February 1874, to Dawes's henchman Edward R. Tinker, plotting out strategy for the confirmation fight and containing several references to "our friends Butler and Dawes." This letter, written more than a week before Simmons's nomination was made public, also contains details of the scheme that led Collector Russell to resign.[61] (2) Dawes's repeated statements to angry reform correspondents during the latter half of February include his "refusing to be a party in this fight" and a vow that "I will not be [responsible] for any appointment [such as the collectorship] in Massachusetts outside my own district."[62] (3) A letter from Simmons to Dawes, just after the former's confirmation, begins: "We have met the enemy and they are ours . . . What we want in the immediate future is *perfect confidence, consultation,* and *organization,* out of which will surely come success."[63] (4) Several missives from Mrs. Benjamin Butler to her daughter chronicle the collectorship campaign; one ends with a note written one week after Sumner's death: "And then the tug and scramble begins for his place. Your father does not want it. . . . If you hear that Dawes is elected, be satisfied."[64]

Although none of the evidence above was publicly accessible in 1874, contemporary speculation about the existence of some arrangement between the two politicians was widespread and open. Two days after

---

59. Nevins, *Fish,* pp. 311–34, 368–83, 449–65, 497–501; Donald, *Sumner,* pp. 436–75; McFeely, *Grant,* pp. 340–53.

60. During the Simmons campaign, the *Nation* reported that Dawes had been defeated for the Senate in 1873 because Butler had swung the support of many legislators to his "candidate and confidant," George S. Boutwell; 26 Feb. 1874, p. 131.

61. Simmons to Tinker, 6 Feb. 1874, Dawes Papers.

62. Dawes to Alanson W. Beard (later collector himself), 19 Feb. 1874, Dawes to editor of the Boston *Advertiser,* n.d. [20 Feb. 1874(?)], Dawes Papers.

63. Simmons to Dawes, 1 Mar. 1874, Dawes Papers.

64. Butler to Ames, 17 Mar. 1874, in Ames, *Chronicles,* 1:661–62.

Sumner's funeral, the *Nation* reported that "The Butler Republicans—said to number sixty [of 212] in the House—are to a man for Dawes; and if Dawes is elected it will be just as clearly a triumph for Butler as it was when Simmons was confirmed." Similarly, Samuel Bowles's Springfield *Republican* argued that Dawes "was above suspicion of bargaining for this support" but declared that "whether consciously or unconsciously, he has been grinding at Butler's mill."[65] Both journals expressed the opinion, however, that the "Butlerization" of the Custom House was too fresh in the public memory to permit Dawes's election, and in this they apparently were correct. After thirty-two ballots, Governor William B. Washburn—"a respectable man, with decided views about Butlerism"—emerged as the compromise choice. The *Nation* asserted that "Mr. Dawes sees in his defeat the natural consequences of his going off and sulking [!] during the Simmons affair," while Bowles editorialized: "Mr. Dawes has only Mr. Dawes and General Butler to thank for the fact that he is sitting to-day in the House and not the Senate . . . He has made a grave political mistake, he has grieved his real friends . . . and he has allowed his candidacy to be used at a critical moment to confuse the minds of the people of Massachusetts. . . . Rightly appreciated and utilized, the mistake may exert a most beneficent influence upon his future."[66]

The last sentence, at least, was prophetic. For if Dawes and his allies lost the battle in 1874, in the long run they won the war. While Butler might not have been able to elect his own favorite, neither could the genteel reformers he so despised. As the *Nation* said of Washburn's victory, it "indicates the fear of the Hoar men that any attempt to do better would probably result in something worse."[67] Moreover, it must be recalled that the original Dawes-Butler plan had been formulated before Sumner's death, and that January 1875 had been its target; the 1874 contest decided only who would fill the remainder of the late incumbent's tenure, a period of less than a year. When balloting occurred for the full term, Dawes did emerge as the winner—with both the formerly disgruntled Brahmins and the Butlerites lending him their support.

Several factors explain why Bowles, the Hoars, and other reformers backed Dawes in 1875. To begin with, they clearly were impressed by Dawes's competence; George F. Hoar, for instance, asserted in his

---

65. *Nation*, 19 Mar. 1874, p. 179; Bowles quoted in Merriam, *Bowles*, 2:266–67.
66. *Nation*, 23 Apr. 1874, p. 259; Bowles, in Merriam, *Bowles*, 2:267.
67. *Nation*, 23 Apr. 1874, p. 259.

memoirs that, while in the House, "no member . . . from Massachusetts and few from any part of the Union had an influence which could be at all compared with his," and upon the occasion of his colleague's retirement from the Senate he declared him to be "a very powerful and logical reasoner. . . . there is none other who has more faithfully and more successfully discharged every duty [and] more constantly represented the interests [of] the Commonwealth, who has maintained a higher or firmer place in her confidence and respect than he."[68] Second, after eighteen months of careful organizing and planning, Dawes had such a commanding advantage over other senatorial aspirants that there were no viable alternatives to him. Third, Bowles, at least, believed that Dawes had sincerely repented his role in the Simmons affair; as he wrote privately in October to the man he had criticized only months before: "I don't believe you are ignorant why we opposed you last winter and are favoring you now. Elected then, you would have been Butler's and Simmons' man this year; now you are, I trust, your own."[69] And there was also the fact that, the Custom House controversy aside, Dawes was hardly a persistent Butler loyalist. Indeed, during their contemporaneous tenures in the House the two Bay State Representatives had more frequently been antagonists than allies.

Finally, and not insignificantly, the Brahmins—most especially George F. Hoar—had senatorial ambitions themselves. Boutwell's term was to expire in 1877, but he made no secret of his desire to run again. Any challenger would face an uphill fight, and endorsement (or, at the very least, lack of opposition) by the popular Dawes would be a strong asset. Certainly a man as intelligent and astute as Hoar realized this, and it may well have determined his and his allies' actions in 1875. In any event, George F. Hoar emerged victorious two years later. And while Dawes had maintained a publicly "neutral" stand—despite an ardent campaign by Boutwell's backers to win his support for their candidate—privately he told Hoar that he hoped soon to be greeting him warmly as a fellow senator.[70]

The immediate consequences of the Simmons affair might suggest that, at least in the short run, both Dawes and Butler managed to get what they wanted, while the Brahmins were forced to retreat. But if the senator subsequently enjoyed a long and satisfying career in the Upper Chamber, the advantage Butler achieved from his collector's con-

68. Hoar, *Autobiography*, 1:228, 231–32.
69. Bowles to Dawes, 16 Oct. 1874, in Merriam, *Bowles*, 2:342.
70. Hoar, *Autobiography*, 2:1–5; Welch, *Hoar*, pp. 71–72.

firmation definitely and rather rapidly diminished. The wholesale housecleaning that followed Simmons's installation and the replacement of "disloyal" workers with "trustworthy" ones were completed quickly, almost assuredly by the end of 1874.[71] Yet even before then, the pejorative label of "spoilsman" had been attached firmly to Butler; its intensification doubtless was the most lasting legacy of his part in the Custom House affair. The characterization was exacerbated further, of course, by the subsequent fight against Dana, something that was by no means unforeseeable.

When William Simmons learned that Butler intended to oppose the British Ministry nomination, he strenuously urged his patron to desist, arguing that, in light of his desire to achieve a congressional comeback that year, "you cannot afford to create any new antagonism or to revive any old ones. . . . I hope, my dear General, you won't get into any fracas that will revive the old spirit of 'cussedness' in our opponents . . . . I am strongly of the opinion that it would be vastly better to let Dana go to England or anywhere else, rather than to give the element which supports him, a new reason to make another war upon you."

Simmons, who had justified his position with the assertion, *"not that I love [sic] Dana less, but that I regard your success next Fall more!"* obviously believed that a struggle was not worth the trouble it might provoke.[72] Butler disagreed completely, though, and gave a response that revealed much about his personality and about the motives underlying his anti-Dana crusade: "To allow Dana to go through simply will be to allow a defeat. If you think to be defeated by my enemies will add anything to my popularity, you look at matters through a different medium from what I do. . . . If you had been followed during your whole life by such men with virulence and persistency without just cause, if they had attempted to make your name a byword, and a reproach, I think with all the philosophy which you invoke for me you would not take the course you have proposed for me to take. They shall feel and fear me if they don't love me; they shall learn that blows are to be given as well as taken."[73]

Thus, the real objective of his lobbying on this occasion was a desire for personal revenge against the "Aristocratic Blue-bloodism" of the anti-Butlerites, led by those old adversaries, the Hoars. In pursuit of

71. Letters in the Butler Papers relating to Custom House jobs taper off sharply by the end of 1874, although they never disappear entirely. But Butler was defeated in the 1874 election, and thereby lost official access to patronage.

72. Simmons to Butler, 16 Mar. 1876, Butler Papers.

73. Butler to Simmons, 18 Mar. 1876, Butler Papers.

this emotional satisfaction, most lesser grievances could be sacrificed; hence, in 1877 he would renege on his confirmation-eve vow of retaliation for the anti-Simmons vote and back Boutwell against George F. Hoar for the Senate.[74] Yet in contrast to the impressive political and patronage leverage he acquired through the collectorship appointment, Butler's subsequent attacks on the Dana-Hoar forces could result in no such tangible rewards. The attacks, however, enabled the Brahmins to accrue tremendous moral capital from their encounter with the vengeful "Beast." The British Ministry appointment did not have the "rippling pool" effect of ever-extending influence that a job like the collectorship carried in its wake; instead, it was an office of largely symbolic significance. As such, it was most valuable—both intrinsically and, after Dana's defeat, as a negative reference—to those who were most concerned with the moral dimensions of politics. And they, of course, were not the unsentimentally realistic Butlerites but, rather, the Brahmin reformers.[75]

Hindsight reveals, then, that 1876 marked the beginning of the end of Butler's reign as powerhouse and patronage boss within the Bay State Republican party. The year that started with his anti-Dana campaign would end with his last personal electoral success as a member of the G.O.P.; when he finally fulfilled his dream to become governor of Massachusetts, he would do it, in 1883, as a Democrat.[76] Furthermore, while "Black Ben" would defeat E. Rockwood Hoar in his 1876 House race, it was a Pyrrhic victory. Only two months later he would fail to prevent the selection of George F. Hoar as Boutwell's replacement in

74. Boutwell, *Reminiscences*, 2:283; Welch, *Hoar*, pp. 70–72.

75. Butler's vendetta against the Brahmins was not without its own symbolic significance. Just as the reformers viewed him as the ultimate "corruptionist," the "gentleman Hoars" and their allies were, in Black Ben's eyes, emblematic of a self-righteous and hypocritical "puritanism," the principal motivation of which seemed to him to be the preservation of patrician hegemony. But regardless of the enthusiasm that his incendiary rhetoric may have inspired among his working-class supporters, the fundamental source of Butler's popularity—and (in contrast to what might have motivated him privately) the more common basis on which he publicly justified his activities—was his advocacy of programs, positions, and, of course, patronage aimed explicitly at providing tangible benefits. The Brahmins, suspicious of an overly active public sector, perceived politics as essentially a moral exercise, and framed their appeals accordingly. Butler, *Butler's Book*, esp. concluding chaps.; Nash, *Stormy Petrel*, chaps. 1 and 20; Trefousse, *Butler*, chap. 19; Blodgett, *Gentle Reformers;* Sproat, *"The Best Men."*

76. And, even then, the Butler-Hoar feud would continue. Prior to 1883, every governor of Massachusetts was awarded an honorary degree by Harvard University. Butler was the first denied the honor; E. Rockwood Hoar was president of the Harvard Board of Overseers, which authorized such awards, at the time. Butler, *Butler's Book*, pp. 975–76.

the Senate. Boutwell's loss was yet another reminder of the ephemeral nature of the Dawes-Butler agreement—entered into by the former strictly out of short-term self-interest—and of the persistence of the "spectre of spoilsmanship" that endured as the latter's legacy. For the reformer's elevation to the Upper House was secured with the assistance of his soon-to-be senior colleague, Henry Dawes. And as Hoar later would reminisce: "Simmons was the manager of Mr. Boutwell's campaign for reelection, and General Butler was his earnest supporter. . . . I am quite sure that but for the determination of the people of Massachusetts not to endure Butler and Butlerism any longer, and probably for the appointment of Simmons, I should never have been elected Senator."[77]

Meanwhile, the new senator had one more time at bat before this inning of the game was over. In April 1877, just days after beginning his term, Hoar would initiate a new "Battle of the Custom House" that eventually led to Simmons's removal. On 18 March 1878, the Brahmin Alanson W. Beard, Hoar's hand-picked nominee, would assume the duties of the collectorship.[78]

It is impossible to untangle the spider web that was the Gilded Age patronage game by examining it solely on a case-by-case basis. Rather, as events in Boston—and even those in the Western Reserve—revealed, distributive decisions and the lobbying they engendered were part of the larger political and policy-making process. Filling an office, or, for that matter, implementing a pension or satisfying a claim, did not occur in a vacuum; the motivations behind and effects of such transactions are integral to understanding them.

Consider, for example, the role that patronage played in Dawes's and Hoar's elections to the Senate, or in the elevation of Chester A. Arthur to national prominence, or in the downfall of Benjamin Butler. These cases suggest the potentially vast influence that allocative business and its pressures could have upon leadership in the federal arena. But this was only one of the consequences that patronage had in the conduct of late nineteenth-century government.

By an avenue much more direct than the electoral route, patronage was responsible for the composition of the public workforce. Virtually all entry-level positions in civil service, and the overwhelming majority of higher ones, were filled by political appointees. Thus, the criteria

77. Hoar, *Autobiography*, 2:3; Welch, *Hoar*, pp. 70–73; *Nation*, 25 Jan. 1877, p. 50.
78. Welch, *Hoar*, p. 76 (note 31).

and methods used to influence who were chosen could have enormous impact on the efficiency and effectiveness generally of nonlegislative activity. If merit was thought to be important, as it was by men like Garfield, then there was no inherent conflict between political and qualitative considerations. If, however, personal or partisan loyalty was regarded as the principal prerequisite to selection, the likelihood of incompetence was increased greatly.[79]

More specifically, any number of appointees had actual substantive responsibility. As scholars such as Leonard D. White, Stephen Skowronek, and William E. Nelson have discovered, "legislation by administration" is by no means a purely twentieth-century phenomenon; even in the 1870s the jurisdiction of departments and agencies went well beyond mere implementation.[80] It is unnecessary to develop this notion further here, but it should be recognized that the policy implications of patronage were evident to Gilded Age Americans both in and outside government. Complaints about red tape and "unresponsive officials" swelled the correspondence of every legislator; less frequent, but similarly revealing, were letters of gratitude for assistance in overcoming bureaucratic roadblocks. Additionally, the most eminent lobbyists of the day all augmented their practices with numerous distributive—and, particularly, patronage—cases. For as William E. Chandler learned during his Reconstruction tenure as assistant secretary of the treasury, and Grenville Dodge remembered from his term in Congress, it never hurt to have "friends at court" whenever subsequent business had to be transacted.[81]

The main concern here, however, is not administration, but Congressional Government. In that context, the sheer size of distributive decision making's burden needs to be emphasized explicitly. As Garfield complained in the *Atlantic Monthly* of July 1877, "one third of the working hours of Senators and Representatives is hardly sufficient to

---

79. There were, of course, exceptions; recall that Charlie Robbins had to be removed from the Niles, Ohio, postmastership. Meanwhile, it appeared that Simmons's regime at the Boston Custom House was as respectable as those of most of his contemporaries, including Chester A. Arthur; in the end, his greatest "crime" was his ardent loyalty to Butler.

80. White, *Republican Era;* Stephen Skowronek, *Building a New American State: The Expansion of National Administrative Capacities, 1877–1920* (Cambridge, 1982); William E. Nelson, *The Roots of American Bureaucracy, 1830–1900* (Cambridge, 1982).

81. Both Chandler-NHHS and the Dodge Papers are filled with examples of their patronage activities; for secondary source summaries, see Richardson, *Chandler,* esp. pp. 59–63, 107; Stanley P. Hirshson, *Grenville M. Dodge: Soldier, Politician, Railroad Pioneer* (Bloomington, Ind., 1967), pp. 31–39, 42–45, 146–51, 173–74.

meet the demands made upon them in reference to appointments to office."[82] And to this obligation one must add those of pensions, claims, patents, and so forth which, if Garfield's own correspondence and diary are reliable indicators, were matters equally voluminous and time-consuming—and equally pervaded with lobbying. All these concerns had visibility and salience to the general public that legislators could not ignore. As representatives of the people, they had to place high priority on response.

Such preoccupation with allocative decisions had serious implications for the overall conduct of Congressional Government, including, as we shall see in the chapter that follows, for the formulation and implementation of *innovative* policy. Overload, after all, was one of the most significant inhibitors of federal business in the Grant years, and a disproportionate part of that load was distributive. Leonard White has called it "administration by legislation," while Garfield regarded it as an "invasion of the executive functions" that was extremely disturbing in its extensiveness. "It is safe to say that the business which now annually claims the attention of Congress is tenfold more complex and burdensome than it was forty years ago," the Ohioan wrote in 1877. "Not the least serious evil resulting from invasion of the executive functions by members of Congress is the fact that it greatly impairs their own usefulness as legislators . . . by diverting [them] from [their] proper sphere of duty." Thus, he concluded, "the evils of loose legislation resulting from this situation must increase rather than diminish, until a remedy is provided."[83] And one remedy, as shall become apparent shortly, would come from the innovations of lobbying.

82. Garfield, "A Century of Congress," p. 61.
83. White, *Republican Era*, pp. 45–46; Garfield, "A Century of Congress," pp. 61–62.

CHAPTER 7

Corruption—or Coherence?
Lobbying and the
Politics of Policy

What the legislator most needs is light upon every subject that can come before him; and whatever contributions to his knowledge of the numerous and complicated subjects with which he has to deal, and of which he must often be profoundly ignorant, is of value. Bad legislation . . . is the fruit of ignorance, not of corruption. . . . . Corruption is frequently wholly absent in cases where the lobby is most industrious, numerous, persistent, and successful.

AINSWORTH R. SPOFFORD, "The Lobby" (1886)

Adolph Sutro was a man with a dream—actually, with a number of dreams.[1] Born in Prussia in 1830, he first came to the United States at the age of twenty, just in time for a trek to California in pursuit of easy affluence through gold. Within a decade, Adolph Sutro had indeed found wealth, but only as a San Francisco merchant. And haberdashery, after all, is hardly the stuff of which serious dreams are made. So on to Nevada and the Comstock Lode, in the wake of the Bonanza strike. And there, in 1862, Adolph Sutro's greatest dream was born. Later on, he would return to San Francisco, make another fortune in real estate, build the still-extant Sutro Baths, compile a library of over 200,000 rare books, and win election as mayor on the Populist ticket in

---

1. General background on Sutro, his life and tunnel, is from *DAB*, 9:223–24; *Nat. Cyc.*, 21:126–27; and Robert E. Stewart, Jr., and Mary Frances Stewart, *Adolph Sutro: A Biography* (Berkeley, Calif., 1962).

1892. Still, all that must have seemed anticlimactic to our hero, who for sixteen years had waged a literally global battle against both mortal and geological antagonists. Surmounting all odds, however, victory was his on July 8, 1878.

The Sutro Tunnel was opened that day: an engineering marvel ten feet high, twelve feet wide, and three miles long, with an additional two miles of branches. Thanks to Adolph Sutro, the Comstock Lode and Carson River were at last connected; silver country's richest vein finally had an adequate source of ventilation, drainage, and easy transport for miners and materials alike. Construction costs were estimated at $6.5 million. But the real price was considerably more. For Adolph Sutro had expended not only the bulk of his personal assets, but also nearly one-third of his life, on this magnificent obsession.[2]

Within a year, Sutro sold the tunnel, wondrous as it was, because the Comstock Lode had passed its prime.[3] And so, in many ways, had Adolph Sutro the dreamer. True, he had won his battle—but with outmoded tactics, in a soon-to-be-outdated sort of war. The era of personal entrepreneurship was coming to an end, both corporately and in the world of politics; the breed of men whom Sutro typified was on its way to practical extinction. Serving as his own lobbyist, Sutro had almost single-handedly procured a charter from the Nevada legislature, right-of-way authorization from Congress, and private funding from American and European investors. He also had persevered— vigorously and lavishly, if ultimately unsuccessfully—in a decade-long campaign for federal subsidy. Nevertheless corporations, and combinations of corporations, were starting to supplant his form of enterprise. Indeed, it was a group of this sort that had comprised his most aggressive opposition. No wonder Adolph Sutro lapsed into disillusion; no wonder, either, that he later joined the Populists!

Adolph Sutro's crusade reveals him to have been neither a quixotic figure nor a man of merely tunnel vision. True, he circulated thousands of brochures and hundreds of gilt-edged, leather-bound yearbooks

2. Secondary source information on the tunnel crusade is drawn from sources above; George D. Lyman, *Ralston's Ring: California Plunders the Comstock Lode* (New York, 1937); and Gilman M. Ostrander, *Nevada: The Great Rotten Borough, 1859–1964* (New York, 1966), esp. chap. 2. Lyman begins his seventh chapter as follows: "It was Adolph Sutro. Tall, dark-haired, massive physically, with the look of a dreamer, and the burning eyes of a seer. Resolution, determination, ambition exuded from every pore" (p. 47). Primary sources include the Adolph Sutro Papers, Henry E. Huntington Library, San Marino, California, and reference below, n. 4.

3. Ostrander, *Nevada*, pp. 65–66.

loaded with hyperbolic encomiums by French engineers and Continental counts on the potential merits of his project.[4] But Tom Scott, Collis Huntington, Jay Gould, and numerous other magnates had inundated both media and the Capitol with similar, if less lavishly illuminated, testimonials.[5] And in contrast at least to the Texas & Pacific's Scott, Sutro actually completed his construction—albeit too tardily to do much good. Sutro, then, may have been a bit fanatical, but he certainly was no fool. His misfortune was one of timing, not intent. During the sixteen years' duration of his crusade, both business and government were being transformed into spheres where his kind of aggressive individualism—however fondly it was regarded by some contemporaries and nostalgic moderns—was coming to seem a little anachronistic. Unintentionally, perhaps, and slowly (but surely), combinations, collective action, and class-based policy response were becoming the common order of the day.

Within a quarter century, that transformation acquired retrospective trappings that would lead scholars, journalists, and other commentators to view its evolution as inevitable. Thus, Arthur Bentley could call his pioneering and now classic study of groups' interactions with policy makers "*The* Process of Government," while protégés of his such as Pendleton Herring alluded to the dominance of that behavior in works like "*Group* Representation before Congress."[6] In *Representative Democracy* and *The Economics of Collective Action,* John R. Commons advocated the reorganization of constituencies to conform to citizens' "natural" memberships in economic categories, and in 1918 Mary Par-

4. Copies of at least some of Sutro's pamphlets were in nearly every collection of congressional correspondence examined in the course of this study. A virtually complete collection of his publications can be found at the L.C. [general call no.: TN413/.N3Z7], where they occupy nearly a shelf in the stacks. Many consist partially of Sutro's congressional testimony, or of documents he prepared for submission to the House Committee on Mines & Mining. But the bindings are definitely his own.

5. Scott's included: *Resolutions of Legislatures, Boards of Trade, State Granges, Etc., Favoring Government Aid to The Texas & Pacific Railway* (Philadelphia, 1874); *Proceedings of the Annual Railroad Convention at St. Louis, Mo., November 23 & 24, 1875, In Regard to the Construction of the TEXAS & PACIFIC RAILWAY . . .* (St. Louis, 1875); and *The Press and the People on the Importance of a Southern Line Railway to the Pacific and in Favor of Government Aid to the Texas and Pacific Railway Co.* (Philadelphia, 1875). An example in behalf of Huntington's interests is: *The Texas Pacific Railway (A Dependency of the Great Pennsylvania Monopoly) Contrasted with A Real Southern Pacific R. R. . . . A Letter to the People of the South by* [Sen.] *Thomas M. Norwood, Of Savannah, Georgia* (n.p., 1878).

6. Arthur F. Bentley, *The Process of Government: A Study of Social Pressures* (1908; Cambridge, 1967) E. Pendleton Herring, *Group Representation before Congress* (1929; New York, 1967).

ker Follett wrote the explicitly titled *The New State—Group Organization the Solution of Popular Government.*[7] Since the early 1900s, in short, both normative pluralists and their critics have presupposed the congruence of clienteles and groups, so that a Lester Milbrath, in the presumably generic *Washington Lobbyists,* could assert, unequivocally and uncontroversially, that "lobbyists are group representatives almost by definition."[8] So studies like David Truman's *The Governmental Process: Political Interests and Public Opinion* and Earl Latham's *The Group Basis of Politics* became standard, while the phrase "interest group" became almost obligatory in titles of texts on pressure politics.[9]

Perhaps Herring set the ground rules as clearly as anyone when, at the outset of his analysis in 1929, he cited groups as the principal phenomenon that distinguished his so-called "Old Lobby" from the "New." And if the latter was exemplified by the "admittedly incomplete" list of 465 organizations that Herring appended to his book, Adolph Sutro may properly be regarded as equally representative of the earlier era.[10] Yet there was a time—Adolph Sutro's time, the early Gilded Age—when groups seemed logical frameworks to neither petitioners of government nor most officials: when practically no one saw groups (other than parties) as especially effective, desirable, or necessary to the presentation or advocacy of substantive interests. Their evolution, however self-evident it might have appeared later on, by no means seemed so to those who lived through the days of their embryonic emergence. Indeed, "combinations" were likely to engender suspicion or outright hostility from even their most probable beneficiaries; epithets like "pool," "conspiracy," "trust," and—especially—"ring" were indicative of popular antipathies.[11]

---

7. John R. Commons, *Representative Democracy* (New York, n.d.), and *The Economics of Collective Action* (New York, 1950); Mary P. Follett, *The New State—Group Organization the Solution of Popular Government* (New York, 1918).

8. Lester W. Milbrath, *The Washington Lobbyists* (Chicago, 1963), p. 28.

9. David B. Truman, *The Governmental Process: Political Interests and Public Opinion,* 2d ed. (New York, 1971); Earl Latham, *The Group Basis of Politics: A Study in Basing-Point Legislation* (Ithaca, 1952); examples of texts include Harmon Zeigler, *Interest Groups in American Society* (Englewood Cliffs, N.J., 1964); V. O. Key, *Politics, Parties & Pressure Groups,* 5th ed. (New York, 1964); Norman J. Ornstein and Shirley Elder, *Interest Groups, Lobbying and Policymaking* (Washington, 1978); and Allan J. Cigler and Burdett A. Loomis, eds., *Interest Group Politics* (Washington, 1983).

10. Herring, *Group Representation,* chap. 3 ("From the Old Lobby to the New"), Appendix 2, pp. 276–83.

11. Note, for example, that the combination of California bankers that opposed Sutro was known as the "Ralston Ring." Lyman, *Ralston's Ring;* see also chap. 1, above.

Yet it was in this far from optimal environment that policy-oriented interest groups started to form among disparate clienteles, including some whose traditional mode of interaction had been competition instead of cooperation. At the same time new procedures and structures—of deliberation, programmatic design, and delivery—were transforming the landscape of federal governance: arising occasionally in response to clienteles' common efforts, occasionally precipitating such combinations, and occasionally appearing almost simultaneously, with or without apparent symbiosis. It would be distortion, of course, to infer from all this any consciously "progressive" intent, any coordinated reaction to a perceived "modernity" or new social or industrial order. But it is in these events, initiated haphazardly, tentatively, and even unconsciously, that we can discern early signs of what recent scholarship has termed "Bureaucratic Democracy," the "Transformation of Federalism," the building of a "New American State" with transformed "National Administrative Capacities," and even (though in a very different sense from ours) "Clientelism." Thus, while another decade would pass before Woodrow Wilson published his presumably descriptive *Congressional Government,* it may not be completely unfair to suggest that the system he characterized and castigated so vigorously was already showing signs of dissolution.[12]

Ridding ourselves of hindsight's advantages, then, we need to ask a number of questions about the transformation that began, however haltingly, in the Grant years. First, why did clientele groups start to appear, both in the course of isolated campaigns and as formally organized instruments of sustained advocacy? Second, how did they come into being and what attracted members to them—especially those to whom benefits did not look obvious or who were inured to acting competitively? Third, why did those in government, and particularly legislators attuned to constituency-based pressures and response, pay attention to these new configurations? Finally, what roles did lobbying play in precipitating these developments, and do they sustain or chal-

---

12. Douglas Yates, *Bureaucratic Democracy: The Search for Democracy and Efficiency in American Government* (Cambridge, 1982); William E. Nelson, *The Roots of American Bureaucracy, 1830–1900* (Cambridge, 1982), esp. chap. 3; Stephen Skowronek, *Building a New American State: the Expansion of National Administration Capacities, 1877–1920* (Cambridge, 1982); Samuel P. Huntington, "Clientelism: A Study in Administrative Politics" (Ph.D. diss., Harvard University, 1950); Christopher Clapham, ed., *Private Patronage and Public Power: Political Clientelism in the Modern State* (New York, 1982); Woodrow Wilson, *Congressional Government: A Study in American Politics* (1885; Cleveland, 1956).

lenge our earlier vision of lobbyists as facilitators, bridge-builders, and catalysts?[13]

By examining the experiences of two prominent clienteles, we can start to generate answers to these questions. One clientele consisted of Union veterans, dependents, and survivors, who inundated 1870s Washington with pleas for pensions and similar benefits. The other was composed of railroads, which spent most of the Grant years (as they had the 1860s) pursuing subsidies, land grants, mail contracts, and other comparably remunerative forms of federal largesse. One included individuals; the other, corporations. One suggests masses of "little people," while the other connotes those "robber barons" who allegedly dominated the late nineteenth century's "Great Barbecue." Despite their obvious differences, however, both groups confronted some surprisingly similar obstacles in obtaining satisfaction for their demands. And the solutions they found to their respective dilemmas were remarkably similar.

Popular assumptions about the era notwithstanding, broad-based success came to the soldiers before it was achieved by the industrialists. So it might be best to begin our discussion with the former: specifically, with the Pension Act of 1862, provisions of which far outstripped those of any previous legislation of its kind. Under its terms, allowances were approved for any Union soldier who incurred disability as a result of his military service, as well as for dependent relatives of men who died in battle or from service-related injury or illness. Applicants for remuneration were required to submit evidence of enlistment and tenure in the armed forces, documentation of the cause of death or disability, and, for those ex-soldiers still alive, a physician's statement as to the

---

13. As presented, all four questions seem almost completely concerned with practical or behavioral matters. This is deliberate, but we ought at least to acknowledge their implicit ideological or normative implications. Since these have been discussed extensively by others, however, I will only briefly refer to them. Twentieth-century political theory, including a number of works cited already in this chapter and previously, has been extremely concerned with the issue of legitimacy—and particularly with whether an "activated pluralism" (that is, conscious attempts by the political system to acknowledge, incorporate, and respond to explicitly defined discrete interests) runs counter to the notion of a "common good" that presumably should supersede more "selfish" loyalties. More recently, and not entirely distinctly, a number of scholars have raised challenges to the "bureaucratization" of policy making: most notably to the fact that it seems to take decisions out of the hands of persons chosen by, and responsible to, the electorate. This, for some at least, raises a danger that outweighs the advantages presumably supplied by administrative efficiency and expertise. Others, meanwhile, including some elite theorists and Marxists, have questioned the very existence, primacy, or beneficiality of pluralism,

"extent of invalidism."[14] Now, these procedures may sound relatively straightforward, but problems often arose in implementing them. First, despite the fact that the Pension Bureau was becoming the largest agency in Washington, it still was too small to process with dispatch (or even completely) the myriad cases that came before it. Prospective pensioners discovered that their chances for success could be improved if someone interceded in their behalf, and, as a result, House members were besieged by constituents begging for their assistance. Second, many veterans and more survivors were unable to come up with all necessary documentation, or could not otherwise comply exactly with the law's specifications. In such instances, a claimant's only recourse was to seek a "special bill"; that naturally required legislators' involvement.[15]

---

or the premise that legislative implementation is necessarily more "democratic" than more purely administrative modes. All these controversies, of course, have precedent or origins long before the twentieth century (and even the Gilded Age): especially in writing from the European Enlightenment and in American efforts such as *The Federalist.* It is true that these debates can be brought to bear on matters of discussion here. My own objectives, though, are different: more closely focused and, at this point, more empirical. On the other hand, by delineating the course of nascent clientele consciousness and activism in the 1870s, this book lays out the events that set the stage for what many modern theorists address. In that sense, *my* discussion bears on *theirs*, principally by providing explicitly historical background and insight. For as more than one of them have appreciated (notably Michael Hayes, William E. Nelson, Stephen Skowronek, and James Sundquist), historical contexts and processes do affect the appropriateness or applicability of many theories and models. [This discursive but, perhaps, necessary aside derives from readings in a large body of literature, including books by Bentley, Herring, Latham, Nelson, Skowronek, Truman, and Yates, all previously cited in this chapter, and Anthony Downs, *An Economic Theory of Democracy* (New York, 1957); Michael T. Hayes, *Lobbyists & Legislators: A Theory of Political Markets* (New Brunswick, N.J., 1981); Samuel P. Huntington, *American Politics: The Promise of Disharmony* (Cambridge, 1981); Theodore J. Lowi, "American Business, Public Policy, Case Studies, and Political Theory," *World Politics,* 16 (1964), 677–715, and *The End of Liberalism: Ideology, Policy, and the Crisis of Public Authority* (New York, 1969); Mancur Olson, Jr., *The Logic of Collective Action: Public Goods and the Theory of Groups* (New York, 1970); Robert H. Salisbury, "An Exchange Theory of Interest Groups," *Midwest J. of Pol. Sci.,* 8 (1969), 1–32; E. E. Schattschneider, *The Semisovereign People: A Realist's View of Democracy in America* (New York, 1960); and James L. Sundquist, *The Decline and Resurgence of Congress* (Washington, 1981). See also other works on representation, especially by Dahl, cited in chap. 3; and Margaret Susan Thompson, "The Decline of Electoral Influence: Political Participation in Modern America," unpublished paper delivered before the Social Science History Association, Nashville, 1981.]

14. John William Oliver, *History of the Civil War Military Pensions, 1861–1885* (Madison, Wis., 1917), pp. 10–12; William H. Glasson, *Federal Military Pensions in the United States* (New York, 1918), pp. 125–34.

15. Leonard D. White, *The Republican Era, 1869–1901: A Study in Administrative History* (New York, 1958), pp. 208–15.

Congress, therefore, became a permanent and decisive component of what originally had been intended as a primarily bureaucratic system of delivery. And there is no doubt that its activity was helpful to some individuals who, without the aid of an ombudsman, would never have received their due. But aside from the erosive impact that the extensive expenditure of resources in this area had on other items of the Capitol's agenda, a more directly relevant question is raised. Of what benefit was this kind of constituent service to would-be pensioners as a class?

For a number of reasons, not always superficially apparent, claimants—collectively as well as individually—suffered from the prevailing mode of doing business. Not all congressmen were equally effectual in providing ombudsmanship; some were uninterested in that facet of their jobs and others, especially the freshmen who often were in the majority, were attentive but unskilled or lacking influence.[16] Since few private bills passed the first time they were introduced, citizens whose cases required persistent advocacy were severely and repeatedly penalized by the constant turnover of House seats. Indeed, the prevalence of this problem, combined with the Pension Bureau's administrative inertia, forced the Forty-second House to enact a law extending the ten-year deadline for submission and resolution of such claims.[17] Further, it was not unheard of for members to act only in behalf of "realistic constituents": those, that is, who had openly supported their candidacies—or, at least, not actively backed their opponents. And consider the plight of former "Boys in Blue" who in ever-growing numbers were being represented in the 1870s by ex-Confederates and Copperheads. How likely was it that their suits would be promoted wholeheartedly?[18]

16. As a freshman in 1873, Richard P. Bland (D-Mo.), later a congressional powerhouse, "received many petitions from individuals seeking pensions and war claims. He religiously brought each to the attention of the proper committee, but never once did he succeed in having one of the bills enacted into law"; Harold Alanson Haswell, "The Public Life of Richard Parks Bland" (Ph.D. diss., University of Missouri, 1951), p. 37.

17. *Cong. Globe*, 42d Cong., 3d sess., p. 1282; Oliver, *Civil War Pensions*, p. 37. Benjamin Butler (R-Mass.), defeated in 1874, received the following not atypical letter shortly before he was due to leave the Capitol: "*Once more* I ask your kind support of the bill, *second* on the private calendar, to pay D. B. Allen & Co. for mail service. You may know that it has passed the Senate *five* times without objection, and the House Claims Com. of the late and present Congress have reported unanimously in its favor"; Horatio King to Butler, 5 Dec. 1874, Benjamin F. Butler Papers, L.C. This bill—S. 439—finally did pass in the 43d Congress and was signed into law on 25 Jan. 1875 (*Sen. J.*, 43d Cong., 2d sess., p. 151); thus, although its bogged-down course was similar to those of most private bills, including those for pensions, its ultimate fate was better than the majority enjoyed.

18. "Confederate Leaders in the Forty-Fourth Congress" and "The Confederate Leaders in Congress," *The Republic*, 6 (1876), 131, 252–59.

Despite de jure guarantees of representational equity, then, there was tremendous de facto disparity in the quality of constituency-based representation. Yet there was another weakness in such a system that was at least as detrimental to the collective interest of claimants. By forcing applicants to present their demands individually through their legislators, and because the capacity for response was finite, the pension distribution process inevitably fostered *competition* among members of what actually was a single, common-interest clientele. So long as each veteran or survivor perceived his or her case as discrete, widespread dissatisfaction would persist, with a mutually antagonistic population of potential beneficiaries wastefully channeling its energies into internecine warfare over procurement of scarce pieces from an insufficient pie. (Clearly, the phrase "brother against brother" did not become entirely inapt in 1865!) Instead, this population needed to work on expanding the pie itself. That required the evolution of what might be called "clientele consciousness." And, due largely to the representational efforts of lobbyists, its evolution began in the Age of Grant.

Veterans naturally had been active participants in their former commander's presidential campaign, but, once Grant was installed in the White House, many began to grumble over what they regarded as his and his party's less than adequate gratitude for their support. Ex-enlisted men were particularly upset by the difficulties they encountered in applying for pensions, the size of which they considered niggardly, and by some Republicans' alleged preference for officers in the distribution of patronage.[19] How, though, was the situation to be rectified? As one historian has suggested: "What was lacking . . . was an agency or individual sufficiently clever to encourage and unify these complaints and thus make them politically effective."[20]

The Grand Army of the Republic, or G.A.R., was the most obvious unifying medium. But it was headed in the early seventies by men with the rather simplistic view that politics consisted solely of electoral activity. Becoming disturbed by well-founded Democratic charges that the G.A.R. was no more than a tool of the G.O.P.—charges that seemed to be hurting its recruitment efforts—the organization's leadership repeatedly declared it to be nonpartisan, and emphatically denied any intention to meddle in politics, at least at the national level. Throughout the immediate postwar decade, therefore, the official

19. Mary R. Dearing, *Veterans in Politics: The Story of the G.A.R.* (Baton Rouge, 1952), pp. 148–84.
20. Dearing, *Veterans in Politics*, p. 187.

Grand Army line emphasized promotion of comradery and voluntary philanthropy; its greatest acknowledged achievement was probably its campaign to secure observance of (Union) Memorial Day.[21] Yet despite aggressive performance by its leaders and frequent, well-publicized, and often well-attended rallies, G.A.R. membership consistently declined after reaching an 1868 peak. Some attributed this to the public's supposed longing to put the War behind it; others believed that the "taint of partisanship"—fostered by behavior in numerous local chapters, and by national figures like Commander (and Republican Senator) John A. Logan—was responsible.[22] Neither explanation is entirely persuasive, however, since the same years witnessed the emergence and rapid growth of alternative veterans' alliances, all of them explicitly political.

Two things distinguished the new groups, which flourished under various names, from the G.A.R. First, while they were formed specifically to engage the political influence of ex-soldiers, they emphasized programmatic objectives, especially pension reform, rather than support of particular parties or candidates—except when such aspirants, regardless of affiliation, promised to work diligently in behalf of veterans.[23] Hence the organizations were able to attract both Democratic and Republican adherents, as well as to exert pressure effectively on decision makers in either camp, which became quite important after 1874, when the G.O.P. lost control of the House. Second, unlike the G.A.R., their chief facilitators were not prominent Union figures. Instead, they were claims agents: lobbyists wise in the ways of Washington and motivated largely by the professional advantages they would gain if measures they espoused were implemented.

The most active and successful of the agent/organizers was a Washingtonian named George E. Lemon. In 1874 he and a few peers initiated a nationwide "Pensioners' Committee" to agitate in behalf of an "arrears" bill, so-called because it would backdate pension payments from the time of death or discharge, rather than just from the time of application.[24] This group operated so as to give the impression that it was a popular, grass-roots lobby and inundated Congress with petitions, resolutions from local meetings, and other memorials—many on

21. Thus, Dearing entitled her chapter on the Grant presidency "The Quiescent Years"; Dearing, *Veterans in Politics*, chap. 6.

22. Clippings Scrapbooks, John A. Logan Family Papers, L.C.

23. Dearing, *Veterans in Politics*, pp. 247–48; Oliver, *Civil War Pensions*, pp. 52–54.

24. The bill, as initially introduced, was H.R. 1179: *Cong. Rec.*, 43d Cong., 1st sess., pp. 205, 2133; see also Oliver, *Civil War Pensions*, pp. 64–69; and Glasson, *Federal Military Pensions*, pp. 149–56.

slickly printed forms supplied by the organizers that belied the spontaneity of the drive.[25] The desired bill passed in the Democratically controlled House during the final days of the Forty-fourth Congress, thereby demonstrating the shrewdness of nonpartisan strategy, but failed to make it through the Senate. Inspired by this partial victory, though, and in anticipation of the new Congress, Lemon started a newspaper, the *National Tribune*, in October 1877. Notwithstanding its nondescript title, it was clearly intended to be an organ for the promotion of arrears, bounties, and other programs that would be of benefit to former soldiers—and their agents. Almost immediately, it became the most widely circulated and influential periodical of its kind.[26]

Grand Army leaders, meanwhile, were not oblivious to what was going on around them. Recognizing the enthusiasm with which their potential constituency had responded to the lobbyists' initiatives, and unwilling to relinquish their claim to being the "true voice of the veteran," G.A.R. officials adopted a new approach in 1878. Encampments that year witnessed the forging of an alliance between the organization and the agents. Lemon and others urged readers of their papers to join the Grand Army, and, after a decade's lag, 1878 marked the start of a rise in its membership. At the same time, G.A.R. rallies became prime occasions for circulating petitions from the agents' journals and for dissemination of their tactical advice.[27] The potency of this combination was soon realized when, in January 1879, President Rutherford B. Hayes signed the Arrears Act into law.[28] And the influence of a cohesive veterans' clientele entered into an upswing that would persist for the remainder of the nineteenth century.

The Arrears Act or, as it was called by some, the "Claims Agents Act" resulted in distribution of more and larger pensions, most of them through simplified procedures of bureaucratic delivery rather than through private legislation, thereby freeing Congress for other things.[29] Thus, applicants and elected officials both benefited from the measure; in a very tangible way, the policy process had been rendered

25. "Report of the Committee on Expenditures in the Interior Department," *Hse. Rpts.*, 43d Cong., 3d sess., No. 189; and petitions in Dockets 43A-H7.1 and 44A-H7.1, Invalid Pensions Committee Petition File, Legislative and Judicial Division, National Archives.

26. Glasson, *Federal Military Pensions*, p. 150; Oliver, *Civil War Pensions*, pp. 68–69.

27. Dearing, *Veterans in Politics*, pp. 248–49; Glasson, *Federal Pensions*, p. 160.

28. Oliver, *Civil War Pensions*, p. 61; Glasson, *Federal Military Pensions*, p. 160.

29. Rep. Edmund N. Morrill (R-Kans.), "Pensions," in *The Republican Party: Its History, Principles, and Policies*, ed. John D. Long (New York, 1888), pp. 124–43; White, *Republican Era*, pp. 214–15; Oliver, *Civil War Pensions*, pp. 70–71.

more effective. And this, of course, was achieved mainly through the representation and expertise offered by lobbyists. Specifically, these men took what had been a group of disgruntled and contentious individuals, divided and internally competitive, and transformed them into a cohesive clientele. Then, informed by their long experience on the Washington scene, agents provided the group with a constructive course of class action. Finally they orchestrated the campaign that ultimately led to victory, by devising strategies that would enable veterans to overcome the dispersive impact of partisanship and constituency-based agitation; instead of viewing Congress as a collection of separate members, each from a particular district and with responsibility only to veterans who lived there, these men understood and lobbied it as a unitary decision-making entity that could be influenced best through nonpartisan pressure focused on it as a body—and one whose own concerns could also be addressed by a revised pension law. For this reason, the arrears campaign was designed to stress the diminished legislative workload that proposed procedural changes would bring, and such an argument was surely persuasive to overburdened members. Claims agents, in short, performed a multitude of tasks, all aimed at enabling their clientele's demands to be both articulated and satisfied more effectively. They acted, in short, as catalysts within the Capitol's policy system.

George Lemon and his colleagues were not, to be sure, particularly altruistic or disinterested; because of the vast increase in business with the Pension Bureau after 1879, most of them—who usually operated on a contingency fee basis—profited handsomely from the change. Moreover, it is likely that, under the newly simplified application procedures, relatively more fraudulent claims may have been paid.[30] But it is not the purpose of this book to assess the particulars of how the Arrears Act worked (in any event, a matter for debate) or to measure it against some hypothetical standard of ideal legislation.[31] The point is that effective lobbying rendered the generally recalcitrant Gilded Age Congressional Government responsive to a clientele's needs, and also helped it to operate more efficiently.

By the end of the 1870s, pensioners probably constituted the largest

---

30. Glasson, *Federal Military Pensions*, p. 168.

31. For President Hayes's defense of the Act, see *Diary and Letters of Rutherford Burchard Hayes*, ed. Charles R. Williams, 5 vols. (Columbus, Ohio, 1922–26), 4:54; see also Morrill, "Pensions," pp. 137–41.

and best-organized national policy clientele. What, then, of the mainly corporate interests that Matthew Josephson, Richard Hofstadter, and others have charged were not only typical, but in control, of this era?[32] Perhaps the most misleading legacy of the "spoilsmen" historiography is the impression it leaves that railroads in the seventies constituted some sort of conspiratorial bloc—a cohesive "interest" with both inclination and ability to force demands down the throat of a reluctant nation.[33] In fact, most early corporate ventures into the public sphere were characterized by competition. Like pensioners and job-seekers, rail executives' initial interests were primarily distributive. But unlike veterans, whose satisfaction was impeded mainly by inadequacies in modes of delivery, the corporations wanted things that were by definition finite: subsidies, land grants and routes, mail contracts, and so on. Most such resources would not or could not be duplicated precisely, so one line's gain was properly regarded as another's loss. For this reason, railroads generally considered their most troublesome and costly adversaries to be, not "the people" or "the government," but other railroads. Thus, one scholar has concluded that "businessmen had no unified economic program to promote. Important business groups," he continued, "opposed each other on almost every significant economic question." And two others have declared, with accuracy and succinctness: "There was no unanimity among industrial businessmen in the 1870's and 1880's in the things they sought from politic[s]."[34]

As long as such attitudes persisted, a "railroad interest," unitary and cohesive, would remain nothing more than a myth. So while "robber barons" and their agents certainly were active and visible during the Gilded Age, their alleged power and performance, at least as long as Grant was in the White House, rarely approached the exalted heights that muckrakers have attributed to them. Despite some of the era's most concerted and sophisticated lobbying, for instance, neither Collis P. Huntington nor Thomas A. Scott was able to secure federal as-

32. See chap. 1, above, and Margaret Susan Thompson, "Corruption—or Confusion? Lobbying and Congressional Government in the Early Gilded Age," *Congress & the Presidency,* 10 (1983), 169–93.

33. Andrew M. Scott and Margaret A. Hunt, *Congress and Lobbies: Image and Reality* (Chapel Hill, 1966), pp. 4–5.

34. Stanley Coben, "Northeastern Business and Radical Reconstruction: A Re-examination," *MVHR,* 46 (1959), 89; Thomas C. Cochran and William Miller, *The Age of Enterprise: A Social History of Industrial America* (New York, 1960), p. 155: see also T. C. Cochran, *Railroad Leaders, 1845–1890: The Business Mind in Action* (Cambridge, 1953), pp. 189–200; and Albro Martin, "The Troubled Subject of Railroad Regulation in the Gilded Age: A Reappraisal," *JAH,* 61 (1974), 339–71.

sistance for a rail route to southern California.[35] Indeed, *no* land grants
of any consequence were approved after 1871; instead, by 1877 the
federal government began a period of recovery and foreclosure that
eventually saw twenty-eight million acres of forfeited land grants returned to the public domain.[36] The extant correspondence of corporate leaders and their lobbyists, in short, has little in it to sustain the
image of gloating plutocrats. Rather, one perceives extensive frustration, forebodings (often accurate) of failure, and widespread conviction
that Washington was a source more of problems than of profits.[37]

Consider, for example, that most notorious of so-called robber barons, Jay Gould, and William E. Chandler, his principal lobbyist through
the later seventies. Gould clearly was desperate in 1874 when he accepted Grenville Dodge's assertion that the Union Pacific he headed
"could not do without" the services of this New Hampshire lawyer;
Chandler, as we know, already had one of Washington's longest lists of
clients.[38] And yet the U.P. retained him for the then-extraordinary sum
of $10,000 per year. For that, to be sure, Gould got more than advocacy
for his railroad; Chandler handled, among other things, matters relating to telegraphs and shipping. To oversee things, Gould communicated almost daily with his agent, by wire and handwritten notes—the
latter known as "Blue Jays," because they were scribbled on tinted paper
and signed only with their author's first initial.[39] Collectively, these
missives reveal the diversity of one man's dealings with the govern-

35. Stuart Daggett, *Chapters on the History of the Southern Pacific* (1922; New York, 1966),
chap. 12; and Lewis Lesley, "A Southern Transcontinental Railroad into California: Texas
and Pacific vs. Southern Pacific, 1865–1885," *Pacific Hist. Rev.*, 5 (1936), 52–60; see also
chap. 5, above.

36. Morton Keller, *Affairs of State: Public Life in Late Nineteenth Century America*
(Cambridge, 1977), p. 388.

37. See, for example, the enormous amount of relevant correspondence in the Grenville M. Dodge Papers, Iowa State Dept. of History & Archives, Des Moines; William E.
Chandler Papers, L.C.; *Letters from Collis P. Huntington to Mark Hopkins, Leland Stanford,
Charles F. Crocker and D.D. Colton. From April 2, 1873, to March 31, 1876*, 3 vols. (New York,
privately printed, 1894), and *Letters from Mark Hopkins, Leland Stanford, Charles F. Crocker
and David D. Colton to Collis P. Huntington, from August 27th, 1869, to December 30th, 1879*
(New York, privately printed, 1891), both in the Henry E. Huntington Library, San
Marino, California.

38. Contract recounted in G.M. Dodge to Chandler, 26 Dec. 1875, Chandler Papers;
see also chap. 4, above.

39. Description of the letters as "Blue Jays" from Leon Burr Richardson. *William E.
Chandler, Republican* (New York, 1940), p. 163. Types of business recounted here are all
documented in the letters, which are in the Chandler Papers, L.C. But because there are
so many of them, arriving so frequently, it is impossible to single out particular ones for
citation here.

ment; in the railroad domain alone, they touched on taxes, sinking funds, bonds, patents, mail and freight contracts, bridges, prorating (which Gould opposed for railroads but wanted for telegraphs), permission for aggregation of new mileage, campaign contributions for friendly legislators, appointments to relevant congressional committees, and so on.

It was Chandler's job, besides everything else, to determine priorities and relationships among the various items, so as to arrive at the best overall strategy for implementation. Through it all, however, his employer's temperament was a constant source of complication. The frantic and omnipresent Blue Jays suggest not complacent plutocracy, but acute insecurity. Thus, one suspects that amateur psychology, aimed at placating the boss, was an added dimension of Chandler's workload— and that in this respect, at least, Gould got his money's worth, at least if value is measured in terms of time. Yet if a Jay Gould, allegedly at the top of the heap and with Washington's number one lobbyist at his beck and call, exhibited such fear, how must those less fortunately situated have felt—and with how much more justification? Indications were that they were hardly unemotional; the overall impression is far from one of relaxed and well-fed diners at the Great Barbecue. What is more, in January 1874 an event occurred that definitely increased their indigestion.

Throughout the late 1860s and early 1870s, "Granger laws" had sought to make state regulation of railroads a reality, especially in the Midwest. Spurred by the same agitation that inspired those measures, and by court decisions connected with them, Congress initiated efforts to follow suit. In January 1874 the House Committee on Railways & Canals, normally a quiescent body, reported favorably on H.R. 1385, which would establish a nine-member commission to regulate interstate rail commerce. After strenuous debate, the bill was passed on March 26 by a vote of 121-115.[40] That same year, the Senate Select Committee on Transportation Routes to the Seaboard issued what became known as the "Windom Report," which endorsed in principle the constitutionality of federal controls over interstate commerce, and which went on to declare such controls to be "expedient and desirable."[41] Thus, while no Senate legislative action occurred immediately, handwriting

40. Balthazar Henry Meyer, *Railway Legislation in the United States* (New York, 1903), pp. 191–94; *Hse. J.*, 43d Cong., 1st sess., p. 655; and *Hse. Rpts*, 43d Cong., 1st sess., No. 26.

41. *Sen. Rpts*, 43d Cong., 1st sess., No. 307; see also Edward Chase Kirkland, *Industry Comes of Age: Business, Labor, and Public Policy, 1860–1897* (New York, 1961), pp. 97–98.

on the wall was plain; whether or not corporate officials liked it, Congress had asserted its jurisdictional authority, and affected parties would have to consider its potential ramifications. The Central Pacific's Collis Huntington responded by complaining that "matters never looked worse in Washington than they do at this time. . . . I think in all the world's history there never before was such a wild set of demagogs [sic] honored by the name of Congress." And his associate, Mark Hopkins, commented wryly, just before these actions occurred: "When we commenced, eleven years ago, Congress and Legislation were gentle steeds. Bless me how they rear and tear now."[42]

The most significant feature of both H.R. 1385 and the Windom Report was their definition of railroads not as discrete entities, but as a class. Any laws that ensued would treat them categorically, an approach entirely distinct from the one that had prevailed before, in regard to matters like bonds and land grants. Those issues had fostered rivalries, but, where controls and other general questions were concerned, former adversaries often had similar stakes in policy outcomes. In these situations, railroad executives with common objectives needed to transcend their traditional competitive inclinations and to start working together as a clientele.

Numerous roadblocks, to be sure, stood in the way of such alliances. Some were obvious and essentially practical; normally antagonistic businessmen could not be expected overnight to unite easily with industrial adversaries. This, we can understand, would never be eliminated entirely since, apart from regulation and similar matters, corporations retained a vast range of particularized interests where competition remained both logical and appropriate. But other impediments were more subtle and harder to contend with, because they stood in the way of any cooperation in the public sphere, even when it was obviously advantageous. Here we are talking about beliefs shared by most nineteenth-century businessmen, as well as by a large percentage of their fellow citizens. Morton Keller refers to them as comprising "hostility to the active state," a sentiment that Samuel P. Huntington sees as "creedal passion": a deep-seated, quasi-religious American antipathy to publicly exercised authority and power.[43] From this perspective, especially in businessmen's minds, government was inherently

---

42. C. P. Huntington to David Colton, 15 Nov. 1877 and 20 June 1878, reprinted in the *Chicago Tribune*, 28 Dec. 1883; Hopkins to C. P. Huntington, 4 Feb. 1873, in *Letters to Collis P. Huntington*, p. 10.

43. Keller, *Affairs of State*, pp. 181–84; Huntington, *Politics of Disharmony*, esp. chap. 3.

mischievious—both to operation of "natural" economic laws and to the broader national ideology of liberty and self-sufficiency.[44] That this latter was not synonymous with "democracy," meanwhile, is demonstrated by industrialists' frequently expressed fears that elected officials, especially in Congress, were little more than "stupid," "empty," and "noisy" men who "devoted themselves to [politics] in order to gain a livelihood" by serving as pawns, "pandering to the caprices" of "brutal," "selfish," and "ignorant" masses.[45] In any event, while such attitudes prevailed, it was difficult for those who held them, particularly in commerce, to regard general legislation affecting their affairs as anything besides anathema—"unnatural" efforts whose legitimacy ought not to be recognized even by explicit opposition. And equally odious was the thought of working in concert with one's "natural" competitors.

As was the case with pensioners, however, lobbyists—as politically experienced Entrepreneurs—were able to encourage necessary changes in attitude and behavior. The best of them, such as Chandler and Dodge, were shrewd and knowledgeable operatives who had already proven themselves with railroad executives during the era of distributive largesse. And as the Gilded Age proceeded, their services continued to be widely sought and used; in 1874 alone, as we have seen, Chandler held retainers from four different lines, and Dodge worked for a minimum of two.[46] By the mid-1870s, based on their broad (and often overlapping) endeavors, it had become obvious to these men that, while some of their employers' objectives remained mutually incompatible, there was a significant amount of common ground, as well. On matters like prorating and patent law, to cite two increasingly prominent issues, they came to appreciate that it was sensible and efficient for at least some railroads to work together—at least some of the time.

Thus, when Chief Counsel Dodge of the Union Pacific had to leave Washington briefly in the spring of 1874, he wrote to Chandler, then in a similar capacity at the Kansas Pacific: "I agreed with Gould to-day that in matters where both companies are interested KP & UP such as Tax Bill or Homestead Bill or that if I was out of reach he should communi-

44. Cochran, *Railroad Leaders*, chaps. 14–15; Edward Chase Kirkland, *Dream and Thought in the Business Community, 1860–1900* (Ithaca, 1956), chap. 5.

45. Kirkland, *Dream and Thought*, pp. 117–18, 129.

46. For general background, see the Dodge and Chandler Papers; Richardson, *Chandler;* Stanley P. Hirshson, *Grenville M. Dodge: Soldier, Politician, Railroad Pioneer* (Bloomington, Ind., 1967); and Jacob R. Perkins, *Rails, Trails, and War: The Life of General G. M. Dodge* (Indianapolis, 1929).

cate direct with you. . . . Seems to me the Attys of all companies interested should act in concert. . . . J. F. Wilson of Iowa Atty of Iowa roads is interested; so are all *Land Grant* Roads. . . . I shall communicate with you—and *will see that you are paid for your services all round.*"[47] The purposes of this letter are clear; Chandler was being asked, first, to lobby concurrently for two separate lines and, second, to coordinate his efforts with agents of additional companies. Moreover, this cooperative endeavor among "Attys" for traditionally contentious entities was proposed as a continuing relationship. The episode suggests that, at least occasionally, an incipient form of clientele consciousness could be discerned within the railroad community.

The qualifications of "incipient" and "occasionally" are, however, critical—one letter, or one ad hoc coalition, does not constitute a revolution. Indeed, less than two months earlier, in March, Chandler had been involved in another K.P. campaign against the Union Pacific; by April he was on retainer for both the Kansas line and Jay Gould; in December the smaller company's president would conclude that his interests were "so far removed" from those of the U.P. that "we must fight our own battles," and he dismissed Chandler from his employ.[48] Nevertheless, some degree of cooperation, however sporadic and limited, was better than none, for congressmen—overburdened and all too used to receiving conflicting and contradictory pressures from petitioners—were likely to listen gratefully and try to act responsively to conveyed consensus.[49] The activation of even embryonic clienteleclasses, therefore, was more apt to serve the needs both of their members and of public officials than were similar, but isolated, actions.

By the mid-1870s, then, even the most hostile antagonists were being encouraged to move, if only tentatively and occasionally, toward cooperative efforts to influence policy. President Tom Scott of the Texas & Pacific and the Central/Southern Pacific's Collis Huntington, for example, spent most of the Gilded Age in a bitter and mutually unproductive fifteen-year rivalry that would extend into the 1880s, aimed at obtaining federal subsidy for their respective southwestern routes.[50] Despite this, each began to appreciate the desirability of working to-

47. Dodge to Chandler, 18 May 1874, Chandler Papers; copy in Dodge Papers.
48. R. E. Carr to Chandler, 7, 12, 18, and 28 Mar. 1874; Dodge to Chandler, 30 Mar. and 19 Apr. 1874; Carr to Chandler, 2 Dec. 1874 (removing Chandler from the KP payroll): all Chandler Papers.
49. See chap. 4, above.
50. Lesley, "Southern Transcontinental Railroad"; see also several letters pertaining to Scott in *Letters from Collis P. Huntington,* vol. 3.

gether when nondistributive legislation was concerned. In late 1876, therefore, although their subsidy war waged fiercely on, the two magnates met and agreed upon a prorating bill that "we can all work for."[51] And both Scott and Huntington, separately and simultaneously, also formed alliances occasionally with another adversary, Jay Gould, as did executives of other competing lines.[52]

When such combinations were effected, the participating firms might hire a single lobbyist to labor collectively for them. So, in 1873, Nebraska attorney J. Sterling Morton was paid $5000 by a consortium of midwestern roads, which included the Burlington and Illinois Central, to promote their common position on regulation; later he was employed again by some of the same companies to work on a pro-rata proposal.[53] An alternative strategy was for agents of various companies to act concurrently in representing mutual interests. This is what Dodge, Chandler, Wilson, and their fellows had done in 1874. But few of these early coalitions lasted for long; just as pooling in the private sector generally had failed to prevent individual railroads from breaking away whenever they saw an economic advantage in doing so, alliances intended to facilitate representation in the public sphere often floundered at the slightest sign of disagreement.[54] The 1870s were transitional in this respect, and both large-scale business and policy-related consolidations would have to wait until later in the century. Nevertheless, even in the Grant years there was a handful of cases in which railroads' clientele consciousness evolved to the point of formal organization.

The head of one early group outlined its benefits in a perceptive and explicit memorandum. Writing to a skeptical subordinate in 1875, Burlington Railroad President Robert Harris explained: "In regard to membership in the Western Railroad Assn—it has seemed to me the

51. Huntington to David Colton, 15 Nov. 1876, published in the *Chicago Tribune,* 27 Dec. 1883.

52. Jay Gould asked Chandler to "look after" Scott and Huntington on prorating, in Gould to Chandler, 11, 18, and 27 Jan. 1876, Chandler Papers; see also Grenville M. Dodge to Rep. George W. McCrary (R-Iowa) on cooperation between the UP and CP, 17 and 22 May and 5 June 1876, Dodge Papers; and Huntington to David Colton, 29 Apr. 1878, published in *Chicago Tribune,* 28 Dec. 1883.

53. L. O. Goddard (president's office, Burlington Railroad) to Morton, 9 July 1873, and Morton to Charles E. Perkins (president, Burlington Railroad), 29 June and 16 Nov. 1876, J. Sterling Morton Papers, Nebraska State Historical Society, Lincoln. See also James C. Olson, *J. Sterling Morton* (Lincoln, 1942), chap. 15.

54. Martin, "The Troubled Subject of Railroad Regulation," 347–51, 364–66; Edward A. Purcell, Jr., "Ideas and Interests: Business and the Interstate Commerce Act," *JAH,* 54 (1967), 569.

advantages were so very decided that there was no room for doubt as to the expediency of being a member. The Tanner Brake case is one of immense importance, involving millions and requiring close study far beyond what any [one] Railroad Counsel can give in connection with his other business. . . . Besides the advantages of combining in suits where all are interested and thus dividing the expenses, there is a very great advantage in having . . . the means of avoiding the most expensive traps to which we have been liable."[55] This particular statement referred only to a specific patent bill, but additional correspondence from Harris's tenure as the Association's leader reveals that it was also involved in taxation, bridges, prorating, and other policy matters.[56] The class basis and breadth of these concerns, combined with formal and continuing structure, marked the Western Railroad Association—like the G.A.R.—as a forerunner of the modern interest group: an apparatus through which clienteles' collective action could become a regular and integral part of the American polity.

In general, however, the Gilded Age railroad experience did not reflect the clear and progressive evolutionary pattern that characterized contemporaneous developments among veterans. Among other things, it was complicated by the initial refusal of a few important entrepreneurs, most notably the Burlington's Charles E. Perkins, to accept the legitimacy of governmental efforts to regulate their affairs.[57] Even among those who conceded such authority, some continued to find it hard to reconcile cooperation on public issues with business competition. Because of their real diversity, and the inevitably dissimilar effects that certain policy decisions could have on their respective economic fortunes, railroads—and most commercial combinations—would rarely achieve the degree of inclusiveness or cohesion that was possible among more homogeneous and narrowly concerned clienteles, such as the G.A.R.

But those late nineteenth-century economic clienteles that did unite, even if only temporarily or incompletely, enjoyed advantages usually inaccessible to noncommercial groups, especially ones less numerous than veterans. In the first place, at a time when professional staff was

55. Robert Harris to Charles E. Perkins, n.d. [spring 1875], Chicago, Burlington & Quincy Railroad Archives, Newberry Library, Chicago.
56. "Robert Harris Out-letters for Western Railroad Association, Feb. 3, 1874-Feb. 11, 1876 (letterpress copybook)," CB&Q Archives.
57. Purcell, "Ideas and Interests," 571–73; Cochran, *Railroad Leaders*, pp. 98, 189, 197–99; Ari Hoogenboom and Olive Hoogenboom, *A History of the ICC: From Panacea to Palliative* (New York, 1973), pp. 32–33.

virtually nonexistent in both Congress and the bureaucracy, experts on private corporation payrolls were sometimes the only, and frequently the best, available sources of technical data on many programmatic questions.[58] Also, these clienteles' generally larger financial assets enabled them to employ the most experienced and skilled lobbyists: Grenville Dodge, for instance, who combined at least some substantive knowledge with his political savvy. As a former Iowa congressman, albeit only for one term, Dodge had an insider's view of how the House worked that unquestionably helped him in devising strategy. But his credibility as a spokesman for Jay Gould and Thomas Scott was enhanced considerably by participation during the 1860s in surveys for the Union Pacific's route. According to a recent biographer, "Dodge's role in construction of the transcontinental road, while important, was less so than he wanted people to believe."[59] Nonetheless, his expertise far exceeded that of most contemporaries, which added greatly to his influence in Washington; his extant letterpress copybooks, almost illegible now, reveal correspondence with federal officials filled with technical data. And responses from these men, unschooled in such matters, suggest the seriousness with which they took his advice.[60]

Still, corporate clienteles were concerned with a variety of public issues—which explains why a generalist like William E. Chandler was even more sought after than Grenville Dodge. To represent a railroad fully, one needed to be able to deal with subsidies and taxation, regulation and contracts, labor laws and tariffs at a minimum. A top-notch Washington counsel had to have a comprehensive understanding of the workings of government, and appreciation of the need to influence *all* stages of the policy process. Chandler, as we know, was involved in elections, media promotion that generated or manufactured "grassroots" support, and Congress's organizational contests that determined construction of relevant committees.[61] But equally crucial was the persistence of his efforts, long after legislation was enacted. For the best Washington lobbyists were aware that, even if a measure they had

58. Key, *Politics, Parties, & Pressure Groups*, p. 132; David J. Rothman, *Politics and Power: The United States Senate, 1869–1901* (Cambridge, 1966), pp. 203–4; and chap. 4, above. Charles Francis Adams II volunteered his expertise on railroads to James A. Garfield when Garfield was on Appropriations: Adams to Garfield, 1 Oct. 1873, James A. Garfield Papers, L. C. And some legislators actively solicited staff support from interested lobbyists: Sen. Stephen Dorsey (R-Ark.) to W. E. Chandler, 30 May 1876, Chandler Papers.

59. Hirshson, *Dodge*, p. 143.

60. For an example, see Dodge to Rep. G. W. McCrary, 22 May 1876, Dodge Papers.

61. Cochran, *Railroad Leaders*, pp. 192–96; Jay Gould to W. E. Chandler, 22 Dec. 1875 and 2 Jan. 1876, Chandler Papers; see also chap. 5, above.

opposed got passed, it was possible to minimize its deleterious potential by constraining—or dominating—its implementation. And as ongoing policy like regulation became prevalent, and as authority for its execution lay increasingly in the hands of unelected officials, clienteles whose agents helped them understand such matters definitely enjoyed an advantage.

Because men like Chandler did their jobs well, railroad leaders' fear declined greatly in the decade after their initial scare from H.R. 1385 and the Windom Report. Instead they got busy and by 1887, when the Interstate Commerce Commission finally was established, they were able to effect considerable influence over its design, composition, and early performance. Thus, they validated a prediction by Charles Francis Adams II, himself a railroad advocate, Union Pacific director, and the man most responsible for determining the form of Massachusetts's pioneering equivalent to the I.C.C. (to which he was appointed immediately). Adams wrote in 1884, three years before the federal body was authorized: "If you only get an efficient Board of Commissioners, they could work out of it whatever was necessary. . . . Everything depends on the men who, so to speak, are inside of it, and who are to make it work. In the hands of the right men, any bill would produce the desired results."[62] Accordingly, a scholar could conclude, in evaluating the relationship between business and policy in the 1880s and 1880s: "Perhaps it was no accident that even though *free* enterprise was beginning to be curbed, *private* enterprise remained as strong as ever."[63]

The effectiveness of commercial clienteles in the late nineteenth century seemed to give them disproportionate influence over public policy. This, as much as anything else, probably accounts for the persistently negative image of Gilded Age lobbying. But as the veterans' earlier success demonstrates, techniques that generated and evolved from clientele consciousness could be adopted profitably by any group with interests that might be affected by government. Indeed, in the half-century following Grant's departure from the White House, more and more kinds of people—from feminists to labor leaders, and from prohibitionists to physicians—caught onto the scheme and enjoyed at

62. Adams to John D. Long, 3 Jan. 1884, quoted in Gabriel Kolko, *Railroads and Regulation, 1877–1916* (Princeton, 1965), p. 36; see also Kolko, pp. 30–53; Robert B. Carson, "Railroads and Regulation Revisited: A Note on Problems of Historiography and Ideology," *The Historian*, 34 (1972), 437–46; see also sources cited in nn. 54 and 57, above.

63. Arthur W. Thompson, "The Gilded Age," in *Main Currents of American History*, ed. Howard Quint et al., 2 vols. (Homewood, Ill., 1964), 2:60.

least some measure of satisfaction.[64] Of course, neither the number of interest groups in the twentieth century nor their generally accepted legitimacy was characteristic of the 1870s and 1880s. Instead, the very scarcity of well-developed, activated clienteles made them anomalous and open to such suspicion that even an ardent pluralist like Pendleton Herring could not see beyond contemporary prejudices as he wrote his analysis of their lobbying.[65]

The examples here, however, should suggest a different, and more positive, interpretation of so-called "special interests" and their agents in the Grant years. Among other things, it ought to be obvious that group efforts were both more fragile and less fearsome than popular mythology would have it. But at a time when federal policy making was overburdened and underequipped to handle the number and range of demands that pressed upon it, lobbyists could and sometimes did serve as facilitators and catalysts, loosing the system from inertia. Far from being disruptive, therefore, clienteles—and their representatives, the lobbyists—helped to focus, to rationalize, and, in the long run, to modernize late nineteenth-century Congressional Government.

64. Maud Wood Park, *Front Door Lobby,* ed. Edna Lamprey Stantial (New York, 1960); Carrie Chapman Catt and Nettie Rogers Shuler, *Woman Suffrage and Politics: The Inner Story of the Suffrage Movement* (New York, 1926); Peter D. Odegard, *Pressure Politics: The Story of the Anti-Saloon League* (New York, 1928); Oliver Garceau, *The Political Life of the American Medical Association* (Hamden, Conn., 1961).

65. Herring, *Group Representation,* pp. 31–38.

Afterword

Henry Adams, writing retrospectively and in the third-person, recalled of his family's return to the United States from Britain in 1868: "Had they been Tyrian traders of the B.C. 1000, landing from a galley fresh from Gibraltar, they could hardly have been stranger on the shore of a world, so changed from what it had been ten years before." Ten years later, his astonishment was gone, replaced by the dissatisfaction and cynicism that persisted for the rest of his life. Ulysses Grant, he would declare with his peculiar cogency, "should have been extinct for ages. . . . The progress of evolution from President Washington to President Grant was alone evidence enough to upset Darwin."[1]

Change was evident, but not necessarily for the better; it was hardly, in Adams's view, synonymous with progress, and the seventies did not give him hope of progress. And one did not need to share all the Brahmin's attitudes to share, at least a bit, in his frustrations. The Age of Grant, particularly in contrast to the years of Civil War, may have seemed a time in which very little really happened—in which political processes and institutions were unable to keep up with myriad developments in the world around them. Even James Garfield, an insider, could see things as "troublesome and uncertain. . . . a bad time to be in public life."[2]

1. Henry Adams, *The Education of Henry Adams* (1918; New York, 1931), p. 237; and Adams quoted in R. P. Blackmur, *Henry Adams* (New York, 1980), p. 79.
2. Harry Brown and Frederick D. Williams, eds., *The Diary of James A. Garfield*, 4 vols. (East Lansing, Mich., 1967–81), 2:243.

Congressional Government and *The American Commonwealth* convey impressions similar to Garfield's and Adams's, and have conditioned historiography more profoundly. Yet within a relatively few years after their masterpieces' publication, both Woodrow Wilson and Lord Bryce became aware that circumstances had altered—that the polity they had described in the 1880s was already a thing of the past, that transformation had been underway even as they wrote, and that its manifestations were not altogether so bad, as Garfield and Adams thought. By 1900 Wilson approvingly noted a pronounced shift of power toward the Executive; the Englishman concurred, and acknowledged as well greater legislative stability and professionalism.[3] The time-lag of the seventies was starting to lessen, as the process of governance adapted itself to the complexities of post–Civil War national life.

This book, like Wilson's and Lord Bryce's, has focused on a rather short-lived and perhaps atypical stage in American political development, an era in which even a sympathetic chronicler had to admit that "sessions were unimportant" and "a large amount of legislation failed to pass both houses."[4] Even so, the Age of Grant has several advantages for my purposes. My concern has been with behavior and process rather than with programmatic substance, and a relative paucity of momentous and attention-grabbing issues has made it easier to avoid distraction from the system itself. Such tensions as did exist, like those surrounding the Texas & Pacific Railroad, provide the opportunity to observe the systemic implications of controversy. But divisive policy matters are precisely those that roll-call analysis can delve into most fully and successfully—and I have tried to avoid well-trodden ground. It is important to remember that politics consists of routines as well as highlights. And times of apparent quiescence permit systemic readjustments, however tentative or unself-conscious—adjustments whose development was too subtle for Bryce, Wilson, Adams, and Garfield to be able to perceive.

I have tried in this study to present the world of *Congressional Government* as it must have appeared to these men and their contemporaries: overburdened, underequipped, populated with tyros, and besieged by ever-growing numbers of disparate clienteles who sought to get demands on the agenda. It was a system more akin and still better suited to conditions of the 1850s than to those it had to address.

3. "Preface to Fifteenth Printing," in Woodrow Wilson, *Congressional Government: A Study in American Politics* (1885; Cleveland, 1956), pp. 19–23; and James, Lord Bryce, *The American Commonwealth,* editions subsequent to the first, esp. Part I.

4. Francis Curtis, *The Republican Party: A History of Its Fifty Years' Existence and a Record of Its Measures and Leaders, 1854–1904,* 2 vols. (New York, 1904), pp. 37–40.

It was the locus in which representation presumably centered, and yet well over half the nation's adults were excluded from selection of its members. The Capitol possessed power without strength, its hegemony dependent more on tradition and Executive passivity than on capacity. Dissatisfaction ran rampant among members and populace alike. Again, in the words of Garfield, everything seemed "to saturate the public mind with suspicion and unfaith and no man is wise enough to see the path through the entanglements."[5]

The circumstances appear much less dismal in retrospect; to some political scientists, the 1870s now even fall well within the perimeter of Congress's so-called "Golden Age."[6] While that assessment may be objectively as misleading as the ones it contradicts, the point is that the perspective of hindsight does have advantages. But it has its dangers, too. Although longitudinal analysis discerns glimmerings of "modernity" during the era of Grant's tenure in the White House, chroniclers like Wilson and Bryce remind us just how dim were those glimmerings' immediate manifestations, and how embryonic their nascent signs of change.

It is in this inchoate situation, as we have seen, that lobbyists provided some essential infusions of know-how, coherence, and representational facility. They helped to transform interests often buried in constituencies into more logically ordered and identifiable clienteles; they called decision makers' attention to particularized needs and sometimes eased the way for their response. Although targets of disdain, excoriation, and even judicial censure, lobbyists nonetheless were indispensable to the conduct of federal business and, consequently—through Hoar's resolution and the like—began to be given, if reluctantly, implicit legitimacy. Whether or not Gilded Age Americans were happy about it, and most were not, the much-maligned "Third House" had—like death and taxes—assumed a certain inevitability.

As has been noted more than once in this book, to recognize either the prevalence or the contributions of lobbying is neither to admire all

5. *Garfield Diary*, 2:243.
6. See, for example, Morris P. Fiorina, *Congress: Keystone of the Washington Establishment* (New Haven, 1977); James L. Sundquist, *The Decline and Resurgence of Congress* (Washington, 1981), esp. chaps. 1–2; James L. Sundquist, "Congress, the President, and the Crisis of Competence in Government," and Lawrence C. Dodd, "Congress, the Constitution, and the Crisis of Legitimation," both in *Congress Reconsidered*, ed. Lawrence C. Dodd and Bruce I. Oppenheimer, 2d ed. (Washington, 1981), pp. 351–70, 390–420; and Alvin M. Josephy, Jr., *On the Hill: A History of the American Congress from 1789 to the Present* (New York, 1979), chaps. 6–7.

of its practices nor to sing an unequivocal paean to it.[7] I appreciate that lobbying and corruption were hardly total strangers a century ago, even as I insist that they were not always bedfellows. I also recognize, and am troubled by, the fact that, now as then, influence too often can be bought—if not through outright bribery and deception, then through well-financed clienteles' ability to hire top-flight advocates and conduct expensive pressure campaigns. But while these are important concerns, they are not the concerns of this book, which is aimed at illuminating historical phenomena and not at normative prescriptions.

The question, then, is not whether lobbying is "good" or "bad"; clearly, it is some of both. Rather, it is what roles lobbying played during the Gilded Age, and to what extent understanding those roles can illuminate the legislative process. My principal contention has been that, because lobbying affects every facet of that process, and because its flexibility allows it to circumvent both the real and artificial constraints of institutional formalism, it is an important subject in its own right; and examining it is a good way to get at the inner workings of Congress, in its legislative and representational capacities. I say *a* good way because obviously other approaches would have been feasible. No single study can do everything that needs doing. I have tried to shed some light on a range of nineteenth-century legislative activities that for too long have been neglected. In addition, I have attempted to suggest some ways that historians can profit from the insights of political science as we proceed with the essential task of generating explicitly historical theories and explanatory models.

Many problems remain to be dealt with—a possibly not inappropriate legacy for a discussion of the 1870s, which also concluded with its share of loose ends, unresolved dilemmas, and more than a touch of uncertainty about just what the future would bring. Like the lobbying that occupied such prominence in the Capitol's domain, perhaps my work, too, will function as a catalyst, facilitating access to Congressional Government.

7. I found neither amusing nor accurate a remark by a onetime colleague that I was "about to do for the lobby what D. W. Griffith did for the Ku Klux Klan."

Index

279

Galloway, George B., 140
Garfield, James A. (R-Ohio), 72, 78–79,
88, 91, 113, 127, 132, 141, 202, 274–75;
Appropriations Committee chairman,
35, 38, 40, 87, 209; assassination of,
218–19; campaign (1874), 223; on Congress, 48, 111, 117, 163, 206, 276; and
constituent interests, 126; and Credit
Mobilier, 35, 38, 210, 223; described,
38, 211, 220–22; and educational aid,
47, 133–34, 154; and free trade, 201;
and Military Affairs Committee, 39–40;
and patronage, 174, 216, 219–30, 249–
50; and Salary Grab Bill, 38, 163, 210–
11, 223; and Union Army, 39, 155, 220–
21; and Ways and Means Committee,
39, 200
Garland, Hamlin, 68–69
George, Kate, 37
Gibson, A. M., 190, 205
Gibson, Randall L. (D-La.), 202–3
Gilded Age: defined, 20; and distributive
politics, 215–16; patronage during,
248–50; political significance of, 20–21,
41–42, 85, 142–44, 275–77. *See also* Lob-
bying
Gilded Age, The, 57–58, 158. *See also* Twain,
Mark; Warner, Charles Dudley
Godkin, Edwin L., 162
Gould, Jay, 27, 188, 253, 267–69, 271; and
William E. Chandler, 264–69
Grady, Henry, 162
Grand Army of the Republic, 133, 259–
61, 270. *See also* Lemon, George E.;
Logan, John A.
Grand Old Party (G.O.P.). *See* Republican
Party
Granger Laws, 46, 265
Grant administration, 21, 37, 58; corrup-
tion during, 34–38, 263–64;
government change during, 33, 38, 41–
48, 60, 65–66, 114–15, 120–21, 137, 142,
255, 259; "unproductivity" during, 38–
40, 145, 250, 274–75
"Grantism," 34, 56, 120, 180, 183, 210
Grant, Ulysses S., 20, 37, 45, 69; concept
of the presidency, 49, 112; election of
(1868), 33; and patronage, 231–33,
236–37, 240–44; and veterans, 259;
"victim" of corruption, 56
"Great Barbecue," 144, 216, 256, 265. *See
also* Grant administration
Greeley, Horace, 107, 161, 227, 234
Greenbacks, 42, 202, 227. *See also* Currency; Ohio Idea; Treasury
Department

Hale, Eugene (R-Maine), 72
Halstead, Murat, 162
Hamilton, Alexander, 119, 121
Hampton Institute (1868), 48
Hancock, John (D-Tex.), 201
Harris, Robert, 269–70
Hawley, John B. (R-Ill.), 213
Hayes, Rutherford B., 167, 206, 226, 261
Hearndon, William (D-Tex.), 125
Henry, Charles E., 220–29. *See also* Gar-
field, James A.
Herring, Pendleton, 136, 253–54, 273
Hesseltine, William B., 33
Hewitt, Abram S. (D-N.Y.), 40, 157
Hinsdale, Burke A., 211
Hiram College, 221
Hoar, E. Rockwood (R-Mass.), 72, 211,
230, 241–43, 247
Hoar, George Frisbie (R-Mass.), 23, 40,
64–65, 72, 79, 93, 158, 163, 172–73, 211,
230, 241, 247; on Congress, 49–50, 89,
91, 94, 108, 110, 213; and Henry L.
Dawes, 245–48; and educational aid,
47, 133–34, 154. *See also* Butler, Ben-
jamin F.; Lobby regulation
Hofstadter, Richard, 21, 144, 173, 263
Holman, William S. (D-Ind.), 91, 108, 183
Hooper, Samuel (R-Mass.), 72, 79
Hoosic Tunnel Commission, 126
Hopkins, Mark, 266
Horr, Roswell (R-Mich.), 126
House Democratic Study Group, 95
House of Representatives, 25–26, 50, 71;
power hierarchy in, 170–71, 177; and
relief legislation, 42–43; size of, 129–30;
and Southern bloc, 86–87, 184
Howard University (1867), 48
Howells, William Dean, 57, 162
Hubbell, Jay (R-Mich.), 124, 157
Huntington, Collis P., 37, 204, 253, 263–
69
Huntington, Samuel P., 51–53, 65, 266–
67
Hurlbert, William Henry, 194

Illinois Central Railroad, 59, 269
Indian rights, 47, 139
Industrialization, 20, 45
Inflation, 42, 202. *See also* Currency; Ohio
Idea
Institutionalization, 73, 85–86. *See also*
Polsby, Nelson
Interest groups, 159–60, 254–73
Interior Department, 216
Interstate commerce, 45–46, 104, 265–66,
270

Library of Congress Cataloging in Publication Data

Thompson, Margaret Susan, 1949–
    The "spider web".

    Includes Index.
    1. Lobbying—United States—History—19th century.
2. United States. Congress. House—History—19th
century.   3. United States—Politics and government—
1869–1877.   I. Title.
JK1118.T38   1986   328.73'078'09   85-47706
ISBN 0-8014-1815-1